European Journal
of
Japanese Philosophy

CHISOKUDŌ

The *European Journal of Japanese Philosophy*, the official academic organ of the European Network of Japanese Philosophy, is a peer-reviewed journal published annually in the fall. Its aim is to provide a forum for critical articles and translations related to Japanese philosophy. Contributions are welcome in English, French, German, Italian, Portuguese, Romanian, Spanish, and Japanese.

> Individual printed copies are priced at approximately $15 US (or its equivalent in euros) and may be ordered directly on-line from Amazon.com.
> Subscriptions (individual or institutional) are priced at €15 and are available from participating agents. For further details, contact us at: ejjp.contact@gmail.com.

Submissions should be made online. Details at: https://ejjp-journal.org/submission/
Books submitted for review should be sent to the address given below.

Cover design by Claudio Bado

Copyright © 2021 by European Network of Japanese Philosophy, ENOJP

All rights reserved. No part of this publication may be reproduced, distributed, or transmitted in any form or by any means, including photocopying, recording, or other electronic or mechanical methods, without the prior written permission of the publisher, except in the case of brief quotations embodied in critical reviews and certain other noncommercial uses permitted by copyright law. For permission requests, write to the publisher, addressed "Attention: Permissions Coordinator," at the address below.

> The European Network of Japanese Philosophy, ENOJP
> Universität Hildesheim, Institut für Philosophie
> Universitätsplatz 1, 31141 Hildesheim, Germany
> www.enojp.org | https://ejjp-journal.org

ISBN 979-8769406676
ISSN 2367-3095 | e-ISSN 2700-0885

Designed and typeset at the Nanzan Institute for Religion & Culture, Nagoya, Japan
Published in collaboration with Chisokudō Publications

ISSN 2367-3095 | e-ISSN 2700-0885

European Journal of Japanese Philosophy

Number 6 · 2021

Articles

Nishida's *An Inquiry into the Good* and Japanese and German Thought in the Late Nineteenth Century
          Mitsuhara Takeshi 7

Permeating Each Others' Hearts: Natsume Sōseki and Watsuji Tetsurō on Ethics and the Unity of Self and Other
          Graham Mayeda 35

D. T. Suzuki e Swedenborg. Una introduzione
          Federica Sgarbi 75

La influencia de Watsuji Tetsurō en el pensamiento de Yuasa Yasuo
          Kuwano Moe 95

Animated Persona: The Ontological Status of a Deceased Person Who Continues to Appear in This World
          Morioka Masahiro 115

Book Symposium

Critical Reviews of David W. Johnson, *Watsuji on Nature* 133

Synopsis
          David W. Johnson 134

Watsuji's Hermeneutics
          Bernard Stevens 139

Response to Bernard Stevens
David W. JOHNSON   142

How to Ignore Mesology
Augustin BERQUE   147

Response to Augustin Berque
David W. JOHNSON   158

和辻はハイデガーから何を継承し、何を継承しなかったか
MINE Hideki   166

Response to Mine Hideki
David W. JOHNSON   176

Japanese Philosophy Beyond Heidegger: David Johnson's Watsuji
Hans Peter LIEDERBACH   184

Response to Hans Peter Liederbach
David W. JOHNSON   208

TRANSLATIONS

Tanabe Hajime: "On Historical Consciousness"
Rossa Ó MUIREARTAIGH   217

Tanabe Hajime: "On Thetic Judgment"
Morten E. JELBY, URAI Satoshi, & Quentin BLAEVOET   227

Nishitani Keiji: "La ciencia y la religión"
Carlos BARBOSA   241

Watsuji Tetsurō: "Middle School"
Kyle Michael James SHUTTLEWORTH   267

Two Texts on Technology
Miki Kiyoshi: "The Ideal of Technology,"
"Technology and the New Culture"
NAKAMURA Norihito & Fernando WIRTZ   323

Ōmori Shōzō: "Die Produktion der linearen Zeit"
Raji C. STEINECK   353

Book Review

杉村靖彦、田口 茂、竹花洋佑 eds.
『渦動する象徴：田辺哲学のダイナミズム』

Inohara Jirō 377

Contributors 381

Mitsuhara Takeshi
Nara Prefectural University

Nishida's *An Inquiry into the Good* and Japanese and German Thought in the Late Nineteenth Century

It is widely accepted that pure experience preceding the separation of subject and object in thought as it appears in Nishida Kitarō's first work, *An Inquiry into the Good*, refers to Zen Buddhist spiritual awakening. The philosophy he proposed is, therefore, Eastern in nature. At the same time, Nishida's thinking in this work shows strong affinities with Wundt's work at several points. At that time, the Japanese philosophical community was strongly influenced by trends in Germany, which drove Nishida's interest in ontology and scientific psychology. Accordingly, he tried to work out his philosophy in reliance on Wundt. As such, the defining characteristics of his philosophy should be sought not in something "Oriental" but in the understanding of pure experience as the self-development of a "peerless entity" in terms of which Nishida attempts to explain all things.

KEYWORDS: Nishida Kitarō—Wilhelm Wundt—*An Inquiry into the Good*—pure experience—direct experience.

Nishida Kitarō's philosophy in his first work, *An Inquiry into the Good*, is often considered to be based on spiritual awakening. Ueda Shizuteru is a typical example of this approach. He begins by citing various remarks of Nishida's indicating that the philosophy of *An Inquiry into the Good* derives from both Zen Buddhism and Western philosophy. On that basis, he sets up spiritual awakening as a disclosure to philosophy of the pre-reflective domain on which critical reflection depends. Finally, he interprets pure experience, which Nishida equates with true reality, as a dynamic connection between pre-reflective experience and reflective explanation. In this way, Ueda interprets pure experience as deriving jointly from Zen Buddhism and Western philosophy.[1]

According to this interpretation, the pre-reflective part of pure experience, characterized as a state in which subjects and objects are not yet separated by thinking, is identified as Zen Buddhist spiritual awakening. Although it has been pointed out that the concept of pure experience derives from William James, it is often emphasized that Nishida's *An Inquiry into the Good* has an Eastern character that stands in contrast to classical European philosophy, which presupposes an antagonism between subject and object.

I find this way of reading Nishida questionable, however, since there is nothing in the work that suggests equating the pure experience that obtains before the separation of subject and object with Zen Buddhist spiritual awakening. On the contrary, Nishida describes pre-reflective pure experience as a normal everyday experience.

At the time Nishida was writing, several philosophers had already begun to pay attention to experiences in which subject and object were not yet

1. Ueda 1991, 219–44.

separated by thinking. Wilhelm Wundt was among them. H[...] neither exceptional nor unconventional, but rather part [of Euro-]pean philosophy, under the influence of which the concept [and experi-]ence in *An Inquiry into the Good* was established. Because the ex[planation] of the pre-reflective domain can be found in both Western philosophy [and] Eastern traditions of thought, there is no basis for the claim that Nishida's notion of pure experience is merely Western or merely Eastern.

I will argue in this paper that Nishida's philosophy is strongly influenced by trends taking place in German philosophy, especially in the work of Wundt, and thereby offer an alternative to the widely accepted view that his conception of pure experience is somehow "Eastern" in character. Moreover, I will try to lay out the defining characteristics of Nishida's philosophy in *An Inquiry into the Good* to show how what has been considered merely Oriental has its basis in the thought of the time.

Nishida's interest in ontology and its background

Nishida was born in 1870 and entered high school in 1887. According to his reminiscences, he was introduced to philosophy by Inoue Enryō's *Philosophy Told in a Night* at that time. In the first volume of Inoue's book, published that very year, a materialist who claims there is only matter in the world and no mind disputes with a spiritualist who argues that the world is in the mind and there is no matter outside of mind. Inoue rejects both positions as one-sided and proposes that neither matter nor mind is the origin of the world.

Ontological themes like this become increasingly central in philosophy in Japan after 1885. After the Meiji Restoration of 1868, there was a great interest in English and French philosophers such as J. S. Mill, Spencer, and Comte. There was a shift in the second half of the 1880s when German philosophy became the mainstream.

Symbolic of the fixation on German philosophy is the fact that teachers of philosophy at Tokyo University (which became the first Imperial University in 1886) were writing exclusively under the influence of German philosophy. In 1887 Ludwig Busse came from Germany to join the staff as a lecturer. In 1890 Inoue Tetsujirō returned from studies in Germany to be appointed a professor at the University. In 1893 Raphael von Koeber, who was born in Russia and completed his doctoral work in Germany, began to teach philosophy there as well.

Under the influence of German philosophy, ontology or metaphysics was frequently discussed in Japan as "pure philosophy" (純正哲学). For example, in his *Introduction to Philosophy* of 1892, Busse described the goal of philosophy or ontology as aimed at a comprehensive view of the general structure of ultimate reality.[2] He understood ontology as a structural account of the antagonism between materialism, asserting that all reality lies in matter, and spiritualism, which considers all reality to be spiritual in nature, lending his own support to the latter.[3]

In 1900 Nakajima Rikizō introduced three ontological standpoints in his work *Recent Problems of Philosophy*. The first is materialism, which regards matter as the substance of all things and tries to explain everything in terms of matter. The second is spiritualism, which regards the mind as the substantive reality of all things and tries to explain everything in terms of mind. The third approach asserts that something neither matter nor mind is the substance of all things. Of these, Nakajima sided with spiritualism.[4]

In a 1902 book based on Friedrich Paulsen's *Introduction to Philosophy* (1892) and entitled *Outlines of Philosophy,* Tomonaga Sanjūrō proposed four ontological standpoints: dualism, which claims that the world consists of matter and mind; materialism, which holds matter to be the ultimate reality; spiritualism, which claims that the mind is reality; and agnosticism, which asserts that we cannot know ultimate reality. He rejects dualism as popular and not properly philosophical. Materialism is discarded because it cannot explain everything, however useful it may be to the natural sciences. Reality as such cannot exist in the material world without the senses, which entails our inner life. Therefore, Tomonaga concludes, spiritualism is the proper standpoint.[5]

Another important philosopher of ontology was Inoue Tetsujirō, who wrote of what he called phenomena-as-reality theory (現象即実在論) in a series of papers beginning with "A Particle of My Worldview" in 1894.

2. Busse 1892, 22, 58.
3. Ibid., 58–66, 110.
4. Nakajima 1900, 211–29.
5. Tomonaga 1902, 64–72, 130.

In these essays, Inoue first describes phenomena as what is knowable and changeable and includes difference. Reality, in contrast, is neither knowable nor changeable and does not include difference.[6] He then distinguishes between ontological standpoints in which the truth is inaccessible and those in which it is accessible. The latter include idealism, which regards objects as the result of subjective activity, and realism, which posits an objective world outside of the subject. Realism further distinguishes between phenomena in the objective world that are not real and those that are. This is what Inoue calls phenomena-as-reality theory, which in one view sees only phenomena as real, and in another sees reality as theoretically distinguishable but ultimately the same.[7]

In a paper published in 1915, "The Philosophical Value of Realism over Materialism and Spiritualism," Inoue compared his phenomena-as-reality theory to the schematic opposition between materialism and spiritualism. He positioned his theory as a third standpoint that unifies matter and mind by means of a third principle of reality, whereas materialism considered only matter, and spiritualism only mind, as the fundamental principle.[8]

Discussions of ontology at the time were not without controversies. For example, in response to Inoue Enryō's attacks on materialism in *Refuting Materialism* (1898), Katō Hiroyuki published an essay "Refuting *Refuting Materialism*" that same year. Or again, in a paper entitled "Reading *A Year and a Half, Continued* by Mr Nakae Tokusuke" (1902), Inoue Tetsujirō took up the cause against the materialism of Nakae Chōmin.

As a high school student, Nishida was exposed to this trend of thought through reading Inoue Enryō. According to Kōsaka Masaaki, Nishida states his thoughts on high school days as follows:

> There was a man who we would now call a materialist or Marxist.... He tried to explain everything in terms of matter. I admit that there is a reasonableness to his position, but I cannot believe that matter is the ultimate reality. His explanation was not false; it just seemed to be abstract or derivative. One day as I happened to be walking around Kanazawa and viewed the city bathed in the setting sun, with the people going by and the sounds of things

---

6. INOUE Tetsujirō 1897A, 385.
7. INOUE Tetsujirō 1894, 491–4.
8. INOUE Tetsujirō 1915, 67.

at dusk, the idea came to me that *these* are reality and that so-called matter is rather an abstraction from it. I suppose this was the germ of *An Inquiry into the Good*.[9]

The view expressed here is spiritualistic and materialism is recognized as false on the grounds that what appears in the mind, like the town bathed in the setting sun, is real and matter is only an abstraction. Already in high school, Nishida had taken sides in the ontological conflict between materialism and spiritualism occasioned by the dominance of German philosophy.

Nishida entered the Imperial University in 1891 and graduated in 1894. He later taught foreign languages, logic, ethics, and psychology at various high schools and published several papers before becoming assistant professor at Kyoto Imperial University in 1910. In 1905, he wrote in a letter to his friend Yamamoto Ryōkichi (山本良吉):

> I have read all usual famous books about ethics for my lectures, but I cannot be satisfied unless I start with metaphysics. I have recently begun to study the history of philosophy and epistemology. Such a study is not necessary for ethics, but I cannot shake myself free of metaphysical doubts.[10]

Nishida wrote of his desire to desire to study metaphysics rather than ethics for his lectures. *The Dictionary of Philosophy*, published in 1905, declared that metaphysics was a systematic investigation into the ultimate problem of reality and that it was synonymous with philosophy if reality is understood in a broad sense and with ontology if reality was seen as opposed to thought.[11] On these grounds, we may say that Nishida's interests lay in ontology at the time.

In 1907 Nishida published a paper entitled "On Reality," which became the basis of a series of papers compiled in 1911 as *An Inquiry into the Good*. The current discussions of materialism and spiritualism, which German philosophy had introduced and which we summarized in the foregoing, stand clearly in the background.

9. Kōsaka 1965, 45–6.
10. Nishida 2006, 74.
11. Tomonaga 1905, 92.

The rise of scientific psychology in Germany and Japan

The philosophical arguments of Nishida's *An Inquiry into the Good* are somewhat distantly related to the Industrial Revolution, which had a great impact on philosophy in the nineteenth century. Beginning in the latter half of the eighteenth century in Great Britain before spreading to other European countries, the United States, and Japan in the nineteenth century, the revolution not only radically changed people's lifestyles through railway factories but also changed the way they thought.

The German Zeitgeist at the time is illustrated in Ludwig Büchner's best-selling book *Force and Matter*.[12] Büchner asserted that philosophers of nature who support idealism should be outcast, since philosophy is the arrogant delusion of those who spin incomprehensible and empty speculations. Inquiry into the world based on thinking had already failed and lost the respect and trust of the public. Our efforts are better spent, he argued, by investigating nature through observation and experience.[13] The revolution had made the results of the natural sciences apparent to everyone. Many had begun to consider philosophy unreliable because it is too etherial and idealistic, whereas the empirical sciences were reliable in that they were based on verifiable observation and experience.

German philosophers at the time had to reckon with this hostile atmosphere to champion the need for and importance of philosophy. According to Schnädelbach, we may classify four emerging groups. The first was modeled on the natural sciences and viewed philosophy as a science of the mind (*Geisteswissenschaft*). Representatives of this group were Eduard Zeller and Kuno Fischer, who treated philosophy as an object of historical study. Other members of this group included figures such as Friedrich Adolf Trendelenburg and Bernard Bolzano, who based their theories on philosophies of the past.

A second group consisted of philosophers who accepted the science of the day as a form of philosophy. Ludwig Büchner and Wilhelm Ostwald were representative of this group, which included thinkers such as Wilhelm

---

12. Ueberweg 1923, 285–6.
13. Büchner 1855, 1–2.

Wundt, Wilhelm Dilthey, and Georg Simmel, who claimed psychology and philosophy as the basis of the science of the mind; Karl Marx and Friedrich Engels, who tried to base philosophy on sociology; and Richard Avenarius and Ernst Mach, whose philosophy was based on biology.

Hegelians such as David Strauß and Bruno Bauer belong to the third group, which viewed philosophy as criticism. For them, philosophy had come to an end with Hegel, and its only remaining task was to adopt his ideas to criticize elements of the current situation which his philosophy had not yet reached.

Members of the fourth and final group sought to provide a new foundation for philosophy by reshaping it into a field of investigation independent from other individual sciences. A typical example here were the approaches to epistemology of Hermann Cohen, Wilhelm Windelband, Heinrich Rickert, and others. Another example is the value philosophy developed by Hermann Lotze, which centered attention on values like the true, the good, and the beautiful.[14]

Wundt, as we said, belonged to the second group. He typified scientific psychology, which partly accounts for his strong influence on Nishida's *An Inquiry into the Good*.

In the nineteenth century, certain psychologists in Germany began to quantify mental states in the attempt to isolate the laws that governed them. For example, Max Weber and Gustav Fechner conducted research on psychophysics and came up with a law now known as the Weber-Fechner law, which demonstrated the relationship between physical stimuli and the strength of perceptions. Wundt, who founded the first Institute of Experimental Psychology at Leipzig University, was drawn to this kind of quantified and experimental psychology, which was gaining increased recognition as a science.

The institute founded by Wundt was introduced to Japan in 1888 in a short essay, probably written by Inoue Tetsujirō, entitled "The Laboratory for Psychology in Leipzig." Psychophysics was also introduced into Japan that year when Motora Yūjirō, who had received his doctoral degree under Stanley Hall, began to lecture on the subject at the Imperial University. As Sawayanagi Seitarō described the situation in Japan in 1888, "It is scientific

---

14. Schnädelbach 2009, 130–53.

or new psychology that appears most frequently in philosophical works and journals, attracts the greatest attention, and is most active."[15]

Nishida, who entered the Imperial University in 1891 and graduated in 1894, wrote a letter to Suzuki Daisetsu in 1907, the same year that he published his essay "On Reality":

> What I just sent you is scientific.... I would like to refine my thoughts further and make them into a book if possible. Most of philosophy so far is founded on logic, but I hope to base my philosophy on psychology. Recently I discovered a very interesting theory of pure experience by W. James, etc....[16]

Considering the time this letter was written, it is clear that Nishida's expressed desire to establish his own philosophy scientifically and to base it on psychology was realized in his first work, *An Inquiry into the Good*, where psychologists like James, Wundt, and Stout are referred to. One of the reasons for this reliance on psychologists is that he was living and writing under the influence of trends spurred by the Industrial Revolution.

Affinity between Nishida's ontological view at his high school days and Wundt's ontology

As mentioned above, Nishida told Kōsaka that when he was walking in Kanazawa and wrapped in the glow of the setting sun, the movements of the people and the sounds of dusk made him think that these things are reality and that "matter" is no more than an abstraction from it. This spiritualistic tendency overlaps with ideas in Wundt's ontology.

Wundt's philosophy is closely tied to his understanding of psychology. In his view, the two dominant strains of psychology in his day were misguided. The first understood psychology as the science of the soul, which he found unacceptable in the light of developments in the empirical sciences and their need to maintain independence from metaphysical theory. The second saw psychology as the study of inner experience, which he considered to be based on an inadequate understanding of inner and outer experiences—an "inner" mind as opposed to an "outer" world. For Wundt, the difference was not one of objects but of standpoints. Inner experiences are rather experi-

---

15. Sawayanagi 1888, 640.
16. Nishida 2006, 107.

ences observed in relation to the subject, and outer experience are those observed independently from the subject. Psychology opts for the former, which Wundt called the standpoint of direct experience, from which subjective elements are not abstracted from experience. In contrast, the natural sciences opt for the latter, which he called the standpoint of mediate experience, from which such subjective elements are abstracted.[17]

Wundt argued that as a standpoint of direct experience, psychology provides a foundation and preparation for the science of the mind, including philosophy, insofar as its content is determined by the interactions of subject and object. He further insisted that psychology is useful for ethics as a philosophical discipline insofar as it investigates the conditions of cognition and action.[18]

Wundt's philosophy was based on his view of direct experience as the object of psychological research. He defined direct experience as an experience that occurs prior to the changes effected by the act of thinking, whereas mediate experience is an experience that has been changed by it. He saw this distinction as necessary because he considered the act of thinking to be one that separates subjective elements like emotions and mental acts from objective elements like physical phenomena. For him, the separation of mind as subjective and matter as objective does not yet arise in direct experience.[19]

Wundt classified ontological standpoints into materialism, idealism, and realism, concluding that it is idealism that must be supported. Realism, which regards both matter and mind as the ultimate grounding, is rejected because it is impossible to posit a third grounding apart from matter and mind. Materialism, which identifies the ultimate ground of everything and the principle of natural events as matter, cannot explain the mind as a subjective element, since matter is only the objective element of direct experience. In contrast to these two positions, idealism, which overlaps the foundational unity of the mental with the mind, can explain both elements. Physical phenomena are contained in direct experience as objects and are experienced as subjective representations. These subjective representations are mental phenomena because they are contained in direct experience; yet they are

17. Wundt 1896, 1–3.
18. Ibid., 4, 19–20.
19. Wundt 1897, 85.

considered physical phenomena when abstracted from the direct experience. He based his idealism on this view that mental phenomena are subjective and physical phenomena are objective elements of direct experience.

Wundt further asserted that direct experience implies cognition in which the subjective representation is the objective reality (*Wirklichkeit*) to which the subjective act corresponds. In most cases, epistemology begins with the antagonism of the subject toward the object and asks how the two can mutually correspond. Wundt insisted, however, that epistemology should begin with direct experience, because the opposition between subject and object arises only after a separation of the two through the act of thinking.

These two claims have affinities with Nishida's thinking during his high school days. Wundt insisted that matter is abstracted from direct experience when the act of thinking separates out objective and subjective elements of experience. Nishida also considered matter to be an abstraction from reality. Moreover, both philosophers agreed that direct experience, prior to being separated out by the act of thinking, is cognition. Nishida argued this position in *An Inquiry into the Good*, where he referred to reality as pure experience and claimed that such experience is the proper starting point of philosophy.

In a word, the spiritualistic standpoint that Nishida adopted during his high school days shows clear affinities with Wundt's philosophy, which was representative of scientific psychology at the time and popular among Japanese philosophers. In a sense, it was only natural that Nishida would follow this trend and seek out clues for his own nascent philosophy from Wundt's philosophy.

Nishida's ontology in *An Inquiry into the Good* and Wundt's ontology

Insofar as *An Inquiry into the Good* developed ideas that had their origins in his high school days and developed further under the influence of Wundt's philosophy, similarities in that work to Wundt's philosophy are hardly to be wondered at.

As we saw, in looking back over his time in high school, Nishida expressed a spiritualistic view in which what appears in the mind, like a city bathed in the setting sun, is ultimate reality, while matter is no more than an abstraction from that reality. In *An Inquiry into the Good*, reality is referred to as pure or direct experience. In the second part of the work, however, Nishida expressed the need for philosophical doubt when it comes to grasping reality: "To understand true reality and to know the true nature of the universe and human life, we must discard all artificial assumptions, doubt whatever can be doubted, and proceed on the basis of direct and indubitable knowledge."[20] He goes on to express the result of pursuing such doubt:

> What is direct knowledge that we cannot even begin to doubt? It is knowledge of facts in our intuitive experience, knowledge of phenomena of consciousness. A present phenomenon of consciousness and our being conscious of it are identical; they cannot be divided into subject and object. Since facts are not separated even a hair's breadth from knowing, we cannot doubt this knowledge.[21]

Nishida contends that the only indubitable knowledge is the knowledge of phenomena of consciousness, because when we are conscious of the presence of conscious phenomena, they cannot be divided into subject and object; knowing is not separated from facts. Declaring the state of consciousness prior to any distinction between subject and object one of "pure" or "direct" experience, Nishida submits that "from the perspective of direct knowledge that is free from all assumptions, reality consists only of phenomena of our consciousness, namely, the facts of direct experience."[22] The phenomena of consciousness and direct or pure experience must be considered reality precisely because they belong to a state prior to the separation of subject and object, which means they precede doubt.

Nishida offers a more detailed explanation of why reality can be seen as pure or direct experience: "At the time of pure experience, there is still no opposition between subject and object and no separation of knowledge, feeling, and volition; there is only an independent, self-sufficient, pure activity." The object does not exist independently of the subject. Rather, "the notions of subject and object derive from two different ways of looking at a single fact."[23]

---

20. NISHIDA 1990, 38; 2003A, 40.
21. NISHIDA 1990, 39; 2003A, 41.
22. NISHIDA 1990, 42; 2003A, 43.
23. NISHIDA 1990; 47, 49; 2003A, 48, 50.

Likewise, matter does not exist independently of the mind. As Nishida states, "Only when we separate the subjective activity from the concrete reality can we think of the grass and trees as purely objective nature." Later he add that "So-called mental phenomena are simply the unifying or active aspect of reality considered abstractly."[24] Matter and nature as objects are extracted when the subjective elements are abstracted from reality as pure or direct experience, and unifying acts as subjects are extracted when the objective elements are abstracted.

Reality as a pure or direct experience that contains mental and physical phenomena is "neither a phenomenon of consciousness nor a material phenomenon," but, as the title of chapter six, "Phenomena of Consciousness Are the Sole Reality"[25] demonstrates, Nishida thinks of reality as simultaneously a phenomenon of consciousness. As a phenomenon of consciousness, reality is not understood in terms of a substantial dualism that assumes the independence of matter from mind but as including nature and matter within it.

The first connection of Nishida's ontology in *An Inquiry into the Good* to Wundt's ontology is that he adopt a spiritualistic or idealistic view in which mental phenomena are subjective and physical phenomena are objective elements of pure or direct experience.

The second is voluntarism. In Wundt's *System of Philosophy*, four types of idealism are distinguished: Herbart's individual intellectualism, Kant's individual voluntarism, Spinoza's universal intellectualism, and Schopenhauer's universal voluntarism. The first two are named individual because they consider mind to be the defining ground of individuality. The last two are referred to as universal because they consider mind to be universal. Intellectualism is the position that regards representation as the essence of mental phenomena, and voluntarism thinks of will as their basis.[26] Of the two, Wundt adopted the position of individual voluntarism.

Wundt argued that universal intellectualism has difficulty dealing with the contradiction between the invariability of an absolute substance and the variability of the individual. From such a position, the ultimate ground is the

24. NISHIDA 1990, 68, 74; 2003A, 67, 72.
25. NISHIDA 1990, 44, 42; 2003A; 45, 43.
26. WUNDT 1897, 200–1.

idea of the infinite unification of all thinkable representations or the idea of an infinite intellect that embraces the totality of thinkable representations and actualizes individual representations in individual consciousness. The idea that representations emerge and change in an unending process of unification is inconsistent with the concept of an infinite intellect. Therefore, infinite unification must be regarded as stationary, and all activities must be brought about in individual consciousness by an infinite intellect. However, this means that while the infinite intellect gives rise to all thought in finite minds, it cannot think because it is itself invariable. This means that we can no longer speak of intellect. An infinite intellect would have to be variable and an active principle of thinking.[27]

Wundt went on to point out three problems with universal voluntarism. First, it is impossible to derive representations from the idea of a universal will. Second, we cannot justify naming the principle preceding all phenomena, because the connection between individual will and representations is inseparable. Lastly, the concept of a world will as opposed to individual will is merely an idea and not the result of research carried out as a supplement to experience.

After he dismissed the above-mentioned two positions in this way, he considered individual intellectualism and voluntarism. In the process, he argues that will cannot exist without representations of its object but will be the only component of consciousness because it remains homogeneous and is always unifying our experience. Meanwhile, representations form groups, but they are often separated from each other. They will retain the unity of our experience, which is constantly developing.[28]

Wundt assigned the function of unification to the will because he identified it with apperception. Whereas perception refers to the appearance of a representation in consciousness, apperception, in Wundt's definition, refers to the appearance of the representation to which one is attentive in the field of consciousness. Inasmuch as apperception points at a representation with the aim of selecting one representation from among others, he looked on apperception as the original activity of the will. Furthermore, since the rep-

27. Ibid., 384–6.
28. Ibid., 374–8.

resentation appears as unified, he believed that it is will qua apperception that is responsible for the unification.[29]

The unifying will makes experience possible by unifying various representations that appear one after the other. Hence, Wundt described will as transcendental and adopted voluntarism in consideration of that point.[30]

For his part, Nishida argued that reality develops through the repeated separation and unification of the contents of consciousness. For example, when we unify blue representations through the concept of blue, the separation of blue things from non-blue things arises simultaneously. By unifying what is separate, new separations appear. In this way, reality continues to be separated without forfeiting its unity as the one and only reality. Because unity is formed by a unifying act, it is the act that makes it possible for there to be only one reality.

Nishida points out that various acts like thinking and recollecting take on the function of unification as a kind of apperception, but the act that unifies the whole of reality is will. The acts of thinking and recollecting only unify ideas, whereas will unifies ideas as well as actions. When we take action with our will to achieve a purpose, the idea that expresses that purpose, as well as the action carried out in its name, are unified by will.[31] Although Nishida's view amounts to a kind of voluntarism that considers will as apperception, his reasons differ from Wundt's.

A final point of contact between the two philosophers lies in their rejection of an unchangeable substratum at the basis of mental phenomena. For Wundt, as a voluntarist, the condition of developing experience was not an unchangeable being but an activity of the will as transcendental apperception which continually unifies the representations of the conscious mind.

For Nishida, reality as direct or pure experience changes through repeated unification and separation. While the basis of this reality is the unifying act of a kind of apperception, he insisted that "the noumenon of a truly active thing must be the unifying power that is the fundamental activity in the establishment of reality." For Nishida, experience unfolds not as the con-

---

29. WUNDT 1880, 206–12, 304–5.
30. WUNDT 1897, 377–9.
31. NISHIDA 1990, 89–91; 2003A, 85–7.

ditioning of an unchangeable substratum of being, but as an activity of the will. To say that "the noumenon refers to the unifying power of reality"[32] does not mean that will is a stationary substance. On the contrary, it is constantly active.

WUNDT'S EPISTEMOLOGY

It is not only in its ontology that *An Inquiry into the Good* was written under Wundt's influence but also in its epistemology. The concept of direct experience plays a defining role here.

Wundt described direct experience in these terms:

> The experience preceding every influence of the functions of thinking, i.e., the concept of cognizing completely detached from the characteristics of thinking, we also call immediate experience and contrast it with mediate experience, which is somehow changed by the effectiveness of the functions of thinking, namely by the formation of concepts obtained through them.[33]

The kind of thinking Wundt has in mind here is classified as a subjective element that is conscious when it is engaged, when it connects and shapes representations and concepts. This last is the most important function of thinking, as, for example, when the concept of wolf is connected with the concept of carnivore and leads to the judgment that wolves are carnivores; or when a particular blue sky is broken up into the two concepts of blue and sky.[34] To name the experience preceding every influence of the functions of thinking direct experience means that the experience preceding every connection and resolution of thought qualifies as direct experience. Hence feeling, willing, perceived objects, and the relations between them all belong to direct experience when they are given without one's having to be conscious of the thought at work. In contrast, when the functions of thinking are employed and relations are formed or resolved in experience, the experience is called mediate experience.[35]

Wundt's understanding of direct experience as "the concept of cognition

---

32. Nishida 1990, 67, 66; 2003a; 67, 66.
33. Wundt 1897, 85.
34. Ibid., 41–3.
35. Ibid., 85–6.

completely detached from the characteristics of thinking" means that correct cognition is always the result of direct experience. While its representation may be in discord with the object of thinking, representation always corresponds to its object in direct experience. Therefore, as mentioned above, Wundt insisted that direct experience is the correct cognition in subjective representation of objective reality.

Wundt's epistemology sought to explain the genesis of knowledge with direct experience as a starting point.[36] His first reason for doing so was that he considered the opposition, separation, and disconnection between the subjective and the objective found in traditional epistemology a poor place to begin a discussion of how to bring the two into harmony. What is given in direct experience is neither a subjective representation nor an objective fact, but a representational object (*Vorstellungsobjekt*) in which the subject is not separated from the object but corresponds to it.

Second, he felt that when we inquire into the correspondence between the subjective and objective, we secure a guarantee of that correspondence which traditional epistemology had not been able to supply. This problem is overcome if we begin with direct experience and agree that the subject already corresponds to the object insofar as there is no need of a third element to guarantee their correspondence.[37]

Wundt observed that representational objects given in direct experience may sometimes appear contradictory. We have then to correct the discrepancy in line with the objective requirements of thinking, finding an object as the basis of the subject, and resolving the contradiction at hand. Although he did not give an example of this process at work, we may consider hallucinations and illusions a case in point. If we heard a sound but no one is around, the initial experience of hearing a sound contradicts the later experience of an absence of a source for that sound. We may therefore conclude that the sound is not a representational object but merely a subjective representation, namely a hallucination.

In other words, wherever there is a contradiction in direct experience, there is a subjective representation to be distinguished from the object of the experience. That said, Wundt maintained that the negation of objectiv-

36. Ibid., 30–1.
37. Ibid., 89–90.

ity and the reality of representation based on such exceptional cases is the wrong place to begin epistemology. As in the natural sciences, Wundt's preferred method was first to approve of the reality and certainty of the representational object and only then correct errors as they arise.[38]

Having established direct experience as the starting point for the emergence of knowledge, Wundt went on to distinguish three stages in cognition. The cognition of representational objects in direct experience and the transformation of the representational object without the aid of conceptualization are located at the stage of perception cognition. The next step is to understand the process of cognition that takes place when a representational object is corrected. Cognition in this stage is gained when the content and connection of representations are improved or supplemented by logical analysis based on perception-cognition. In the last stage, the connections gained through understanding are brought together into a single whole. The cognition of the whole into a worldview is a function of reason-cognition.[39]

Wundt explained the genesis of cognition in his epistemology in terms of stages. The origin of the distinction between various things is described as a process of perception-cognition. First, sensory content as perceptual matter is distinguished from space and time as perceptual form of perception, based on the variability and independence of matter from form and the invariability of form. Next, space is distinguished from time where changes in properties are thought to be purely temporal events, whereas movement is considered to be change in time and space. Furthermore, subjects and objects are distinguished by reason of the fact that various things have value specifications based on feeling and that only the movement of the perceiving subject connects feelings that precede, accompany, and resonate with the movement.[40]

Once the genesis of the distinction between subject and object has been taken into account, imaginary objects produced by the subject need to be distinguished from things produced by influence from the object on the subject. The question naturally arises as to what belongs to the subjective dimension in our representations and what to the objective. Wundt's

38. Ibid., 98, 102–3.
39. Ibid., 104.
40. Ibid., 111–13, 124–30.

response was that a representation is initially a representation of an object, and that if a contradiction arises in perception or representation as a result of thought, the representational object may be corrected, with a part of the representational object being regarded as subjective and detached at the stage of understanding-cognition. After the detachment, the representational object remains objective insofar as the part that was not corrected corresponds to objective reality, while the part that was regarded as subjective loses its objectivity.[41]

For thinking to function, it must follow the laws of thinking. But these laws only mark the range of the possible; they do not tell us what reality is. Accordingly, Wundt argued that it is necessary to design hypotheses to uncover and resolve contradictions in perception or representation. In this way, the linking of the entire contents of experience at the stage of understanding-cognition is made possible by a principle of sufficient reason linking multiple things through relationships of cause and effect. We are thereby able to rise above the contents of experience at the stage of reason-cognition, where we cognize what is beyond the actual contents of experience.[42]

As shown above, Wundt's epistemology is a three-staged process whereby first we gain representational objects in direct experience at the stage of perception-cognition, then correct the representational object at the stage of understanding-cognition, and then move beyond experience at the stage of reason-cognition.

Nishida's Epistemology in *An Inquiry into the Good*

Let us return to a passage cited earlier from Nishida:

> What is direct knowledge that we cannot even begin to doubt? It is knowledge of facts in our intuitive experience, knowledge of phenomena of consciousness. A present phenomenon of consciousness and our being conscious of it are identical; they cannot be divided into subject and object. Since facts are not separated even a hair's breadth from knowing, we cannot doubt this knowledge.[43]

41. Ibid., 132–6.
42. Ibid., 133, 168–9, 180–1.
43. Nishida 1990, 39; 2003a, 41.

Nishida, like Wundt, argues here that correct cognition is grounded in an "intuitive experience" in which the subject and object are not yet separated. The mistaken cognition associated with hallucinations or illusions seems to argue against such a view. Nishida counters that "at that time, not intuition but judgment based on it makes a mistake,"[44] giving as an example the way a stick inserted into the water appears to be bent. The illusion itself is not a mistake but an indubitable fact. It is the judgment that the stick is bent that is in error.

At the beginning of *An Inquiry into the Good*, Nishida says, "to experience means to know facts just as they are." He calls such an experience direct or pure experience and determines it as one that precedes the act of judgment and in which "there is not yet a subject or an object, and knowing and its object are completely unified."[45] As the example of the bent stick illustrates, we are always able to carry out correct cognition and gain indisputable knowledge in such direct or pure experience.

Nishida observes that

> the purpose of my discussion in the first section 'Pure Experience' is not to distinguish pure experience from mediate and non-pure experience but to argue rather that perception, thinking, will and intuition have the same form.[46]

This indicates that it is not correct to define pure experience as "to know facts as they are" or as experiences in which "there is not yet a subject or an object, and knowing and its object are completely unified."

The most important character of pure experience lies in its "independent, self-sufficient, pure activity" in the form of "the self-development of a peerless entity."[47] Pure experience develops through the unification and separation of its content. Although unified as a whole, pure experience contains separation and does not stipulate a unified consciousness. As Nishida states, not only does "the directness and purity of pure experience derive… from the strict unity of concrete consciousness," but "we see that even these uni-

---

44. Nishida 2008, 40.
45. Nishida 1990, 3–4; 2003a, 9.
46. Nishida 2003b, 241.
47. Nishida 1990, 47, 53; 2003a, 48, 54.

ties and disunities differ only in degree"[48] and that "there is neither absolutely pure nor absolutely non-pure experience. Every experience is pure, depending on how we look at."[49] The degree of unity of pure experience is different, and the experience with a greater degree of unity is purer than an experience with less unity.

Hence, in addition to arguing that the criterion of truth lies in pure experience,[50] Nishida remarks:

> There are various classes of experiences.... If various direct experiences exist in this way, then one may wonder how we can determine their truth or falsehood. When two experiences are enveloped by a third, we can judge the two according to the third.[51]

As a pure activity that marks the self-development of a "peerless entity," pure experience displays various classes of development. Of these, pure experience as the criterion of truth is the greatest and displays the highest degree of unity, one which envelops other less pure experiences.

Although Nishida does not provide an example of pure experience with such a highest degree of unity, the stick in the water may serve the purpose. If a child who is unaware of the phenomenon of light refraction were to notice that the same stick looks straight when placed on the ground, they would not be able to determine which judgment is correct: "the stick is bent" or "the stick is straight." In Nishida's words, the two experiences are contradictory and in a state of separation.

However, once the child learns about light refraction, the contradictory experiences are resolved in a third insight, namely that a straight stick looks bent when inserted into water, and they are then able to make a corrected judgment on the matter. Nishida's remark that "in the course of its [conscious] development various conflicts and contradictions crop up in the system, and out of this emerges reflective thinking" speaks to the contradiction between the child's first two experiences and their ensuing reflection on it. Only then are they able to proceed to a third experience with a higher degree of unity. As Nishida continues, "when viewed from a different angle,

---

48. Nishida 1990, 6, 9; 2003a, 11, 14.
49. Nishida 1990, 6, 9; 2003a, 11, 14.
50. Nishida 1990, 26, 2003a, 30.
51. Nishida 1990, 26–27, 2003a, 31.

that which is contradictory and conflicted is the beginning of a still greater systematic development; it is the incomplete state of a greater unity."[52]

Pure experiences with a greater degree of unity arise by thinking about and judging different experiences that at first appear to be contradictory. Accordingly, it is not correct simply to claim that the criterion of truth lies in pure experience "without the least addition of deliberative discrimination" and "prior… to thought."[53] The criterion of truth lies in the greatest pure experience, that is, the one that attains the highest degree of unity after thinking and judgment.

Understood in this way, Nishida's epistemology in *An Inquiry into the Good* shows remarkable affinities with Wundt's. In fact, he himself states that "pure experience is identical with direct experience."[54] Pure or direct experience in Nishida and direct experience in Wundt are identical in character in the sense that both precede thinking and the separation of subject and object. Just as Wundt maintains that correct cognition is established in direct experience, Nishida claims that knowing facts as they are is established in pure experience.

Or again, Wundt asserted that in the attempt to connect and unify the contents of multiple direct experiences through thinking, the subject is distinguished from the object in order to resolve contradictions that arise in thought, a hypothesis is formed, and the contents of the experience are corrected. This claim is similar to Nishida's argument that "with the development of consciousness, because of conflict among various systems—which is an advance toward a still greater unity—one can distinguish between ideals and facts; the subjective and the objective worlds diverge."[55] Like Wundt, Nishida proposes that the dichotomy of subject from object emerges out of conflicts in pure experiences.

Nishida goes on to say that "the fulfillment of the will or the culmination of truth thus means that from a state of disunity one has arrived at the state of pure experience" and that "just as one's scientific conjectures are proven through experimentation, what becomes manifest when the will has been

---

52. Nishida 1990, 16, 2003a, 21.
53. Nishida 1990, 3, 2003a, 9.
54. Nishida 1990, 3, 2003a, 9.
55. Nishida 1990, 26, 2003a, 30.

fulfilled in the external world is the most unified, direct experience, which has broken through the subject-object distinction."[56] When our conjectures are proven through experimentation, the subject and object that were separated and in a state of distunity become unified again and we are able to attain truth. Here again, Nishida shares Wundt's view that we can know the truth by forming hypotheses and correcting our experience through the provisional separation of subject and object.

Characteristics of Nishida's philosophy

As we can see from the above, Nishida's philosophy shows remarkable affinities with Wundt's ontology and epistemology. Still, there are important characteristics of Nishida's thought that stand in contrast to Wundt's.

Nishida claims that the division of subject and object emerges out of internal conflicts among experiences but can be reunified, and that we can come to know the truth through such things as testing and proving conjectures. In contrast, Wundt does not think that subject and object can be reunified, even though he agrees that we can reach truth by forming hypotheses and correcting our experiences despite the separation of subject from object.

This tells us that one feature of Nishida's view is that pure experience can be reunified, or that it develops and differentiates by itself in the form of "the self-development of a peerless entity" and is pure because it is unified.[57] This idea was originally presented in the context of ontology. In *An Inquiry into the Good*, after asserting that the phenomenon of consciousness is the ultimate reality in chapter six, Nishida attempts to explain what he means by reality. It is in this context that pure experience is characterized as an activity in the form of the self-development of a peerless entity.

Nishida also adopts the same characterization for epistemology, arguing that development and differentiation are processes aimed at reaching the truth. Of the many pure experiences that develop and differentiate with various degrees of unity, the criterion of truth is to be sought in the greatest

---

56. Nishida 1990, 26–7:, 2003a, 30–1.
57. Nishida 1990, 53, 6; 2003A, 54, 11.

pure experience with the highest degree of unity that can be attained after thinking and judgment. In short, to attain the greatest form of pure experience is equivalent to attaining the truth.

I will not go into further detail here but would only add that Nishida contends that the criterion of goodness is also to be found in pure experience. We feel satisfaction and happiness when our actions realize an ideal, thus bringing about a unity of action, ideal, and reality. The happiness generated through this unity is the criterion of goodness. He further states that the deepest form of religion is based on experiences in which God and human beings are unified. And inasmuch as God is the power unifying the universe, pure experience evidences unity with that power.[58]

In the preface to *An Inquiry into the Good*, Nishida admits, "for many years I wanted to explain all things on the basis of pure experience as the sole reality."[59] Clearly his aim was to resolve problems in ontology, epistemology, ethics, and religion by means of the idea of pure experience as the self-development of a peerless entity. This, above all, is what sets his thought off from Wundt's philosophy.

Conclusion

When Nishida was first introduced to philosophy, the Japanese philosophical community was strongly influenced by trends in contemporary German thought. Their central concern was with ontology and the dispute between materialism on the one hand and idealism and spiritualism on the other. Nishida tried to work out an original response to this problem with the aid of psychology, which had drawn increasing attention in both the Japanese and German philosophical communities.

Nishida attraction to Wundt's philosophy was based on the popularity of scientific psychology among German and Japanese philosophers, but ideas germinating in his high school days already showed affinities to Wundt in terms of matter being an abstraction from reality and in the insight into direct or pure experience as a state prior to the separation of subject and object in thought. For these reasons, he was persuaded to take elements of

58. Nishida 1990, 122–5, 151–7; 2003a, 114–17, 137–41.
59. Nishida 1990, xxx; 2003a, 6.

Wundt's ontology over into the philosophical position he developed in *An Inquiry into the Good*.

From the above it should be clear that the widely accepted views that identifies pure experience prior to the subject-object dichotomy with spiritual awakening in Zen Buddhism, and that therefore the philosophical position espoused in *An Inquiry into the Good* should be classified as Eastern philosophy are not sustainable. Rather, what Nishida called pure experience and Wundt referred to as direct experience must be identified with everyday experience. Insofar as *An Inquiry into the Good* was composed under the strong influence of trends in nineteenth-century German philosophy, one of the most important characteristics of Nishida's philosophy in his maiden work is his insight into pure experience as an activity that takes the form of the self-development of a peerless entity and that he adopts in the attempt to explain all things.

> * The author would like to thank Richard Stone and Editage (http://www.editage.com) for editing and reviewing the English of this essay.

References

Abbreviation

NKZ 『西田幾多郎全集』[Complete Works of Nishita Kitarō] (Tōkyō: Iwanami Shoten, 2003), 24 vols.

Anon.
1888 「ライプツィヒの心理試験室」[The Laboratory for Psychology in Leipzig], 『哲学会雑誌』[Journal of the Philosophical Association] 2/19.

Büchner, Ludwig
1855 *Kraft und Stoff* (Frankfurt am Main: Meidlinger).

Busse, Ludwig
1892 *Introduction to Philosophy: Dictated Portions of the Lectures* (Tokyo).

Funayama Shin'ichi 舩山信一
1999 『舩山信一著作集』[Collected Works of Funayama Shin'ichi] (Tokyo: Kobushi Shobō).

Inoue Enryō 井上円了
1887 『哲学一夕話』[Philosophy Told in a Night] (Tokyo: Tetsugaku Shoin).
1898 『破唯物論』[Refuting Materialism] (Tokyo: Shiseidō).

Inoue Tetsujirō 井上哲次郎
    1894   「我世界観の一塵」[A particle of my worldview], 『哲学雑誌』[*Journal of Philosophy*] 9/89.
    1897a   「現象即実在論の要領」[An outline of the phenomena-as-reality theory], 『哲学雑誌』[*Journal of Philosophy*] 12/123.
    1897b   「現象即実在論」[The phenomena-as-reality theory], 『哲学雑誌』[*Journal of Philosophy*] 12/124.
    1901   「認識と実在の関係」[The relationship between knowledge and reality], in 『巽軒論文二集 [*Second Tatsumiken Collection of Essays*] (Tokyo: Fuzanbō).
    1902   「中江篤介氏の『続一年有半』を読む」[Reading Nakae Tokusuke's *A Year and A Half, Continued*], 『哲学雑誌』[Journal of Philosophy] 17/180.
    1915   「唯物論と唯心論とに対する実在論の哲学的価値」[The philosophical value of realism over materialism and spiritualism 『哲学と宗教』 [Philosophy and Religion] (Tokyo: Kōdōkan).

Katō Hiroyuki 加藤弘之
    1898   「破『破唯物論』」[Refuting *Refuting Materialism*], 『哲学雑誌』[*Journal of Philosophy*] 13/142.

Kosaka Kunitsugu 小坂国継
    2008   『西洋の哲学・東洋の思想』[Western Philosophy, Eastern Thought] (Tokyo: Kōdansha).

Kōsaka Masaaki 高坂正顕
    1965   『西田幾多郎先生の生涯と思想』[The Life and Thought of Nishida Kitarō], in 『高坂正顕著作集』[Collected Works of Kōsaka Masaaki], vol. 8 (Chiba: Risōsha).

Nakae Chōmin 中江兆民
    1901   『続一年有半』[A Year and A Half, Continued] (Tokyo: Hakubunkan).

Nakajima Rikizō 中島力造
    1900   『現今の哲学問題』[Recent Problems of Philosophy] (Tokyo: Fukyūsha).

Nishida Kitarō 西田幾多郎
    1907   「実在に就いて」[On reality], 『哲学雑誌』[Journal of Philosophy] 22/241.
    1990   *An Inquiry into the Good*, trans. by Masao Abe and Christopher Ives (New Haven, cn: Yale University Press).
    2003a   『善の研究』[*An Inquiry into the Good*], in nkz 1.
    2003b   「高橋（里美）文学士の拙著『善の研究』に対する批評に答う」[A Reply to Takahashi (Satomi)'s criticism of my work *An Inquiry into the Good*], in nkz 1.
    2006   『書簡集 2』, nikz 19.
    2008   『初期草稿』, nikz 16.
    2009   「鎌倉雑談 (一九三六)」[A chat in Kamakura (1936)] nkz 24.

Nishitani Keiji 西谷啓治
　1987　『西谷啓治著作集』[Collected Works of Nishitani Keiji], vol. 9 (Tokyo: Sōbunsha).

Paulsen, Friedrich
　1892　*Einleitung in die Philosophie* (Berlin: Hertz).

Sawayanagi Seitarō 澤柳政太郎
　1888　「新心理学と哲学 [The new psychology and philosophy],『哲学雑誌』[Journal of Philosophy], 2/23.

Schnädelbach, Herbert
　2009　『ドイツ哲学史 1831–1933』[A History of Philosophy in Germany, 1831–1933], trans. by Toshiaki Funayama et al. (Tokyo: Hōsei Daigaku Shuppankyoku).

Tomonaga Sanjūrō 朝永三十郎
　1902　『哲学綱要』[Outlines of Philosophy] (Tokyo: Hōbunkan).
　1905　『哲学辞典』[Dictionary of Philosophy] (Tokyo: Hōbunkan).

Ueberweg, Friedrich
　1923　*Grundriss der Geschichte der Philosophie*, iv, *Die Deutsche Philosophie des xix, Jahrhunderts und der Gegenwart*, 12th revised edition (Berlin: E. S. Mittler und Sohn).

Ueda Shizuteru 上田閑照
　1991　『西田幾多郎を読む』[Reading Nishida Kitarō] (Tokyo: Iwanami Shoten).
　2002　『上田閑照集 [The Ueda Shizuteru Collection], vol. 2 (Tokyo: Iwanami Shoten).

Wundt Wilhelm
　1880　*Grundzüge der physiologischen Psychologie*, vol 2 (Leipzig: Wilhelm Engelmann).
　1896　*Grundriss der Psychologie*, 2nd edition (Leipzig: Wilhelm Engelmann).
　1897　*System der Philosophie*, 2nd edition (Leipzig: Wilhelm Engelmann).

Graham Mayeda

University of Ottawa

Permeating Each Others' Hearts

Natsume Sōseki and Watsuji Tetsurō
on Ethics and the Unity of Self and Other

It is well known that philosopher Watsuji Tetsurō (1889–1960) was influenced by his teacher, author Natsume Sōseki (1867–1916). There are many indications of how profoundly Watsuji was touched by Sōseki's unrelenting devotion to justice and fairness and his rejection of selfishness. However, the influence goes beyond this personal level: there are many aspects of Watsuji's ethics that can be clarified through a comparison with Sōseki's ethics of the artist set out in his works such as *Theory of Literature* and "The Philosophical Foundations of the Literary Arts." This article focuses on four points at which the ethics of Sōseki and Watsuji touch: the possibility of ethics depends on the interpenetration (浸透) of the experience of self and the group; the tension (張り) inherent in human relations; the importance of pursuing ideals, which are embodied in relationships; and the transcendent status of experiencing in itself. While these basic elements of the ethics of Sōseki and Watsuji overlap, Watsuji's phenomenological method enables him to overcome the essentialism inherent in Sōseki's psychologism. It also enabled him to use not only the interpenetration of thoughts and experiences but also the interconnection of human acts to demonstrate the fundamental characteristics of human existence that make ethics possible—indeed, that *are* ethics..

KEYWORDS: Watsuji Tetsurō—Natsume Sōseki—phenomenological ethics—ethics in art

Many researchers have noted the influence of author Natsume Sōseki 夏目漱石 (1867–1916) on the young philosopher, Watsuji Tetsurō 和辻哲郎 (1889–1960).¹ For instance, Karaki Junzō believed that Watsuji's interaction with Sōseki prompted the philosopher to shift from his initial interest in Søren Kierkegaard and Friedrich Nietzsche to the study of ethics.² In this light, it makes sense to study Sōseki's ethics of the artist to help us understand some of the features of Watsuji's ethics such as his notion of betweenness (間柄 *aidagara*), which plays a key role in his three-volume *Ethics* (『倫理学』), written between 1937 and 1949. A comparative study can shed light on Watsuji's understanding of the nature of the relationship between the individual and the group, which has remained controversial in the literature: Yuasa Yasuo points to the common criticism that Watsuji prioritized the group over the individual,³ while Utsunomiya Yoshiaki

---

1. Watsuji's first positive impression of Sōseki seems to have been when the young man read the author's short novel "London Tower" (『倫敦塔』), published in 1905 (Watsuji 1916, reprinted in Karaki 1963, 414; see also wtz 18: 312), although he had read Sōseki's poem "Military Service" published the previous year (wtz 18: 311). Watsuji first corresponded with Sōseki in 1913, and he also met him by chance that same year. Thereafter, he frequently visited Sōseki at home, where he took part in a study group. Shortly after Sōseki's death in 1916, Watsuji wrote a tribute to his teacher titled "A Reminiscence of Natsume Sensei" (『夏目先生の追憶』), which attests to the deep impression he made on Watsuji. Dilworth, Viglielmo and Jacinto Zavala briefly discuss the influence of Sōseki on Watsuji in the introduction to the selections of his work in their *Sourcebook for Modern Japanese Philosophy* (1998, 223). Karaki Junzō and T. James Kodera also write about Sōseki's influence (Karaki 1963, 11–14; Kodera 1987), and likewise Yuasa Yasuo and Katsube Mitake in a discussion recorded in Yuasa 1973, 20–22 (see also Yuasa 1981, 29, 31).

2. Karaki 1963, 14.

3. "In Watsuji's ethics, the whole always takes precedence over the parts; the individual takes on a 'persona' only in specific relationships" [translation] (Yuasa 1981, 271). Yuasa writes that this precedence should really be recognized simply as a feature of some societies, rather than as a

reproached Watsuji for modeling the relationship between the group and the individual on the relationship between the whole (全体) and its parts (部分).[4] While provocative in itself, such criticism also highlights the need to clarify exactly what Watsuji's views were. An examination of how Sōseki's ethics might have influenced Watsuji sheds light on such questions.

This paper focuses on four ways in which Sōseki's philosophy of literature may have influenced Watsuji's ethics. First, both thinkers argued that the possibility of ethics depends on the interpenetration (*shintō* 浸透) of the experience of the self and the group. Second, human relations involve an inherent tension (*hari* 張り). For Sōseki, this tension exists within human experience: there is a tension between the flow of consciousness, which we habitually follow, and the resistance against this flow that the ethical actor must demonstrate. Rather than focusing on the tension within experience, Watsuji points to the tension between the group and the individual—to be human is to exist within the dialectical movement between these two poles.[5] Third, both had a relational understanding of ethical ideals: ideals are not simply abstract ideas; they only exist within a particular relationship or way of being with others. This is evident in Sōseki's description of the role of

---

universal characteristic. In this light, he believes that Watsuji's ethics has some value, because it sheds light on the societies for whom this precedence holds true (276).

4. Utsunomiya writes:

[B]ut can the individual really only be a negative moment (*hiteiteki keiki*) of the whole?… Does the individual really only exist in relationship to the whole? Is it not rather the case that the individual is an individual only in relationship to another individual? Perhaps the true meaning of the individual whom [Watsuji] contrasts with the whole is not really an individual per se, but more like a part of a whole, similar to [the relationship] between each cell and an organism; in other words, [the individual is] nothing other than a structural element of the whole. In order to capture the relationship between individuals as such, Watsuji introduced the category of the 'many,' thus creating the scheme "individual"—"the many"—"the whole." The whole is made up of many individuals, and yet in order to constitute the whole, the many individuals must 'abandon their individuality and become one.' However, if we accept that the individual is only truly an individual within the relationship between individuals, then the individual loses her own individuality, and the problem of [understanding] the relationship between each individual vanishes. (translation, Utsunomiya 1980, 107)

For an excellent summary of the criticism of Watsuji by both Utsunomiya and Yuasa, see Honda 2019.

5. Watsuji 1996, 124.

the author, which is to communicate ethical ideals by placing the people about whom they write in relationships that embody them. Similarly, for Watsuji, an ethical life, like that of Jesus or the Buddha, is a life in which one's experience of the absolute is embodied in one's relations with others.[6] Finally, both recognize a transcendent aspect to reality that manifests itself as our capacity for relating to others. Adopting the phenomenological psychology of William James (1842–1910), Sōseki considered this reality to be the flow of consciousness, which is at the same time the flow of life itself.[7] In contrast, adopting a phenomenological stance, Watsuji considered the relational nature of human experiencing itself to be a manifestation of the "absolute" (絶対者).[8] The absolute is not a transcendent reality in the sense of something separate from the reality of each human being: rather, Watsuji conceived of it as an experience of the inter-relationship of all beings as the unfolding of experience in general.[9]

The primary task of this paper will be to elaborate on these four resonances between the theory of experience underlying Sōseki's philosophy of literature and Watsuji's phenomenological ethics. However, before pursuing this task, I would like to explain briefly why it is justified to study these resonances.

The relevance of Sōseki's philosophy of literature for interpreting Watsuji's ethics

The suggestion that we study Watsuji via Sōseki may at first seem puzzling. Sōseki was a writer, not a philosopher, and he focused solely on the ethics of artists rather than develop a general ethical theory. Moreover,

---

6. Watsuji 1996, 122.

7. For a thorough discussion of the resonance between Sōseki's theory and that of William James, including the elements of Zen Buddhism that Sōseki mixed in, see Lamarre 2008.

8. Watsuji 1996, 122; wtz 10: 129.

9. Watsuji had in mind the examples of Jesus Christ and Gotama Buddha, who experienced an awakening to the Absolute which they then sought to integrate into their everyday relationships (Watsuji 1996, 122; wtz 10: 129). The experiential nature of the Absolute is most clear when Watsuji writes about the voice of conscience as "a voice invoking absolute negativity" (絶対的否定性への呼び声), which he describes as "a voice of negation from one's innermost" (自己の内奥から否定の声) and "a negation at the rear of one's self" (自己の奥底に否定が存する) (Watsuji 1996, 137; wtz 10: 145).

his theory of literature was inspired by philosophers who were not of interest to Watsuji such as William James and Herbert Spencer. Finally, there was a long gap between Sōseki's writing on the subject, which was roughly between 1903 and 1907, and Watsuji's ethics, of which the first volume was published in 1937.[10] However, when one reads Sōseki and Watsuji together, the similarities become clearer. In a talk on the philosophy of literature in 1907, Sōseki wrote:

> [T]he excellent character of the author will permeate (浸みわたる) the hearts of readers, spectators, or listeners.... It will become part of their flesh and blood, handed down to their children and grandchildren.[11]

The writer relates to others through her novels, but this relationship is not just indirect; through her texts, the author embeds her ethical views into the "flesh and blood" of her readers. Her writing enables her to permeate the being of readers so thoroughly that their whole way of seeing the world is affected.

In *Ethics*, Watsuji wrote in similar language about the interpenetration of the experience of oneself and another. Just as the ethical views of the author permeate her audience, according to Watsuji, my experience is influenced by that of the other:

> Activity inherent in the consciousness of "I" is never determined by this "I" alone but is also determined by others. It is not merely a reciprocal activity in that one-way conscious activities are performed one after another but, rather, that either one of them is at once determined by both sides; that is, by itself and by the other. Hence, so far as betweenness-oriented existences are concerned, each consciousness interpenetrates the other (浸透する). When Thou gets angry, my consciousness may be entirely colored by Thou's expressed anger, and when I feel sorrow, Thou's consciousness is influenced by I's sorrow. It can never be argued that the consciousness of such a self is independent.[12]

In this passage, Watsuji, much like Sōseki, emphasizes that the relation-

---

10. Of course, Watsuji's reflection on ethics began far earlier, in part since he was hired to teach ethics at Kyoto Imperial University in 1925.
11. Natsume 2009a, 197–198; Natsume 1986, 90.
12. Watsuji 1996, 69; WTZ 10: 73.

ship between people is not a relationship between two completely separate individuals, but rather a sort of interpenetration or "permeation" (浸透) of the consciousness of one by the other. As David Dilworth writes, Watsuji "points to an experiential horizon… which transcends the plane of abstract individuals," a "horizon of dialectical immediacy prior to the subject-object and self-society dichotomies."[13]

The similarity that is evident in the juxtaposition of the two passages justifies a comparative study of Sōseki and Watsuji.[14] Sōseki's views may have helped Watsuji to formulate the basic philosophical question in his mature work, which is an inquiry into the relationship between the individual and the group. And perhaps it also provided the outline of an answer—this relationship is one of tension (*hari* 張り) that is premised on a fundamental interpenetration of self and other (*hitari* 浸り). Indeed, betweenness (*aidagara* 間柄), Watsuji's term for the relational nature of the human mode of being (人間存在), is essentially a combination of these two features—tension and interpenetration.

A comparative study is also justified based on Watsuji's own account of his relationship to the author. When one reads Watsuji's reminiscence of Sōseki, written eight days after the author's death, it is clear that he was deeply moved by his character, and that the ethics in his novels had a profound effect on Watsuji's outlook. Indeed, he was most impressed by Sōseki's love of humanity, and yet surprised by how it manifested itself as a desire for justice and a deprecation of individualism. Watsuji wrote,

> One cannot understand Sensei's personality without thinking about his passion for justice and his effort to drive out selfishness from love. Sensei could not forgive individuals for loving themselves even though self-love is

---

13. DILWORTH 2005, 47. Dilworth does not mean that the "horizon of dialectical immediacy" is prior to the splitting of subject and object in the sense of temporally prior. Nor do either he or Watsuji mean that it is transcendentally prior. For Sōseki, the priority is dependent on the degree of focusing—what Sōseki calls differentiation—that occurs within the flow of consciousness itself. In the case of Watsuji, both the individual and the community are moments in the development of the absolute as experience.

14. Other scholars have noted the influence. David Dilworth refers to a passage in Karaki Junzō's *Watsuji Tetsurō* (Tokyo: Chikuma Shobo, 1963), where Karaki maintains that the expression *hito to hito no aidagara* used by Watsuji in his works was inspired by a passage in Sōseki's *Kōjin* (*The Wayfarer*) (KARAKI, 12; DILWORTH 2005, 47).

naturally the strongest form of love. Sensei was constantly vigilant against such selfishness within himself. As a keen observer of human psychology, he expressed to us [his students] how this selfishness constituted a grave dark side of human nature.... For Sensei, it was more important to treat others justly than to love.[15]

As we have already indicated, the influence of Sōseki on Watsuji perhaps contributed to the latter's shift from what Kōsaka Masaaki calls his "Sturm und Drang" period toward ethics.[16]

What unites Watsuji and Sōseki is the view that ethical ideals are embodied in concrete relationships; they are in no way simply abstract ideas. In Sōseki's literary theory, the novelist expresses ideals through a description (in a novel or poem) of a particular relationship between people, or in some cases a relationship between people and objects, especially natural ones. Watsuji's contention in his middle and late philosophy that human existence is characterized by "betweenness" (*aidagara* 間柄) is a theoretical way of explaining Sōseki's intuition that ethical ideals are not abstract but must be expressed through concrete relationships.

In the remainder of this article, we will undertake a comparison of the similarities between the views of Sōseki and Watsuji by showing four different ways in which their philosophies resonated with each other.

Resonance one: Interpenetration between individual and group

Tension and unity are two sides of the same coin: tension presupposes a relationship. For Sōseki, the flow of consciousness is what gives each individual's life a sense of unity,[17] and it also unifies groups that share ideas and feelings. In *Theory of Literature,* he discusses in detail how individual consciousness can affect the consciousness of the group,[18] and he also points out how the participation of all humans in the flow of consciousness allows a skilled author to portray relationships whose ideals "permeate the hearts" of

---

15. Translation of Watsuji 1963, 416.
16. Kōsaka discusses the four periods of Watsuji's philosophy in Kōsaka 1964, 176–181.
17. Natsume 2009c, 126.
18. Natsume 2009c, 136–142.

her readers.[19] In the case of Watsuji, it is because the thoughts and feelings of each person penetrate those of others and because the acts of each individual occur within the interconnected acts of others that communication is possible and individual acts have meaning.

Despite the different philosophical bases for their theories—Sōseki's philosophy is rooted in psychology while Watsuji's is phenomenological—the two use similar terms to refer to unity: Sōseki writes about "permeation" (*hitaru* 浸る), whereas Watsuji tends to use "penetration" (*shintō* 浸透). Let us now examine how each characterizes the unity at the heart of human experience.

Permeation in Sōseki's ethics

Sōseki's ethics presupposes that human experience is intersubjective and dynamic: each person's experience offers a perspective on a single continuous flow of experiencing that we all share. Sōseki refers to this shared consciousness as "group consciousness" (集合意識)[20] or "mutual consciousness" (相互意識).[21] He explains the nature of consciousness by drawing on William James' phenomenological psychology,[22] from which he adopts the idea of a "continuous stream of consciousness" (意識の連続).[23] This stream is at once the stream of our experience and that of life itself.[24] It is in constant "flux" (推移),[25] and its apparent unity gives rise to the assumption that if follows the laws of cause and effect, with each new moment of consciousness affecting the next.[26]

Of course, just because the flow of group consciousness is shared, this does not mean that the content of each individual's consciousness is the same: we are not all mind readers. In fact, the opposite is true, and Sōseki

---

19. Natsume 2009a, 198.
20. Natsume 2017, 420.
21. Natsume 2017, 446.
22. Matsui, 119–120; Yamoto 1971, 88–92. Sōseki relies on other psychologists in addition to James such as Lloyd Morgan (1852–1936), author of *Introduction to Comparative Psychology* (London: Walter Scott, 1894), and Karl Groos (1861–1946).
23. Natsume 2009a, 163.
24. Natsume 2009a, 165.
25. Natsume 2009a, 164; Natsume 1986, 39
26. Natsume 2009a, 163.

sets up a dialectic within the flow of consciousness—a dialectic of self and other, sameness and difference—which has profound implications for how we understand the nature of interpersonal relationships. This is most obvious in his explanation of why some individuals are more attuned to the trends of group consciousness than others. While we all share in the flow of consciousness, some individuals are better at noting its patterns and directions.[27] This differentiation gives rise to what Sōseki calls the "three types of focus within group consciousness" (三種の集合的F).[28] Each of these types represents a different way in which the consciousness of one person is able to penetrate group consciousness. The first type is "imitative consciousness" (模擬意識),[29] which is the ability to imitate others—to cry "Fire! Fire!" upon hearing another do so and then to flee. It is evident that the ability to imitate others is essential for our survival as a society.[30] The second type is intuition—some people are able to anticipate the direction in which social trends are going without knowing how they do so.[31] Sōseki calls this the consciousness of those with "talent" (能才) because one must have attained a certain level of understanding in order to have such insight.[32] Finally, there is the consciousness of the genius (天才).[33] Such a person can do more than foresee the next trend, the next cresting wave of group consciousness.

27. Sōseki writes:
The consciousness of ordinary people comes and goes according to the dizzying multiplicity of phenomena; they are as easily fooled as those monkeys in the Chinese legend who were kept happy with four acorns in the morning and three at night. They are easily manipulated by appearances; they sink or swim and run themselves ragged at the prospect of whatever treasure is before them at the moment. The things they encounter every day are myriad and multiple, but they are simply carried away by them into a glimmering confusion. It is a continuous stream, like a procession of carriages, horses, and people endlessly reflected in a mirror. But those [like the genius] who are able to screw themselves tightly to that single core and remain forever unmoved will, according to the form and quality of this core, be able to gather together the limitless floating dust and discover for themselves one or two perspectives to live by. (Natsume 2009c, 130–131; Natsume 2017, 430)
28. The "F" is shorthand for "focus," meaning here the "focus of consciousness." Natsume 2017, 420.
29. Natsume 2017, 420–423.
30. Natsume 2009c, 123.
31. Natsume 2009c, 125–127.
32. Natsume 2017, 423–427.
33. Natsume 2017, 427–435.

Rather, she is able to see many steps ahead. To use a phrase from Friedrich Nietzsche, her meditations are "untimely"—she sees so far ahead that her thoughts are disruptive for ordinary society.[34]

Sōseki is clear that what distinguishes the ordinary person from the genius is not the content of consciousness (for everyone who shares in its flow will eventually arrive at a particular idea if it becomes sufficiently prevalent in society), but rather the speed and timing with which each develops this content. He writes:

> …[T]he waves of consciousness of the genius differ from those of everyone else only in terms of stage, while the process and order of their transformations do not contradict each other in the slightest—indeed, they are in perfect accord with one another.[35]

This "perfect accord" is what permits ideas developed by one person to "penetrate" (染み渡る) the heart and mind of another.

As we have seen, for Sōseki, our experience of life is a continuous flow of consciousness shared by all of us. However, the content of the consciousness of two individuals is not identical at any given moment. Nevertheless, the more attuned we are to the trends of the era in which we live, the more often we are able share thoughts and feelings. What is not yet clear, especially in Sōseki's *Theory of Literature,* is what the relationship is between the self, the other, and group consciousness. As we will see in the next section, Sōseki characterizes the relationship between self, other and the flow of consciousness as a kind of tension. It is this model of "tension" (*hari* 張り) within shared consciousness that has similarities with Watsuji's understanding of betweenness (*aidagara* 間柄), the term he uses to characterize the relational character of humans.

Permeation in Watsuji's ethics

In the case of Watsuji, interpenetration takes place at two levels: at the level of the dialectic of individual and group, and at the level of the movement of absolute negation itself. In the first case, human existence is characterized by moments in which individualism is asserted and the group is rejected,

---

34. Natsume 2009c, 128.
35. Natsume 2009c, 130; Natsume 2017, 429.

but also moments in in which we identify completely with a social group by adopting their values and norms and adhering to social rules.[36] Watsuji calls this back and forth process a "negative interdependent relationship" (否定的な相依関係).[37] In the second case, the condition for the possibility of this negative interdependent relationship is the emptiness in which the movement of negation of absolute negativity (絶対的否定性の否定の運動) that characterizes this relationship takes place.[38] Watsuji calls this a "kind of absolute wholeness,"[39] thus indicating the interpenetration that it presupposes. It may be difficult to think of this wholeness as being a kind of interpenetration, but Watsuji tries to make this clear when he writes that

> an established betweenness is, in its extreme, the absolute wholeness that consists of the nonduality of the self and the other.... [I]t is authenticity (*honraisei*) as the ground out of which we, fundamentally speaking, come forth.[40]

Watsuji associates this ground with what is called in Buddhism "the original face before your parents were born" (本来の面目),[41] a reference to a famous *kōan*, a tool of Zen practice for helping the Zen practitioner to align with reality.[42]

Let us begin by examining the first aspect, the negative interdependent relationship. In Watsuji's account, this kind of interpenetration has both a subjective and an objective aspect. The subjective element is the interpenetration of my experience with yours. The objective element is what Watsuji calls the "practical interconnection of acts" (実践的行為的連関): all of my acts take on meaning because they are embedded in a network of the acts of others.[43]

In regard to the subjective aspect, Watsuji's explains that our experience

---

36. Watsuji 1996, 145, 186; wtz 10: 152, 195.
37. Ibid.
38. Watsuji 1996, 117, 124; wtz 10: 124, 131.
39. Ibid.
40. Ibid. I do not really like the translation of *honraisei* (本来性) as "authenticity" because it loses the connection with the Zen kōan of the original face (本来の面目) that Watsuji invokes. I discuss this point further below.
41. Watsuji 1996, 187; wtz 10: 195.
42. For more on the use of *kōan* in Rinzai Zen practice, see Hori 2003, 3–90.
43. For a description of Watsuji's view, see Sevilla 2017, 11 and 42.

is inherently relational: we cannot find an experience of the pure "I." He explains this relational nature of experience as follows:

> My seeing Thou is already determined by your seeing me, and the activity of my loving Thou is already determined by your loving me. Hence, my becoming conscious of Thou is inextricably interconnected with your becoming conscious of me. This interconnection we have called betweenness is quite distinct from the intentionality of consciousness. Activity inherent in the consciousness of "I" is never determined by this "I" alone but is also determined by others. It is not merely a reciprocal activity in that one-way conscious activities are performed one after another but, rather, that either one of them is at once determined by both sides; that is, by itself and by the other. Hence, so far as betweenness-oriented existences are concerned, each consciousness interpenetrates the other. When Thou gets angry, my consciousness may be entirely colored by Thou's expressed anger, and when I feel sorrow, Thou's consciousness is influenced by I's sorrow. It can never be argued that the consciousness of such a self is independent.[44]

Watsuji follows up this theoretical description with a practical example—the streetcar.[45] Even though we may be surrounded by strangers on a streetcar, our thoughts and feelings are influenced by those around us: we all feel impatient when the streetcar is delayed as we are rushing to work, we all feel apprehensive if one passenger yells at another, and we share a common joy when every passenger on the car is going to a sporting event (as long as no fans of the opposing team are onboard!). These shared feelings point to the subjective form of interpenetration—the "interpenetration of consciousness" (意識の浸透)[46] or the "consciousness of betweenness" (間柄的意識).[47]

While what Watsuji calls the subjective aspect of shared consciousness takes on the principal role in Sōseki's account, for the former there is another

---

44. WATSUJI 1996, 69; WTZ 10: 73.
45. WTZ 10: 70.
46. WTZ 10: 64.
47. WTZ 10: 73. Johnson calls this the "porosity or openness of one consciousness to another" (JOHNSON 2019, 90). He also highlights this porosity as a feature that distinguishes Watsuji's notion of the relationship to others from that of Heidegger. He writes: "Watsuji arrives at a very different conception of the self from that found in the notion of Dasein. The practical subject differs from Dasein first, to the extent that direct relational interaction is constitutive for it, and second, insofar as the kind of self it is that is so constituted is able to be continuous with and extend into others, who, in turn, are able to extend into and be continuous with it" (ibid., 99).

way in which each person is always together with others—through human acts. This is the objective aspect of relationality—each act takes on a meaning in relation to the context of human actions in general (行為的連関). Our association and interdependence with others are thus not only subjectively experienced but objectively manifest through our acts.[48] The recognition of an active facet to human existence gives rise to its dynamic dialectical structure, as acts unfold in time.

Watsuji gives many examples of the objective manifestation of the interconnection between individuals: roads, traffic patterns, railroads, radio broadcasts, the postal system, indeed, communication in general.[49] Such interactions are objective not simply because they are physical but rather because they are "public." For instance, public paths and alleys reflect the historical pattern of movements in a village, and they develop and extend over time as villages become connected, prefectures or provinces form, and the public road system emerges to reflect the political organization of the state.[50] In this way, the public forms of transportation and communication point to our fundamental interconnection.

As we have seen, Watsuji's ethics presupposes a profound interrelationship between the self and the group, which Watsuji captures in regard to the subjective element using a term similar to that used by Sōseki—*interpenetration* (浸透). Moreover, in the realm of action, acts are "interconnected" (連関). Everything we do and experience as humans implies that we are always already in a relationship with others. This is *betweenness* (*aidagara* 間柄), a fundamental feature of human existence.

As we can see, there are correlates to Sōseki's notion of "penetration" (浸り) in both the subjective (experiential) aspects of Watsuji's philosophy, in which case the term he uses is "interpenetration" (浸透), and in the objective aspects, in which case the term he uses is "interconnection" (連関). The intersubjective nature of experience evokes the "flow" of the consciousness that Sōseki describes in his theory of literature. The objective aspect evokes Sōseki's account of the role of the author, which is to portray in a poem or a novel the relationship between the characters by reproducing a con-

48. Watsuji 1996, 18.
49. Watsuji 1996, 155, 159, 163.
50. Watsuji 1996, 161.

versation or describing the way they act toward each other. These physical and communicative acts can have meaning precisely because they take place against a background of shared human feeling. However, while Watsuji's objective aspect is embodied in the patterns of interrelated activities that exist outside of our mind, this aspect remains interiorized in Sōseki's psychologistic analysis.

I mentioned earlier that there is another level of Watsuji's philosophy—the level of the absolute—at which interpenetration takes on an important role. We will discuss this below in the section on transcendence in Watsuji's philosophy.

Resonance two:
the role of tension in sōseki and watsuji

Tension in Sōseki's theory of literature

In *The Theory of Literature* and "Philosophical Foundations of the Literary Arts," Sōseki notes that tension is a fundamental feature of human existence, which exists between two poles, the undifferentiated wholeness of the "flow of consciousness" (意識の連続), and the differentiated consciousness (分化した意識) that results when self and other emerge from the flow of consciousness in a process of differentiation and distancing.[51] The tension that Sōseki points to between the undifferentiated and differentiated consciousness is the difference between simply following one's habits of thought, which he considers to be an immersion in the undifferentiated flow of consciousness, and adopting an ethical standpoint, which requires one to focus on particular parts of one's experience (through differentiation and distancing) and directing this experience along particular "vectors."[52] In

---

51. Natsume 2009a, 173. To demonstrate the tension that is created between self and other, Sōseki uses a fun metaphor: the process of making *mochi* covered in *kinako*. He writes: "We latch on to our consciousness and throw it out there, latch on to it and throw it out there— throw it out there just like an *awamochi* maker plucks out individual bits of pounded rice *mochi* and tosses them into a dish of *kinako* soybean flour" (Natsume 1986, 51). Of course, once thrown into *kinako*, the tension between *mochi*-maker and *mochi* is gone; but in the case of consciousness, the tension persists—as Sōseki says, we "latch on to our consciousness" (意識を攫む, Natsume 1986, 172) in a way one does not do with *mochi*.

52. Ibid., 171. The reader may find this distinction between immersion in undifferentiated consciousness and taking a standpoint within this consciousness by differentiation and distanc-

this way, each human is torn between wanting to simply remain immersed in the flow of undifferentiated consciousness and following her habits, and wanting to assert her individuality by taking up a stand within the flow and making choices to direct it.

As we saw in the previous section, according to Sōseki, consciousness, like life itself, is continuously unfolding and is characterized by a kind of unity. However, tension can be created within the flow of experience by those who seek to direct how their lives, and hence their conscious experience, unfolds. To account for this, Sōseki explains that it is possible to focus on particular aspects of the flow of consciousness and so differentiate those aspects of the flow from others. When individuals begin to focus on differences within the flow of consciousness, they recognize that they have a choice at each moment whether to follow along with the flow or direct it in a particular way. To make this point clear, Sōseki compares himself with a visual artist—both may observe the grass, but only a painter can differentiate the many shades of green. Indeed, Sōseki writes that Titian could distinguish fifty shades where he sees only one.[53] The artist is able to distinguish particular kinds of experiences within the general flow of consciousness and interrupt the flow by focusing on it from a particular perspective. This power of differentiation then gives the artist a choice, for instance when selecting a colour for painting the sea of grass waving in a field. Sōseki explains:

> The differentiation among the contents of consciousness indicates that there is a wide range of possible streams of continuity these contents can follow, which, in turn, indicates that there is a considerable latitude in choosing among the possible ideal forms—that is, among the specific types of continuity of consciousness from which we choose in leading our own lives....[54]

As we will see in the case of Watsuji's philosophy, an inherent tension—

---

ing to be a bit imprecise: it is. The metaphor is evocative, but it lacks philosophical precision. However, I think the association of the flow of consciousness with habit and the process of differentiation as a resistance of habit can be helpful: one may observe the cherry blossoms every spring and share in the feelings this habitual practice engenders, but one can also inquire into the nuances of feeling and how they are evoked. It is in doing the latter that the artist can evoke similar feelings in her readers by depicting the cherry blossoms or blossom viewing in a particular way.

53. Natsume 2009a, 174; Natsume 1986, 53–54; see also Natsume 2009c, 133.
54. Natsume 2009a, 177; Natsume 1986, 54.

a push and pull—exists between the individual and society. This tension between the individual and the person who merely follows along with the group also exists in Sōseki's philosophy: the artistic genius resists the flow of consciousness that carries most of us along most of the time by focusing on an aspect of it. In so doing, he is able to identify the nuances within it, to "see within it what others fail to notice, to hear what others do not hear, and to feel or think what others have missed."[55] The genius is so fascinated by the area of consciousness on which he concentrates that he becomes an "oddball" who "will not comprehend the customs of society, nor will he conform to the niceties of the world. In some cases, he will lack even the most basic moral sensibility."[56] Thus, for Sōseki, to assert individualism requires resistance to the group, but at the same time, the group reacts to this resistance with fear and loathing. And so, similar to Watsuji's philosophy, when we make a choice in life and assert our individualism, our inherent connection with others creates a tension (*hari* 張り) within the flow of consciousness,[57] and as a result, geniuses who choose to focus in ever greater detail on a particular aspect of the flow find themselves in "conflict with the trends of the age."[58]

Tension also surfaces in Sōseki's philosophy of literature because we have a tendency to assert our difference from others and then lapse back into normalcy. In this way, our existence is an inherent tension between asserting individuality and reabsorption into the group. We may live selfish lives by simply allowing experiences to take us where they may; or we can take a stand and pursue ideals that we perceive within its currents. But we can never do wholly one or the other thing; we shuttle back and forth between the two. This dynamic tension is dependent on the underlying unity that Sōseki sees as the possibility of ethics: the creation of ideals depends on the one hand on differentiating the otherwise unitary flow of consciousness— literally pulling it apart and examining it more closely, as if in freeze-frame

---

55. Natsume 2009c, 132; Natsume 2017, 432.
56. Natsume 2009c, 134; Natsume 2017, 434; see also Natsume 2009c, 131.
57. Natsume 2009c, 132, 135.
58. Natsume 2009c, 128. Sōseki doesn't directly use the term tension (*hari*), but such a tension is clearly evoked not only by his description of how the talented person pulls consciousness in a particular direction but also in the social consequence of doing so, which creates a "conflict with the trends of the age" (Natsume 2017, 427).

—but in order for ethics to be possible, the ideals articulated by the author or poet must be able to permeate the consciousness of the readers.

Tension in Watsuji's ethics

Tension also plays a key role in Watsuji's ethics: he characterizes the relationship between self and the group, which he terms "betweenness" (*aidagara* 間柄), as a kind of tension rather than as relationship of contradiction.[59] In other words, the assertion of the individual is not simply the negation of the group and vice versa.[60] Instead, human existence, conceived relationally as betweenness, exists between the assertion of individuality and assertion of the group. He writes:

> From the standpoint of subjective spatiality, an individual cannot simply be a disconnected point. Of course, an individual obtains her individuality precisely through the negation of community, and precisely because of this, she cannot have an independent subsistence. That she is established through the negation of community means that she finds that other individuals exist and she distances herself from them. This gives rise to the opposition between subjects, such that the self stands opposed to the other, and there appears also a "tension" (*hari* 張り) that spreads over these subjects. The self and the other are distanced from one another, so it does not follow that they are self-subsistent without connection. Rather, the truth is exactly the contrary. It means that they become relative to one another. For this reason, this distance turns out to be, at the same time, a field in which the movement of the connection as well as the unification of subjects, takes place. What was grasped as subjective spatiality is exactly the connection between subjects who stand opposed to each other in the form of self and other.[61]

As we can see, the relationship between the individual and the group is not one of contradiction but of tension.[62] Humans exist within a field of relations that Watsuji calls "subjective spatiality" or "subjective extendedness" (主体的空間性). The individual is not just an isolated point, but rather

---

59. WATSUJI 1996, 346–7.
60. WATSUJI 1996, 187–8.
61. WATSUJI 1996, 187; WTZ 10: 187.
62. See also WTZ 10: 187–8 and WTZ 10: 236.

exists in a web of dynamic relationships with others. This field or web maintains the tension between its points.

In practical terms, what Watsuji is describing is the fact that each human has moments in which he struggles to pull away from the group, but also moments in which he returns to it, though the group to which he returns may take on a different form from the one that he left, and his relationship to the group may also evolve. Whereas for Sōseki it is only the genius and ethical author who feel the tension between acting justly and fairly and acting in one's self-interest, according to Watsuji, to be human is to constantly be located in inherent tension between individual and group, and thus *betweenness*, the fundamental characteristic of human existence, is likewise characterized by a tension between the two moments of the self and the group. Thus whereas Sōseki juxtaposed selfish and ethical action, Watsuji sees all human activity as "ethical" in that it operates within this fundamental tension between individual and group.

As we have seen, in Sōseki's approach, the flow of consciousness—the flow of life itself—takes on a foundational status as that which is most real.[63] Watsuji departs from this problematic essentialist psychologism; in adopting a phenomenological method, he clarifies that the tension between self and the group is in fact a facet of relationality—of betweenness—and therefore a fundamental feature of human existence (*ningen sonzai* 人間存在).[64]

---

63. Sōseki writes: "Consciousness is the only thing that can be said to exist—to really exist" (Natsume 2009a, 163). Watsuji notes a similar tendency to essentialism in Edmund Husserl's phenomenology. According to Watsuji, for Husserl, there is still something primordial that does not exist in subjective space and time: consciousness. Watsuji writes:

> Husserl argues that basic temporality is precisely the intentionality of consciousness itself and that this intentionality is constructed within basic consciousness. Therefore, basic consciousness is itself not temporal because it is the ground of temporality. That is to say, in the nontemporal stream of consciousness, the primary contents of experience (i.e., "consciousness of …") are discriminated from each other and the intentionality of these experiences turns out to be prephenomenal temporality that serves to construct phenomenal time.
> (Watsuji 1996, 212)

64. As Erin McCarthy explains, citing John Maraldo, "*Ningen* is a dynamic concept of self, one that John Maraldo has suggested be understood, not as a metaphysical entity, rather as an interrelation" (McCarthy 2011, 13; citing Maraldo 2002, 185). She goes on to write, "*ningen* is *both* an individual *and* in relation at the same time, and to isolate either of these two aspects of being human, for Watsuji, does not express the fullness of what it is to be a human being" (ibid.).

He thus abandons Sōseki's psychological materialism by reconceiving the tension between the moments of human existence as a feature of our capacity to enter into relationships rather than positing an entity like the flow of consciousness. The unity at the base of existence in Sōseki's model is thus replaced by a dynamic movement of difference—the movement of the tension between the individual and the group.

While Watsuji's philosophy is in some sense an improvement over Sōseki's problematic adoption of Jamesian phenomenological psychology, it introduces difficulties of its own. One of the most pernicious is the nature of the tension (*hari*) that constitutes betweenness (*aidagara* 間柄): while it is clear that one pole of the tension is the individual, it is not always clear what constitutes the other. Is it the group? Is it the other? Is it society? I suggest that if we take the influence of Sōseki on Watsuji seriously, we should abandon the view that the tension is between two entities, either the individual and the other or the individual and a specific group. Rather, the tension is simply a feature of betweenness itself: it is a tension between the individual and *any possible group*.

Because relationality has both a subjective and an objective aspect in Watsuji's philosophy, the tension manifests itself both in our experience and in our acts. For instance, when we leave home for the first time to go to school or to work, we feel free, but at the same time, we sense the tug of family and friends. However, the relationality is not reducible to the experience of tension; the tension between individual and group also manifests itself "outside" our thoughts and feelings in the world of action. Each time we act, it is against a background of the acts of others. And many of these acts follow long-established patterns. Thus when we choose how to dress for the first day of work or school, or when we decide how to comport ourselves in the classroom or the workplace, the meaning of our forms of dress and comportment are derived from pre-established norms. Each person acts out their individualism within, or at least in relation to, the network of acts of those around us. Thus betweenness, the fundamental characteristic of human existence as relational, involves both these sorts of tension—an experiential tension and tension between the acts of the individual and the group.

As we have seen, in Watsuji's philosophy, tension is a fundamental feature of human existence as ethical existence. While for Sōseki, the tension is between the individual who "goes with the flow" and the genius who pursues ideals and arouses ethical motives in others, Watsuji explains how this tension is manifest both at the level of subjective experience and at the objective level in terms of the interconnection of human acts.

Resonance three: a relational notion of ideals

In regard to the third resonance, the ethics of both Sōseki and Watsuji depend on a relational notion of "ideals": ideals are defined through our relation to others, and we actualize them by acting in a way that helps others to realize and align with the relational nature of human existence. Sōseki explicitly uses the term "ideals" (理想). The role of the ethical artist is to focus on and then express particular streams within the flow of our shared experience that express ideals such as bravery, truth or authentic feeling. Because of the power of her vision, which his rooted in a shared flow of consciousness, the artist is able to express something true about human existence. Watsuji rarely uses the term "ideals," preferring instead to speak of the realization of "supreme values" (最高の価値) or "goodness" (善),[65] which is the manifestation of what he calls "absolute wholeness." When our actions express goodness, they manifest absolute wholeness in concrete relationships.[66]

While they share similarities, there are also marked differences between the views of Sōseki and Watsuji that result from the philosophical orientation each adopts: the former adopts a psychologism with a tendency toward essentializing consciousness, while the latter arguably avoids essentialism by rooting his ontology of relationality (*aidagara*) in the movement of absolute emptiness. The difference in orientation can be seen in their explanation of how we discover and manifest ideals. Sōseki's ideals correspond to a particular focus within consciousness which he calls a "continuity of consciousness."[67] In contrast, for Watsuji, Christian love or Buddhist compassion, the two exemplary values to which he consistently returns, are not simply aspects of experience, but rather, they are ways of taking responsi-

---

65. Watsuji 1996, 134.
66. Ibid.
67. Natsume 2009a, 173.

bility in our relationships that we discover once we align ourselves with the movement of absolute negativity that constitutes human existence as relational.[68] For Watsuji, the fundamental principle of ethics is the dual existence of humans as both individual and social, and moral action the manifestation of the "absolute wholeness" that makes this dual existence possible.[69] Thus the pursuit of ideals is the infusion into social relationships of the absolute wholeness that such relationships presuppose. In practical terms, moral action is pointing to how reality is freely and spontaneously expressing its fundamental nature.

Ideals in Sōseki's philosophy

For the most part, we are self-absorbed, simply going where the flow of our consciousness and our inclinations take us: in other words, we live by habit.[70] But we are also able to direct the flow of consciousness in a particular way—in essence, direct our life down a particular stream within the flow of consciousness as a whole. When we choose to do this, we are living in accordance with what Sōseki calls an "ideal." He writes:

> [O]ur ideals gradually evolve as we make choices concerning what sort of sequence we want our continuous consciousness to follow and what sort of contents we want to include in it.[71]

Thus, for Sōseki, an ideal is a "kind of life," i.e. a story about it—the meaning we want our life to have.[72] The story helps us to make choices: it provides a focus within the flow of consciousness, a way of discerning among otherwise undifferentiated experiences and choosing meaningful ones.

It is important to note that not just any ideal—not just any story—will do. Rather, Sōseki is clear that the various ideals one pursues in life are ways of "understanding… the problem of how one should live."[73] Thus, to make choices in pursuit of an ideal is to touch what Sōseki calls the "essence of life"; some ideals, some stories, are closer to the essence of life than others.

68. Watsuji 1996, 139.
69. Watsuji 1996, 124; wtz 10: 131.
70. Natsume 2009c, 131, 138.
71. Natsume 2009a, 168; Natsume 1986, 44.
72. Natsume 2009a, 168, 207; Natsume 1986, 44.
73. Natsume 2009a, 208; see also 212.

Thanks to the fact that ideals touch the essence of life, a life lived in accordance with an ideal will not be purely selfish, because it will be aligned with this essence and inspire others to resist lapsing into habit to instead pursue ideals themselves. For instance, Sōseki explains that the role of the ethical author is to create a "receptive affinity" between herself and the reader[74] by means of which she can influence the choices the reader makes and encourage them to realize this essence.

Sōseki distinguishes three primary ideals within the flow of consciousness: streams of consciousness dominated by the intellect, streams dominated by feeling, and streams dominated by heroic action. For instance, the philosopher focuses primarily on the intellectual experiences within the flow of consciousness,[75] leading her to see the world in an abstract way through the lens of generalizing ideas. The author follows a different stream—a different "continuity of consciousness":[76] she analyzes objects in terms of emotions and seeks to clarify the nature of a relationship "in order to savor those relationships more fully than before."[77] The person of action is animated by values such as heroism or decisiveness. Individuals may choose to pursue one of these streams in its pure form or mix them together.

Because ideals are not mere ideas but rather streams within the flow of consciousness, they can be embodied not just in thoughts but in the con-

---

74. NATSUME 2009A, 208. Watsuji clearly felt that Sōseki was the type of author who could achieve this. He wrote:

> Sensei was not a writer of the eye but of the mind. He was a psychologist, not a painter. He was a thinker more than an observer. He was much closer to being a philosopher than a novelist. As a result, one should not mind too much that his works lack an air of realism. (Although if one accepts realism in the sense that Dostoyevsky used the term in characterizing his own works, then Sensei, too, was a realist.)
>
> I myself observed Sensei's remarkable [fixation] on the idea. I believe that it is entirely the way he communicated it that made his work so splendid. What I mean by this is that Sensei's text gave one the strong feeling that it had been (carefully) crafted. However, this feeling quickly disappeared in the face of the idea it embodied. In it, the reader felt as if he were standing before Sensei's naked mind.
>
> In reading his work, we are not simply hearing the report of a person's life; we hear rather the divulging of the interior journey, the experience of a person who has sought the way (*michi*). (translation, Natsume 1963, 419)

75. NATSUME 2009A, 176.
76. NATSUME 2009A, 209.
77. NATSUME 2009A, 178; NATSUME 1986, 59.

crete relationships between individuals or between humans and non-human objects. The role of the author is to express the insights that she gains about emotions by means of the relationships she describes between objects or people. Sōseki gives the example of expressing love:

> [O]ne can express a relation of love via some thing—well, this is much clearer if we make it a person rather than a thing. To express a relation of love via a person is the ideal of eight or nine out of ten people we call novelists. This relation of love can be further differentiated into various types. For example, there is the love that results in a marriage, or the feverish love one succumbs to like a disease—but these old-fashioned kinds hardly ever appear in novels nowadays. More cynical varieties might include a woman who marries even as she remains infatuated with another man, or a couple who finally realize their dream of being together and who begin fighting the very next day.[78]

The example of love focuses on the ideal of feeling. But authors can also address the forms of relationships particular to other ideals. An author might choose to depict the relationship that a hero has to a particular object or toward other humans, for instance by depicting a mountaineer who, foolish though it may be, bravely decides to climb Mount Fuji in winter.[79] Or she might describe a person resolving to cross a desert or to swim across an ocean strait. The continuity of consciousness that embodies the ideal of the hero is portrayed through a particular relationship of the hero to an object like a mountain, a desert or an ocean. Of course, they can also be portrayed in human relationships, as Sōseki did with such tenderness in all of his novels.

To summarize, for Sōseki, to live ethically is to pursue an ideal. An ideal is more than just an abstract idea: it is a particular stream within our consciousness on which we focus and which we develop. These ideals include truth (the ideal of the philosopher), heroism (the ideal of the person of action), or the expression of emotions (the ideal of the artist). These ideals are embodied in relationships between objects or humans. This is why the goal of the writer is to describe certain objects (natural objects and people) and the relationships between them in a way that depicts a particular pos-

78. Natsume 2009a, 183; Natsume 1986, 67.
79. Natsume 2009a, 184.

sibility of being—the instantiation of a particular ideal.[80] The pursuit of these ideals involves the selection within the continuity of consciousness of certain experiences that together give meaning to the undifferentiated flow. Through the pursuit of such ideals, Sōseki explains, we "render the purpose of our existence into something higher and more distinguished" because life is now lived for some identifiable purpose.[81] Indeed, these ideals are not just a way of giving our individual lives purpose—they can serve as the ideals for the group as a whole.

While superficially compelling, Sōseki's theory of ethical ideals lacks philosophical precision; indeed, he has some difficulty explaining what an ideal is within the terms of his Jamesian theory of consciousness. He proposes that an ideal is a particular way of directing the stream of consciousness that involves taking up a standpoint within it and then noting how certain patterns—ideals—can be observed in the flow. However, Sōseki is not especially clear about what it means to adopt a standpoint within the flow of consciousness; sometimes, this seems to be no more than a metaphor. Moreover, it is hard to know how these standpoints can be established if they themselves are abstractions from the flow of consciousness:[82] how can the self be part of the flow of consciousness and at the same time separate itself sufficiently from it to identify within it elements that are consistent with the ideal which that part represents?[83] It was not Sōseki's concern to explain in detail how this occurs; his general point was that the author must be able to identify gradations within a general social understanding of what it means to be a hero or a person embodying one of the other virtues.

Ideals in Watsuji's ethics

Ideals play an important part in Watsuji's ethics. Human existence is inherently relational: it is the relationship between group and individual, which is dynamic and constantly changing. But while human existence is always ethical in nature and each of our choices affect others, it is nonetheless better to

---

80. Natsume 2009a, 212.
81. Natsume 2009a, 198.
82. Natsume 2009a, 171.

83. Perhaps Sōseki would have acknowledged that such a separation is impossible. The model of a feedback loop similar to Heidegger's notion of the hermeneutic circle would have worked better.

make good choices and to promote harmonious relationships. Unsurprisingly, this is the role of ideals. In European philosophical traditions, we tend to think of ideals as ideas or concepts. But in Watsuji's philosophy, because human existence is inherently ethical in the sense that all of our thoughts, feelings and actions are rooted in this dynamic relationship to others, ideals, too must be conceived of relationally. To pursue an ideal for Watsuji means to treat others in a way that is consistent with relational structure of human existence itself. Or as John Maraldo explains in an essay on human dignity and human rights:

> [I]f to be human means to be in reciprocal relationships in which we bestow dignity on one another through respect, then the claim to rights would be a claim to enjoy appropriate relationships, namely, those that realize this law or structure.[84]

I would go a step further and argue that Watsuji explains what an appropriate relationship is: it is one animated by Christian love or Buddhist compassion.[85]

To live in a way that our relationships take the appropriate form, we must first come to understand the nature of human relationships. Watsuji does not explain how we do this, but he does describe what we learn: when we understand the tension in which we all exist between individualism and responsibility to others, we are able to realize Buddhist compassion or Christian love.[86] Thus within any given relationship, we have the possibility of understanding it from the standpoint of the absolute unity of self and other. However, we can only discover this by abandoning unquestioned notions of self and other, most of which are based on conventional group norms. Ideals must be realized within relationships such as the family, the

---

84. MARALDO 2019, 144.

85. The list is not meant to be limited to these two relationships. Similar notions exist in every religion. However, these are the two religions that Watsuji discusses in depth in *Rinrigaku*.

86. Watsuji explains: "[O]bedience to gods or to the authority of the whole, that is the abandonment of individual independence, and the manifestation of love, devotion, or service have always been proclaimed as 'goodness.' This can be illustrated through a simple expression, the Japanese term *nakayoshi*, which refers to the realization of socio-ethical unity" (Watsuji 1996, 134). In other words, when we realize the relational nature of human existence (its "socio-ethical unity"), we express love and compassion.

workplace, the neighbourhood, the nation and so on.[87] However, these relationships are not bound to take on their traditional forms; rather, because of the relational nature of human existence, the forms are just the location where our understanding of the absolute unity of self and others can be actualized. Watsuji explains:

> [H]uman existence… infinitely aims at the realization of communal existence by virtue of the fact that human beings are *ningen*. Because of this, *the pattern of practical connections already realized serves, at the same time, as a pattern yet to be achieved*. Therefore, although ethics is already what is, without being merely what should be, it is also regarded as what should be achieved infinitely, without thereby being a mere law of being.[88]

The forms of relationships may be an inheritance, but they are also "patterns yet to be achieved." This is because the evolution of these patterns is itself a reflection of the inherent relational nature of human existence which is in a constant state of flux or development. Confucius inherited the rites of the Zhou dynasty, but he sought to breath new life into them by seeing them as the manifestation of the four virtues (human-heartedness, righteousness, wisdom and ritual propriety).[89] Old forms can be revitalized: what it means to be a "family" today is much different than what it meant one hundred years ago, and yet the family continues to be a form of human relations in which one can act morally.

My contention that Watsuji's ethics involves the pursuit of ideals differs somewhat from that of other scholars. Kyle Michael James Shuttleworth has suggested that the ideal in Watsuji is authenticity (*honraisei* 本来性). *Honraisei*, he writes, is "an ethical ideal which regulates [the dynamic between individual and community],"[90] and therefore ethics is the pursuit of authenticity. I take a slightly different view because I do not interpret *honraisei* as being itself the ethical ideal. *Honraisei* is something to be realized, but it actualizes itself in human relations as the ideals of love and compassion. This is why Watsuji writes that when we awaken to emptiness, we realize

---

87. For a discussion of how Watsuji's ethics is instantiated in concrete communities, see Sevilla 2017, §1.3.
88. Watsuji 1996, 12; wtz 10: 14. Author's emphasis.
89. Shen 2014, 46.
90. Shuttleworth 2019, 247.

Buddhist compassion, or when we put ourselves entirely in God's hands, we realize Christian love.[91] Part of the confusion can be traced to the fact that Carter and Yamamoto translate *honraisei* as "authenticity." In my view, this is a poor translation because *honraisei* is meant to evoke the *kōan* of the "original face," which in Japanese is called *honrai no menmoku* (本来の面目), and reliance on the translation is what leads Shuttleworth to describe *honraisei* as a regulative ethical ideal. The realization of the emptiness of "self" and "other" is an essential pre-requisite to ethical action, but this realization manifests itself in the ideals of infinite love and compassion. As Watsuji writes,

> regarding the possible connection of human beings, people show a concern so great that it is beyond imagination. This is so because the direction of this possible connection is, in the extreme *the direction in which a human being tries to return to her [original face]*. The present concern is not with ["one's original face"]; nevertheless, this concern does lurk in the background in the form of possibility.[92]

What this quote points to is that ethical action is the consequence of or manifestation of the process of returning to one's original face (*honraisei*). This means that ethical action is the manifestation of this original face (the absolute or simply reality) unfettered by the petty preoccupations of individuals or the tyranny of unquestioned community norms.

This interpretation is consistent with the way that Watsuji discusses freedom, which he acknowledges is "a basic concept of ethics."[93] While in the philosophy of liberalism, freedom is conceived negatively as freedom from coercion,[94] the kind of freedom that is essential to ethics is freedom to "self-initiate without a cause outside of itself."[95] We have the capacity to act freely in this way, Watsuji explains, because we share with "God as Creator" the freedom to realize ourselves in the created. In ethical terms, the manifestation of this freedom is the movement of negativity, which gives us as indi-

---

91. Watsuji 1996, 123.
92. Watsuji 1996, 188. I have substituted "original face" for "authenticity" and "one's authentic countenance," the terms used in the translation of Carter and Yamamoto.
93. Watsuji 1996, 137.
94. Watsuji 1996, 138.
95. Ibid.

viduals the ability to revolt against social norms, but in so doing, to realize our socio-ethical obligations to others by breathing new life into the forms of social relations. As Watsuji writes, this is "the freedom of revolting against one's own foundation… [that] can be *developed from the foundation itself*."[96] Understood in this way, Watsuji's claim that ethics is "the study of human existence" (人間の学としての倫理学) takes on a dual meaning: the nature of human existence is relationality (*aidagara*), and it is because human existence is at its base ethical that we are able to express the Absolute, which is constantly expressing itself freely as the movement of negation.[97] To act ethically, then, is not simply to realize our authentic self, but to act from out of our original nature (*honraisei*).

Thus, Watsuji points to Jesus and the Buddha as paragons of virtue because the ideal in accordance with which they lead their life is that embodied in the very nature of human existence itself, i.e., in relationality (*aidagara*), a fundamental feature of human existence that is in turn rooted in a fundamental feature of reality itself. Both the individual and the group are possible only because the nature of human existence is betweenness; and therefore, neither the individual nor the group alone are authoritative unless their ideals and goals reflect this nature.

My contention that Watsuji's ethics relies on ideals is consistent with the fact that he resorts to aspects of Confucian philosophy to illustrate his theory that human existence is inherently ethical. Indeed, many scholars have rightly pointed to his repeated references to Confucian concepts such as the Five Relationships (*gorin* 五倫: ruler-ruled, older-younger, parent-child, husband-wife, friend-friend).[98] Jordančo Sekulovski has proposed that the forms of concrete relationships should take a primary place in Watsuji's thought, and that the goal of his ethics is to "empower the *rin* (as a form)" by means of *aidagara*, the fundamental nature of human relationality, in order to allow these basic forms to be realized in ethical life.[99] I would agree if what is meant by this is that the patterns of human relationships such as the Five Confucian Relationships are where compassion or love can be

---

96. WATSUJI 1996, 138. Author's emphasis.
97. Ibid.
98. DILWORTH 1974, 17,
99. SEKULOVSKI 2019, 202–204.

realized, or as Maraldo writes, community is a place where people can live together in harmony.[100] Such a view is consistent with the fact that Watsuji conceives of the patterns of human existence as the "noematic meaning" (ノエーマ的な意味) of "dynamic human existence."[101] The ethical ideal is to see that well-established forms of human relationships are just the manifestation of the movement of the Absolute. To use Confucian terms, the fact that this dynamic activity is the movement of negation and that it is empty (空) means that the Five Relationships can be places in which to manifest the foundational Confucian value of *ren* (*nin* in Japanese; 仁), variously translated as "humanity" or "human-heartedness."[102]

Thus for both Sōseki and Watsuji ethical ideals manifest themselves relationally. In Sōseki's case, the ethical task of the author is to study human relationships and to distinguish fine gradations within them. Through this study, she is able to depict relationships that evoke ideals that resonate with the age in which she lives, thereby touching the hearts and minds of her readers and inspiring them to pursue similar ideals within their relationships.[103] Similarly, in the case of Watsuji, divine love and compassion—the forms that the absolute interconnection between people takes—must manifest themselves in actual "socio-ethical organizations" (人倫的組織) and "socio-ethical wholes" (人倫的全体)[104] such as monastic communities, families, neighbourhood or friendship communities and the state.[105] By returning to the absolute and awakening to the ideal of interrelatedness in which the movement of sameness and difference between self and the totality is realized, avatars of ethical life such as Christ or Gotama Buddha were able to realize love and compassion as ideal forms toward which to strive in actual concrete relationships.

100. Maraldo 2019, 144.
101. Watsuji 1996, 11.
102. See Katsube Mitake's explanation of the nature of emptiness in Watsuji's philosophy in Yuasa 1973, 27–28. As Katsube explains, "emptiness" (空) is meant to point to the fact that experience is just a series of moments of experience. This is what he means when he says that "emptiness" does not mean the absence of something (何もない), but rather that the essence of that thing, be it an individual thing or the whole, is emptiness (個別性も全体性も「空」に帰してしまう). Cf. Yuasa 1973, 27.
103. Natsume 2009a, 197–8.
104. wtz 10: 127.
105. Watsuji 1996, 122–3.

To complete this section, I would like to emphasize that we should not simply gloss over the differences between Sōseki and Watsuji's understanding of ideals. For Sōseki, ideals are essentially patterns of consciousness such as "righteousness," "justness" and "bravery" that are acted out in real life. It is not surprising that this model of ethics led Sōseki to be constantly disappointed by human selfishness, because he searches for ideals within the flow of shared human consciousness rather than recognizing the nature or source of this consciousness. For this reason, the ideals expressed in poems, novels, and other art forms are too fragile—too human—to guide human behaviour in the push and pull of social convention and individual desire. In contrast, ideals for Watsuji are not ideas or patterns of consciousness—they are ways of acting in particular forms of relationships that reflect the fundamental unity of all beings. Buddhist compassion and Christian love are only realized through constant mindfulness of the dependence of myself on others. When one lives with such interdependence in one's heart, Watsuji believes, any form of relationship, be it family or friendship, can glow with the light of life itself. While Sōseki's approach was very intellectual, Watsuji's was experiential and embodied—our experience of the interrelationship of self and other must animate how we treat those with whom we have concrete relationships such as our parents, our siblings, our friends and so on.

Resonance four: transcendence

A persistent puzzle in Watsuji's thought is the role of the transcendent dimension, which he calls "absolute totality" (絶対的全体性),[106] and which he characterizes as the dialectical movement of negation within absolute emptiness (絶対空).[107] Does Watsuji intend for the relationship between concrete human existence and the transcendent dimension to be understood as transcendental, meaning that the absolute is the condition for the possibility of concrete existence? Or is the relationship meant to be metaphysical, in which case the experience each person has of being

---

106. Watsuji 1996, 23, 224; wtz 10: 26, 236.
107. Watsuji 1996, 68; wtz 10: 71. For a discussion of the Buddhist influence in Watsuji's theory, see Sevilla 2017, Chapter 5, and Sevilla 2016.

stretched between the individual and the group is simply a moment of the development of the transcendent itself?[108]

A comparison with Sōseki's philosophy can help us to resolve this issue. As we have seen, implicit in Sōseki's adoption of William James' phenomenological paradigm is a metaphysical proposition—our experience is simply "the flow of consciousness," and the self is therefore a fragment of or limited perspective on this flow.[109] Thus, the assertion of individuality—the taking up of a standpoint from which to make choices—is a manifestation of a moment in the flow of consciousness through internal self-differentiation (分化).[110] I suggest that there is a similarity between this model and Watsuji's, except that the latter has eliminated the psychologism from Sōseki's model. The key feature of that model is that the individual subject is an abstraction from the self that is always embedded in and inseparable from the flow of experience. However, within the flow of experience, there are moments of differentiation and focusing: they are like waves, with the apex being a moment of focusing, and the trough being indistinct as we approach the threshold of consciousness. Sōseki explains that as we grow older, we develop a "capacity for distinction" which allows us to see in the waving grasses not just a green mass but a myriad of different shades of green.[111] Also, the refinement of consciousness develops over the ages of history as societies evolve.[112] Thus within consciousness, there develops moments of clear seeing—the focus of consciousness—and moments of unclarity at the threshold or "periphery" of consciousness.[113]

Similarly, for Watsuji, the moments in which we assert individuality are simply an extreme within the movement of negation between the poles of individual and community.[114] And similar to Sōseki, these poles are actually moments of awareness—the assertion of the individual is a moment of "self-awareness," and the assertion of community is awareness of the community

---

108. I call this "metaphysical" because it implies a certain relationship between the immanent and the transcendent, between everyday individual experience and the transcendent.
109. See also LAMARRE 2008, 60–1.
110. NATSUME 2009A, 166–7; NATSUME 1986, 42–3.
111. NATSUME 2009C, 76.
112. NATSUME 2009C, 57.
113. Ibid.
114. WATSUJI 1996, 23.

will (Watsuji uses the term "superindividual will").[115] However, Watsuji manages to avoid the essentialism inherent in Sōseki's psychologism, in which consciousness appears to be a kind of substance, by explaining that both the individual and the community are "empty." However, by this he does not mean that they are non-existent or non-being, but rather that they are "absolute totality."[116] Thus absolute totality—reality—is the movement of emptying—of the coming and going of phenomena. And because human existence is also characterized by this coming and going, which Watsuji terms the "movement of negation," ethics is simply "the negation of negation" which is "the self-returning and self-realizing movement of the absolute totality."[117] Watsuji's metaphysics thus avoids essentialism by recognizing reality, not as a series of focused and unfocused conscious experiences, but by pointing out that the flow of our experience is the manifestation or result of the constant emptying out that constitutes reality: life comes and goes, and thus experiences arise and recede. Thus one way of understanding Watsuji's model is to see its similarities with that of Sōseki, but then acknowledging that the difference lies in the use of European philosophy, especially phenomenology, to describe this characteristic of reality as emptiness.

However, Watsuji was not satisfied with the presuppositions of most Western philosophy, which in his view assume an "ego [that] exists as independent from the outset,"[118] rather than presupposing relationality and deriving independence as a moment of relations. To avoid swinging to the opposite extreme and prioritizing the group or the community over the individual, Watsuji explains that by relationality he means "subjective practice," the "activities inherent in human relationships" that "do not allow themselves to be contemplated," but which nonetheless demonstrate interconnection. Communication and transportation cannot be directly observed—they are not reduceable to newspapers, roads or trolley cars. Rather, these objects are the physical manifestation of a subjective practice that displays the relational quality of human experiencing.[119]

115. Ibid.
116. Ibid.
117. Ibid.
118. Watsuji 1996, 68.
119. Watsuji 1996, 177.

The interpersonal nature of the phenomena that Watsuji investigates allows him to avoid the essentialism to which psychologism is prone: consciousness is not in itself a substance—it is simply subjective experiencing. But it also allows him, like Sōseki, to consider the individual's experience as derivative of or a manifestation of subjective experiencing itself, which is, as the movement of negation, absolute totality. When one expresses it this way, Watsuji's approach may seem obscure. But the model that he has in mind here is that which the Zen monk Dōgen expressed as "dropping through bodymind" (身心脱落), which Carter and Yamamoto translate as "dropping off of body-mind." Watsuji explains that there is a point in meditation when one is conscious, one is experiencing, and yet the sense of being separate from the experiencing itself disappears. Writing about the fact that human bodies are never absolutely separate, he explains:

> The second example [of this lack of absolute separation] is that a human body that, while carrying on its subjectivity to an extreme, finally dissociates itself from every sort of relational capacity. This body is neither that of a man nor a woman nor is it to be conceived of as a believer belonging to any religious association. A believer possesses one of the capacities prescribed by a betweenness-oriented existence, and hence, a believer's body has a necessary connection with some religious association. Then, is what remains left at the extremity a human body standing before God as one of His creatures? Even she who prays alone in separation from all connection still has her body that kneels and clasps its hands in veneration. But this is precisely a body that is affiliated with God, which is obviously revealed through this prayerful facial expression. Thus, it is not so much an absolute independent body as an absolutely dependent body. That is to say, in the extremity in which we examine the individual independence of a body, we reach a point at which individual independence necessarily perishes. This is what in Buddhism is described as "the dropping off of body-mind." Even Buddhists who abandon every kind of human privilege in aid of gaining absolute enlightenment and who remain tenaciously engaged with Buddhist truth with a willingness to kill even the founder of Buddhism in order to detach from a connection with all religious association, nonetheless finally ends up sitting meditation, which is to a great extent a bodily activity. When they break through this bodily meditation, their body becomes entirely emptied. That is to say, the subjective body terminates in absolute emptiness (*zettaikū*), when its individuality is carried to

the extreme. This is a real feature and characteristic of the individuality of a human body.[120]

In both the Judeo-Christian and the Buddhist examples in the above paragraph, absolute subjectivity is experienced as an awareness without conditional subjectivity—without the everyday sense of a self separate from others. But whereas for Sōseki, each person's consciousness is part of a reified flow of consciousness, in Watsuji's model, each person has the capacity to "drop through body-mind" and realize that their experience is simply *being aware*: not some substance, but simply experiencing—the original face (*honrai no menmoku*).[121] Or to use the Christian terminology Watsuji invokes, we experience our absolute dependency on God as the creator of each moment. It is at this point, Watsuji writes, that the individual realizes themselves, but paradoxically, it is the moment in which a sense of individuality dissolves: "the pursuit of the absolute independence of the individual terminates, in truth, not with the individual but with the Absolute, where the individual is more than likely to lose its own reality."[122] And it is at this point that ideals such as love, which is the "consciousness of the 'unity of the self and other'"[123] manifest themselves, not as ideas, but as experiences.

Watsuji's position is not meant to be a mystical one—he does not require you to have sat zazen in order to understand the nature of absolute emptiness. Nor does he think that through zazen you will gain some special type of experience. Indeed, he also uses the example of activities other than sitting zazen. The nature of human existence as *ningen sonzai* (人間存在) is manifest simply in the fact that we ride the streetcar, drive an automobile, use a letterbox or public telephone, listen to the radio (or a podcast), read the newspaper and so on.[124] According to him, the fact that we participate in such activities or use such objects tells us something about the intersubjective nature of human existence:[125] the fact that we do these things indicates that

---

120. Watsuji 1996, 67–8; WTZ 10: 70–1.
121. I just wish to emphasize that we are dealing here with Watsuji's understanding of the *kōan* of the Original Face, not the understanding of the Zen teacher that must be realized by the student.
122. Watsuji 1996, 81.
123. Watsuji 1996, 83, citing Hegel's analysis of love.
124. Watsuji 1996, 39.
125. Watsuji 1996, 40.

each of our acts is oriented towards the world and to others, and therefore each act manifests our nature as betweenness. But he goes even further—these activities are a manifestation of life itself. He explains:

> Even though one personality performs her self-creative activity in entirely her own way, she consists, nonetheless, in the creative activities of a superindividual life. The past, which we understand in the sense that we manifest the totality of the past in our activities, is both the past peculiar to our personality and, at the same time, the past of a superindividual life. This means precisely that we possess the past in betweenness. We grasp this fact through the existence of *ningen*.[126]

Here, Watsuji uses language much like that of Sōseki: our experience actually points to experiencing in general, which is the "activity of superindividual life."[127]

Watsuji's ethics is a study of the nature of human modes of being (人間の学としての倫理学); and this study reveals that human activity and human experience are always the manifestation of the possibility of experience itself unencumbered by what Sōseki called the abstract differentiation into self and other. Thus Watsuji's ethics shares with Sōseki the view that experiencing is fundamental to human existence; but he avoids giving to this experience the status of a substance, the "flow of consciousness." Rather, for Watsuji, the fundamental nature of human existence as experiencing is what is meant by Watsuji's description of betweenness as "subjective spatiality," the relationship that emerges from experiencing itself.[128] Insofar as our experience contains moments of experiencing our separation from others and our unity with them, this points to the whole of our experiencing as the movement of what he calls "the Absolute," understood as the movement of negativity within absolute space. By comparing and then distinguishing Sōseki's psychological model with the intersubjective phenomenology of

---

126. Watsuji 1996, 206; wtz 10: 218.

127. Unfortunately, Watsuji sometimes mixes up the level of experiencing as "the activity of superindividual life" and ordinary experiencing that presupposes a self separate from others. Thus when he points to fashion as an example of the manifestation of experiencing in itself, he steps down to the level of "communal experience" (Watsuji 1996, 74–5), mistaking this for the experiencing that is the "activity of superindividual life."

128. Watsuji 1996, 166.

Watsuji, we gain some insight into the role of the transcendent in the latter's philosophy: my experience is always the manifestation of the movement of reality—its coming and going—which is not a substance, but a constant movement of emptying and creating.

Conclusion

Sōseki was an inspiration to Watsuji. The purpose of this paper was to show that the influence was not just of a general nature: Watsuji's ethics engages with issues originally taken up by Sōseki in his work on the ethics of the author. The similarities include the notion that we live together with others not simply on the sociological level, but also on the experiential level: our experiences and ideas are able to penetrate (浸る, 浸透) the experiences and ideas of others. Likewise, both thinkers see an inherent tension at the base of ethical action, be it a tension within the flow of consciousness (in the case of Sōseki) or a tension inherent in relationality itself due to the natural evolution of the relationship between individual and group (in the case of Watsuji). The difference is that penetration and tension are interpreted by Watsuji through the phenomenological lens that he adopts in his work rather than by means of a theoretical consciousness. The categories of temporality and spatiality that are essential to that lens enable him to show that it is not just our experiences that interpenetrate—our acts, too, all occur within a web of interconnected actions (実践的行為的連関).

While Sōseki was clear that the ethical author must embody ideals and inspire others to live likewise, he was not that clear about the fundamental mechanisms underlying his ethics. When pressed, he threw up his hands. For instance, when questioning what the cause is of the flow of consciousness that constituted life itself, he said that this constituted an aporia—a *kōan*[129]—that he could not himself penetrate. However, Watsuji was able

---

129. Sōseki wrote:
[W]hat we call life consists of a continuity of consciousness…. We wish nothing more than for this continuity to continue. I can't explain why we wish for this. Nobody can explain that. All we can do is acknowledge it as a fact…. [T]o proceed further and try to determine the ultimate cause behind this tendency is futile. It would require us to resort to something like a Zen kōan, such as the one that asks: If all things can be returned to a single cause, then what is the cause of that cause? (Natsume 2007a, 167; Natsume 1986, 41)

to dissolve this aporia to some degree through phenomenological analysis. Ethical ideals, it turns out, are not just ideas or patterns of consciousness, as Sōseki thought, but ideal forms of relationships such as parent-child or friend-friend: relationships that are given life by our awakening to our original or true selves—the absolute unity between self and others. This absolute unity is something that we experience when we are able to set aside the abstractions of the everyday self and realize "the flow of consciousness" without adopting a perspective: it is simply experiencing itself as the movement of negation within absolute emptiness.

Watsuji managed to turn Sōseki's pessimism into a form of optimism. For while Sōseki recognized the tension between the self and the continuity of consciousness which is life itself, he felt that to maintain ideals, one had to constantly struggle against reabsorption into the whole. It is for this reason that he considered a love of truth to be utterly incompatible with love of oneself: to emphasize oneself is to give up ideals and to simply seek one's own pleasure within the flow of consciousness, i.e., to let the tension between the ethical standpoint and the flow of consciousness utterly collapse. However, for Watsuji, the tension between self and community is positive even though he calls it the movement of negation.[130] While Sōseki constantly sought the unattainable ideal, Watsuji sees the struggle itself as ethics; indeed, this struggle is the basic law of human existence as ethical existence: it is the manifestation of "the movement in which absolute negativity returns back to itself through negation."[131] Thus Watsuji, whose disposition was naturally sunnier than that of Sōseki, manages to transform the latter's pessimism about human nature into a positive feature of human existence. For Watsuji, the inability to reach the ideal is not a problem; to strive to realize it is itself to live ethically as *ningen sonzai*.

Bibliography

Abbreviation

WTZ 『和辻哲郎全集』[*Complete works of Watsuji Tetsurō*] (Tōkyō: Iwanami Shoten, 1961–1963).

130. WATSUJI 1996, 22.
131. WATSUJI 1996, 119.

Dilworth, David A.
- 1969 "The Initial Formations of 'Pure Experience' in Nishida Kitarō and William James," *Monumenta Nipponica* 24/1–2: 93–111.
- 2005 "The Phenomenology and Logic of Interpresence in Watsuji Tetsurō and Nishida Kitarō" in Nobuko Ochner and William Ridgeway, eds., *Confluences: Studies from East to West in Honor of V. H. Viglielmo* (Honolulu: University of Hawai'i Press), 43–55.
- 1974 "Watsuji Tetsurō (1889–1960): Cultural Phenomenologist and Ethician," *Philosophy East and West* 24/1: –22.

Dilworth, David A., Valdo H. Viglielmo, and Agustín Jacinto Zavala
- 1998 *Sourcebook for Modern Japanese Philosophy: Selected Documents* (Westport, CT: Greenwood Press).

Honda Takahiro 本田隆裕
- 2019 『和辻倫理学における「人間」の構造』[The structure of *ningen* in Watsuji's ethics], MA Thesis, on file with author (Kyoto: Kyoto University).

Hori, Victor Sōgen
- 2003 *Zen Sand: The Book of Capping Phrases for Kōan Practice* (Honolulu: University of Hawai'i Press).

Horowitz, Asher
- 2008 *Ethics at a Standstill: History and Subjectivity in Lévinas and the Frankfurt School* (Pittsburgh: Duquesne University Press).

Johnson, David W.
- 2019 *Watsuji on Nature: Japanese Philosophy in the Wake of Heidegger* (Northwestern University Press).

Kalmanson, Leah
- 2010. "Levinas in Japan: The Ethics of Alterity and the Philosophy of No-Self." *Continental Philosophy Review* 43: 193–206.

Karaki Junzō 唐木順三
- 1963 「和辻哲郎の人と思想」[Watsuji Tetsurō: The man and his thought], in Karaki Junzō, ed., 『和辻哲郎』[*Watsuji Tetsurō*] (Tokyo: Chikuma Shoten), 7–52.

Kodera, T. James
- 1987 "The Romantic Humanism of Watsuji Tetsurō," *Dialogue & Alliance* 1/3: 3–11.

Kōsaka Masaaki 高坂正顕
- 1964 『西田幾多郎と和辻哲郎』[*Nishida Kitarō and Watsuji Tetsurō*] (Tokyo: Shinchōsha).

Lafleur, William R.
- 1978 "Buddhist Emptiness in Watsuji Tetsurō," *Religious Studies* 14: 237–50.

Lamarre, Thomas
    2008   "Expanded Empiricism: Natsume Sōseki with William James" *Japan Forum* 20/1: 47–77.

Levinas, Emmanuel
    1998   *Otherwise Than Being or Beyond Essence*, trans. by Alphonso Lingis (Pittsburgh: Duquesne University Press).

Maraldo, John
    2019   "Dignity and Respect: Conceptualizing their Relationship," in J. Maraldo, *Japanese Philosophy in the Making 2: Borderline Interrogations* (Nagoya: Chisokudō), 97–144.
    2002   "Watsuji Tetsurō's Ethics: Totalitarian or Communitarian?" in Rolf Elberfeld and Günter Wohlfart, eds., *Komparative Ethik: Das gute Leben zwischen den Kulturen* (Köln: Ed. Chōra).

Matsui Sakuko 松井朔子
    1975   *Natsume Sōseki as a Critic of English Literature* (Tokyo: Centre for East Asian Cultural Studies).

Murphy, Joseph A.
    2001   "The Fourth Possibility in Soseki's Theory of Literature: Towards a General Economy of Literature and Science," in *Approches critiques de la pensée japonaise du xxe siècle* (Montréal: Presses de l' Université de Montréal).

Nagami Isamu 永見 勇
    1981   "The Ontological Foundation in Tetsurō Watsuji's Philosophy: *Kū* and Human Existence," *Philosophy East and West* 31/3: 279–96.

Natsume Sōseki 夏目漱石
    1986   『文芸の哲学的基礎』[*The Philosophical Foundations of Literature*] (Tokyo: Iwanami Shoten), 29–113.
    2009a   "Philosophical Foundations of the Literary Arts," in Michael K. Bourdaghs, Atsuko Ueda, and Joseph A. Murphy, eds., *Theory of Literature and Other Critical Writings* (New York: Columbia University Press), 159–213.
    2009b   "Statement on Joining the Asahi," ibid., 155–18.
    2009c   *Theory of Literature*, ibid., 38–152.
    2017   『文学論』in 『漱石全集』, vol. 14 (Tokyo: Iwanami Shoten).

Sekulovski, Jordančo
    2019   "Watsuji's Ethics from the Perspective of *Kata* as a Technology of the Self," *European Journal of Japanese Philosophy* 2: 199–208.

Sevilla, Anton Luis
    2016   "The Buddhist Roots of Watsuji Tetsurô's Ethics of Emptiness," *Journal of Religious Ethics* 44/4: 606–35.
    2017   *Watsuji Tetsurô's Global Ethics of Emptiness: A Contemporary Look at a Modern Japanese Philosopher* (Cham: Springer).

SHEN, Vincent
 2014 "The Fading of Political Theology and the Rise of Creative Humanism," in V. Shen, ed., *Dao Companion to Classical Confucian Philosophy* (Dordrecht, Springer).

SHUTTLEWORTH, Kyle Michael James
 2019 "Watsuji Tetsurō's Concept of 'Authenticity'" *Comparative and Continental Philosophy* 11/3: 235–50.

UTSUNOMIYA Yoshiaki 宇都宮芳明
 1980 『人間の間の倫理』[*Between Human Beings and Ethics*] (Tokyo: Ibunsha).

WATSUJI Tetsurō 和辻哲郎
 1916 「夏目先生の追憶」[Remembering Natsume Sensei], Karaki Junzō 唐木順三, ed., 『和辻哲郎』[*Watsuji Tetsurō*] [*Watsuji Tetsurō*] (Tokyo: Chikuma Shoten, 1963), 412–23.

YAMOTO Tadayoshi 矢本貞幹
 1971 『夏目漱石：その英文学的側面』[Natsume Sōseki: Aspects of English Literature] (Tokyo: Kenkyūsha).

YUASA Yasuō 湯浅泰雄
 1973 (ed.) 『人と思想：和辻哲郎』[*Watsuji Tetsurō: The Man and His Thought*]. (Tokyo: San'ichi Shōbō).
 1981 『和辻哲郎：近代日本哲学の運命』[*Watsuji Tetsurō: The Fate of Modern Japanese Philosophy*].(Kyoto: Minerva).

Federica Sgarbi
Dōshisha University

D. T. Suzuki e Swedenborg
Una introduzione

Il filosofo giapponese Daisetsu Teitarō Suzuki (1870–1966) è noto per i suoi contributi circa il buddhismo zen e per l'intensa opera di divulgazione di esso in Occidente. Tuttavia, esiste un campo d'indagine ch'egli coltivò assiduamente, alquanto trascurato in termini di ricerca: quello relativo al mistico svedese Emanuel Swedenborg (1688–1772). Suzuki fu un devoto estimatore dell'autore europeo: identificava nelle sue opere un valido punto di riferimento per il superamento della profonda crisi spirituale, dilagante nel Giappone di fine '800. Egli, pertanto, si prodigò per la diffusione di tali opere, sia attraverso la traduzione in lingua giapponese da lui stesso curata, sia tramite i suoi scritti. Essi offrono, in termini di ricerca, contributi originali in tema di filosofia e storia della religione e un'inedita interpretazione della figura di Swedenborg, nota forse più per la critica mossagli da Kant che per i contenuti in ambito teologico.

Il presente articolo mira ad introdurre tali contributi, ripercorrendo la vita e le opere del mistico svedese, con specifico riferimento alle analogie che Suzuki individuò tra il pensiero di Swedenborg e quello buddhista.

KEYWORDS: buddhismo—Kant—religione—esoterismo—cultura—Suzuki Daisetsu—Swedenborg—filosofia occidentale—filosofia orientale—Beatrice Erskine Lane

Suzuki Daisetsu definì Swedenborg «un genio scientifico e religioso» ed enfatizzò l'importanza della sua intera produzione, non solo di quella teologica. Il valore degli scritti e delle scoperte scientifiche dello studioso svedese, che di fatto caratterizzarono la prima metà della sua vita, fu, in effetti, elevato e venne riconosciuto anche istituzionalmente: Swedenborg fu membro dell'Accademia delle Scienze di Parigi, oltre che di quella di San Pietroburgo. La sua carriera di studioso e inventore fu folgorante, portandolo a lavorare anche a servizio della corona svedese.

Tale carriera venne, però, subitamente abbandonata in seguito ad una profonda crisi spirituale che lo portò ad una vita ritirata, dedita alla sola stesura dei suoi scritti mistici.

Le fasi della vita di Swedenborg, seppur apparentemente molto diverse, furono, invece, legate da uno specifico e immutato argomento di ricerca: il rapporto tra corpo e anima.

L'educazione

Nato Swedberg – il cognome sarebbe stato modificato successivamente – nel 1688 a Stoccolma, era il terzo figlio dell'influente vescovo di Skara, Jesper Swedberg (1653–1735). Nel 1699, entrò all'Università di Uppsala, presso la quale completò i suoi studi in filosofia nel 1709.[1]

Come prevedeva la consuetudine per i giovani rampolli di famiglia benestante del suo tempo, si recò poi all'estero al fine di approfondire le conoscenze apprese: la prima tappa fu l'Inghilterra, riconosciuto centro di cultura e grande potenza marittima, dove studiò le tecniche di osservazione dell'astronomo reale John Flamsteed (1646–1719), frequentando i circoli

---

1. L. R. WILKINSON 1996, 59–60.

intellettuali di luminari come Isaac Newton (1643–1727) e Edmund Halley (1656–1742). Si dedicò anche alla geologia, botanica, zoologia e alle scienze meccaniche, continuando a coltivarle successivamente ad Amsterdam e Parigi.

Al suo rientro in Svezia, avvenuto più di cinque anni dopo, fu assunto come assistente dell'inventore svedese Christopher Polhem (1661–1751), posizione che gli valse la presentazione ufficiale a Corte. Il re di Svezia Carlo XII (1682–1718), impressionato dall'intelletto del giovane scienziato, lo fece assumere in qualità di assessore presso il Consiglio delle Miniere. Tale incarico, significativo e prestigioso in considerazione del ruolo vitale delle risorse minerarie nell'economia svedese, consentiva ampie opportunità di ricerca scientifica che lo scienziato sfruttò a fondo. Dopo la morte di Carlo XII avvenuta nel 1718, salì al trono la sorella Ulrika Eleonora (1688–1741) che, nel 1719, conferì il titolo nobiliare alla famiglia Swedberg, modificandone il nome in Swedenborg. Il giovane ottenne, così, il diritto di voto nella casata svedese dei nobili che esercitò per la maggior parte della sua vita. Nel 1723, ottenne ulteriori incarichi nel Consiglio delle Miniere, che ricoprì, con prolungati congedi per studio all'estero, fino al 1747.

Del corpo e dell'anima. l'approccio scientifico

Negli anni immediatamente successivi al suo ritorno in Svezia, la maggior parte dell'energia intellettuale di Swedenborg venne incanalata nel lavoro scientifico e tecnico. Nel 1716, pubblicò, inusualmente in lingua svedese, il primo numero della rivista scientifica *Daedalus Hyperboreus*. Sebbene essa avesse lo scopo di evidenziare i risultati di Polhem, includeva anche la pubblicazione di progetti e invenzioni dello stesso Swedenborg. Seguì la stesura di testi di chimica e fisica, nonché del primo libro, in lingua svedese, sull'algebra, di natura per lo più speculativa.

La prima pubblicazione importante fu *Opera philosophica et Mineralia*, una serie di tre volumi stampata nel 1734. *Opera philosophica et Mineralia* fu redatta in latino e pubblicata all'estero nella speranza di una divulgazione a livello internazionale. Il secondo e il terzo volume furono dedicati, rispettivamente, alla trattazione del ferro, del rame e dell'ottone e attirarono l'attenzione per le loro informazioni tecniche sulla metallurgia; il primo volume, intitolato *Principia rerum naturalium* [Principi fondamentali della natura], gettò le basi filosofiche per le successive indagini di Swedenborg sulla natura dell'anima.

Tra il 1720 e il 1730, egli si distinse tra i più quotati scienziati di Svezia, divenendo membro dell'Accademia delle scienze di San Pietroburgo.[2]

Alla fine degli anni '30, i suoi interessi scientifici volsero verso la fisiologia umana, con un focus specifico sulle questioni di psicologia speculativa. I due volumi di *Oeconomia regni animalis* [Dinamica del Regno Animale], furono pubblicati rispettivamente nel 1740 e nel 1741. Il primo di essi era incentrato sulla trattazione del cuore e del sangue; il secondo, sulla trattazione del cervello, del sistema nervoso e dell'anima con il persistente intento di individuare una connessione tra il mondo spirituale e quello fisico. Attingendo alle opere di scienziati e filosofi contemporanei, il testo sosteneva l'esistenza di un fluido spirituale presente in tutte le creature viventi, alimentato da una fonte divina.

Successivamente, Swedenborg iniziò a lavorare a *Regnum animale anatomice, physice et philosophice perlustratum* [Il Regno Animale ispezionato anatomicamente, fisicamente e filosoficamente] che trattava, in modo più approfondito, di materia anatomica. Altri scritti vennero abbozzati, ma poi interrotti in seguito ad un repentino quanto profondo cambiamento avvenuto nella vita dello scienziato.

Del corpo e dell'anima. l'approccio mistico

Nei suoi diari, Swedenborg asseriva di aver vissuto, da bambino, esperienze mistiche sotto forma di visioni. Purtroppo si hanno scarse informazioni circa la sua infanzia; le voluminose memorie del padre lo menzionano una volta soltanto per annotarne la nascita e il significato del nome: Emanuel, «Dio con noi». Esse, tuttavia, forniscono una chiara idea della forte personalità del vescovo, delle sue solide scelte religiose e del misticismo delle sue convinzioni e dei suoi costrutti mentali, che arricchivano di un significato ultraterreno oggetti ed eventi anche quotidiani. Fu proprio in seguito alla morte del padre (1743) che ebbe inizio la crisi spirituale di Swedenborg.[3]

---

2. White 1878, 46.
3. L. R. Wilkinson 1996, 60.

Durante il 1743 e per tutto il 1744, infatti, egli visse intense esperienze mistiche che registrò nel proprio diario personale. Inizialmente, molte di esse ruotavano attorno a un senso di indegnità spirituale e di una necessaria purificazione dal peccato. La prima fu una visione, avvenuta di giorno, nell'aprile del 1745 in prossimità della Pasqua. Da quel momento in poi, Swedenborg iniziò a riportare regolari esperienze di contatto con il mondo spirituale.

In seguito a ciò, egli avviò la stesura di uno scritto mirato all'esplorazione del testo biblico, reinterpretato alla luce delle conoscenze acquisite durante i suoi episodi visionari.

La crisi spirituale e le ripetute esperienze mistiche spinsero Swedenborg a dimettersi dall'incarico di pubblico ufficiale per dedicarsi esclusivamente alla stesura di testi religiosi. Il suo interesse per la connessione tra il mondo spirituale e quello fisico continuò così come la sua ricerca in merito, ma fu modificato l'approccio d'indagine: in luogo di quello scientifico, subentrò quello mistico.

La prima opera teologica di Swedenborg fu *Arcana Coelestia quae in Scriptura Sacra, seu Verbo Domini sunt, detecta. Hic primum in Genesi.* [Rivelazione dei misteri celesti contenuti nella parola del Signore, a partire dal libro della Genesi]: un'analisi condotta capillarmente, verso per verso, del significato recondito della Bibbia, circa i libri della Genesi e dell'Esodo.

Il presupposto dello studio di Swedenborg era la chiave simbolica del testo, la cui comprensione era possibile solo attraverso un'interpretazione del testo letterale:

> Dalla semplice lettera della Parola dell'Antico Testamento nessuno potrà mai discernere il fatto che questa parte della Parola contiene profondi segreti celesti [...] Eppure la verità è che ovunque in quella Parola ci sono cose interne che non appaiono affatto nelle cose esteriori, eccetto pochissime che il Signore ha rivelato e spiegato agli apostoli.[4]

Inframmezzata tra i capitoli di commento, appariva la presentazione di principi che sarebbero diventati parti fondamentali della teologia di Swedenborg; fra essi, il più importante era quello delle «corrispondenze» tra il mondo fisico e il mondo spirituale e tra l'anima e il corpo.

---

4. SWEDENBORG 1749, 1.

Swedenborg pubblicò l'*Arcana Coelestia* nel 1749, eccezion fatta per l'ottavo e ultimo volume, uscito nel 1756. Scelse di pubblicare il libro a Londra, sia per evitare le rigide leggi svedesi anti-eretiche, sia per l'aperta e vivace atmosfera intellettuale regnante nella città inglese, presupposto e auspicio per un modo completamente nuovo di recepire le Sacre Scritture.

Sebbene Swedenborg avesse, inizialmente, l'intento di dedicarsi all'interpretazione dell'intero testo biblico, non procedette in tal senso. Fece, infatti, ritorno a Londra nel 1758 con nuovi titoli da pubblicare: *De coelo et eius mirabilibus et de inferno, ex auditis et visis* [Del cielo e delle sue meraviglie e dell'inferno secondo quel che si è udito e veduto], dedicato alla descrizione dell'aldilà e della vita dei suoi abitanti; *De equo albo de quo in Apocalypsi* [Del cavallo bianco menzionato nel libro dell'Apocalisse], dedicato al significato recondito della Bibbia; *De telluribus in mundo nostro solari, quae vocantur planetae, et de telluribus in coelo astrifero, deque illarum incolis, tum de spiritibus et angelis ibi, ex auditis et visis* [Delle terre nel cielo stellato, dei loro abitanti, dei loro spiriti e angeli secondo quel che si udito e veduto], dedicato alle forme di vita sugli altri pianeti; *De ultimo judicio* [Del giudizio universale] e *De Nova Hierosolyma et eius Doctrina Coelesti. Quibus præmittitur aliquid de novo coelo et nova terra* [Della nuova Gerusalemme e della sua dottrina celeste secondo ciò che è stato udito dal cielo, con un proemio sul nuovo cielo e sulla nuova terra]. Questi ultimi due poggiavano su un presupposto ferreo della teologia di Swedenborg: quello del significato simbolico delle Sacre Scritture. *De ultimo judicio* era, infatti, un rimando al Giudizio Universale interpretato non come evento profetico nella storia dell'umanità, bensì come una fase spirituale nell'evoluzione di essa, mentre Gerusalemme, in *De Nova Hierosolyma,* era concepita come il simbolo della nuova chiesa e dei suoi principi generali.

Ad eccezione del *De ultimo judicio*, il contenuto dei cinque volumi da lui pubblicati nel 1758 era tratto dall'*Arcana Coelestia*, talvolta con scarsissime revisioni.[5]

In *De coelo et ejus mirabilibus, et de inferno, ex auditis et visis*, vi si ritrovava, infatti, un intero capitolo dedicato alle «corrispondenze»:

---

5. Essa era stata pubblicata, inizialmente, in forma anonima e le vendite erano risultate molto scarse. Separare gli elementi dell'opera in volumi più piccoli potrebbe essere stato un tentativo di rendere il contenuto più accessibile.

Al giorno d'oggi l'uomo ignora che cos'è la corrispondenza; la ragione principale di questa ignoranza è che l'uomo si è allontanato dal Cielo per amore di sé e del mondo. In effetti, colui che ama sé stesso e il mondo al di sopra di tutte le cose, non considera altri oggetti che quelli del mondo, perché sono gradevoli e soddisfano i suoi desideri. Non presta alcuna attenzione agli oggetti spirituali che soddisfano soltanto la sua interiorità e la sua mente, e li rifiuta trovandoli troppo elevati per essere oggetto del proprio pensiero. Gli antichi si sono comportati in modo completamente diverso: la scienza delle corrispondenze è stata per loro la prima di tutte le scienze. Attraverso tale scienza hanno acquisito intelligenza e saggezza e anche comunicazione col Cielo, perché la scienza delle corrispondenze è la scienza angelica. I primi uomini, che erano uomini celesti, pensavano in base alle corrispondenze, come gli angeli. È per questo che si intrattenevano con gli angeli e il Signore sovente si mostrava a loro e li istruiva. Oggi si ignora che cos'è una corrispondenza perché questa scienza è totalmente perduta.

Senza la percezione di ciò che è la corrispondenza, non si può avere alcuna chiara nozione del mondo spirituale, del suo influsso nel mondo naturale, dello spirituale relativamente al naturale; e neppure alcuna nozione dell'anima umana, della sua azione sul corpo, della condizione dell'uomo dopo la morte. Di conseguenza è necessario descrivere cos'è la corrispondenza.

Il mondo naturale corrisponde al mondo spirituale non soltanto nelle linee generali, ma ancor più in ognuna delle cose che lo compongono. Ogni cosa che esiste nel mondo naturale deriva dal mondo spirituale ed è definita corrispondenza. Occorre sapere che il mondo naturale esiste e sussiste grazie a quello spirituale, come l'effetto deriva dalla causa. È chiamato mondo naturale quello che si trova sotto il sole e dal sole riceve luce e calore, e tutte le cose che esistono in questo mondo. Il mondo spirituale è il Cielo, e a questo mondo appartiene tutto ciò che è nei Cieli.

Poiché l'uomo è il Cielo e anche il mondo nella loro forma più piccola, ad immagine di quella più grande, in lui c'è il mondo spirituale e quello naturale. La sua interiorità, che appartiene al suo animo ed è fornita di intelletto e volontà, costituisce il suo mondo spirituale. La sua esteriorità, che appartiene al suo corpo e si riferisce ai sensi e alle azioni del corpo, costituisce il suo mondo naturale. È per questo che è chiamato «corrispondente» tutto ciò che si manifesta nel mondo naturale, ovvero nel suo corpo, derivando dal mondo spirituale, ovvero dalla sua mente, dalla sua ragione e dalla sua volontà.[6]

6. Swedenborg 1758 (2005), 64.

Negli ultimi anni della sua vita, Swedenborg pubblicò molte altre opere teologiche determinanti nella sua produzione: *De cultu et amore Dei* [Dell'amore e saggezza di Dio] (1763), *De Divina Providentia* [Della provvidenza divina] (1764), *Apocalypsis revelata: in qua deteguntur arcana quae ibi praedicta sunt et hactenus recondita latuerunt* [Dell'Apocalisse rivelata, svelando i segreti che vi erano stati predetti e che sono rimasti nascosti fino ad ora] (1766) e *Delitiae sapientiae de Amore conjugali, post quas sequuntur voluptates insaniae de Amore scortatorio* [Del piacere della saggezza dell'amore coniugale: seguito dal piacere insano dell'amore promiscuo] (1768). *De cultu et amore Dei* e *Sapientia Angelica de Divina Providentia*, sebbene pubblicate separatamente, erano entrambe incentrate sull'indagine dell'essenza divina, sviluppandone due aspetti diversi. La prima, infatti, trattava della natura di Dio, in guisa di amore e saggezza e fonte di ogni forma di vita, come già appariva nelle prime opere di Swedenborg. *Sapientia Angelica de Divina Providentia* affrontava, invece, il tema del libero arbitrio e la natura del male e della sofferenza, descrivendo le leggi spirituali che governano il mondo.

L'*Apocalypsis revelata* era un ritorno al primo discorso di Swedenborg sul significato della Bibbia e inclusivo degli eventi memorabili [*memorabilia*] ovvero le descrizioni di incontri con creature della realtà ultraterrena, di solito portatori di contenuti teologici specifici.

Delitiae sapientiae de Amore conjugali era, invece, incentrato sull'amore in tutti i suoi aspetti, con un focus sul principio di complementarietà tra i sessi.

Nel 1771, oramai in tarda età, Swedenborg pubblicò il suo ultimo lavoro, *Vera Christiana Religio, continens universam Theologiam Novae Ecclesiae, a Domino apud Danielem* [Della vera religione cristiana: contenente tutta la teologia della nuova Chiesa, predetta dal Signore in Daniel].

L'anno seguente, 1772, egli si spense in una pensione di Londra, mantenendo sino all'ultimo uno stile di vita ritirata, dedita solamente alla stesura dei suoi scritti.

Suzuki: swedenborg, buddha del nord

Suzuki aveva scoperto la mistica di Swedenborg durante un periodo di profonda crisi spirituale del Giappone,[7] causata da un materialismo

---

7. Yoshinaga 2009, 123.

dilagante, fautore dell'indebolimento significativo della coscienza religiosa e spirituale e dei sistemi di credenza e fede ad essa collegati.

Con lo scopo di trovare validi spunti per una risposta a tale crisi, Suzuki si era recato negli Stati Uniti, attraversati da un fervido dibattito filosofico-religioso influenzato anche da tendenze orientali.[8] L'attività della casa editrice Open Court era incentrata sui temi del dibattito: Suzuki vi lavorò a lungo, sotto la guida dello studioso Paul Carus (1852–1919), autore dei testi *Religion of Science* [La religione della scienza] del 1893 e *The Gospel of Buddha* [Il Vangelo di Buddha] del 1894. La devozione di Suzuki alla religione scientifica di Carus, che sembra aver preceduto il suo soggiorno americano, fu seguita da un interesse per la teosofia che Suzuki mantenne e sviluppò.[9]

Al suo ritorno in patria, tradusse in giapponese quattro opere di Swedenborg: nel 1910 『天界と地獄』[Del cielo e delle sue meraviglie e dell'inferno secondo quel che si è udito e veduto], nel 1914 『新エルサレムとその教説』[Della nuova Gerusalemme e della sua dottrina celeste] e 『神知と神愛』[Dell'amore e saggezza divina) e, nel 1915, 『神慮論』[Della provvidenza divina]. Sempre nel 1910, partecipò al Congresso Internazionale dedicato a Swedenborg, svoltosi a Londra, in veste di vicepresidente. Suzuki dedicò, inoltre, due scritti al mistico svedese: il primo, pubblicato nel 1913, intitolato 『スエデンボルグ』 [Swedenborg]; il secondo, 『スエデンボルグ(その天界と他力観)』[Swedenborg (la sua concezione del paradiso e del potere «dell'Altro»)], pubblicato nel 1924.

Il primo scritto fu redatto con lo scopo di presentare la figura di Swedenborg e il suo pensiero mistico, all'epoca pressoché sconosciuti in Giappone[10]. Il secondo, con lo scopo di divulgare in modo più approfondito la teoria filosofica e religiosa dell'autore svedese, arricchito di un aspetto predominante nella ricerca del filosofo: le similarità con il pensiero buddhista.

Gli scritti di Suzuki trasmettono molta ammirazione per la vita e l'opera dello scrittore svedese, enfatizzandone il valore e riflettendo tutto l'impatto che la crisi spirituale di Swedenborg – capace di segnare il passaggio dall'approccio d'indagine scientifico a quello mistico circa il tema dell'ani-

---

8. Ibid., 129–30.
9. Ibid., 105–6.
10. Fatta eccezione per una traduzione in giapponese, edita nel 1910, di *De Coelo et Eius Mirabilibus et de inferno*.

ma – ebbe sul filosofo giapponese. Vi era in essa, infatti, un forte punto di contatto con l'esperienza dei praticanti buddhisti, quale era lo stesso Suzuki.

Suedenborugu

Il testo del 1913 è una dettagliata ricostruzione della vita, della carriera e delle opere di Swedenborg. Nella prefazione, Suzuki spiegava le ragioni d'interesse ispirato dalla figura del mistico:

> Innanzitutto, Swedenborg asserisce di aver viaggiato nell'inferno e in paradiso, e di aver potuto osservare in dettaglio la reale condizione delle persone dopo il trapasso: le sue asserzioni suonano sincere. Esse sono prive della benché minima esagerazione e, se analizzate sotto il profilo del senso comune, sembrano accordarsi in tutto con la verità. Questa è la prima ragione che rende il personaggio di Swedenborg di sicuro interesse. In questo nostro mondo sembra esserci un reame spirituale separato da quello dei cinque sensi; e quando entriamo in un certo stato psicologico, parrebbe che noi siamo effettivamente in grado di comunicare con detto livello ultramondano. Anche se pensiamo che le condizioni di questo livello di esistenza non abbiano alcuna relazione in termini di morale con il reame mondano in cui viviamo, sotto il profilo della scienza o della filosofia, in questa scoperta c'è molto di rilevante. Questa è una seconda ragione per esaminare Swedenborg.
>
> La dottrina teologica di Swedenborg ha, inoltre, molti punti in comune con il buddhismo. Egli spiega che, avendo abbandonato il «proprium», ciascuno debba agire in accordo con il lavoro del Divino, che la vera salvazione sia l'unificazione di fede e azione, e che il Divino si manifesti in termini di saggezza e amore. Inoltre, egli afferma che l'amore è più grande e profondo della saggezza e che non c'è nulla, grande o piccolo che sia, che è al di fuori della sfera d'azione della divina provvidenza. Non c'è una sola cosa al mondo che sia lasciata al caso, e si può testimoniare la rivelazione della divina saggezza e amore anche nel tratto tracciato da una penna, in quanto essa è pervasa dalla provvidenza. Questo genere di questioni attraggono l'interesse degli studiosi di religioni, particolarmente di buddhismo. Questa è la terza ragione, nell'ordine, per la quale Swedenborg andrebbe studiato a fondo. Anche solo una delle motivazioni qui presentate dovrebbe convincere del fatto che Swedenborg sia un filosofo che è necessario conoscere e studiare.[11]

---

11. Suzuki 1913, 3. Ove non altrimenti indicato, tutte le traduzioni dal giapponese sono dell'autrice.

Un'esplorazione della dimensione post-mortem, restituita nei suoi testi con sincerità e sobria moderatezza e percepibile come verosimile: questa era la prima ragione d'interesse individuata da Suzuki in Swedenborg. L'asserzione di una dimensione spirituale – parallela a quella sensoriale – percepibile solamente in presenza di uno stato psicologico specifico, era la seconda. La similarità della dottrina teologica di Swedenborg al buddhismo, la terza, con uno specifico riferimento alla tensione verso l'elevazione spirituale massima e il raggiungimento della relativa salvazione e ad un sistema che provvede, mai casuale nelle sue concessioni.

A questi elementi, se ne aggiungevano degli altri:

> Il fatto che un genio scientifico e religioso insieme si sia così combinato in una persona di tale profondità è un ottimo materiale non solo nell'ambito della ricerca psicologica, ma dato che egli era un uomo di grande vitalità e un intelletto fine che si era affrancato dal materialismo allora vigente, anche il suo esempio di vita può fungere da modello per il lettore, cui indirettamente impartirà una grande lezione. Non ci sono grandi cambiamenti nello snodarsi dei fatti che costituiscono la sua biografia, e pertanto non c'è nulla che veramente catturi la nostra attenzione, ma nei suoi ottantaquattro anni di vita egli fu totalmente devoto alla scienza e alla religione, la sua esistenza nel quotidiano fu riempita di ogni genere di atti stupefacenti. Era un uomo di alto spirito e noi uomini del XX secolo possiamo solo essere commossi dalla sua personalità; se non fosse altro per questo, dovremmo studiarne la biografia.[12]

In un periodo nel quale le fondamenta della spiritualità giapponese stavano vacillando a causa del materialismo dilagante, la figura di Swedenborg, che si era distinta nei costumi e valori contro un materialismo di due secoli più antico, aveva affascinato Suzuki, rinvigorendo l'idea di una possibile sortita dalla crisi spirituale che tanto toccava il filosofo giapponese e, come lui, una generazione di giovani con una forte coscienza sociale e culturale, oltre che spirituale.

Suzuki aveva avuto cura di evidenziare anche «il genio scientifico e religioso» di Swedenborg, valorizzando le due fasi, diverse e ben distinte, della vita dell'autore svedese: la prima, quella del valente scienziato, devoto servitore di corte, oltre che quella del mistico, dalla vita ritirata e dedita alla trascrizione delle proprie esperienze spirituali.

12. Ibid., 4–5.

La prima parte del testo, in effetti, ricostruiva la carriera di studi e gli impegni di Swedenborg sino al 1744. Tale carriera era incentrata sui suoi interessi scientifici e i contributi da lui apportati, con un'attenta disamina delle opere e degli argomenti approfonditi nella sua ricerca, il cui focus verteva su un tema di grande interesse per Suzuki, il rapporto tra corpo e anima, mantenuto costante nelle due fasi di vita di Swedenborg:

> Tuttavia, da ciò che posso osservare dalla mia prospettiva, non c'è un grande divario fra la cosiddetta «carriera mondana» di Swedenborg e la sua carriera spirituale; dico ciò riflettendo su come i suoi primi pensieri e sentimenti, che hanno animato i primi anni di attività, siano in fondo consonanti con la sua vita spirituale posteriore. Naturalmente, non si può negare la completa rivoluzione occorsa nella sua scrittura, nelle sue idee, nei suoi concetti e nei suoi ragionamenti; tuttavia ci sono stati aspetti del passato rimasti sullo sfondo. Per investigare le tracce di questa connessione, possiamo rivolgerci a ciò che Swedenborg scrisse nell'opera *Il regno animale*, per vedere dove le sue idee lo avrebbero poi condotto.[13]

Di seguito, Suzuki riportava il seguente passo dell'opera di Swedenborg:

> Intendo esaminare sotto il profilo fisico e filosofico l'intera morfologia del corpo: l'anatomia delle viscere, delle cavità toracica e addominale, degli apparati genitali in entrambi i sessi e degli organi dei cinque sensi. Parimenti, mi soffermerò sull'anatomia di tutte le parti che compongono il cervello, il cervelletto, il midollo spinale e la *medulla oblongata*. Dopo procederò a descrivere la sostanza corticale dei due sistemi nervosi e le fibre, le cause organiche delle forze e del movimento dell'organismo intero, le condizioni patologiche, in particolare quelle della testa e quelle che derivano da fenomeni di deflusso dall'encefalo.
>
> Mio scopo susseguente sarà fornire un'introduzione alla psicologia razionale, consistente in alcune nuove dottrine mediane il cui ausilio il lettore sarà condotto dall'organismo materiale del corpo a una conoscenza dell'anima, la quale è immateriale: queste sono la dottrina delle forme, la dottrina dell'ordine e dei gradi, e inoltre le dottrine delle serie e associazioni, degli influssi, delle corrispondenze e rappresentazioni, e da ultima, la dottrina delle modificazioni. Da queste dottrine procederò a stabilire la scienza della psicologia razionale in sé, la quale comprenderà i soggetti di azione; sensi interni ed esterni; immaginazione e memoria; da ultimo, le affezioni dell'animo.

---

13. Ibid., 22.

Dell'intelletto, ovvero sia del pensiero e la volontà e le affezioni della mente razionale, così come l'istinto.

Da ultimo, parlerò dell'anima, e del suo stato nel corpo, le sue interrelazioni, affezioni e immortalità, e dello stato che essa assume dopo che il corpo è decaduto. Il lavoro si chiuderà con una concordanza che teorizzerò fra tutti questi sistemi.

Dal sunto dell'opera così come espresso sopra, il lettore avrà a osservare che lo scopo ultimo che mi pongo nel lavoro è proprio la conoscenza dell'anima, dacché è detta conoscenza che rappresenta il coronamento di tutti i miei studi pertanto, per dare il giusto seguito alle mie investigazioni e risolverne le criticità, ho scelto di procedere in maniera analitica, e credo di poter affermare di essere il primo ad adottare esplicitamente tale approccio.

Nei tempi antichi, prima che ogni gareggiante potesse aspirare alla corona, gli veniva richiesto di correre sette volte intorno all'obiettivo, cosa che io stesso mi sono proposto di fare in questa occasione.

Spero pertanto che orientando la mia corsa circolare progressivamente verso il centro, io riesca nell'impresa di aprire tutte le porte che conducono all'anima, e entrare direttamente al suo interno, con il divino benvolere.[14]

E così Suzuki commentava le parole di Swedenborg:

Possiamo osservare che non ci fosse una separazione completa della vita spirituale di Swedenborg negli anni della maturità rispetto alla sua vita intellettuale dei primi anni. Nel 1744, quando compì cinquantasei anni, egli vantava un'esperienza spirituale senza precedenti, e si imbarcò in una nuova vita. Ciò non significa che essa non avesse connessioni con il suo passato. Per altri versi, anzi, essa non dovrebbe essere considerata altro che un'estensione della vita interiore del filosofo nella sua fase precedente. Naturalmente, la sua cosiddetta «contemplazione del Divino» in realtà sarebbe stata alquanto diversa da quanto forse egli stesso avrebbe potuto anticipare; ciò però non è da considerarsi incongruo con le continue evoluzioni del punto di vista maturato dal filosofo nell'intero suo arco di vita.

Swedenborg tentò di scandagliare l'essenza del Divino dal punto di vista intellettuale analitico; appunto inizialmente fece uno studio attento a livello chimico, fisico e meccanico; poi, da questa base, si addentrò nella ricerca anatomica e biologica. Fu allora che, usando tutto il suo genio teoretico, tentò di penetrare il mistero del Divino, rimanendo, tuttavia, ancora insoddisfatto. Come risultato di meditazioni e pratiche esoteriche, l'occhio della sua mente

14. SWEDENBORG 1744, 79.

acquisì gradualmente la capacità di vedere e pare che lui ottenne la capacità di entrare e uscire dal reame divino a suo piacimento.[15]

Le parole di Suzuki davano grande risalto alla presenza continua, attraverso le due fasi della vita di Swedenborg, della ricerca circa il tema dell'anima e all'interesse per esso, aprendo alla vera e unica esperienza che aveva diviso l'esistenza dello svedese in un «prima e dopo»: la «connessione con il reame spirituale» ovvero con la «sfera del Divino» che Suzuki identificava come «reale vocazione» di Swedenborg, di cui le opere del periodo scientifico erano rimaste avulse. Tale aspetto non poteva non sfuggire a Suzuki per una palese similarità con l'esperienza del *satori* buddhista.

Nelle considerazioni del filosofo giapponese emergeva anche l'osservazione circa i differenti criteri d'indagine in materia di anima: inizialmente, quello «intellettuale e analitico» della fase scientifica, capace di produrre approfonditi studi, dapprima nell'ambito della chimica, della fisica e della meccanica e, successivamente, nell'ambito dell'anatomia e della biologia. Tale approccio, con l'inizio della fase mistica seguita alle «meditazioni e pratiche esoteriche», era stato sostituito da quello «dell'occhio della mente».

Il primo criterio e il secondo sarebbero diventati, anni dopo, oggetto di un'approfondita analisi nel testo *Zen Buddhism and Psychoanalysis*: qui Suzuki, infatti, concludeva come tali criteri, definiti rispettivamente «intellettivo» e «intuitivo», fossero il frutto corrispondente delle culture di provenienza, ovvero quella occidentale e quella orientale, e come essi conducessero a risultati d'indagine dissimili proprio in virtù della differenza degli strumenti utilizzati: l'intelletto e l'intuizione appunto. Il primo, proprio delle indagini circa le verità manifeste, scientificamente misurabili e il secondo, proprio della dimensione spirituale.

Swedenborg li aveva saputi impiegare entrambi in un campo d'indagine caro a Suzuki: quello circa l'anima. I risultati di tale indagine avevano portato ad una conoscenza filosofico-religiosa profonda, contenente similarità con la tradizione buddhista, come si vede nel riferimento alle «meditazioni e pratiche esoteriche».

Nel testo, il riferimento all'esoterismo (密教), citato in merito alla fase mistica della vita di Swedenborg, era un rimando ad una tradizione di saperi

---

15. SUZUKI 1913, 22–4.

approcciata dall'autore svedese nel corso delle sue indagini, ma era anche un rimando ad un campo d'interesse che andava diffondendosi negli Stati Uniti nel periodo in cui Suzuki vi aveva lavorato e soggiornato e a cui appunto, anche lui si era approcciato: quello della teosofia. Un orientamento disgiunto dal culto religioso e completamente volto all'esplorazione dell'esperienza spirituale e del rapporto tra l'anima e l'essenza divina, a cui si votava la neonata Società Teosofica, istituita a New York nel 1875. Tra i numerosi adepti della teosofia figurava anche Beatrice Erskin Lane (1878–1939), la moglie di Suzuki. Entrambi continuarono a coltivare tale disciplina anche in Giappone, attraverso incontri e conferenze che coinvolsero diverse personalità intellettuali e accademiche, nel contesto di vere e proprie logge.

La seconda fase della vita di Swedenborg coincide con la seconda parte del testo di Suzuki. Entrando nel vivo del pensiero mistico dell'autore svedese, Suzuki delineò con maggiore precisione anche le analogie da lui riconosciute rispetto al buddhismo. Egli individuava proprio nel percorso di vita di Swedenborg il primo punto di similarità in tal senso, definendolo «analogo a quello di un praticante degli insegnamenti buddhisti», ed enfatizzandone il culmine ovvero la traslazione dall'idea di un «proprio potere» a quella del «potere dell'altro»:

> Il suo percorso di vita è, per esempio, analogo a un praticante degli insegnamenti buddhisti, inizialmente seguace della scuola di pensiero del «proprio potere», che facesse dietrofront, per diventare un credente nel potere dell'altro. La fede nel potere esterno delle deità illuminate appare semplice, ma le sue austerità non sono diverse da quelle che comporta l'affidarsi al potere interno.
>
> Coloro che devolvono la loro vita alle pratiche religiose conoscono questo cambiamento intimamente, in base alla loro esperienza personale.[16]

L'abbandono del «proprium» e la sinergia con l'opera del Divino erano dunque un punto chiave dell'opera di Swedenborg, simile al pensiero buddhista e familiare alla cultura giapponese. Tale opera costituiva allora non solo un elemento d'interesse per Suzuki, filosofo e studioso delle religioni, ma anche un valido punto di riferimento per la critica situazione spirituale del paese alla quale egli cercava risposta.

---

16. Suzuki 1913, 26.

Un'altra similarità con il buddhismo era il presupposto della «provvidenza»:

> Swedenborg spiega la ragione per cui c'è il male e la falsità nel mondo. Questa sezione rassomiglia agli insegnamenti dei mezzi abili del buddhismo Mahāyāna: ovvero, è la divina provvidenza che permette al male e alla falsità di affermarsi temporaneamente, così che questi possano essere sopraffatti dal buono e dalla verità. Questo non vuol dire che la provvidenza non si manifesti sia nelle persone buone sia in quelle cattive. La divina provvidenza invita continuamente l'individuo a entrare in paradiso. Ciascuno è libero di rispondere e agire bene, ma le persone sono anche libere di non rispondere e agire male. Un uso cattivo di questa libertà è il risultato dell'attaccamento al sé (*proprium*). Ogni persona ha la predisposizione e la capacità per essere salvata; e non essere salvati, o cadere in disgrazia, deriva dal non salvare sé stessi. La strada per la salvazione comporta il riconoscimento di vari mali come peccati contro la provvidenza divina e la loro elusione. Quindi, compiere un'azione malvagia, ripetutamente, dopo averla riconosciuta come male e un'offesa alla provvidenza. Non è abbastanza ammettere di aver compiuto il male; bisogna percepirne il suo più grande significato religioso e bisogna evitarlo al meglio delle proprie abilità, tendendo sempre solo al buono. Questa è la via più veloce per la salvazione. Essa arriva gradualmente; non si attualizza immediatamente attraverso la diretta grazia di Dio, poiché ciò sarebbe contrario alla divina provvidenza. La salvazione basata solo sulla fede è impossibile; bisogna riconoscere che il frutto della salvazione nasce solo quando la carità e l'amore sono raggiunti. Condurre una vita commettendo peccati, anche se si dicesse sul letto di morte «ti prego, Dio, salvami», non cancellerebbe in un sol colpo il peso dei demeriti degli anni precedenti. È importante avere un cuore penitente fin dal principio e, riconoscendo i propri peccati, è importante accumulare buone azioni che si addicano all'amore e alla saggezza. In questo modo, può essere ottenuta una morte pacifica.[17]

Non seguivano significativi commenti nel testo e nemmeno altri riferimenti al buddhismo: d'altronde, come annunciato, 『スエデンボルグ』 [Swedenborg] aveva una pura funzione introduttiva della figura dell'autore svedese e delle sue opere.

Tali analogie sarebbero state sviluppate, ben undici anni dopo, nell'altra opera di Suzuki dedicata al mistico: 『スエデンボルグ(その天界と他力観)』

---

17. Ibid., 37.

[Swedenborg (la sua concezione del paradiso e del potere «dell'Altro»)]. Come recitava il titolo, lo scritto si proponeva di indagare la concezione che aveva Swedenborg del reame divino e del «potere dell'altro» di cui, appunto, Swedenborg si era diffusamente occupato e che Suzuki aveva identificato come tema analogo nel buddhismo. Non a caso, nel testo sono rintracciabili riferimenti alle «corrispondenze» presenti in diverse opere del mistico svedese e non a caso citate da Suzuki sul finire dello scritto del 1913:

> Per comprendere correttamente la visione spirituale del mondo oltre questa vita propugnata da Swedenborg, è necessario conoscere a fondo le sue dottrine della rappresentazione, corrispondenza, dei gradi, e degli influssi [...] Swedenborg insegna che la vita umana è amore, e che questo amore non è differente da Dio. Quindi, Dio è la vita umana e le persone sono i *recipient* (consegnatari) di questa vita. Inoltre, nella natura divina esiste una divergenza tra *Esse* (natura) ed *Existere* (apparenza visibile): questi sono due, eppure sono uno. L'amore è la natura, la saggezza è forma esteriore e l'amore dipende dalla saggezza come la saggezza dipende dall'amore. Il Divino è pertanto una combinazione di queste. Esso si manifesta nel mondo spirituale come un sole, il cui calore è amore e la cui luce è saggezza. Il sole del nostro mondo dipende dal sole spirituale. Ricevendo il suo calore vivente e la sua luce vivente, il sole naturale dà luogo all'intera creazione e la fa prosperare. Lo scopo della creazione dell'universo è ricondurre ogni cosa alla propria origine, il Signore, ovvero il Divino, e stabilire così una corrispondenza e una congiunzione tra loro.[18]

Conclusioni

Swedenborg racchiudeva in sé numerosi elementi d'interesse nella prospettiva di Suzuki, ovvero quella di un filosofo buddhista e storico delle religioni alla ricerca di un valido riferimento per la crisi spirituale del proprio paese: in primo luogo, una coscienza circa le conseguenze delle azioni della propria vita terrena nel post-mortem. In secondo luogo, il presupposto dell'esistenza di una dimensione spirituale e, dunque, di una prospettiva non materialistica che si contrapponeva, evidentemente, a quella materialistica del Giappone contemporaneo a Suzuki. In terzo luogo, il pensiero del mistico

18. Ibid., 36.

svedese abbracciava una serie di presupposti spirituali accomunabili a quelli del buddhismo e, pertanto, vicini e cari alla cultura del popolo giapponese.

Swedenborg, dunque, si prestava molto bene come riferimento per la fondazione di un nuova coscienza spirituale e religiosa del paese. Inoltre, il suo sistema teologico aveva il vantaggio di farsi portatore di radici consolidate, ma in una guisa rinnovata, dal sapore moderno e accattivante perché occidentale e quindi papabile per il clima culturale giapponese, rinnovato dall'apertura delle frontiere, dopo secoli di clausura. A questo si aggiungeva il valore del pensiero di Swedenborg, di doppia fattezza perché sia scientifico sia religioso, sdoppiatosi nel presupposto diverso dell'uno e dell'altro tipo di approccio: intellettivo il primo, intuitivo il secondo. Il tutto era poi coronato dall'esperienza del risveglio spirituale, di cui il mistico svedese era stato protagonista, nei fatti – anche se non nella definizione – di quella illuminazione evocata ed invocata dal buddhismo.

Le ragioni elencate da Suzuki motivavano perfettamente quell'appellativo di «Buddha del Nord» coniato per Swedenborg. Esse credo rispondano anche all'intento del presente articolo il quale mirava, oltre che a ricostruire la vita e l'opera dell'autore svedese, a delineare gli elementi d'interesse ravvisati, in lui, da Suzuki.

In altra sede, si proporrà un'indagine filosofica approfondita volta a spiegare nel dettaglio le reali analogie dei due sistemi di pensiero individuate dal filosofo giapponese, con uno specifico riferimento «al potere dell'altro» citato nella Prefazione di *Swedenborg*. Tale «potere», infatti, si costituisce come il fulcro attorno al quale è redatto il secondo testo di Suzuki, nel quale egli richiama l'esoterismo già citato in questo lavoro.

Qui si è voluta fornire una ragionata rassegna di elementi necessari al fine della comprensione della dedizione, filosofica e non, di Suzuki verso Swedenborg, il quale costituì un suo soggetto di ricerca e indagine per quasi un ventennio.

Bibliografia

Kant, Immanuel
    1992   *Dreams of a Spirit-Seer Elucitaded by Dreams of Metaphysics*. Trans. by David Walford. Cambridge: Cambridge University Press.

NAGASHIMA Tatsuya
- 1996 Foreword, in *Swedenborg: Buddha of the North*. West Chester: Swedenborg Foundation.

SUZUKI Daisetsu Teitarō 鈴木大拙 貞太郎
- 1910 『天界と地獄』[*Del cielo e delle sue meraviglie e dell'inferno secondo quel che si è udito e veduto*]. Tokyo: Yūrakusha.
- 1913 『スエデンボルグ』[*Swedenborg*]. Tokyo: Heigo Shuppansha.
- 1914 『新エルサレムとその教説』[*Della nuova Gerusalemme e della sua dottrina celeste*] Tokyo: Heigo Shuppansha.
- 1914 『神知と神愛』[*Dell'amore e saggezza di Dio*]. Tokyo: Heigo Shuppansha.
- 1915 『神慮論』[*Della provvidenza divina*]. Tokyo: Heigo Shuppansha.
- 1924 『スエデンボルグ：その天界と他力観)』[Swedenborg. La sua concezione del paradiso e del potere «dell'Altro»] 『中外日報』2/3-8.
- 1996 *Swedenborg. Buddha of the North*. West Chester: Swedenborg Foundation.

SUZUKI, D. T., et al.
- 1960 *Zen Buddhism and Pyschoanalysis*. New York: Harper and Brothers.

SWEDENBORG, Emanuel
- 1758 *Del cielo e delle sue meraviglie e dell'inferno secondo quel che si e udito e veduto*. Roma: Edizioni Mediterranee, 2005.
- 1749 *Arcana Coelestia, quae in Scriptura Sacra, seu Verbo Domini sunt, detecta. Hic primum in Genesi. Una cum mirabilibus, quae visa sunt in mundo spirituum, et in Coelo angelorum*, vol.1. West Chester: Swedenborg Foundation, 2009.

TWEED, Thomas A.
- 2005 American Occultism and Japanese Buddhism: Albert J. Edmunds, D. T. Suzuki, and Translocative History. *Japanese Journal of Religious Studies* 32/2.

YOSHINAGA Shin'ichi 吉永進一
- 2009 Theosophy and Buddhist Reformers in the Middle of the Meiji Period. *Japanese Religions* 34/2.
- 2012 After Olcott Left: Theosophy and New Buddhists at the Turn of the Century. *The Eastern Buddhist* 43/1–2.
- 2014 Suzuki Daisetsu and Swedenborg: A Historical Background. Paul. L. Swanson and Hayashi Makoto., eds. *Modern Buddhism in Japan*. Nagoya: Nanzan Institute for Religion and Culture, 112–43.

WILKINSON, James. J. G.
- 1842 *A Sketch of Swedenborg and Swedenborgians*. Boston: Clapp.

WILKINSON, Lynn R.
- 1996 *The Dream of an Absolute Language: Emanuel Swedenborg and French Literary Culture*. Albany: State University of New York Press.

WHITE, William M.
- 1878 *Life of Emanuel Swedenborg*. Philadelphia: J. P. Lippincott & Co.

Kuwano Moe
Kanazawa Seiryō University

La influencia de Watsuji Tetsurō en el pensamiento de Yuasa Yasuo

El tema principal de este artículo es cuestionar cuál es el legado de Watsuji para Yuasa y para nosotros hoy, así como indagar en qué consiste la aportación de Yuasa. Consideraremos este tema desde tres perspectivas: el tema ético de la pregunta intercultural por el Sí-mismo y el tema metafísico (que Yuasa prefiere llamar meta-psíquico) acerca del camino a través de la interioridad hacia la trascendencia; el tema del mundo, espacio, *aidagara*, interrelación y corporalidad; el tema de la unidad corpóreo-espiritual como clave de la unidad entre praxis y teoría. En este artículo, expondré brevemente los puntos principales de la filosofía de Watsuji que Yuasa incorpora en su planteamiento filosófico: la filosofía comparada; la filosofía del cuerpo y la relación entre filosofía y espiritualidad o autocultivo.

PALABRAS CLAVE: filosofía intercultural—antropología de Watsuji—pregunta por el Sí-mismo—unidad corpóreo-espiritual

El tema principal de este artículo es cuestionar cuál es el legado de Watsuji para Yuasa y para nosotros hoy, así como indagar en qué consiste la aportación de Yuasa. Consideraremos este tema desde tres perspectivas: el tema ético de la pregunta intercultural por el Sí-mismo y el tema metafísico (que Yuasa prefiere llamar meta-psíquico) acerca del camino a través de la interioridad hacia la trascendencia; el tema del mundo, espacio, *aidagara*, interrelación y corporalidad; el tema de la unidad corpóreo-espiritual como clave de la unidad entre praxis y teoría. En este artículo, expondré brevemente los puntos principales de la filosofía de Watsuji que Yuasa incorpora en su planteamiento filosófico: la filosofía comparada; la filosofía del cuerpo y la relación entre filosofía y espiritualidad o autocultivo.

Yuasa Yasuo (1925–2005) pertenece a la generación siguiente a la de las grandes figuras de la filosofía moderna japonesa, como Nishida Kitarō (1870–1945) y Watsuji Tetsurō (1889–1960). Yuasa es el discípulo principal de Watsuji y recoge también la herencia de Nishida. Watsuji y Nishida buscaron las raíces de la filosofía japonesa en el marco del encuentro entre Occidente y Oriente dentro de la propia interioridad. Ambos influyeron muy decisivamente en el alumbramiento de las ideas filosóficas principales de Yuasa, especialmente su teoría sobre el cuerpo humano como realidad unificada de lo corpóreo y lo espiritual. En este artículo, voy a plantear brevemente los puntos principales de la filosofía de Watsuji incorporada en la filosofía de Yuasa, especialmente por lo que se refiere a la filosofía intercultural. Enfocaremos los siguientes tres puntos: la filosofía comparada; la filosofía del cuerpo y la relación entre filosofía y espiritualidad o autocultivo. Cada uno de estos enfoques requiere una consideración más profunda y crítica, pero mi objetivo aquí es sólo presentar una visión general del modo en que Yuasa incorporó el legado del pensamiento de Watsuji en su propia visión filosófica.

Yuasa, siguiendo la línea de Watsuji cuya antropología está centrada en la noción clave de *aidagara* 間柄, da mucha importancia a la inserción de la filosofía en la vida cotidiana (clima, historia, cultura y sociedad) de manera que forme parte constitutiva de la existencia humana. Para Yuasa, la filosofía originalmente es una sabiduría interdisciplinaria e integral que reflexiona sobre el ser humano y el mundo desde una perspectiva de los principios últimos que generan y orientan el pensar. Es decir, la filosofía tiene que estar íntimamente relacionada con nuestra propia vivencia de estar en el mundo y con el contexto circunstancial en el que se desarrolla nuestra vida. En este sentido, dice Yuasa, es necesario el renacimiento de una filosofía arraigada en la circunstancia espiritual de la vida humana en la actualidad para poder cuestionar las incógnitas y el sentido de la vida humana personal y convivencial. Podríamos aducir, como ejemplos de dicha metodología, teniendo en cuenta la situación espiritual presente, la destrucción del medio ambiente, el estado psíquico de la persona humana o los conflictos étnicos o religiosos.[1]

Otro punto importante es el método de la filosofía comparada en la que caracteriza la filosofía de Yuasa. El método principal de Yuasa es la filosofía comparada, reflexionar en profundidad sobre la totalidad del pensamiento, tanto de Occidente como de Oriente. El pensamiento occidental se refiere aquí especialmente al racionalismo moderno occidental, mientras que por pensamiento oriental se entiende la filosofía moderna japonesa cuyo núcleo está basado especialmente en la tradición budista y confuciana, del mismo modo en que el pensamiento occidental arraigaría en la tradición cristiana. A pesar de que Yuasa habla de dos pensamientos, el de Occidente y el de Oriente, es evidente que no se puede distinguir fácilmente, con formula estereotipada, qué es pensamiento occidental y qué es pensamiento oriental.

Hay que tener en cuenta que Yuasa evita empezar comparando a nivel superficial pensamientos ya constituidos y prefiere remontarse a las raíces tradicionales de los respectivos pensamientos en su génesis y desarrollo. Por eso la filosofía comparada según Yuasa conlleva siempre un reflexionar en profundidad sobre la totalidad de cada pensamiento, tanto en su cuestionamiento de pensamientos diferentes como en la afirmación consciente de sus propias raíces tradicionales. Yuasa intenta esclarecer dichas

---

1. Yuasa 1993, 224.

cuestiones yendo más allá de diferencias culturales o contextuales entre Occidente y Oriente, así como respecto a los condicionamientos del pensador por sus circunstancias temporales, regionales y biográficas, marco ineludible de sus enfoques. Así es como Yuasa trata principalmente la temática de la interioridad humana en la experiencia contemplativa, tanto en obras sobre historia del pensamiento occidental como en obras sobre historia del pensamiento oriental.

En el campo de la filosofía comparada
El legado de Watsuji en el tema ético de la pregunta intercultural por el Sí mismo

Watsuji, utilizando el método comparativo, coteja y contrasta semejanzas y diferencias entre la diversidad de climas, ambientes y culturas.[2] En ese proceso de comparación, el pensador que entra en contacto con la alteridad de la otra cultura, toma conciencia así de la mismidad de su propia circunstancia cultural, como primer paso para trascenderla y hacer posible mutuamente la fecundación filosófica intercultural.

A lo largo de todas las obras de Yuasa, podemos encontrar las preguntas radicales sobre sí mismo, sobre el mundo y sobre el fundamento que los trasciende. Diríamos, con una expresión de la tradición filosófica occidental, que están presentes en él las preguntas metafísicas. El núcleo de este pensamiento es la teoría de la corporalidad (身体論) y la teoría sobre la importancia filosófica de las prácticas de autocultivo espiritual (修行論). Esta forma del pensamiento filosófico de Yuasa proviene de la filosofía moderna japonesa, especialmente la de Watsuji Tetsurō y Nishida Kitarō. Según Yuasa, tanto Nishida como Watsuji afrontaron la modernización occidental e intentaron captar el encuentro entre la tradición occidental y su propia cultura tradicional; pero no lo hicieron como quien analiza y compara desde fuera, histórica o sociológicamente, dos culturas diversas, sino como quien vive el encuentro o desencuentro entre ambas en forma de conflicto existencial vivido dentro de la propia interioridad.[3] Ambos buscaron, a través

---

2. Sobre este tema véase Watsuji 1935.

3. Sobre la característica de los filósofos modernos japoneses, Yuasa menciona: «Para nosotros, los orientales, la relación entre Occidente y Oriente es un encuentro en el interior de noso-

de este encuentro divergente, las raíces de la filosofía japonesa. El interés principal de Yuasa, concerniente a su investigación de la filosofía japonesa, es cómo adoptar y heredar la forma de pensamiento de Nishida y Watsuji, quienes reflexionan sobre su propio pensamiento tradicional y la dimensión religiosa (incluyendo la universalidad) a través del encuentro con diferentes culturas y tradiciones. Esta pregunta intercultural por el Sí-mismo estuvo en la base de la teoría del cuerpo de Yuasa.

Ahora bien, reflexionemos sobre cómo ahonda Yuasa en la indagación sobre esta pregunta fundamental y cuáles son las coincidencias o diferencias de actitud filosófica entre él y Watsuji.

En la actitud de Yuasa de reflexionar sobre sí mismo como problema ético se halla la influencia de la filosofía de Watsuji[4]. Es decir, la actitud de preguntar sobre sí mismo a través de un enfoque fenomenológico de cuestionar cómo arraiga el pensamiento en la circunstancia ambiental de la propia cultura. Yuasa comenta sobre Watsuji calificándolo como «buscador del valor y del destino del yo».[5] En sus primeras obras, dice Yuasa, se halla una actitud que da mucha importancia a la experiencia interna del yo. Es decir, una pregunta por sí mismo y sobre cómo deberíamos vivir. Sin embargo, en el sistema ético de sus últimos años, el problema del yo desapareció totalmente. Yuasa cuestiona el paradero de este yo oculto de Watsuji para poder comprender su ética. Según opinión de Yuasa, la pregunta hacia el yo de Watsuji desapareció desde que Watsuji empezó a buscar el modo de salir de sí mismo negando el yo reducido a la racionalidad.

Sin embargo, dice Yuasa, la estructura del sujeto de Watsuji consiste

---

tros mismos, más que un encuentro entre lo interior y lo exterior» (YUASA 1970, 140).

4. Para Yuasa, la ética (倫理) señala la pregunta por sí mismo, sobre cómo debería vivir su propia vida. Es decir, la cuestión ética está profundamente relacionada con la filosofía existencial. Yuasa empezó a interesarse por la filosofía al recibir clases de Watsuji sobre ética, como comenta al reflexionar sobre sus clases tras la derrota de Japón en la Segunda Guerra Mundial: «Cuando escuchaba la explicación de Watsuji sobre Kant y Dilthey en su curso de ética, sentía por primera vez que mis ojos estaban abiertos a la filosofía» (YUASA 1981, 189). Según Yuasa, en el pensamiento de Watsuji se encuentra la cuestión sobre sí mismo. En el concepto de *aidagara* de Watsuji es donde arraiga el Sí-mismo y el fundamento de su ética.

5. Yuasa comenta así sobre Watsuji: «En el fondo de la formación del pensamiento de Watsuji está oculto un enigma. En la época de adolescencia, Watsuji investigó y presentó rigurosamente el pensamiento existencial. Además era un buscador apasionado 'valor y del destino del yo' [como un Sí-mismo]» (YUASA 1970, 234–55).

meramente en negar el yo racional y no ha tocado el problema de las emociones o de superar los deseos del yo. Es decir, la visión del sujeto de Watsuji «ha llegado a la puerta del camino de sumergirse hacia atrás, pero se negó a entrar dentro de este camino».[6] Esta actitud de Watsuji de negar el yo racional, según el análisis de Yuasa, está reflejada en su ética. Para Watsuji, «la relación entre los seres humanos *(aidagara)* es, para el ser humano, más fundamental que el sujeto personal; es decir, *aidagara* o la interrelación es nuestra existencia originaria». Pero esta idea de Watsuji «se desarrolla siempre dentro de la dimensión cotidiana»,[7] es decir, en el nivel del ser humano cotidiano y consciente, por contraste con la filosofía de Nishida que busca la causa latente de la existencia del yo dentro de la interioridad humana. Watsuji mostró personalmente su falta de interés hacia la religión.[8]

Hay en Yuasa una actitud de reflexionar sobre sí mismo y sobre el pensamiento transmitido por la propia tradición cultural. Esta reflexión se lleva a cabo mediante un enfoque fenomenológico, en el que se nota el influjo de Watsuji, porque plantea la reflexión sobre la propia historia y cultura a partir de la reflexión sobre la diferencia geográfica y climático-ambiental, que es como planteaba Watsuji la pregunta por la identidad. También Yuasa pone en el punto de partida de la ética la pregunta antropológica por Sí mismo. Pero hay un punto de diferencia en el enfoque ético de ambos pensadores. Watsuji, en su investigación antropológica, da importancia a la comprensión hermenéutica de la realidad cotidiana, individual y social; en el contexto concreto, espacial y temporal, de la tradición histórica y la cultura. Pero se detiene ahí, en la horizontalidad de esa indagación; se abre a la socialidad, a través de la interrelación (*aidagara*), pero no va más allá, ni trata de ahon-

---

6. Yuasa 1970, 242–3.
7. Yuasa 1970, 251, 252.
8. Lo que pretende Nishida es investigar la esencia invisible de la existencia del yo, mientras Watsuji desarrolla sus ideas dentro de la dimensión antropológica (Yuasa 1970, 252–3). Sobre este punto comenta Yuasa que:

> El hecho de que a Watsuji no le interesó la religión, al final, coincide con su problema fundamental que le llevó a eliminar toda la conciencia del yo. Efectivamente, la esencia de la religión no puede reducirse a lo meramente cultural, conecta con la cuestión sobre la causa absoluta de la existencia del sujeto, ya que la esencia de la religión conecta con la pregunta hacia el fundamento absoluto de la existencia del yo. (1970, 255)

Por otro lado, hay otras investigaciones que consideran la relación de la idea de Watsuji con la religiosidad y la fe como, por ejemplo, Inuzuka 2018.

dar a través de la interioridad hacia la dimensión última, radical. Contrasta esto con Yuasa que trata de penetrar en la dimensión de ultimidad y profundidad del sujeto humano. Yuasa, a través de la pregunta ética práctica sobre cómo vivir la propia vida, se encamina hacia la pregunta religiosa por el fundamento último de la existencia humana. Para Yuasa la ética está en una relación de inseparabilidad con la cuestión religiosa, que trasciende la mera cotidianidad. ¿Cómo será entonces posible acercarse al fundamento último de la existencia humana que trasciende la cotidianidad? Sobre esto, Yuasa afirma: «Hay que seguir preguntando por el sí mismo existencialmente hacia ese fundamento oculto».[9] Solamente así se puede avanzar hacia la interioridad y por ella hacia la trascendencia.

Aportación de Yuasa

Como hemos visto antes, la consideración de Watsuji sobre la estructura del sujeto está limitada dentro del nivel del ser humano cotidiano y consciente, mientras que Yuasa intentó superar esta dimensión cotidiana e ir más allá. Es decir, Yuasa intentó llegar a la dimensión religiosa, el fundamento absoluto de la existencia humana a través de la cuestión práctica de cómo vivir nuestra vida. Es decir, para Yuasa la ética es inseparable de la cuestión metafísica que va más allá de la cotidianidad. La aportación de Yuasa a partir de la pregunta ética por sí mismo de Watsuji es la revisión de las raíces tradicionales de la mismidad y de la alteridad: en vez de comparar los frutos, prefiere remontarse a las raíces de cada árbol para encontrar el terreno común en el subsuelo.[10] Profundizando en lo particular se llega a lo universal. En vez de trascender negando el yo y ascendiendo a lo alto, se trasciende descendiendo, es decir, profundizando en lo propio, en lo particular y tradicional, para encontrar en el fondo lo universal.

---

9. Yuasa 1970, 25. Dice así Yuasa: «El fundamento último de la existencia humana como absoluto (絶対) o vacuidad (空) no se puede captar desde fuera mediante la hermenéutica sino que hay que seguir preguntando por el Sí mismo existencialmente hacia este fundamento oculto» (かくれた根拠にむけてみずから実存的に問うてゆくこと).

10. Sobre este método de comparar teniendo en cuenta el ejemplo de las raíces del árbol, remito a la obra de Thomas Kasulis 2002.

En el campo de la filosofía del cuerpo
La herencia de Watsuji en el tema de «mundo, espacio, aidagara, interrelación».

El segundo punto importante para poder considerar la herencia de Watsuji para Yuasa y para nosotros es el tema del mundo, el espacio y *aidagara*, la interrelación. Según Yuasa el concepto de *aidagara* es palabra clave en la ética de Watsuji.

Watsuji analiza en su obra *La ética como Antropología*, la palabra *ningen*. Se usa en japonés con ambigüedad. Sirve para decir lo que se dice en lenguas europeas con palabras como *anthropos, homo, man, Mensch*. También se usa con sentidos semejantes la palabra *hito* para referirse al individuo de la especie humana. El término *aida* o también leído *ma*: intervalo, espacio intermedio, relación, entre) se junta al de *hito* y tenemos la palabra *ningen*. Al juntar así el «individuo» y el «entre» se obtiene la palabra *ningen* (con pronunciación castellana, *ninguén*), que sería, al pie de la letra, «individuo humano entre o en medio de...»; es decir, se hace humano el individuo entre los humanos, no aislado y solo. Según Watsuji, «la particular amplitud de *hito* (que, también se lee y pronuncia *nin*) no se altera al añadírsele *gen* para formar la palabra *ningen*: ser humano. *Ningen* no significa solamente «entre los humanos» o «en medio de los humanos», sino existir entre los humanos en cuanto que cada ser humano es un «yo», es «otra persona» como yo, y es también lo que llamamos «la gente». No es solo la relación «tú-yo» sino la relación «nosotros-ellos». Por otra parte, resulta claro el hecho de que cada ser humano, como «yo» u «otra persona», se fundamenta siempre en la interrelación humana. Al definirse una relación humana, surge tanto el «yo» como la «otra persona». Es decir, el que el ser humano sea «yo» u «otra persona» no es más que una restricción del sentido de *ningen*. Aquí encuentra también su fundamento la constitución del ser humano en cuanto tal por el lenguaje. Con estos análisis pretendía Watsuji explorar el peso histórico de la palabra *ningen*.[11]

Teniendo en cuenta este pensamiento, ha desarrollado Watsuji la inseparabilidad de cuerpo y mente, persona y ambiente o entorno natural. La convivencia con lo otro y la naturaleza es una base muy importante para la

---

11. Watsuji 1934, 13–21.

reflexión sobre el ser humano en el marco de la antropología filosófica en Oriente.[12] Por ello, Watsuji reflexiona en su obra *Fūdo* (*Antropología del paisaje*), sobre la ambientalidad —clima y paisaje— como algo que forma parte de la estructura de la existencia humana. Dice así en el primer capítulo de dicha obra: «La vivencia del paisaje forma parte de nuestra vida cotidiana».[13]

Existir en *aidagara* es existir en la vida cotidiana, en el paisaje, en la naturaleza viviente. Se puede decir, desde la perspectiva espiritual, que existir en *aidagara* es el punto de partida y llegada de lo humano.

Por tanto, según Watsuji, el comienzo de un gran error en la modernidad ha sido captar el problema de la ética meramente a nivel de la conciencia de un individuo. Desde el punto de vista de la corporeidad humana, el ser humano nace por la relación de los padres y existe en su propio cuerpo. Desde el momento del nacimiento, el ser humano está inserto en la relación interpersonal. Este hecho es precedente a la lógica.[14]

La inseparabilidad entre la mente y el cuerpo y la naturaleza, según Watsuji, es la visión de la vida propia de la antigüedad japonesa. Además, la palabra *aidagara*, que indica para Watsuji el sentido de la vinculación subjetiva de la «vida-en el espacio-con los demás», debería captarse, como comenta Yuasa, en términos de una vinculación auténticamente corporal. Esta vinculación no es meramente una relación psicológica ni una relación física, ni la mera unión entre ellas.

El mérito de Watsuji frente a la filosofía contemporánea, según opinión de Yuasa, es que ha fijado la cuestión de la relación entre el cuerpo y el espa-

---

12. Yuasa considera que la diferencia sobre la visión de la naturaleza entre Occidente y Oriente influye en el desarrollo del pensamiento antropológico de ambas culturas: En la tradición judeo-cristiana en Occidente, donde se considera el ser humano como «*Imago Dei*», imagen de Dios, la naturaleza es vista como criatura que está por debajo de él y sometida a su dominio. Por tanto, la naturaleza puede ser un objeto a captar. Por el contrario, en Oriente, se da mucha importancia a la armonía de la vida humana con la naturaleza. Es decir, se considera que los seres humanos originalmente forman parte de la naturaleza. (Yuasa 1990, 153–9).

13. Watsuji 1935, 7 (2006, 24). Watsuji habla sobre la convivencia del ser humano con la naturaleza desde su experiencia. Dice así en el prólogo: «la relevancia que adquirió esta dimensión se debió quizá a que, al dedicarme a analizar pormenorizadamente la temporalidad, bullían en mi interior las impresiones de diversos climas y paisajes, recogidas a lo largo de mi viaje de Japón a Europa y en mis viajes por el continente» (Watsuji 2006, 18).

14. Yuasa 1999, 776–7.

cio y ha subrayado la interrelación entre los humanos en la mediación de la corporalidad: la relación humana está originalmente arraigada en la vinculación corporal.

Aportación de Yuasa

La herencia de la filosofía de «aidagara» de Watsuji[15]

Yuasa capta el concepto de *aidagara* desde un enfoque de gramática de primera-segunda-tercera persona, para poder comparar con la visión del hombre en la modernidad occidental.[16] Normalmente al observar al ser humano nosotros distinguimos tres posiciones: primera persona, segunda persona y tercera persona. Cuando observamos al hombre desde la tercera persona, dice Yuasa, captamos al hombre como un cuerpo observable y medible de un modo cuantificable. Por ejemplo, para expresar la población de Japón o España o números de víctimas de desastres naturales o accidentes, captamos al ser humano con parámetros numerables, cuantificables, que son aplicables a un objeto físico para determinar su corporeidad. En este caso las dimensiones personal y psíquica están olvidadas. La actitud de la tecnología científica observa al hombre desde la perspectiva de la tercera persona y esta manera de observar al hombre es necesaria para su desarrollo. Por otro lado, cuando hablamos de la primera persona, se capta el hombre desde el punto de vista de un yo o sujeto. En este caso, captamos la existencia del sí mismo como existencia personal irrepetible basándonos en la mente. Esta manera de captar al hombre, podemos encontrarla en la actitud de la conciencia del yo en la filosofía moderna a partir de Descartes. Y aquí acentúa Yuasa que es importante aclarar el contenido psicológico de la mente.[17] Cuando Des-

---

15. Sobre la filosofía de Watsuji he tomado el texto de Yuasa 2000.

16. Considero muy importante esta parte sobre todo porque aquí podemos encontrar el desarrollo de la teoría del otro (他者論) de Yuasa basándose en la herencia de la filosofía de Watsuji. Yuasa da mucha importancia a la segunda persona, la relación interpersonal, relacionándola con la corporalidad.

17. Psicología para Yuasa es «psicología profunda» que busca la parte inconsciente del ser humano. Según Yuasa la psicología está vinculada con la historia del pensamiento y de la religión. En este punto, Yuasa recibió una gran influencia del psiquiatra suizo Carl G. Jung que analiza la diferencia de la forma del pensamiento ontológico y epistemológico entre Oriente y Occidente desde la perspectiva psicológica. De esta manera de captar historia de la filosofía comparativa surgió la idea de la metapsíquica, sobre la que insiste Yuasa, precisando que se desarrolla especialmente en la tradición oriental y además es una clave para encontrar unos puntos comunes al

cartes dice «yo existo porque yo pienso», se considera que esta conciencia y yo del «pensar» está basada en la función del pensamiento intelectual. A partir de aquí surgió la visión racional del hombre que tiene como condición esencial la racionalidad. Sin embargo, en esta visión racional el cuerpo del hombre está totalmente olvidado. La subjetividad según la filosofía moderna es un sujeto centrado en el *logos* es decir, la conciencia humana que ignora la corporalidad.[18]

Sin embargo, dice Yuasa, todas las cosas de este mundo existen concretamente en el mundo de la extensión espacial. Aquí aparece un concepto de objetividad como objeto de la cognición. Basándose en esa relación conflictiva entre sujeto y objeto, surgió el dualismo que separa claramente la materia y la mente, con las consiguientes dicotomías que afectan a las diversas metodologías académicas. Este hecho provocó la tendencia a separar la filosofía y las ciencias al observar al hombre. Es decir, surgieron problemas éticos especialmente al introducir el método dicotómico en el campo de la tecnología médica en la segunda mitad del siglo XX.[19]

Por el contrario, subraya Yuasa, la base de la segunda persona es la relación interpersonal, es decir, una relación entre personas que se conocen.[20] Aquí hay una interconexión de la mente y se conocen mutuamente como existencia corporal. Por ejemplo, podemos tener en cuenta distintos tipos de comunidades como la relación familiar, la relación entre amigos, de colegas de trabajo, de la gente local, es decir, desde la relación como miembro de la organización cultural o académica hasta la relación pública que se estabiliza por ley. La palabra *aidagara* señala originalmente esta relación interpersonal de la segunda persona. En este caso, podemos captar el ser humano como unidad de cuerpo-mente. El ser humano experimenta inmediatamente la

---

nivel del psiquismo humano más allá de las diferencias tradicionales de Occidente y Oriente. Sobre la relación de la filosofía comparada con la psicología profunda, véase YUASA 1979.

18. Sobre el problema de la conciencia del yo y racionalismo en la filosofía moderna, véase YUASA 1970, especialmente el capítulo III.3.

19. Sobre el problema del dualismo y de la dicotomía en diversas metodologías académicas, véase YUASA 1983.

20. Yuasa dice 「顔見知りの関係」 (la relación de cara-cara) sobre la relación entre personas que se conocen. Además, esta relación es precisamente lo que llama Watsuji como *aidagara*, la relación interpersonal. La idea de Yuasa sobre la segunda persona como relación interpersonal, se puede comparar con la filosofía del Otro de Pedro LAÍN ENTRALGO (1991).

unidad del sujeto y del objeto mediante su propio cuerpo. Pero este tipo de relación no está creada por la lógica intelectual, sino que está fundada en la relación psicológica de los miembros que están sometidos a la comunidad. Las leyes y contratos son un mecanismo para mantener y asegurar la estabilidad de la relación comunitaria. La relación psicológica, que está oculta en la forma lógica, está vinculada con sentimientos y deseos de la corporalidad. Así concluye Yuasa que el *aidagara* es la relación que surge basándose en la comunidad psicológica.

Ahora bien, ¿por qué Yuasa consideró este concepto de *aidagara* como una idea principal e importante de Watsuji? Yuasa tiene en cuenta dos grupos de problemas como tarea de investigación para el futuro: los problemas relacionados con la bioética en el campo de la medicina y los problemas relacionados con la psicología clínica. En primer lugar, en el campo clínico, la relación entre médico y enfermo era originalmente una relación interpersonal de la segunda persona; sin embargo, en la situación real de hoy, hay una tendencia a tratar al enfermo como tercera persona, es decir, se le considera meramente como «un objeto enfermo». Aquí hay una doble dimensión de la realidad clínica, que es una condición de destino inevitable: una es la del médico; trata el cuerpo del enfermo como objeto de la observación científica (como tercera persona); pero, al mismo tiempo, también es cierto que el médico trata al enfermo como segunda persona, con la que mantiene una relación de *aidagara*. Podemos encontrar en el fondo de estos problemas datos históricos que muestran como la teoría y tecnología de la medicina contemporánea, especialmente a partir de la mitad del siglo xx, se desarrollaron desde la perspectiva dicotómica. Sin embargo, el ser humano vive en la inseparabilidad entre cuerpo y mente. Este es un hecho que nadie podrá negar, incluidos los médicos. Para poder reflexionar sobre la esencia del ser humano desde el punto de vista filosófico, dice Yuasa, tenemos que partir de este sentido común de unidad corpóreo espiritual. En segundo lugar, hay que considerar los problemas sociales relacionados con el campo de la psicología clínica. Por ejemplo, en los países avanzados, se producen casos de violencia irracional y sin sentido como la violencia doméstica y problemas como 引きこもり (encerramiento en sí mismo) que padecen personas que rechazan la relación social y familiar. Yuasa analiza que en el fondo de estos problemas hay una pérdida de la vinculación psicológica o capacidad de conectar con la interrelación de *aidagara* y surge una situación psicológica de *bellum omnium contra omnes,* como dice Hobbes. A partir de esta psicología surge la condición de la pérdida de identidad que solo puede confirmar su propia existencia por reacción apresurada hacia el estímulo sensitivo corriente. La identidad señala la confirmación del propio sí mismo, pero se puede observar que en los jóvenes de ahora hay una condición psicológica que se puede definir como pérdida del sentido de su propia vida. Aquí, dice Yuasa, hay que reflexionar sobre el sentido de la tercera persona y primera persona que surge de la relación interpersonal de *aidagara*: la posición de tercera persona conectaría con la consideración crítica hacia el método de la ciencia, conectaría más propiamente con la tercera persona. En cambio, la primera persona conectaría con problemas de la formación personal, es decir, la cuestión sobre cómo tiene que vivir su propia vida. Ante este problema sobre formación personal es importante recuperar el auténtico sentido del cultivo de las virtudes personales desde la perspectiva de la psicología y del cuerpo, que se han perdido en la ética moderna por generalizar sobre las virtudes de manera abstracta. La clave de esa recuperación es la relación interpersonal de *aidagara*.

De aidagara a la filosofía del cuerpo

Yuasa interpreta y desarrolla la idea de *aidagara* de Watsuji al sugerir que el ser humano que existe en el espacio, en la relación, en la naturaleza, es el propio cuerpo que dice «yo estoy aquí». No es solamente un cuerpo físico que está aquí, sino un cuerpo-sujeto que dice «yo estoy aquí». Es decir, el cuerpo no es la posesión del yo, sino que es un cuerpo que dice yo, el cuerpo temporal y espacial, el cuerpo vivo o el cuerpo animado, cuerpo consciente y conciencia encarnada. Igualmente, el esquema corporal no es una idea que yo tenga de mi cuerpo, ni es un cuerpo pensado, sino un cuerpo viviente (o vivido). El ser humano es, como dice el filósofo español Pedro Laín Entralgo, un cuerpo que tiene capacidad de decir de sí mismo «yo».[21] En este sentido, la corporalidad es el camino para la pregunta hacia lo trascendente, partiendo de un cuerpo que es «cuerpo-espíritu». El cuerpo en japonés se escribe 身体 (*shintai*) indicando el ser propio (身) cuerpo (体). Por ello, aquí preferimos designarla como la unidad corpóreo-espiritual, más que decir solamente el cuerpo o la corporalidad. Es decir, estamos tratando sobre un

21. Laín 1991, 243.

cuerpo que conlleva inseparablemente las dimensiones física, psíquica y espiritual.[22]

En el campo de la relación entre filosofía y espiritualidad o autocultivo
La herencia de Watsuji en el tema de la teoría y la praxis, o de la filosofía y la espiritualidad.

Para poder hablar de la relación entre filosofía y espiritualidad, hay que ver la característica que Yuasa considera propia de Asia oriental de la unidad entre la sabiduría teórica y la práctica. Según Yuasa, «la sabiduría del cuerpo» es clave para poder pensar la relación entre la sabiduría de la teoría y la de la praxis.[23]

Aquí me quisiera fijar especialmente en la que Yuasa llama «sabiduría del cuerpo» (*shintai no chi*), considerándola desde el punto de vista de la relación entre el saber teórico y la sabiduría práctica[24]. El problema de la sabiduría del cuerpo ocupa para Yuasa un lugar preferente y juega un papel indispensable para aclarar las tensiones entre teoría y praxis. Pero hay que tener en cuenta la delimitación de sentido con la que él precisa estos dos términos. El saber teórico está representado por la ontología y metafísica occidentales, mientras que la sabiduría práctica sigue el ejemplo de la «ética como filosofía de lo humano», propuesta por Watsuji como método de pensamiento sobre la acción humanamente justa y correcta.

En la tradición occidental, basándose en la cultura griega y romana, hay una tendencia a acentuar la teoría como algo que se presupone y precede a la praxis. Por eso, a la hora de aplicar criterios teóricos al campo de la práctica, se tropieza inevitablemente con la dificultad de articular bien la unidad entre la praxis y la teoría. Esta forma de pensar provocó una separación entre

---

22. Kuwano 2012, 199.

23. Sobre la sabiduría del cuerpo y la relación entre la praxis y la teoría he tomado el texto de Yuasa sobre la recuperación de la filosofía (1993: 216–33).

24. Sobre la sabiduría del cuerpo desde el punto de vista de la unidad entre el saber teórico y la sabiduría práctica, véase el capítulo primero del Kuroki et al. 2015). La sabiduría del cuerpo indica sabiduría de la experiencia práctica, es decir experimentar a través del propio cuerpo (身をもって体験すること).

la sabiduría de la teoría y la de la praxis, especialmente a partir de la modernidad occidental.[25]

En cambio, en las tradiciones budistas y confucianas, en la que arraigan las filosofías de Watsuji o Nishida, se puede encontrar más fácilmente el camino hacia la unidad entre la praxis y la teoría. Yuasa se planteó cuestionar nuevamente el sentido y el puesto de la ética, ya que lo consideraba clave para poder reconsiderar la relación de ambas. En efecto, la clave para poder pensar esta unidad entre praxis y teoría es el cuerpo personal, es decir, la trasformación de cuerpo-mente a través de la práctica del autocultivo corpóreo-espiritual (修行 *shugyō*). Siguiendo la línea de la filosofía moderna japonesa, subraya Yuasa que hay una inseparabilidad entre la teoría (cognición) y la praxis, entre el conocer y el actuar, como se veía también en la manera de concebir la relación entre receptividad y creatividad en el análisis de la acción libre humana, para lo cual Nishida acuñó la noción de «intuición agente» (行為的直観)[26]. Cuando habla del budismo primitivo como filosofía práctica, incluye el sentido de la filosofía teórica (KUWANO 2012: 93). Pero se trata de una reflexión teórica que no precede a la práctica, sino, por el contrario, presupone la práctica de experiencias de sentido como las que se dan en la meditación, por ejemplo, en el yoga o el zen. Tanto Nishida como Yuasa distinguen dos modos de filosofar teóricamente sobre el tema de la religiosidad o espiritualidad: la reflexión teórica antes de tener experiencias de practicar la espiritualidad; la reflexión teórica que presupone esas prácticas y reflexiona teóricamente sobre ellas. La reflexión sobre la transformación de cuerpo y mente, que resulta de la práctica de *shugyō*, nos descubre el significado del cuerpo personal.[27]

Aportación de Yuasa

La idea de Yuasa sobre la relación entre la filosofía y la espiritualidad es más parecida a la de Nishida. Además de continuar con la tradición oriental de

---

25. KUWANO 2015, 83–4.
26. Sobre la «intuición agente» Niishida dice lo siguiente:
La intuición agente consiste en observar las cosas a través de la actuación de la realidad. Ese actuar de la realidad constituye el ver. En este caso no es que desaparezca el yo o simplemente se cosifique, sino más bien que el yo se transforma en el yo auténtico (真の自己), que es creativo a partir de su receptividad para la actuación de la realidad. (NISHIDA 1937: 343)
27. KUWANO 2015, 82.

ver la unidad cuerpo-espíritu como un logro del autocultivo. Yuasa precisa que se trata de un camino de retorno a la unidad originaria. Con otras palabras, el camino de retorno a la unidad originaria es expresión de la trasformación de cuerpo-mente a través de la práctica de *shugyō*. Es decir, es un intento de la trasformación de cuerpo-mente para poder llegar a la óptima condición para la persona que practica el autocultivo.

La praxis se refiere aquí al concepto oriental de *shugyō*. ¿Qué es *shugyō*? ¿Cuál es su finalidad? La noción de *shugyō* implica varios sentidos que se desarrollaron en el contexto filosófico oriental; por tanto, no significa exactamente lo mismo que la práctica a la que se hace referencia en la filosofía occidental.

Dentro del concepto de *shugyō*, Yuasa distingue entre el ámbito de las prácticas preceptivas o normativas: *sīla* (戒), en japonés, *kai*: preceptos o mandamientos del campo ético y el ámbito de las prácticas contemplativas: *samādhi* (定) en japonés, *jō*: concentración receptiva, contemplativa. Recordamos que el concepto de *sīla* (戒) indica «los preceptos de la vida cotidiana que se impone uno a sí mismo», o dicho más claramente, «imponerse a sí mismo la normativa ética de la vida cotidiana, mientras el *samādhi* significa la actividad contemplativa que «se orienta hacia la propia interioridad de sí mismo sumergiéndose en su propio fondo».[28] En el pensamiento de Yuasa, los preceptos *sīla* se llaman praxis exterior (外交的実践), mientras la contemplación es llamada la praxis interior. La praxis interior (内向的実践) es la actividad que se orienta hacia la propia interioridad del ser humano, cuyo significado equivale a la vida contemplativa en el término occidental.[29]

La idea de *shugyō* es, según Yuasa, una de las características propias de los fundamentos filosóficos en Asia oriental[30]. La verdadera sabiduría se puede alcanzar en el cuerpo-mente. Como afirma Yuasa: «*shugyō* es la praxis para poder alcanzar la sabiduría mediante la dedicación con todo el cuerpo-mente». Es decir, la sabiduría no se alcanza con la reflexión teórica, sino que se realiza a través de la experiencia del propio cuerpo (体得).[31] El juicio consciente no puede captar la autenticidad de la interioridad humana. Esto

---

28. Yuasa 1990, 204.
29. Kuwano 2012, 235.
30. Yuasa 1970, 143.
31. Yuasa 1990, 145, 143.

es lo que expresa Dōgen como *shinjin-datsuraku* 身心脱落),[32] cuestionar el auténtico sentido del alma o de la interioridad humana precediendo la autopercepción de la corporalidad.[33]

Yuasa subraya de este modo la inseparabilidad del cuerpo y de la mente en la perspectiva de la tradición de *shugyō*. Precisamente ahí surge la característica propia de la tradición oriental especialmente de la tradición chino-japonesa. El método del *shugyō* es, como define Yuasa, «el entrenamiento práctico para alcanzar a elevar y a desarrollar la mente o la virtud de uno mismo» (YUASA 1990, 200). Pero, al mismo tiempo, Yuasa subraya la unidad originaría entre el cuerpo y el método del *shugyō* y la coloca como característica propia de la tradición oriental. Es decir, Yuasa considera el *shugyō* en la base de la unidad corpóreo espiritual.[34] Como dice Yuasa:

> La palabra *shugyō* implica depurar la mente humana o elevar la personalidad. Por tanto, considero que en el pensamiento del *shugyō*, se capta la corporalidad dentro de la inseparabilidad entre el cuerpo y la mente.[35]

Herencia y tarea para el futuro

Hemos visto las ideas filosóficas principales que Yuasa heredó de su maestro Watsuji y su aportación para nosotros, en la actualidad, desde tres perspectivas: en el campo de la filosofía comparada; en el campo de la filosofía del cuerpo; en el campo de la relación entre filosofía y espiritualidad o autocultivo.

En primer lugar, hemos considerado el método comparativo de Watsuji

---

32. 身心脱落: diluirse las fronteras entre cuerpo y mente y entre los diversos cinco sentidos. Esto indica, según Dōgen, el camino hacia la sabiduría búdica de la iluminación. Es decir, diluirse los lindes de cuerpo y mente es superar la manera dualista de distinguir entre el cuerpo y la mente, y entre el sujeto y el objeto en la conciencia cotidiana y recuperar la interrelación originaria de cuerpo-mente. Yuasa descubre además la clave de su respuesta en la idea de Dōgen: en primer lugar, para evitar la actitud del pensamiento cotidiano, hay que fijarse en el propio cuerpo y mente del yo. Negando la comprensión cotidiana de que la mente domina el cuerpo, hay que seguir la actitud de que en realidad el cuerpo domina a la mente. El «sentarse a contemplar» o «postura del loto» indica precisamente descubrir el auténtico estado del cuerpo-mente (YUASA 1990, 242–3).
33. KUWANO 2012, 236.
34. KUWANO 2012, 238.
35. YUASA 1986, 399.

mediante la toma de conciencia y trascendencia de la mismidad del propio clima y cultura al entrar en contacto con la alteridad del clima y cultura diferentes. La aportación de Yuasa fue cuestión ética o antropológica como pregunta por sí mismo, para llegar a las raíces del ser humano, en una tradición universal más allá de las tradiciones culturales diferentes. Pero a esa universalidad se llega ahondando en la particularidad de la propia cultura, en la que nos sumergimos adentrándonos en la propia interioridad. Según Yuasa, la filosofía es como una búsqueda de la eternidad, pero al mismo tiempo, como una actividad que siempre se realiza dentro de las circunstancias de cada contexto histórico.[36]

En segundo lugar, hemos visto la herencia de Watsuji por lo que se refiere a concretar el ser-en-el mundo y en el tiempo heideggeriano en el ser-en el-espacio, ser-en-relación y el ser-en el-clima y la cultura. La aportación de Yuasa fue ampliar y profundizar el tema de la corporalidad, especialmente ahondando en la interioridad del propio ser, que es un ser-en-el-mundo y el ser-con-los-otros-*aidagara*. Pero Yuasa insiste en añadir que el ser con los demás siempre es «en, con y a través del cuerpo».[37]

En tercer lugar, hemos visto que, aunque es parte del legado de Watsuji dar importancia a lo existencial y a la práctica, en la contribución de Yuasa pesa más la interioridad que la exterioridad, destaca más lo místico o lo espiritual que lo cultural. Yuasa es, en este punto, más parecido a Nishida; además, recoge la tradición oriental de ver la unidad cuerpo-espíritu como un logro del autocultivo, que es un camino de retorno a la unidad originaria.

Yuasa fue, según la referencia de su discípulo Watanabe Manabu, casi el único discípulo de Watsuji que recogió plenamente en su aprendizaje la herencia del maestro.[38] El interés de Yuasa por la ética y la influencia de Watsuji se puede observar en todas sus obras.

En el núcleo de la filosofía de Yuasa, se puede encontrar una pregunta hacia la interioridad de sí mismo: ¿cómo voy a vivir mi propia vida y cuál es mi misión como filósofo para la sociedad de hoy y para el mundo contemporáneo? Filosofar significó para Yuasa, la práctica del *shugyō* a lo largo de toda su vida.

36. YUASA 1970, 139.
37. YUASA 1990, 159–62.
38. WATANABE 2006, 58.

* Este artículo se basa en parte de la investigación que llevé a cabo en mi tesis doctoral *El 気 (=ki) en la filosofía de Yuasa: La unidad corpóreo-espiritual como clave antropológica de la apertura personal a la transcendencia* presentada y defendida en el Centro Facultad de Filosofía y en el Departamento de Filosofía Teorética y de Historia de la Filosofía y de la Ciencia en la Universidad Ramon Llull (Barcelona, 2012).

Referencias bibliográficas

Abreviaturas

WZ   『和辻哲郎全集』[*Obras completas de Watsuji Tetsurō*], Tokyo, Iwanami Shoten, 20 vols., 1961–1963.

YZ   『湯浅泰雄全集』[*Obras completas de Yuasa Yasuo*], Tokyo, Hakua Shobō, 17 vols., 2002–2012.

Fuentes primarias

Nishida Kitarō 西田幾多郎

1937   『哲学論文集 2』, en 『西田幾多郎全集』[*Obras completas de Nishida Kitarō*], Tokyo, Iwanami Shoten, 1965, 8: 296–589.

Watsuji Tetsurō 和辻哲郎

1934   『人間の学としての倫理学』[*La ética como antropología*, 1ª edición), en WZ 9: 1–192.

1935   『風土：人間学的考察』 primera edición), en WZ 8: 1–256. ,

2006   *Antropología del paisaje: Climas, culturas y religiones*, trad. Juan Masiá Clavel. Salamanca, Sígueme.

Yuasa Yasuo

1970   『近代日本の哲学と実存思想』[*La filosofía moderna de Japón y el pensamiento existencial*], YZ 5: 136–489.

1979   「比較思想研究の方法としての深層心理学」[*La psicología profunda como método de la investigación sobre la filosofía comparada:*], YZ 5: 51–102.

1981   『和辻哲郎：近代日本哲学の運命』[*Watsuji Tetsurō: Destino de la filosofía japonesa*], YZ 13: 188–35

1983   「東洋の身体論をめぐる諸問題」) [Problemas acerca de la teoría del ser cuerpo en Oriente], YZ 14: 78–119.

1986   『気・修行・身体』[*La historia de ideas en Japón, 6*], YZ 14: 398–610.

1990   『身体論：東洋的心身論と現代』[*La teoría del cuerpo en Oriente y la actualidad*], YZ 14: 136–395.

1993   『宗教と科学の間：共時性・超心理学・気の科学』[*Entre la religión y la ciencia: Sincronicidad, parapsichología, filosofía del «ki»*], YZ 17: 214–350.

1999   「身体論の展開」[*El despliegue de la teoría del cuerpo*], YZ 14: 776–7.

2000   「和辻倫理学の遺産と課題：風土・身体・芸術」[*La herencia y la tarea de la ética de Watsuji: Clima, cuerpo, arte*), YZ 13: 156–71.

Fuentes secundarias

INUZUKA Yū 犬塚 悠
2018 「和辻哲郎における「信仰」と「さとり」：近代日本倫理学の一軌跡」）[«Fe» y «alumbramiento» en Watsuji Tetsurō: Una trayectoria en la ética moderna de Japón], 『国際日本学』[*Estudios japoneses globales*] 15: 257–79.

KASULIS, Thomas
2002 *Intimacy or Integrity: Philosophy and Cultural Difference*, Honolulu: University of Hawai'i Press.

KUWANO Moe 桒野 萌
2012 *El 気 (=ki) en la filosofía de Yuasa: La unidad corpóreo-espiritual como clave antropológica de la apertura personal a la transcendencia*, TDX 10803/80061, [https://www.tdx.cat/handle/10803/80061#page=1], consulta 20,08. 2018)
2015 「湯浅泰雄の修行論と身体の知をめぐって」[El autocultivo espiritual y el conocimiento del cuerpo en Yuasa Yasuo], en 黒木幹夫 Kuroki Miki, 鎌田東二 Kamata Tōji y 鮎澤聡 Ayusawa Satoshi, eds, 『身体の知：湯浅哲学の継承と展開』）[*Conocer el cuerpo: La herencia y el despliegue de la filosofía de Yuasa Yasuo*], Sagamihara, Big Net Press, 76–95.

LAÍN ENTRALGO, Pedro
1991 *Cuerpo y alma: Estructura dinámica del cuerpo humano*. Madrid, Espasa-Calpe.

WATANABE Manabu 渡邊 学
2006 «In memoriam Yuasa Yasuo (1925–2005)», *Bulletin of the Nanzan Institute for Religion and Culture* 30: 55–61.

Morioka Masahiro
Waseda Univversity

Animated Persona
The Ontological Status of a Deceased Person Who Continues to Appear in This World

In this paper, I propose the concept of the "animated persona," a soundless voice that says, "I AM HERE" and appears on the surface of someone or something. This concept can bring clarity to the experience of perceiving a kind of personhood on a corpse, a wooden mask, or even a tree. In the first half of this paper, I will examine some Japanese literature and a work of Viktor Frankl's that discuss these phenomena. In the second half, I will analyze the concept of *animated persona* from five perspectives: (1) a compelling power, (2) surface-ness, (3) religious experience, (4) universality, and (5) the meaning of "I." Lastly, I will discuss the relationship among the three layers of biological object, animated persona, and self-conscious being. My aim is to shed new light on the meaning of the encounter between the living and the dead.

KEYWORDS: person—death—Watsuji Tetsurō—Tanabe Hajime—Victor Frankl—phenomenology

Since the great East Japan earthquake of 2011, many tsunami victims who lost family members are reported to have encountered their loved ones in their homes, at the seashore, and in other nearby places. Some saw their images in living rooms, some heard their voices in the wind. From the perspective of modern science, these phenomena would be interpreted as delusions brought about by overwhelming emotions over the tragedy of family members lost to the disaster.

In this paper, I would like to propose a new philosophical framework to have another look at these phenomena, which occur to ordinary people in everyday settings, and offer an alternative explanation. In the first half of this paper, I will examine some of the literature that discusses these phenomena from a philosophical point of view. In the second half, I will propose the concept of *animated persona* and attempt a phenomenological and ontological analysis of it. My discussion relies heavily on the writings of Japanese authors, but I believe that the theory of the *animated persona* applies equally to a variety of phenomena experienced by ordinary people around the world. The central challenge of this paper is to examine how we might interpret the encounter between the living and the dead from the perspective of contemporary philosophy.

Conversations with a Brain-Dead Body

It is interesting that even those who do not believe in the existence of a soul can have this kind of experience. For example, Yanagida Kunio (1936–), a well-known Japanese journalist with a rigorously scientific mind, acknowledged the experience of having "conversations" with his brain-dead, unconscious son Yōjirō in the hospital.

In his autobiographical memoir *Gisei (Sacrifice)*, published in 1995,

Yanagida recounts his experience of sitting at the bedside of his brain-dead son, taking hold of the still warm hands and calling him by name as he reminisced on their time together in life.

"My son's body 'converses' with me without spoken language," Yanagida wries. "This is a mysterious feeling."[1]

> Even though Yōjirō was brain-dead, when Ken'ichirō and I talked to his body, he "talked back" to us. This was a truly mysterious experience. Perhaps it is something that can be understood only by members of a family who have shared happiness and sorrows with each other. Despite the scientific evidence that a brain-dead person is literally a dead person who has no consciousness or use of the senses, I was convinced that the brain-dead body of our beloved held great meaning for those of his family who were joined by a living, spiritual bond.[2]

This was a very strange experience for Yanagida, who had the strong feeling that there was someone, some living person, in front of him, although his son was in the state of brain death, lying unconscious on a bed. As an objective observer, Yanagida clearly understood that a brain-dead patient has lost self-consciousness permanently, but as a father, he could not help noticing "a remnant of personhood" on his beloved son's brain-dead body.

We find similar narratives in the memoirs of any number of families of brain-dead patients. In an impressive memoir, the parents of a brain-dead daughter write vividly of their attempt to communicate with her. Her mother would put perfume on their daughter's warm feet, and every time her father would leave the hospital room, he would call out to his daughter, "*Gambariya* (Hang in there)!" They understood that their daughter had lost self-consciousness in the state of brain death, but at the same time, they perceived a mysterious something on their daughter's body. It was the overwhelming power of that "something" that prompted them to act in this way.[3]

Another example is taken from a letter to a newspaper written by Watanabe Ryōko. She had requested that in the event she were to become brain dead, her organs were to be donated immediately. One day, her father fell into a deep coma (in his case, brain death was not diagnosed). She writes:

---

1. YANAGIDA 1995, 129.
2. YANAGIDA 1995, 129. Ken'ichirō was Yanagida's first son.
3. FUJIWARA 1993, 21.

> To touch the body of my unconscious father and to feel its warmth is *the sole dialogue between us* at present. It is different in quality from everyday communication through words and expressions. As I do so, I feel my sensitivity broaden and deepen limitlessly. I soothe myself and make preparations for the inevitable parting with my father.
>
> It may be that my father's warmth heals me. His present condition may go against his will, but it is of great significance for those of us who keep holding his hands in ours.
>
> I myself wish to be an organ donor. But having gone through this experience, I have come to think that I should forgive my family if they wish to share my warmth for as long as possible—for a day, or even for just an hour. Just as things are with my father now.[4]

What is most impressive about these narratives is that those who recount them believed that *a dialogue or conversation without spoken language* had taken place between a brain-dead person (or a person in a deep coma) and their family members. Scientifically, it makes no sense to claim that one can converse with someone who is unconscious. But then, who were the family members talking with?

Watsuji's concept of *persona*

Let us now turn to the important Japanese philosopher Watsuji Tetsurō (1889–1960). In his essay "Mask and Persona," published in 1935,[5] Watsuji talks about the Japanese Nō play and its relationship to the idea of *persona*, a Latin word that originally referred to the "mask" worn by an actor.

An actor in a Nō play dances on stage while wearing a mask. Watsuji remarks that, by itself, the mask looks like the face of someone who has died a sudden death, but once worn, it becomes expressive like the face of a living person. The bodily movements of the actor seem to breathe "life" into the dead mask and allow it to show various emotions of a living person. What at first appears to be a death mask is gradually transformed into a thing of beauty through the dance of the actor until at last it seems to sparkle with life. In the dreamlike illusion of a *mugen* Nō (夢幻能), the protagonist is a

---

4. Watanabe 1997; emphasis added. For further examples, see Kinjō and Morioka 2011.
5. Watsuji 1935.

departed soul wandering the world, and it is on his mask that the soul alights to restore life to the deceased. The mask is the point at which life and death intersect in the one who has died.

Watsuji identifies two phases occurring on the Nō stage. In the first, the actor's bodily movements breathe "life" into the mask he is wearing. At this point, the mask is being controlled by the dance and gestures of the actor's bodily movement. This is followed by a second phase in which the Nō mask, which the actor has made to come "alive," becomes the locus of personhood and begins to control the body and limbs of the dancer as if they were its own. In the first phase, the actor is the subject of the body; in the second, the mask takes over as subject. This conversion of actor and mask is one of the most impressive parts of Watsuji's argument.

A Nō mask on its own lacks any self-consciousness or rationality. It is nothing more than a wood carving. But no sooner is it worn by an actor performing in front of an audience than it takes on personhood and begins to govern the whole body of the actor. Watsuji calls what appears on the surface of the mask "*persona*."[6] It is not the inner personality of the actor, but rather a mysterious something that emerges from the interaction among the protagonist, the other actors, the audience, the story line, and the music.

Watsuji's theory of *persona* as outlined above suggests that even a wooden mask, devoid of self-consciousness and rationality, becomes a kind of person when animated by an actor's movement or some other force. I propose to call this type of personhood *animated persona*. In doing so, I am fully aware that such an idea contradicts the modern European concept of person as a self-conscious subject equipped with free will and the power of reason.[7]

---

6. Watsuji writes, "The mask or face has a central significance for human existence. It is not only a part of the body, but also the locus of the subject that governs its body, that is to say, the locus of personhood. All things considered, it is very natural here to imagine (the word) *persona*" (Watsuji 1935, 21.) Here he himself writes the word "persona" in Latin, and later in katakana.

7. Two years later, in 1937, Watsuji published the first volume of his *Ethics*, where he systematically discussed the concept of person in the opening chapter, where the idea of the *animated persona* is present in germ. For example, Watsuji writes that when we go to meet up with a friend, we never try to find a body that resembles our friend, and then try to find our friend in that body. However, he does not proceed here to a discussion of the *animated persona*, which for some reason I cannot fathom he seems to have kept separate from his philosophical system of

I would argue that the mysterious "something" that made its presence felt on the body of Yanagida's brain-dead son is none other than the *animated persona* Watsuji identified on the Nō mask. I am also persuaded what many authors who write about the relationship between the living and the dead mean by "the deceased" also falls under the definition of the *animated persona*.

An *animated persona* appearing on a Nō mask (Watsuji) and an *animated persona* appearing on the body of a brain-dead patient (Yanagida) should not be considered *merely* an illusion or projection. It is something *actually perceived* by the audience or the family members. Of course, this does not commit us to believe in *the soul as an entity* present in the corpse, on the surface of a mask, or somewhere in one's imagination. We cannot directly see, touch, or hear an *animated persona* as such, but we can perceive its appearance with our whole body and communicate with it without spoken language. In other words, the *animated persona* is a "soundless voice" that can be heard by those with a special relationship to a deceased person in a state of brain death, or by an audience deeply immersed in a Nō drama being enacted before them. The message of that soundless voice is simply "I am here." This is the essence of the appearance of an *animated persona*.

Viktor Frankl and the *animated persona*

The phenomenon of the *animated persona* is hardly unique to Japan or other cultures where an animistic worldview seems to have survived the test of time in a large portion of the population. I would point out similar descriptions in Viktor Frankl's masterpiece *Man's Search for Meaning*.[8]

In the concentration camp, where he was forced into hard labor, Frankl remembers the image of his beloved wife, who had been sent to another camp and of whom he does not know whether or not she is still alive:

Ethics. For my part, the idea of an *animated persona* is more attractive than the idea of person discussed in his *Ethics*, especially when it comes to the relationship between the living and the dead. See Watsuji 1937, 99.

8. Frankl 2011.

> I resumed talk with my loved one: I asked her questions, and she answered; she questioned me in return, and I answered.... A thought crossed my mind: I didn't even know if she were still alive. I knew only one thing—which I have learned well by now: Love goes very far beyond the physical person of the beloved. It finds its deepest meaning in his [the beloved person's] spiritual being, his inner self.[9] Whether or not he [the beloved person] is actually present,[10] whether or not he is still alive at all, ceases somehow to be of importance.... There was no need for me to know; nothing could touch the strength of my love, my thoughts, and the image of my beloved. Had I known then that my wife was dead, I think that I would still have given myself, undisturbed by that knowledge, to the contemplation for her image, and that my mental conversation with her[11] would have been just as vivid and just as satisfying....[12]
>
> Once again I communed with my beloved. More and more I felt that she was present, that she was with me; I had the feeling that I was able to touch her, able to stretch out my hand and grasp hers. The feeling was very strong: she was there [*sie – ist – da!*].[13]

Frankl's experience of conversing with his beloved wife and feeling that she is in his presence is an impressive example of the appearance of an *animated persona* in sense I have just described.

Frankl also writes of a young woman who is set to die shortly:

> This young woman knew that she would die in the next few days.... Pointing through the window of the hut, she said, "This tree here is the only friend I have in my loneliness."... "I often talk to this tree," she said to me.... Anxiously I asked her if the tree replied. "Yes." What did it say to her? She answered, "It said to me, 'I am here [*ich bin da*] – I am here – I am life, eternal life.'"[14]

Here, too, Frankl talks about an *animated persona*, a soundless voice that announces, "I AM HERE"—this time through a tree. I am struck by the fact that the young woman uses the words "I am here (*ich bin da*)." She may or

---

9. "das geistige Wesen des geliebten Menschen, sein 'So-sein.'"
10. "seine körperliche Existenz."
11. "diese geistige Zwiesprache."
12. FRANKL 2011, 31; German, 64–5.
13. FRANKL 2011, 33; German, 68.
14. FRANKL 2011, 56, German: p. 107. "Er hat mir gesagt: Ich bin da – ich – bin – da – ich bin das Leben, das ewige Leben...."

may not have heard that voice as an actual sound wave, but she believed she could perceive an *animated persona* actually appearing on the tree. This would seem to indicate that not only a deceased person but also a God or spirit can appear as an *animated persona*. If so, the range of the concept of *animated persona* is broader than we at first thought.

Because Frankl was a Jewish thinker, it may seem misleading to speak of him as having perceived an *"animated"* persona. Nonetheless, I believe his case is a clear indication of how people throughout history can experience such phenomena irrespective of time and place; it is a truly universal experience.

Interaction between the living and the deceased

Before moving on to a philosophical analysis of the *animated persona*, I would like to take up other discussions in Japanese philosophical literature on the interaction between the living and the dead.

The philosopher Tanabe Hajime (1885–1962) wrote in an essay entitled "An Ontology of Life or a Dialectics of Death?" that living persons can communicate with the deceased and establish an "existential cooperation" with them.[15] Tanabe argued that the love of the deceased toward the living person and of the living toward the deceased resonate in a mutual "existential cooperation" of love that amounts to a "resurrection from death."[16] He calls it "a cooperative sympathy through mutual love between the living and the dead."[17] What is unique about Tanabe's thinking here is that he believed that the living and the dead can *actually* communicate with each other in this world, reminiscent of conversations between brain-dead patients and the members of their family. He argues that cooperative sympathy involves, first, a catharsis of the deceased and then, secondly, a purification of the living under the influence of the deceased. This suggests that the starting point is the deceased, not the living.

Tanabe's concept of "existential cooperation" is echoed in the historian Uehara Senroku's (1899–1975) book *The Living and the Dead*. Uehara writes

---

15. 実存協同, TANABE 1958, 245.
16. 死復活, TANABE 1958, 293.
17. 死者生者の交互愛における協同感応, TANABE 1958, 294.

that he *actually* felt the continued existence of his late wife when he sat in front of her Buddhist memorial tablet.[18] It was "a presence that is not dead in spite of having already died."[19]

Uehara then came to think that he *actually* existed with his late wife, lived with her, and fought social injustice with her. He calls this "a co-existence, co-living, and co-struggling that goes on between the deceased and the living."[20] He appended a special chapter to the book to expose what he saw as the medical misconduct his wife suffered while hospitalized. The chapter was written as a result of their joint struggles against injustice in which his wife had been the leading figure, so that it was the deceased and not the living who was passing judgment. It is also worth noting that in the course of this confrontation he could *actually* hear his late wife's voice at times. Furthermore, he was persuaded that it was the deceased and not the living who initiated the communication between the living and the dead.

The critic Wakamatsu Eisuke (1963–) also speaks of the presence of his late wife and refers to her ontological status as "the living dead."[21] In his words, "The deceased accompany us. They actually feel pain, grieve, feel sorrow, and rejoice with us."[22] For Wakamatsu, the deceased have their own inner emotions:

> The deceased always exist side by side with the living, and have to look at the face of the living who are weeping over them. The deceased also feel the living in the midst of their sorrow. The sorrow indicates a cooperation taking place between the living and the deceased.[23]

All three authors mentioned above believe that they have had *actual* interactions with a deceased person. In my view, their accounts can be interpreted as examples of the *animated personae* I have been discussing in these pages.

18. Uehara 1988, 40.
19. Uehara 1988, 16.
20. Uehara 1988, 3.
21. 生ける死者, Wakamatsu 2012, 7.
22. Wakamatsu 2012, 221.
23. Wakamatsu 2012, 222. In his book, he discusses the philosophies of death in Frankl, Tanabe, and Uehara. I consulted his work frequently in composing this paper.

A philosophical analysis of the *animated persona*

The concept of *animated persona* as I am describing it differs from the concept of *persona* as understood in mainstream European philosophy, which requires self-consciousness, free will, and rationality as necessary conditions for identifying a person. In a word, I would define *animated persona* as "*a soundless voice saying I AM HERE' that appears on the surface of something or someone.*" Based on the brief explanation given above, I would now like to consider some salient characteristics of the *animated persona* in more detail.

1. *A compelling power and the reaction to it*

A striking feature of the *animated persona* is that it has a compelling power to make the one who perceives it react in some fashion. Sitting alongside his brain-dead son, Yanagida unintentionally began "conversations" with him, and Frankl, perceiving the appearance of his wife in the air, began "conversations" with her.

Once a voice that makes no sound has come to me, it is difficult to ignore it or erase it from my mind. An *animated persona*'s compelling power *forces* me to react to the voice in some way. Whence does this power arise? One possible explanation is that the ultimate cause is located outside the body or object in which the *animated persona* is thought to reside. For example, in the case of the brain-dead son, the ultimate cause would lie in the father's overwhelming emotions, or in the case of the wooden mask, in the movements of the actor and the setting of the play.

That said, if we put ourselves in the position of the perceiver, the situation changes dramatically. We may describe it as follows: In the first case, the appearance of an *animated persona* in the brain-dead body of the son was followed by a reaction to the soundless voice emerging from it. In the second case, the appearance of an *animated persona on the wooden mask* in the course of a beautiful dance moved the audience.

From the position of a detached bystander, then, we see things one way; from the position of the actual perceiver, we see them another. Here I have been taking the second standpoint, obliging me to pay special attention to the latter perspective: an *animated persona* appears first on the surface of someone or something, which triggers the perceiver to recognize its appearance and react to it. We recall that Tanabe and Uehara emphasize that the starting point of the communication between the living and the dead is in the dead, not the living.

2. The surface-ness of an animated persona

An *animated persona* appears on the surface of a body or an object. In the case of the brain-dead patient, the soundless voice comes from the surface of the brain-dead body, not from within. The place that emits the voice is the surface, not the interior.

Here we need to make a "Copernican revolution." As moderns, we are inclined to think that what is most essential about a human being is hidden beneath the surface. We tend to think that our inner character is more important than our exterior appearance or behavior. When it comes to the *animated persona*, however, the reverse is true. An *animated persona* appears only on the surface of the object. The *animated persona* originates from the surface. It is impossible for it to exist inside something.

For an *animated persona*, what appears on the surface is everything. There is nothing that is hidden inside. The essence of the *animated persona* and what gives it its ontological status is its *surface-ness*.[24]

Husserl's concept of other minds is different from the concept of *animated persona* being proposed here. When Levinas talks about "the face," he views it as the trace of the advent of "the Other," which is destined to escape from my every endeavor to grasp it. But here, too, Levinas's "Other" differs from the *animated persona*, even though his concept of "face" shares with the *animated persona* its attention to the surface. Moreover, in our experience of an *animated persona*, there is no delay in Levinas's sense. The soundless voice reaches me simultaneously with my perception of the *animated persona*. In the future I plan to return to a more detailed analysis of the difference between *animated persona* and these kinds of phenomenological concepts, giving special attention to the relationship between the perceptible and the imperceptible.

Where might an *animated persona* appear? It appears on the surface of something, but it can also appear in the wind, in my memory, or in my imagination. In each case, *animated personae* do not occupy a physical place. This suggests that there are two kinds of *animated persona*: those that have a

---

24. Surface-ness does not entail shallowness; it can have depth.

physical place and those that do not. The question then arises as to whether an *animated persona* that occupies no physical place can be said to appear on the surface of something. This is complicated, but in the case of an *animated persona* that appears in memory, we may say that it appears on the surface of memory because there is no "inside" to memory. The same applies to imagination. This, too, calls for further investigation.

3. The resemblance to religious experience

Each time I perceive the appearance of an *animated persona*, I hear a soundless "I AM HERE" emerge from the *animated persona*. This is not unlike what we call religious experience.

There are numerous accounts of people hearing the voice of God or spirits without the use of their auditory organs. Frankl's second example is instructive here. The young woman heard the voice of God proclaim, "I AM HERE" when looking at a tree outside her window. This is a typical religious experience of encounter with the divine, but it is also quite similar to the experience of perceiving an *animated persona* on the body of a brain-dead family member or on a Nō mask.

In this sense, we may say that the perception of God or spirits and the perception of an *animated persona* share an important characteristic, namely, that while I do not see, hear, or touch anything clearly, I am able to directly perceive with my body as a whole a soundless voice telling me, "I AM HERE." This perception is so real that it is almost impossible for me to doubt the truthfulness of the presence of an *animated persona*. In the Spanish movie *Marcelino, pan y vino* (1955), the protagonist, a boy called Marcelino, sees an apparition of Jesus on a crucifix hanging on the wall of a monastery cell, reaching out to gently take hold of the boy's body. From the boy's perspective, he hears the voice of Jesus and sees the movement of the arm. In the movie the movement of Jesus's arm and his voice are beautifully depicted to show something that actually occurred in the boy's subjective perception at that moment, but I would suggest that it is an artistic visualization of the boy's encounter with a soundless voice telling him, "I AM HERE."

Strange as it may seem, this may further suggest that the very act of encountering someone might itself be a kind of religious experience. That is to say, each time I encounter a human being and perceive an *animated persona* on that body, I am swept up in a religious experience in the midst of everyday life. As will I discuss later, we can perceive an *animated persona* not only on dead bodies, but also on living human bodies and other material objects. When I see a friend in the classroom, I can hear the soundless voice that says, "I AM HERE" on the body of that friend. Everyday experience may well be filled with small religious experiences like this. Meeting someone, in essence, is a kind of a religious event.

4. The universality of the animated persona

Is the appearance of an *animated persona* on another's body an objective or a subjective event? If subjective, we have to say that it is a phenomenon peculiar to the subject who perceives it and hence lacks universality.

For example, a brain-dead patient may appear as an *animated persona* to family members, but may not appear as such to a hospital doctor or a bystander. In this case, we can say that the appearance of an *animated persona* is a particular subjective phenomenon and not a universal one. This is the reason the *animated persona* is often dismissed as an illusion or projection. While I disagree with the conclusion, I have to admit that *animated persona* seems to lack universality.

For some, an *animated persona* is an irreplaceable reality; for others, it is nothing more than a subjective phenomenon limited to those close to the subject. An *animated persona* is not an external object open to everyone to see or touch or smell. Its appearance is restricted to a select group of people. This does not necessarily mean that an *animated persona* is not important, or without value. When the family member of a brain-dead patient perceives an *animated persona* on the patient's body, the appearance is invaluable and irreplaceable to the perceiver. There is no cause to heartlessly negate the experience. On the contrary, we have every reason to respect and protect the experience even when it cannot be shared. This must be our basic moral attitude toward those who undergo the experience of an the *animated persona* in someone close to them.[25]

Imagine a sacred statue revered by a certain religious group. Most if not all of the believers are able to perceive a certain kind of *animated persona* on the surface of the statue, perhaps because their teachings or beliefs lead

---

25. This is what I argued in my book *Brain Dead Person* published in 1991. An English translation is available for download on the internet.

them to accept it as sacred. In this case, we may say that an *animated persona* appearing on the statue has universality within the confines of the religious community. But now, what if this religious group spreads rapidly until almost everyone on earth has become an ardent believer? Then, perhaps, we may speak of the *animated persona* of the statue as having attained universality, even if some continue to dismiss it as an illusion. Theoretically speaking, it is sometimes hard to distinguish collectively held subjective beliefs from what we consider to be objective reality. This opens the possibility of a subjective universality in addition to our usually objective understanding of universality.

5. What is "I" in the "I am here"?

The *Animated persona*, as we have been saying, implies a soundless voice announcing its presence. What are we to make of the "I" in the phrase "I am here"? In my view, the "I" stands for the subject that appears on the *surface* of a body or an object, not the subject that exists *within* the body or the object.

Then, what exactly can such a surface "I" mean? I have not yet made up my mind on this question, but my sense is that this "I" signals the "starting point" of the voice. In other words, the soundless voice comes into being at that point, which the perceiver regards as a subject, an "I" that can deliver messages to others. When I perceive an *animated persona* on the surface of a body or an object, what I perceive is a *soundless voice* emitted from the body or the object, and I think of the "I" in this voice as the starting point of a trajectory that reaches me as its end.

I cannot intentionally control where and when this starting point makes itself manifest. In this sense, it transcends the realm of my control. This means that the advent of the starting point, which can also be named the advent of the "I," resembles the advent of "the Other" in Levinas's sense. Earlier I noted that Levinas's idea of "the Other" differs from my idea of the *animated persona*, but I would now add that the "I" perceived as the starting point of the soundless voice could also be considered another name for "the Other." The question then arises as whether there was anything there before the starting point. Did it appear *ex nihilo* or was there something or someone who prepared the way for the voice? I leave this question for future research.

Conclusion

Up to this point I have centered my remarks mainly on the concept of *animated persona* as a kind of personhood appearing on the corpse of a brain-dead patient, on someone fallen into a coma, or on the surface of a mask. But this concept can also be applied to living human beings and to other non-living objects, like robots and dolls.

Say I enter a classroom and find one of my friends there. She smiles at me and I say hello to her. Why did I say hello to her? The reason is that I noticed someone who can have a conversation with me. But why did I think that she was such a person? Because when I caught sight of my friend, I perceived an *animated persona* on the surface of her body. The reason was not that I noticed a human being equipped with self-consciousness inside her body. She might actually have turned out to be a well-engineered robot without any self-consciousness at all.

And what of Watsuji's example of the Nō player? Clearly the members of the audience do not believe that the wooden mask has some kind of inner self-consciousness. Still, they are able to perceive the appearance of an *animated persona* on the surface of the wooden mask. In short, the appearance of an *animated persona* is independent of any belief about the presence of self-consciousness behind the mask.

All of this leads to the hypothesis of three layers of perception that can be applied to any object, human beings included. First is the layer of the biological object. Second is the layer of the *animated persona*. And third is the layer of the self-conscious being.

For example, a friend sitting opposite me is a biological object, but also appears as an *animated persona* and is someone I consider to be self-conscious. In the case of the Nō actor, the mask is not a biological object (it is made of a piece of wood) and while it nevertheless appears as an *animated persona* to the audience, it is not considered a self-conscious being.

Animated persona is not just another name for the soul or spirit of a dead person. It is a layer that can be found as well in living human beings as in brain-dead human beings, and in inanimate masks and mementos. It is also interesting to imagine whether we can perceive an *animated persona* on the surface of a well-engineered robot. Theoretically, an *animated persona* could indeed appear there as well as on any inanimate doll.

This suggests that our theory of the *animated persona* could have implications on robotic studies and AI research which has begun to question whether robots could be engineered to such a level of AI that they might be regarded as a true person. In any event, we are driven to reconsider just what it is that constitutes personhood. As for myself, I am inclined to take the possibility seriously and not dismiss it simply on the grounds that something lacks a "human soul."

Finally, I would like to add a brief comment on an *animated persona* and the process of human death. Futuristic discussions aside, I accept as fact that an *animated persona* can appear distinctly on the body of a person approaching death or who has just passed away. My reasoning is as follows. When someone is still alive, even though I perceive their *animated persona*, the power of linguistic communication overshadows it. But when that same person is approaching death or has already died, communication through language disappears and in its place the presence of their *animated persona* suddenly looms large. To use a well-known analogy, the sun and the stars are all out in the daytime, but the light of the sun blocks out that of the stars. Only when the sun has set do the stars that were there all along begin to shine for us.

The appearance of an *animated persona* becomes most visible in the starlight that the darkness of death brings with it. Just then, for the first time, am I able to notice the *animated persona* appear and to hear the tiny soundless voice that says, "I AM HERE."

* This paper was presented as a keynote speech at the 5th Conference of the European Network of Japanese Philosophy held at Nanzan University, Nagoya, on 31 August 2019. I would like to express my deepest gratitude to the organizers of the conference and the participants who asked me helpful questions.

    The work was supported by a "Kakenhi" Grant-in-Aid for Scientific Research 20K00042, 17H00828, and 20H01175.

References

FRANKL, Viktor E.
 2011 *Man's Search for Meaning* (London: Rider); German original, *…trotzdem Ja zum Leben sagen* (München: Kösel, 1977).

FUJIWARA Fumikazu 藤原史和 and FUJIWARA Yasuko 藤原康子
 1993 『飛翔』[*Flight*] (Self-published).

KINJŌ Takanobu 金城隆展 and MORIOKA Masahiro 森岡正博
    2011   "Narrative Responsibility and Moral Dilemma: A Case Study of a Family's Decision about a Brain-Dead Daughter," *Theoretical Medicine and Bioethics* 32/2: 91–9.

MORIOKA Masahiro 森岡正博
    1991   『脳死の人』[*Brain Dead Person*] (Kyoto: Hōzōkan, 2000).
    2010   「パーソンとペルソナ」[Person and persona], in 『人間科学：大阪府立大学紀要』[*Human Science, Bulletin of Osaka Prefecture University*] 5: 91–121.

TANABE Hajime 田辺 元
    1958   「生の存在学か死の弁証法か」["An ontology of life or a dialectics of death?], in 藤田正勝編『死の哲学』[*The Philosophy of Death*] (Tokyo: Iwanami Shoten, 2010), 219–392.

UEHARA Senroku 上原専禄
    1988   『生者・死者』[*The Living and the Deceased*] (Tokyo: Hyōronsha).

WAKAMATSU Eisuke 若松英輔
    2012   『魂にふれる』[*Touching the Soul*] (Tokyo: Transview).

WATANABE Ryōko 渡辺良子
    1997   投書 [Letter] 『朝日新聞・大阪版・ひととき欄』[*Asahi Shimbun*, Osaka Edition, Hitotoki Column], 20 October.

WATSUJI Tetsurō 和辻哲郎
    1935   「面とペルソナ」[Mask and persona], in 坂部恵編『和辻哲郎随筆集』[*Collected Essays of Watsuji Tetsuro*] (Tokyo: Iwanami Shoten, 1995), 21–9.
    1937   『倫理学（一）』[*Ethics*, vol.1] (Tokyo: Iwanami Shoten, 2007).

YANAGIDA Kunio 柳田邦男
    1995   『犠牲』[*Sacrifice*] (Tokyo: Bungei Shunjū).

Book Symposium
David W. Johnson, *Watsuji on Nature*

David W. Johnson, *Watsuji on Nature: Japanese Philosophy in the Wake of Heidegge*r

Evanston, IL: Northwestern University Press, 2019
242 pages. $34.95. ISBN: 978-0810140462

"Synopsis," David W. Johnson *134*
"Watsuji's Hermeneutics," Bernard Stevens *139*
"Reply to Bernard Stevens," David W. Johnson *142*
"How to Ignore Mesology," Augustin Berque *147*
"Reply to Augustin Berque," David W. Johnson *158*
「和辻はハイデガーから何を継承し、何を継承しなかったか。」、
 嶺 秀樹 Mine Hideki *166*
"Reply to Mine Hideki," David W. Johnson *176*
"Disclosure without Normative Background?"
 Hans Peter Liederbach *184*
"Reply to Hans Peter Liederbach," David W. Johnson *208*

KEYWORDS: Watsuji Tetsurō—nature—Martin Heidegger—*fūdo*—climate—environment—normativity—*aidagara*—mesology

David W. Johnson

Synopsis

In the remarks that follow I begin with a short summary of the book's central thesis. After this I set out what I take the main contributions of this study to be, and then conclude with an excerpt taken from the introduction, which summarizes the major questions that inform the book.

Watsuji on Nature reconstructs Watsuji Tetsurō's astonishing philosophy of nature, situating it in relation both to his reception of the thought of Heidegger and to his renewal of core ontological positions in classical Confucian and Buddhist philosophy. I show that for Watsuji we have our being in the lived experience of nature, one in which nature and culture compose a tightly interwoven texture called *fūdo* 風土. By unfolding Watsuji's novel and radical claim that this is a setting that is neither fully external to human subjectivity nor merely a product of it, this book also sets out what still remains unthought in this concept, as well as in the relational structure that underwrites it. I argue that what remains unarticulated is nothing less than the recovery of a reenchanted conception of nature and an elucidation of the wide-ranging implications of a relational conception of the self for questions about the disclosive character of experience, the distinction between fact and value, and the possibility of a place-based ecological ethics.

In taking up what is unthought in Watsuji's retrieval of the concept of *fūdo*, this study attempts to move beyond the scholarly analysis and interpretive reconstruction of Watsuji's work to win a new and even radical understanding of this term through a series of engagements with Heidegger, Herder, and others. These exchanges bring Watsuji's views into an intercultural philosophical conversation, and lay the groundwork for a philosophy of nature that can transcend particular worldviews and cultural perspectives. By showing in this way what Watsuji's work has to offer to a global philosophical conversation this book also aims to expand the English-language reception and appreciation of Watsuji's philosophy, which remains relatively unknown in the West. The following is excerpted from the Introduction.[1]

Excerpt

The Japanese philosopher Watsuji Tetsurō (1889–1960) was a thinker whose work extended across a remarkable range of topics in cultural theory, intellectual history, religion, the arts, and, above all, philosophy. Watsuji's overall philosophical project can be understood as an attempt to reconceive the relations between selfhood, ethical life, and the natural world by reinterpreting and interweaving philosophical concepts found in Confucianism and Buddhism with ideas drawn from Western philosophy, especially hermeneutics, phenomenology, and the philosophy of Hegel. This is a way of approaching the human and natural worlds that opens genuinely original themes and questions, while also offering a creative array of responses to these issues.

This study focuses on Watsuji's philosophy of nature. At the heart of his thinking about nature is the novel and radical claim that nature as it is experienced and lived through is part of the very structure of human existence, such that the self is immersed in, and continuous with, this dimension of nature. This means that the human being can be what it is only through its living in, incorporating, and giving cultural expression to a region of nature, and, furthermore, that a particular region of nature can fully be what *it* is only through its being part of and disclosed through the world of human culture. Watsuji calls this geocultural environment, which we both open up and belong to, a *fūdo* 風土.

This concept is built upon an ordinary Japanese word whose usage and history are connected to texts, practices, and ways of thinking that link self with place, and nature with culture, and whose constituent sinographs extend the semantic range and depth of these associations. Watsuji draws on this background and these connotations to express the way nature and subjectivity are ontologically interwoven with rather than exterior to one another. While he sets out this philosophical interpretation of *fūdo* primar-

---

1. I thank Northwestern University Press for permission to reprint this excerpt from *Watsuji on Nature: Japanese Philosophy in the Wake of Heidegger*. Copyright © 2019 by Northwestern University Press. Published 2019. All rights reserved.

ily in response to related problems and themes he encounters in the work of Herder and, above all, Heidegger, the importance of this idea for philosophical inquiry extends well beyond these concerns.

The Relational Self

The central claim of this study is that the concept of *fūdo* has significant implications for two important issues in contemporary philosophy. The first question concerns how we understand the self; the second, how we understand our experience of nature. In the former case, the claim that the lived experience of nature is part of the very structure of subjectivity challenges the problematic modern understanding of the self as a self-contained, individuated center, completely encased in a biological profile that fully divides it from the world. Instead the notion of *fūdo* enables us to uncover the way in which the self, in, for instance, its sensibility, preferences, imagination, has its being in the places and spaces of the natural world. This mode of being also makes possible an essential form of self-understanding, one that varies across regions of nature.

Thus rather than an individual subject decoupled and sealed off from that which surrounds it such that it remains the same in all places and in any set of circumstances, we find that the self is continuous with its environment in and through a space that is constitutive of its being rather than external to it. Because this relational space is also an intersubjective one, we discover that we have our being in others, too. The self is present to, overlaps with, extends into, and is continuous with others who help to compose it. In uncovering this dimension of the basic space and place in and through which the self is able to be continuous with the human and natural worlds, Watsuji advances a new conception of the self as a relational structure open to that which is constitutive for it. This understanding of the self allows us to circumvent central aspects of ontological dualism and, by doing so, to dispense with some of the philosophical difficulties and problems that this dichotomy entails.

Fūdo and the Reenchantment of Nature

The concept of *fūdo* also has significant consequences for the pressing question of the appropriate relation between what has been called the "manifest" image of nature, or nature as it appears to us, with its characteristic qualities, meanings, and values, and the scientific image of nature, or the qualitatively bald and value-free world of nature as described by science. When these images collide, the dominant approach to resolving this conflict has been to fold the manifest image into the scientific one. The consequences of this move are immense and manifold; numbered among them is the abolition of a large expanse of the world of meaningful human experience. Yet this approach has also become entangled in serious philosophical difficulties, such as in the various problems posed by the attempt to account for mental states from the external or third-person standpoint of physicalism, or in the controversies generated by naturalistically reductive accounts of ethical and aesthetic experience. As many have argued, the attempt to reduce lived experience to purely objective elements has led to incoherence, to the loss of insight, and even to the loss of the phenomenon that was to be explained.

I argue that Watsuji's work contains an account of the appearances of nature that avoids these difficulties by showing that the essential reality of nature in this dimension is neither merely phenomenal and subjective, nor is it "really" an objective domain of bare entities, independent, self-contained, and complete in themselves. Rather nature as it appears in the lifeworld possesses a nascent intelligibility that is completed only in the experience of those who encounter and perceive it. This experience is not, however, an encounter with a "pristine" nature standing outside of all mediation. Watsuji's work can be situated within a hermeneutical tradition that includes Herder, Humboldt, Heidegger, and Gadamer, one that, as John Maraldo has observed, has now become international.[2] For Watsuji and other thinkers in this tradition, the intelligibility of nature, like the whole content of human experience, is disclosed and so mediated through our language, practices, and culture, and brought in this way to a kind of expressive articulation. And because the intelligibility of nature is completed in culture, it can be said that nature has a history—as many histories as there are cultures.

So disclosure as expressive articulation is not simply the articulation of something already known and fully formed; in this process there is a complex interaction of making and showing, discovery and creation. Yet insofar

---

2. See John Maraldo, "Between Individual and Communal, Subject and Object, Self and Other: Mediating Watsuji Tetsurō's Hermeneutics," in Michael F. Marra, ed., *Japanese Hermeneutics: Current Debates on Aesthetics and Interpretation* (Honolulu: University of Hawai'i Press, 2002), 76–86 (77).

as the disclosive activity of the self and the being of nature unfold together in *fūdo*, nature as it appears in the lifeworld is not an "objective" entity onto which we project "subjective" meanings; rather it is an always already meaningful setting in which subjective and objective elements form a unity.

In this regard, the concept of *fūdo* returns us to a richer, premodern conception of experience, one that, by restoring the "weight" of the things, holds out the promise of a partial reenchantment of nature. Although the philosophical implications of the concept of *fūdo* are novel, wide-ranging, and dramatic, the idea that the appearances of nature are "saved" in the event of disclosure is only incipient but never fully realized in Watsuji's thought. This study shows that this aspect of Watsuji's philosophy of nature can be more fully developed through a richer account of the disclosive capacity of actions, practices, language, and emotions.

This book thus offers a critical interpretation of Watsuji's thought, but it does not aim to present an assessment of his *oeuvre* as a whole, or even to provide an interpretive reconstruction of the entirety of Climate and Culture (*Fūdo*), which is his main text on the theme of nature. To fully grasp Watsuji's theory of *fūdo*, Climate and Culture must be read together with the third volume of Ethics (倫理学). There Watsuji supplies many more of the ingredients needed to fill out the highly compressed philosophical insights that were presented in the preface, first chapter, and last chapter of Climate and Culture. Nevertheless, my primary interest is less in the granular details of Watsuji's texts themselves than it is in what I see as fundamental and original philosophical insights which emerge from them concerning the relation between fact and value, the nature of the self, the structure and status of experience, and, at the end of this study, the implications of the concept of *fūdo* for problems in phenomenology, for questions in environmental ethics, and for the recent turn to place and space in contemporary philosophy. In this regard this book belongs among recent works that seek, as James Heisig observes, "to put the ideas of the Kyoto School to use in rephrasing a range of traditional philosophical questions. This, in turn, has led to a *creative rethinking of some of their core ideas* in order to accommodate them to new modes of thought and problems specific to our own times."[3]

---

3. James Heisig, Foreword to Christopher Goto-Jones, *Re-Politicising the Kyoto School as Philosophy* (New York: Routledge, 2008), xiv.

Bernard Stevens

Watsuji's Hermeneuti

Among Western academics concerned wit[h ...] in these early decades of the 21st centur[y ...] in Watsuji Tetsurō (1889–1960), a philosopher obviously [...] philosophy, although he cannot be considered to be part of the schoo[l ...] *sensu*. And among recent publications on his work (translations, books, articles, …), one of the most outstanding is the study by David W. Johnson, *Watsuji on Nature: Japanese Philosophy in the Wake of Heidegger*. Although the book focuses on Watsuji's philosophy of nature, centered around the notion of 風土 *fūdo* (often mistranslated as "climate"), it presents more globally the thought of the Japanese philosopher in its attempt to reinterpret the relations between selfhood (主体性), ethics (倫理学), history (歴史) and nature (自然), in the light of both Asian notions (mainly Confucianist and Mahāyāna Buddhist) and European concepts (drawn mostly from Hegelian dialectics, Husserlian phenomenology and Heideggerian hermeneutics). The author shows remarkably how Watsuji's work is clearly situated within a hermeneutical tradition that includes Herder and Heidegger—to name just the two philosophers that have influenced him the most. "For Watsuji and other thinkers in this tradition, the intelligibility of nature, like the whole content of human experience, is disclosed and so mediated through our language, practices, and culture, and brought in this way to a kind of expressive articulation." (p. 5). For these thinkers, in order to fully understand a phenomenon, it must be put in relation to the things that surround it, while these, in turn, need to be situated in a still larger contextual field. All this is done through a usage of language as disclosive, rather than designative, and it operates at the point where separate domains of intelligibility intersect. This includes methods that enrich the phenomenological descriptions of intentionality with the hermeneutic usage of etymology and philology.

Watsuji elaborates here on the word *fūdo* through a reappropriation of *Being and Time*'s notion of "being-in-the-world" (*in-der-Welt-sein*), unveiling the spatial dimension belonging to it that Heidegger's stress on temporality had neglected. At the two poles of this phenomenological

(1) the individual ek-sistent *Dasein* becomes a social human being (人間存在 *ningen sonzai*) constituted by its relations to others, it's "practical interconnection of acts" (実践的行為的連関), while (2) the world (*Welt*) incorporates nature (風土性 *fūdosei* rather than 自然 *shizen*), as it is experienced and lived through by the self. *Fūdo* is a "moment" (契機) in the structure of human life.

Nature is not just an objective reality facing a subjective cogito: it is part of the very structure of human existence. The human being cannot exist without being part of nature and nature cannot be what it is without being disclosed by the world of human culture. This ontological interweaving is precisely what is expressed by the word 風土 *fūdo*, an ordinary Japanese term from which Watsuji derives very rich philosophical significance. In sum: we have our self not just in an individual and bodily subjectivity, but also "outside" of us: in our other fellow humans and in our surroundings, which are altogether natural and cultural. A human (人間 *ningen*: person+relation) is ontologically a relational structure (間柄 *aidagara* : relation+quality). So the isolated individual is an abstraction from this more primordial relational human reality: a negation of it. The full human being is formed by the dialectic unity of the person and the group, giving an identity to both the individual and the whole, which otherwise are both "empty" (空 *kara*). And the group cannot be understood in its very identity apart from its integration in its surroundings—which is discovered through the combination of a practical disposition, an affective orientation and a linguistically disclosive comportment.

Watsuji's reinterpretation of all the above-mentioned expressions is enriched by Asian reflections on self and other (自他), such as the Confucian description of human relations (*aidagara*), or the Buddhist metaphysics of non-dualism (不二) and of conditioned co-production (因縁).

The most notable effort of David W. Johnson in this context lies in his endeavour to not just repeat and summarize Watsuji's philosophy but to also show all the implications of his thinking, developing what remains unthought and finally proposing a speculative reconstruction of that which lies beyond what Watsuji actually said. So, for example, the "disenchanted" dualistic objectivism of modern scientific thought is dissected in order to obtain a better view of how hermeneutic phenomenology (from Merleau-Ponty and Heidegger to Watsuji and Berque) manages to overcome it; the hybrid nature of the self (individual and social) is illustrated by a number of concrete descriptions that make the point undisputable; and the same thing happens when this social space of the self is enlarged to its cultural, "atmospheric" and natural dimensions (where a clear limit between the natural and the artificial cannot always be drawn). The author also shows how the profound logic of Watsuji's thought is not compatible with the geographic determinism nor with the "national environmentalism" some critics have seen in occasionally ambiguous aspects of his writings.

After having developed and illustrated the rich consequences of Watsuji's hermeneutics of *fūdo* and having tried to make explicit what often remains unsaid in his philosophy of nature by giving both more weight and clarity to an often elliptical style, David W. Johnson shows us how the disclosive capacity of expressing the interweaving between man and nature, in all their liveliness, opens the horizon of a "reenchantment" of nature. Beyond new developments in phenomenology, this includes new horizons in environmental ethics which should help us address some of the specific ecological problems of our time. All this effort can contribute to "the promise of a reconciliation with the world" (209), and to the hope of finding ourselves at home in nature once again.

Notwithstanding the remarkable quality of this book, the reader might want to ask a couple of questions.

The first question: At a certain point, during his discussion of the interaction between person and group, Watsuji tends towards a dialectic of mutual negation between the individual and the totality which obviously merges with Nishidian metaphysics. To what extent is this metaphysical dimension an essential point in his argument? Could it not just be a stylistic subtlety to show his proximity with Kyoto School philosophy?

The second question: Watsuji's reinterpretation of the notion of *fūdo* obviously offers a better understanding of how man is rooted in nature, but in what way does it really help us address the specific environmental problems of our time?

David W. Johnson
Reply to Bernard Stevens

I would like to begin by thanking Professors Stevens, Berque, Mine, and Liederbach for their close and careful attention to this book and for so generously taking the time to respond in such thought-provoking ways to it.

The first question that Prof. Stevens poses is, "At a certain point, during his discussion of the interaction between person and group, Watsuji tends towards a dialectic of mutual negation between the individual and the totality which obviously merges with Nishidian metaphysics. To what extent is this metaphysical dimension an essential point in his argument? Could it not just be a stylistic subtlety to show his proximity with Kyoto School philosophy?" This certainly seems to be the view of commentators such as William LaFleur, who claims, as I have noted, that this dialectic is "never integrated well into the architecture of his philosophy." I show that one reason for this is Watsuji's confusing attempt to identify the movement of the self between individuation and community with the metaphysical structure of the nondual whole of human existence *as such*. As Thomas Kasulis observes, Watsuji sometimes fails to distinguish between

> the betweenness of emptiness that logically precedes and makes possible the differentiation and logical tension between *nin* and *gen* (also called the *originary totality*) vs. the betweenness inherent in the collective pole, the *gen* of the *ningen*. That is, *ningen* is one kind of betweenness, namely, one that exists in the tension between the individual and the collective. The other kind of betweenness is that of collective itself (*gen*); as a collective, it is a totality between or among people.[1]

The metaphysical dimension of the dialectic of mutual negation between the individual and the totality which Stevens alludes to refers in my view to the betweenness that is that of "the totality between or among people." In short, Watsuji's notion of mutual negation is another way of expressing the nondual character of the "collective itself (*gen*)." And while the vocabulary

---

1. Thomas P. Kasulis, *Engaging Japanese Philosophy: A Short History* (Honolulu: University of Hawaiʻi Press, 2017), 514.

that Watsuji deploys to articulate the nonduality of human existence may be clumsy (as well as needlessly technical), what emerges is something much more than a metaphysical construction that signals his affinity with the Kyoto School. As I show in Sec. IV of Chapter 5, the nondual structure of human existence necessitates that self and other also be distinct and differentiated entities in order for them to be situated in a relation of dependence on one another. And this means that there must be a certain kind of separation between the two. Because the relation between self and other is also a relation between physical entities, this separation is a physical separation—in space—between them. Space is what makes this mode of relational unity possible; it holds together and separates at the same time since there must be a distinction in and through space between one thing and another that separates the things related. Hence the nondual structure of human existence—in which one self exists in relational continuity with another—entails a space that both subtends the relation between practical subjects (inasmuch as space connects selves to one another) and links them to a world, and ultimately, to the lifeworldly dimension of nature that is disclosed through this world, namely, a *fūdo*.

In his second question, Stevens asks: "in what way does [the notion of *fūdo*] really help us address the specific environmental problems of our time?" In my study I tried to show that an understanding of the natural world in terms of *fūdo* entails an at least partially reenchanted concept of nature, namely, a nature characterized by qualities and values (such as beauty and sublimity) that we are entitled to take at face value, that is, to take as features of the natural world itself rather than as projections of the human mind. One of the ideas I drew on to support this claim was John McDowell's argument that secondary qualities can be understood as subject-dependent entities that nevertheless count as real. I will not repeat the way that his argument establishes this claim; instead I would like to pursue more fully the way in which McDowell extends this argument to moral and aesthetic experience.

McDowell argues that the entities that populate the ethical and aesthetic domains are like secondary qualities in the relevant respects. In the same way that our everyday experience gives us secondary qualities as if they were features of things, our moral and aesthetic experience presents itself as an encounter with a value or disvalue residing in an object, and so suggests to us that normative facts are "part of the fabric of the world."[2] More specifically, the ethical and aesthetic component of our evaluative thought presents itself as a sensitivity to normative facts, i.e., as properties residing in objects in the manner of a secondary quality, and the phenomenology of this experience allows one to make an analogy between the awareness of moral and aesthetic value in evaluative thinking and the perception of secondary qualities.

If we have found McDowell's argument for the reality of secondary qualities persuasive, there does not seem to be any obstacle to accepting in addition at face value the appearances in evaluative thinking. But McDowell does not want to press the analogy too far, and notes that whereas secondary qualities may be said to elicit responses, values can be said to merit them, and that the presence of values are contentious, whereas that of secondary qualities is not. I suggest, loosely following J. L. Mackie, that what is philosophically contentious about values understood as properties of entities is that, on the one hand, they are supposed to exist independently of human beliefs or attitudes (like McDowell's secondary qualities) and so can be understood as facts of the matter, while on the other, they are (unlike secondary qualities) intrinsically motivating and action-guiding.

To say that such properties are intrinsically motivating and action-guiding is to say that there would be something about the facts *themselves* that appealed to the agent or was felt to be compelling such that they either merit responses (such as particular attitudes or states of will) or give us good reasons for acting. In the former case, these properties demand an affective attitude such as being enchanted by (e.g., the beauty of a waterfall), being overwhelmed by (e.g., the sublimity of a canyon view), or simply appreciating what we are confronted with. This is a kind of awareness that is similar to an aesthetic response to an object. In the latter case, such properties are a feature of the world that seems to make a demand on us, that seems to require us to act—and this give us a good reason or motive to act that is independent of our own interests, desires, and goals (e.g., such as protecting a primeval forest landscape from developers who want to build a resort on the same site).

In short, the suggestion here is that we can be motivated to refrain from

---

2. See John McDowell, "Aesthetic Value, Objectivity, and the Fabric of the World," in *Mind Value, and Reality* (Cambridge, Mass.: Harvard University Press, 1998), 122–4.

harming or destroying the environment because the metaphysical status of such properties entails that the natural world possesses features that are intrinsically valuable, and that this sense of its value is no merely "subjective" construal. Nevertheless, one might object that it seems highly unlikely that the mere recognition of intrinsic value will necessarily motivate or provide reasons for action regardless of the interests, desires, or psychological make-up of the agent. As Chad Engelland observes, "Mind bogglingly, intrinsic values can deliberately be ignored; they can fail to move us. It is therefore not enough to iterate intrinsic values; it is also necessary to give an account of the kind of disposition one must have in order to be receptive to them."[3] The notion that we may need to become a certain kind of person to engage the world in fuller and truer ways is, of course, something that is thematized in the injunction to self-cultivation in classical Asian philosophy. This is also a project that can be pursued and developed, as I have tried to show elsewhere, by bringing Nishida's work together with elements of the phenomenological tradition.[4]

But a conception of nature as at least partially reenchanted is not the only way that the notion of *fūdo* can motivate us to address the specific environmental problems of our time. As I observed in the concluding chapter of the book, the convergence of nature and culture in *fūdo* allows us to see that the damage we do to nature through our practices is also a form of self-harm, one whose consequences and ultimate losses are more than merely physical. Jonathan Lear's philosophical meditation on the collapse and death of the (native American) Crow life-world at the end of the nineteenth century has shown quite clearly just what such a loss comes to.[5] It is a loss different in

---

3. Chad Engelland, "Naturalizing Heidegger: His Confrontation with Nietzsche, His Contributions to Environmental Philosophy," *Notre Dame Philosophical Reviews,* Department of Philosophy, University of Notre Dame, Sept. 11th, 2015, https://ndpr.nd.edu/news/naturalizing-heidegger-his-confrontation-with-nietzsche-his-contributions-to-environmental-philosophy/

4. See David W. Johnson, "Perception, Expression, and the Continuity of Being: Some Intersections Between Nishida and Gadamer," *Asian Philosophy* 24/1 (2014).

5. See Jonathan Lear, *Radical Hope: Ethics in the Face of Cultural Devastation* (Cambridge: Harvard University Press, 2006). It is no coincidence that after John Haugeland moved to the University of Chicago in 1999, he co-taught *Being and Time* with Lear, who, according to Richard Polt, "would credit Haugeland with helping him explore the phenomenon of the end of a community's way of life." See Richard Polt, "Nailing It Down: Haugeland's Heidegger," *Graduate Faculty Philosophy Journal*, 34/2 (2013), 457–81 (458).

kind and substance from something as grave as defeat in war or even as catastrophic as the Holocaust. In the aftermath of such occurrences the defeated or the victims have the capacity to try to make sense of what has happened to them; but while the Crow people, like others who have suffered, continue to exist, their world does not. And with the end—after their move onto a reservation—of the traditional Crow way of life as warriors, hunters, and nomads, comes the end of the social and political structure, the celebrations and religious ceremonies, the narratives and rituals, the adult roles of men and women, and the education, play, and games of children that were directly tied to this life-way. With this the higher aims and values that govern a life are lost such that actions become unmoored from all meaning.

This loss, says Lear, "is a *real loss*, not just one that is described from a certain point of view. It is a *real loss of a point of view*." And this means that the loss of a life-way "is not itself a happening but is the breakdown of that in terms of which happenings occur." To lose a world is to lose the ability to make sense of one's actions, projects, and very existence. This is the frame in which Lear interprets enigmatic statement of the Crow Chief Plenty Coups to a white interlocutor at the end of his life: "when the buffalo went away the hearts of my people fell to the ground, and they could not lift them up again. After this, nothing happened."[6] This example enables us to see in a particularly acute manner that there is no way to adequately compensate for this kind of destruction—the kind of damage and loss here is not only environmental, but also existential.

6. Ibid. The quotations in this paragraph are from—in the order in which they appear—pages 32, 38, and 2.

Augustin Berque

How to Ignore Mesology

The author is an associate professor of philosophy at Boston College. The book consists of seven chapters, entitled 1. *Fūdo*: History, Language and Philosophy; 2. The Scientific Image of Nature: Dualism and Disenchantment; 3. Beyond Objectivism: Watsuji's Path through Phenomenology; 4. The Relational Self: a New Conception; 5. The Hybrid Self: Oscillation and Dialectic; 6. The Space of the Self: Between Culture and Nature; 7. Self, World and *Fūdo*: Continuity and Belonging; 8. Self in Nature, Nature in the Lifeworld.

The last few lines of the conclusion aptly sum up the author's judgment:

> Watsuji's theory of *fūdo* thus offers a novel, wide-ranging and complex view of how the self comes to be what it is—a view that moves beyond the problematic modern understanding of human beings as individual subjectivities ontologically decoupled from the natural and social environment that surrounds them. In this vision, we find instead that the self and its consciousness are rooted in a source far greater and more profound than the awareness of a single individual: not only are we immersed in, and emerge from, the depths of the historical and social world, but our lives both shape, and flow from, the vast life of nature (214).

The Japanese word *fūdo*, written 風土, is composed of the two elements "wind" (風) and "earth" (土). Let us first remark that it is not a very current word. I have met young Japanese who, hearing it for the first time, confused it with フード (food), and consequently confused *fūdogaku* 風土学 (the study of *fūdo*) with dietetics. This phenomenon enabled sociologist Miura Atsushi to publish in 2004 an essay which became a bestseller, entitled *Fast-fūdoka suru Nippon* ファスト風土化する日本. This title was rendered in French with "Le *fūdo* devient Macdo," but a more respectful English equivalent might be *The fast-fūdoisation of Japan*.

These puns are far from being only jocular, because what is at stake here is exactly what Watsuji's classic, *Fūdo* (1935) defines in its first line: "What this book aims at is to make clear *fūdosei* 風土性 as the structural moment of human existence (人間存在の構造契機 *ningen sonzai no kōzō keiki*)."[1] An immediate translation of this concept, *fūdosei*, would be "*fūdo*ity" or "*fūdo*ness": the quality of *fūdo*, the manifestation of *fūdo*. Johnson for his part uses the following periphrases to render its meaning: "nature as it is experienced and lived through" (6), "a *fūdo* as it is encountered in experience, as part of a world, …a particular region of nature as it is disclosed through the activities, practices, affective possibilities, and language that characterize a world" (15), "the concrete character of a human *fūdo* as it is lived through" (48), "the character and quality of *fūdo* as it is experienced and lived through" (26), "the experience of *fūdo*" (42), "the concrete character of a region of nature as lived through" (107).

One may first wonder why Johnson does not take advantage of Watsuji's proper definition in order to define this watsujian concept (*fūdosei* is indeed a concept created by Watsuji), which might possibly have led him to propose an English translation of that concept. Yet the fact is that Johnson is reluctant to translate Watsuji's main concepts, to begin with *fūdo*. The first chapter is dedicated to an excellent historical presentation of that word, starting with the *fūdoki* 風土記 ("official eighth-century reports on the history, geography, and customs of the provinces," p. 18), up to its emergence as a philosophical concept in Watsuji's works, in the sense which the above quotation of Johnson's conclusion convincingly sums up. Yet I should like to add that, although *fūdo* is widely recognized as one of the flagships of Japanese philosophy in the twentieth century—and the existence of such a book as *Watsuji on Nature* precisely testifies this—the fact is that most of its Japanese readers have misunderstood its purpose and purport. On the one hand, it is often considered as a *Nihonjinron* (an essay on the unique uniqueness of the Japanese), which it is indeed to some degree, but it is also much more: first and foremost, as its first line declares, it is a clarification of "the structural moment of human existence." Second, although the second sentence of the book clearly dismisses determinism ("Therefore, the question here is not how the natural environment determines human life," many readers, typically so geographers like Suzuki Hideo or Yasuda Yoshinori, have unshakeably interpreted it as a deterministic thesis, and used it to war-

---

1. In the Japanese text : この書の目指すところは人間存在の構造契機としての風土性を明らかにすることである。

rant their own. More generally, Japanese readers have understood *fūdo* just as if they had not read its first sentence (which is hard to digest, it must be said), thus ignoring Watsuji's definition of *fūdosei* and inferring the meaning of this concept from the average understanding of the word *fūdo*, which stresses the singularity of a certain region or country. In that sense, *fūdosei* might be rendered with *Gegendheit* in German, *comarcalidad* in Castilian, and *contréité* in French.

Then what about English? Since *country* derives from *contrée*, *fūdosei* might then be translated with *countriness*. Yet, the meaning of *country* has evolved since that origin; and in particular, this word has now foremost the acceptation of *nation*, which is totally absent from *fūdo*. Moreover, and, in my eyes, mainly, *countriness* would have not much to do with Watsuji's definition of *fūdosei*.

Now, what does this definition mean? The decisive word here is *keiki* 契機, which in Japanese philosophy has translated the German *Moment*. Not *der* Moment (a short lapse of time), but *das* Moment, which is a power of moving. Of moving what? In this instance, moving the relationship between the human and nature, and acting on both; and it is this moment which produces what nature (that universal) historically becomes: a singular *fūdo*.

Johnson for his part does not delve into Watsuji's definition of *fūdosei*, but the paraphrases through which he expresses the meaning of this concept are entirely compatible with the above interpretation. So what is the problem? To put it in the worst sense, it is that, by refusing to translate both *fūdo* and its derivative *fūdosei*, he *countrifies* these concepts; he reduces them to two more unique nipponese notions, though—and this is an oximoron— classically "in the wake of" something Western (Heidegger in this instance). This locks out the possibility to have these concepts, and the related term *fūdogaku* 風土学 (the study of *fūdo*), display their true potential; that is, to overcome onto/logically (that means: both ontologically and logically) the modern classical Western paradigm, which has come to a dead end—let us rather say: a *deadly* end, that of the Sixth Extinction of life on this planet.

Let me precise immediately that this alone would be too harsh a judgment. I shall not forget to stress the evident qualities of this book, which presents clearly, concretely and in a pleasant-to-read manner—even for an unanglo (非英) being such as I—what I do think is the essence of Watsuji's message. Yet a problem there is, because translation, in this case, is more than putting or not Javanese into Tagalog, or Japanese into English. The reason for that is clearly expatiated upon by Johnson himself: language discloses a certain reality. And the time being what it is (that of the Anthropocene), we *have to* disclose a reality other than that which leads us toward the Sixth Extinction (which, of course, will comprise our own, not only that of pangolins). For such a task, we must have at our disposal, in each of our proper mother tongues, among other concepts, the equivalent of what Watsuji defined as "the structural moment of human existence."

This need is demonstrated by the fact that, outside of Japan, the diffusion of the ideas of *Fūdo* has been more than hindered: blocked by its translation in English, due to Geoffrey Bownas and sponsored by the UNESCO.[1] One cannot but say that this translation completely misses the purport of the book, leaving only its deterministic side (that of the non-theoretical chapters II to IV, based on Watsuji's impressions as a traveller, not on his conceptual framework), which is nothing but mundane. Later a German version[2] was published, a better one but still approximate about Watsuji's essential concepts.

Fūdo (1935): here we have a book written by a philosopher, and which revolves around a concept: *fūdosei* 風土性, enunciated and defined, as we have seen, in the first sentence of its first line. In the two above translations, this becomes respectively: "My purpose in this study is to clarify the function of climate as a factor within the structure of human existence," and "In der vorliegenden Studie möchten wir zeigen, daß *fūdosei*, das Klimatische, zur Struktur des menschlichen Dasein gehört." The two main difficulties of this sentence are the translation of the concept of *fūdosei* and that of its definition as *ningen sonzai no kōzō keiki* 人間存在の構造契機. One can see that the concept is rendered differently: "the function of climate" on the one hand, "das Klimatische" on the other hand; and its definition too: "a factor within the structure of human existence," and "die Struktur des menschlichen Daseins." *Keiki* is not translated in the German version, although, in the Japanese philosophical vocabulary, this word, as we have

---

1. *Climate. A philosophical study* (1960), which later became *Climate and culture. A philosophical study*, New York, London, Westport (Connecticut): Greenwood Press, 1988.

2. By Dora Fischer-Barnicol and Okochi Ryōgi, *Fudo. Der Zusammenhang zwischen Klima und Kultur*, Darmstadt: Wissenschaftliche Buchgesellschaft, 1992.

seen, has rendered the German *Moment*, frequently used for example in Hegel, and of primary importance for the Japanese philosophers of Watsuji's generation.

That two different translations render differently a difficult sentence, nothing surprising here. Yet although the entry into this book is arduous— actually, this first sentence is certainly the most recondite in the whole book —its rigorous coherence with the theoretical construction of the introduction and the first chapter makes it luminously clear *a posteriori*. Not only does the whole of *Fūdo* revolve around the concept of *fūdosei*, but the text displays about that same term a conceptual apparatus of no less consistency. Now the two translations, as for them, do not respect this consistency: they fluctuate from page to page. To take here only the example of the introduction, which is short and where the word *fūdosei* occurs five times, it is respectively rendered as follows:

English version	German version
the function of climate	*fūdosei*, das Klimatische
"human climate"	das klimatische Bestimmtsein
climate	*fūdo*, Klima
climate	das Klimatische

Thus, for one and the same word, each of the two versions adopts three different translations. Moreover, *climate* or *Klima* translating on the other hand another word in the same book, *fūdo*, an interference occurs between the two terms *fūdo* and *fūdosei*; whereas, in Japanese, these words are no less distinct than are in English *history* and *historicity*, or *space* and *spatiality*. As Watsuji, besides *fūdosei*, also derives from *fūdo* the adjective *fūdoteki* 風土的 (relative to *fūdo*), the adverb *fūdotekini* 風土的に (relatively to *fūdo*), as well as *fūdoron* 風土論 (*fūdo*-logy) and *fūdogaku* 風土学 (the science or study of *fūdo*), one can imagine the knock-on effects of such sideslippings in the two translations.

Still, the main problem is indeed, in both cases, the defaulting translation of *fūdo* and of its deriving concept *fūdosei* (the suffix *-sei* 性 being the equivalent of the German *-keit*, the Castilian *-idad*, the English *-ness* etc.). In the German text, this concept is not rendered with an adequate term, but the general frame of the problematics is nonetheless respected. In Bownas' text, on the other hand, it is that whole frame which remains misunderstood; which, in some cases, leads the translator to surrealistic digressions, for lack of a conceptual seamark as regards the meaning of the book.

There exists also a Spanish translation,[3] conceptually more successful, first published in 1973 but out of sale for a long time, which was republished in 2006. It is remarkable because, here, *fûdosei* is effectively translated, as testifies the first sentence: "El objeto de esta obra es resaltar la importancia de la ambientalidad—clima y paisaje—como elemento estructural de la existencia humana." Yet one can see that the idea of structural moment, which is absolutely central in Watsuji's conception of *fûdosei*, is padded out into a trite "structural element," which straightaway occults the Watsujian conception of human existence. As for the abovesaid five occurrences of *fûdosei* in the introduction, they are rendered in the following way:

English version	Spanish version
the function of climate	ambientalidad, clima y paisaje
"human climate"	ambientalidad climático-paisajística
climate	ambientalidad
climate	ambientalidad existencial

The distinction between *fûdo* and *fûdosei*, for its part, is rather well respected, the first term being rendered with *clima y paisaje* ; but there remain some overlappings, as in the first occurrence above, or on the following page, where the brief expression *fûdo no mondai* 風土の問題 (the question of *fûdo*) is rendered with a periphrastic "[el] clima y paisaje como ambientalidad constitutiva de la vida humana." Besides, the derivatives of *fûdo* are not arrayed into a genuine conceptual apparatus, but casually rendered in various ways. To sum up—and this corroborates the fact that the definition of the concept of *fûdosei* is not rendered in the first sentence –, Watsuji's problematics does not clearly appear.

Finally, there exists of *Fûdo*—among the works which I have been able to consult—a Chinese version,[4] which should have been supposed to respect Watsuji's conceptual apparatus, since the sinographs could have been reproduced just as they are; but in fact, Watsuji's problematics is erased, leaving

---

3. *Antropología del paisaje. Climas, culturas y religiones*, trans. by Juan Masiá and Anselmo Mataix (Salamanca: Sigueme, 2006).

4. *Fengtu*, trans. by Chen Liwei (Beijing: Shangwu yin Shudian, 2006).

only a thesis of gross environmental determinism, as the first sentence testifies straightaway, since the concept of *fūdosei* (*fēngtǔxing* 风土性) as well as its definition—and at the same time Watsuji's conception of *ningen* 人間 (the human as a relational being, or more accurately, the human interlink) and that of *ningen sonzai* (human existence), which are no less central than *fūdosei* in Watsuji's conception of *fūdo*—are squeezed out into in a flat "What this book aims at is to make clear the relation between the human's existential modes (*rén dē cúnzài fāngshì* 人的存在方式) and milieu (*fēngtǔ* 风土)." Correlatively, the distinction between *fūdo* (*fēngtǔ*) and *fūdosei* (*fēngtǔxing*) is not respected, to the detriment of the concept of *fūdosei* (*fēngtǔxing*). Consequently, in the introduction, the five occurrences of *fūdosei* become:

English version	Chinese version
the function of climate	...
"human climate"	*fēngtǔxing* 风土性
climate	*fēngtǔxing* 风土性
climate	*fēngtǔxing* 风土性

This is to say that the central idea of the book went up in smoke.... Because, for a Chinese reader, the word *fēngtǔ* 风土 evokes nothing more than the objective environment[5]; and it is to that objective environment that the improper simplifications of the translator tend to reduce the purpose of the book.

As can be seen, the fact is that the translators of *Fūdo*—as far as I know, that is, comparing only the English, German, Spanish and Chinese versions—have most of the time not been able to translate properly, or translate at all, the concept of *fūdosei*. As one of these translators, but also as a geographer, I have argued that it should be rendered with *médiance*, a neologism which I derived from the latin *medietas*, same root as *medius* (central, in the middle, intermediate) which, combined with *lieu* (place), gave *milieu*. *Medietas* means "half," which is to say that the human's Being is both inside the self and *ek-sists* outside in her/his milieu; and that is indeed what Watsuji

---

5. The *Xiandai hanyu cidian* (The Chinese equivalent of the Oxford Concise) defines this word as follows : "A general term comprising the natural environment (land, mountains and rivers, climate), productions etc., the customs and mores proper to a certain region."

means with his definition of *fūdosei* as a "structural moment" between these two "halves" of the human's Being: self and milieu, as Johnson makes evident though he does not delve into that definition and does not translate *fūdosei*.

This is not all; using the latin root *med-* and its Greek equivalent *meso-* enables one to display in French the whole fan of Watsuji's terminology : *milieu, médiance, médial (fūdoteki* 風土的*), mésologie (fūdogaku), mésologique (fūdogakuteki* 風土学的*)*, and so on. This is a conceptual apparatus homologous to that of Watsuji, and it is all based on his own definition of *fūdosei*: "the structural moment of human existence." *Noblesse oblige*, English has the capacity to assimilate all these words almost just as they are in French: *milieu, mediance, medial, mesology, mesological,* and so on.

By the way, the word *mesology* has been around for a long time in English, where it was "introduced by the English colour theorist and philosopher George Field (1777–1854) in a book published in 1839, *Outlines of Analogical Philosophy*" (Wikipedia). I have not read that book, but it manifestly relates with colour, a topic discussed by Johnson. *Milieu* for its part is defined by the *Concise Oxford Dictionary* (5th edition, 1964) as: "Environment, state of life, social surroundings." Nothing here dissonant with *fūdo*. Nevertheless, Johnson dismisses *milieu* on the ground that "in English *milieu* primarily connotes a social environment, and it does not really convey the vital and all-important sense of nature as the ground of *fūdo*" (24). As for the first point, from beginning to end, and rightly so, Johnson relates *fūdo* with *aidagara* 間柄, which he defines as "being in relation to others" (79, and *passim* about the same). I wonder why this should not be compatible with "a social environment"…

It remains to be seen whether Johnson's second argument for not translating *fūdo* with *milieu*, viz. that in English, *milieu* "does not really convey… nature as the ground of *fūdo*" is compatible with the Oxford Concise's definition of that word. As we have just seen, this definition begins with the word *environment*. Now, doesn't the idea of nature linger somewhere in the connotations of that word? To be sure, φύσις δὲ κρύπτεσθαι φιλεῖ (Heraclitus, Fragm. 123: Nature loves to hide), but environmental philosophers do not exclude nature from their concern (nor the reverse, environment from nature). Watsuji, for one, systematically associates the two terms in the syntagm *shizen kankyō* 自然環境 (natural environment). For certain, this is precisely in order to distinguish it from the concept of milieu (*fūdo*), but the idea of nature is evidently present in both cases. Johnson himself, in fact, here and there in his own book, uses *milieu* to convey the idea of *fūdo*; e.g. p. 210: "...the notion of *fūdo* enables us to see that natural environments—and their climates and geographies above all—afford ways of being. These shape the structure of cities and schedules, buildings and interactions as well as the structure of ideas, habits and values. Given that climate change alters such a milieu...."

The problem here is not that I should have liked Johnson to adopt my own translation of *fūdo* with *milieu*. It is that, by translating neither *fūdo* nor *fūdosei*, he bars himself from the whole problematics of mesology, the cornerstone of which was laid as soon as Plato's *Timaeus* with the notion of χώρα, as both the matrix and the imprint of relative being (γένεσις). This mediance was already nothing else than what Johnson shows about the reciprocal relationship of self and *fūdo*. Yet, as we know, Plato's rationalism, based on the principle of identity and its correlate, the principle of contradiction, eventually excluded the possibility to define such a relationship. For the same reason, afterwards, it took more than two millenia for Western thought to reach anew the stage of conceiving of mediance, but this time with the methods of the natural sciences, thus experimentally proving it; namely with Jakob von Uexküll's mesology (*Umweltlehre*).

It is not clear whether Watsuji, during his stay in Germany, or back to Japan, had or had not heard of Uexküll's mesology, but the fact remains that his own mesology (*fūdogaku*) relies on the two same pillars which Uexküll had established: 1. the subjecthood (*Subjektität*, *shutaisei* 主体性) of the concerned being (in Uexküll's case the animal, or the living in general, and in Watsuji's case the human); 2. correlatively, the necessity to distinguish the objective environment (*Umgebung*, *kankyō*, under the gaze-from-nowhere of modern science) from the milieu (*Umwelt*, *fūdo*) of such situated subjects (*Subjekten*, *shutai* 主体), living this milieu through their own flesh.

It may be that Heidegger's thought was the medium between Watsuji (1889–1960) and Uexküll (1864–1944), because Uexküll profoundly influenced Heidegger (1889–1976), who even dedicated half of his seminar of 1929–1930 to Uexküll's ideas, making them heideggerian. Indirectly and unconsciously though it may be, Johnson propagates this influence when he writes for example the following: "perception is never the simple mirroring of what is present; it always includes and involves meaning, and so the understanding of something 'as' something" (196). This "something as something" is word for word that which in Heidegger was expressed as "etwas als etwas," and which, in the above seminar, was construed in the following way: "[Aristotle] wants to say what we call the structure of 'as' (*die >als<-Struktur*). That is what he wants to say, without really advancing expressly into the dimension of that problem. The *structure of 'as'*, the *precedingly unifying perception* (vorgängige einheitbildende Vernehmen) *of something as something* (etwas als etwas), is the *condition of possibility* of the *truth* or of the *falseness* of the λόγος."[6]

Now, if Heidegger was able to write the above, it is because he knew about Uexküll's findings, which have experimentally proved that an object never exists as such for an animal, but necessarily in a certain "tone" (*Ton*), which depends on this animal's species. For example, a same tuft of grass will *exist as* food (*Esston*) for a cow, *as* an obstacle (*Hinderniston*) for an ant, *as* a shelter (*Schutzton*) for a beetle, etc. Later, Heidegger developed the same idea in *Der Ursprung des Kunstwerkes*, in which the famous "dispute" (*Streit*) between "earth" (*die Erde*) and "world" (*die Welt*) is manifestly derived from the enactment (ἐνέργεια, as Aristotle would have put it) of the *Umgebung* "as" a certain *Umwelt*; in other words, the historical incarnation of nature's universal virtuality "as" the singularity of a concrete milieu.

The developments of post-uexküllian and post-watsujian mesology have founded anew the problematics of the nature/culture relation.[7] Yet it must be stressed that this relation, being concretely nothing else than the relation of Humankind with the Earth, has been questioned for more than two millenia by geography. No surprise that Johnson, in the last pages of his book, uses repeatedly such words as *geography* or *geocultural*, though he did not notice (or does not mention) that Watsuji himself, in his 1948 codicil to the

---

6. Martin Heidegger, *Die Grundbegriffe der Metaphysik. Welt–Endlichkeit–Einsamkeit*, Frankfurt am Main: Vittorio Klostermann, 1985, p. 456. Italics of Heidegger. Note: This book, published after Heidegger's death, is the text of his 1929–1930 seminar.

7. See for instance my *Poetics of the Earth. Natural history and human history* (London: Routledge, 2019) trans. by Anne-Marie Feenberg from *Poétique de la Terre. Histoire naturelle et histoire humaine, essai de mésologie* (Paris : Belin, 2014); or more generally Marie Augendre, Jean-Pierre Llored, and Yann Nussaume, eds., *La Mésologie, un autre paradigme pour l'anthropocène?* (Paris : Hermann, 2018).

second edition of *Fūdo* (287 in the 1979 *bunko* edition, Iwanami), explicitly refers to Vidal de la Blache's *Principes de géographie humaine*, which he regrets not having read before writing his own essay (as a matter of fact, Vidal's book, published posthumously in 1922, translated by Iizuka Kōji, was published in Japanese only in 1940). Why that? Because Vidal's *géographie humaine*, reacting against the determinism prevailing at the time in German and Anglo-Saxon geographies, had shown that, even in comparable natural environments, human societies can historically develop completely different *genres de vie* (a concept which Iizuka rendered with *seikatsu yōshiki* 生活様式). This idea—which Lucien Febvre later qualified as "possibilisme"—was indeed consonant with Watsuji's opposition to determinism. Yet he adds, rightly so, that even if he had known of Vidal's theory before, that would not have changed his basic point of view. He does not say why, but we know the answer: whereas Vidal's standpoint was classically that of positive geography, and therefore does not distinguish environment from milieu, Watsuji's standpoint, as we have seen, is truly mesological.

Let me conclude in stressing, once again, that Johnson's book gives us an excellent presentation of Watsuji's problematics of *fūdo*, while adding the wish that he may some day, why not, *de-countrify* it and delve further into that of mesology as such.

David W. Johnson

Reply to Augustin Berque

Prof. Berque's essay approaches my book through the erudite rehearsal of an argument he has long made—one which, however, I have not taken up or made my own. This is the claim that the term *fūdosei* 風土性 should be translated with the word *médiance*, which is a neologism Berque derives from the Latin *medietas* (center; half; intermediate state; amidst). He wants to use this term to capture the way the human being for Watsuji is not a self-contained silo, a being closed up on itself, but one that exists only in and through its natural milieu. Berque points out that this "is indeed what Watsuji means with his definition of *fūdosei* as a "structural moment" between these two "halves" of the human's Being: self and milieu.... This is not all; using the latin root *med-* and its Greek equivalent *meso-* enables one to display in French the whole fan of Watsuji's terminology: *milieu, médiance, médial (fūdoteki* 風土的*), mésologie (fūdogaku), mésologique (fūdogakuteki* 風土学的*)*, and so on." He observes that his conceptual apparatus maps onto Watsuji's own, and contends that "English has the capacity to assimilate all these words almost just as they are in French: *milieu, mediance, medial, mesology, mesological,* and so on."

These claims and the impressive evidence assembled to support them (etymological investigations, comparative analyses of translations of the term *fūdosei* across different languages, and so on) have appeared in multiple places; they are repeated in his essay first, in order to highlight where the basic outlines of our respective interpretations of Watsuji overlap and second, in order to show why there is a substantive complaint to be lodged against my decision to leave *fūdosei* untranslated. With respect to the former, Berque acknowledges that my study does make the mediating and mediated character of *fūdosei* evident. Regarding the latter point, the difficulty for Berque appears to be that I do not "delve into that definition [of *médiance*]."

Although in the book I do not explicitly address why I do not make use of and expound on the term *médiance* in particular (as well as the closely connected *medial* and *mesology*), the reason for this should be clear from two of the central claims that I defend and substantiate there. The first problem with making use of the word *médiance* is that it only covers one dimension of the sense in which the human being "stands outside" of itself (*ex-sistere*), namely the self as it exists outside of itself and has its being in the natural world (recall that for Berque *médiance* = *fūdosei*), yet the terms *médiance/medial* at once connote something far broader and more general than this, namely, the self as mediating and mediated *in toto*. Despite this connotation, Berque's narrower definition of *médiance* means that in his hands it does not capture the other essential sense in which the self is mediating and mediated for Watsuji, namely, the way that the self stands outside of itself and has its being in others (*aidagara* 間柄). Others are also a key dimension of the self's transcendence, one which is inseparably interwoven with *fūdosei*—as I show in extensive discussions in the book of phenomena such as "shared intentionality" (*kyōdōshikō* 共同志向), and the historicity of nature. The use of the term *médiance* to convey *fūdosei* alone causes confusion, unfortunately, because its etymology suggests something much wider; this has the consequence of obscuring what must be opened up, namely, the totality of the mediating and mediated structure of the self; this is a unified structure whose central dimensions are nevertheless analytically distinguishable. To express this, both in this study and elsewhere, I have instead mapped out a *topology* of the self through the planes of nature and sociality.

The second reason that I do not employ the term *médiance* is that I espouse and defend a conception of language as fundamentally disclosive and expressive rather than designative and referential. Although Berque indicates that he is aware of this rationale he does not engage with this standpoint or its philosophical consequences, which are considerable. I will not repeat here what I have already laid out in a series of arguments in the book (see "Translating *Fūdo*," 21–6, as well as 173–6, 238–41) except to note the most prominent landmarks. The first of these is that Watsuji's work can be situated within an international hermeneutical tradition that includes Herder, Humboldt, Heidegger, Gadamer, and Ricoeur inasmuch as the conception of language as a holistic and disclosive medium that emerges from this tradition has deep intellectual and historical affinities and overlaps with Watsuji's own philosophical stance (see Chapter 7, 155–80, as well as 281–6). This conception of language and linguistic meaning poses serious obstacles to the adequate translation of terms such as *fūdo* and *fūdosei*. This is because what is disclosed by terms like these depends upon an adequate grasp of the rich semantic, cultural, and historical background in which they are situated. Without this context, a loss in translation occurs insofar as the original language can disclose something which cannot be made manifest in another language. In short, my claim is that different languages can disclose different things, and no single language is able to say or show everything.

Moreover, because these terms have been appropriated by Watsuji as *philosophical concepts*, that is, concepts which bring to light new realities and give us novel ways of understanding the world, translating these terms undermines (and sometimes distorts) their disclosive force as philosophical concepts, just as would be the case were we to translate *Dasein* with terms such as *subject* or *consciousness*, or *phronêsis* with *prudence*. Watsuji was aware of this problem, which is why he rejects the translation of *ningen* 人間 (which was another key philosophical concept for him) with words from Western languages such as *anthropos*, *homo*, *man*, or *Mensch*. One needs more than a "translation" of Dasein, *phronêsis*, or *fūdo* to see what these terms make manifest—one needs a translation of the philosophical account which accompanies and explains the use of these terms; *Watsuji on Nature* is in part an attempt to provide just such an account.

What is disclosed by *fūdo* and *fūdosei* as philosophical concepts, moreover, can be made intelligible even—and perhaps especially—if these terms are left untranslated, just as in the case of the examples from German and ancient Greek. In carrying these words over into the target language and working with them over time, we develop a fuller sense of the network of ideas, values, practices, narratives, texts, related terms, and claims that surround these terms and fill out their sense and significance. An example of this approach in our own philosophical tradition is the way in which we work with Greek or Latin terms, no longer automatically translating *logos* into reason or *arête* into virtue. The process of struggling to incorporate these terms into our already existing philosophical vocabulary, in turn, enlivens and enriches it. This kind of contact with radically other vocabularies and ways of thinking can also provide a powerful stimulant to the linguistic imagination. Through this attempt to say something in a novel way with foreign words, new meanings come into being and new realities are brought to light. And this, in turn, can open up new ways of being and thinking.[1]

It would be good to know what Prof. Berque makes of any of this—the philosophical claims and arguments about the disclosive nature of language, the attendant obstacles to translation for such a conception, the special challenges posed by philosophical concepts from another language, the examples of precedents in German and Greek, or the convergence of these points with Watsuji's own views. But he unfortunately says nothing about any of these issues. A response of some kind, I respectfully suggest, would have given his complaint more substance.

Rather than engage with any of these questions, Berque maintains that "The problem here is not that I should have liked Johnson to adopt my own translation of *fūdo* with *milieu*. It is that, by translating neither *fūdo* nor *fūdosei*, he bars himself from the whole problematics of mesology." This proclamation comes as something of a surprise. On page 49 I provide a translation of the key line from Watsuji that Berque places at the center of mesological thinking: "The aim of this book is to elucidate the character of *fūdo* as it is lived through and experienced (*fūdosei* 風土性) as a moment (*keiki* 契機) of the structure of human existence (*ningen sonzai no kōzō* 人間存在の構造)." I go on to state that "the full meaning of this passage will become apparent only at the end of our own study." By the end of the study I have set out some of the main ingredients of a mesological ontology of the lived experience of nature: the return to the lifeworld that is made possible by Heidegger's phenomenology, an extensive account of our linguistic, affective, and practical modes of disclosing nature, an analysis of the composite process of collective and historical change (Chapter 8, "Nature, History, Transcendence") based on an analysis of structure and agents that does not give primacy to either, an exhibition of the mutually constitutive unity of self-understanding and disclosure with one another in *fūdo* (this demonstration of an interactional domain underlying the unity of the subjective and objective and the physical and phenomenal is at the very ground of mesological thinking, see, e.g., 196–7), and, in the final chapter, an argument advancing the idea that the

---

1. I have recently set out these ideas and arguments in "The Limits of Language: Philosophical Hermeneutics and the Task of Comparative Philosophy," *Journal of Speculative Philosophy* 14/3: (2020).

reality of our world is emergent rather than sheerly and objectively there, already complete in itself—that it comes most fully into being in unfolding with and through the active participation of human and animal perception. The last three items in this list are all intimately connected, moreover, to what in Berque's *mesological* terminology is called *trajection*.

In short, rather than use the term *mesology* (partly for the reasons already given) I have instead *shown* what lies at its philosophical heart. One wishes in all sincerity that Berque had come to grips with the main themes and claims of *Watsuji on Nature* in relation to his own thinking about *mesology*. It would have been enlightening and fruitful, for instance, to compare my re-reading of philosophers such as Heidegger and Merleau-Ponty with what he has set out in his own system. It would have been good to know in this regard what he thinks of Merleau-Ponty's account of perception as an opening onto a world that it simultaneously belongs to and emerges from. As I attempt to show, insofar as the capacity to perceive belongs to the things perceived, the comportments and dispositions that realize these capacities can also be said to belong to what they would disclose. This idea, in turn, underlies my claim that "in our encounter with nature as *fūdo*, it can be said that this experience is the disclosure of a nature which presents *itself* to us." I can only wonder what Berque would have made of these points in light of his affirmation of Uexküll's relativism about human and animal perception.

I turn now to address two final points. First, Berque maintains that the idea of the perception (*Vernehmen*) of something "as" something in Heidegger was made possible "because he [Heidegger] knew about Uexküll's findings," and suggests that the "as" structure is derived from the notion of "tone" (*Ton*) in Uexküll. For philosophers working in this area the connection between Heidegger and the theoretical biology of Uexküll has long been well-known. And while not wishing to downplay this link, it must be said that the precise nature and extent of Uexküll's influence on Heidegger is unclear. In his authoritative study titled *The Genesis of Being and Time*, Theodore Kisiel notes only that "the young Heidegger was clearly aware of Uexküll's then-popular notion of *Umwelt*."[2] But if, as Berque contends, there

---

2. Theodore Kisiel, *The Genesis of Being and Time* (Berkeley: University of California Press, 1993), 506.

was a direct connection between Heidegger's notion of the "as" structure of perception and the results of Uexküll's forays (*Streifzüge*) into the *Umwelt* of animals, the relationship was not that of model and copy. In fact, in the text which Berque draws our attention to (*Die Grundbegriffe der Metaphysik. Welt – Endlichkeit – Einsamkeit*), insofar as Heidegger examines Uexküll's ideas, this is done in order to *contrast* the animal as world-poor (*weltarm*) with the human being as world-forming (*weltbildend*). The animal has access to the entities in its environment only insofar as these stimuli initiate or inhibit its drives. Since it is absorbed (*benommen*) or captivated within the circle of its drives, it never reaches entities in their being. Heidegger maintains that the animal is carried away (*hingenommen*) by what is in its environment such that its behavior (*Benehmen*) does not involve apprehension (*Vernehmen*).[3] Since the animal cannot "apprehend something as something, something as an entity at all," "the animal is separated from man by an abyss."[4] What is at stake here, then, is the chasm opened between Watsuji's Heideggerean understanding of *fūdo* and Uexküll's notion of the animal *Umwelt* by the transcendence of Dasein and the concomitant phenomenon of the ontological difference. If we truly want to understand the origins and development of Heidegger's notion of the hermeneutic *as*, we must set this *as* side by side with the apophantic *as* in his thought and begin to excavate and work through the many thinkers that had a decisive influence on the development both of these concepts, a list that would include Aristotle, Herder, Humboldt, Schleiermacher, Dilthey, Scheler, and Husserl.

Finally, I would like to offer a minor correction to Berque's last point in which he states that

> [...] Johnson, in the last pages of his book, uses repeatedly such words as *geography* or *geocultural*, though he did not notice (or does not mention) that Watsuji himself, in his 1948 codicil to the second edition of *Fūdo* (p. 287 in the 1979 *bunko* edition, Iwanami), explicitly refers to Vidal de la Blache's *Principes de géographie humaine*, which he regrets not having read before writing his own essay (as a matter of fact, Vidal's book, published posthu-

---

3. Martin Heidegger, *Die Grundbegriffe der Metaphysik: Welt–Endlichkeit–Einsamkeit. Gesamtausgabe* 29–30 (Frankfurt: Klostermann, 1983), 360.

4. Martin Heidegger, *Fundamental Concepts of Metaphysics: World–Finitude–Solitude*, trans. William McNeill and Nicholas Walker (Bloomington: Indiana University Press, 1995), 264.

mously in 1922, translated by Iizuka Kōji, was published in Japanese only in 1940). Why that? Because Vidal's *géographie humaine*, reacting against the determinism prevailing at the time in German and Anglo-Saxon geographies, had shown that, even in comparable natural environments, human societies can historically develop completely different *genres de vie* (a concept which Iizuka rendered with *seikatsu yōshiki* 生活様式). This idea—which Lucien Febvre later qualified as "possibilisme" – was indeed consonant with Watsuji's opposition to determinism. Yet he adds, rightly so, that even if he had known of Vidal's theory before, that would not have changed his basic point of view. He does not say why, but we know the answer: whereas Vidal's standpoint was classically that of positive geography, and therefore does not distinguish environment from milieu, Watsuji's standpoint, as we have seen, is truly mesological.

But in note 13 of the eighth chapter I observe that

> Jeff Malpas reminds us that the same kind of integrated spatiotemporal analysis is especially prominent within twentieth-century historiography, which has explicitly thematized the interplay of climactic, geological, and topographical factors and human action, society and culture. He observes that Paul Vidal de la Blache and Lucien Febvre played a foundational role in the rise of this kind of geographically oriented history. See *Heidegger and the Thinking of Place*, 138–40. Watsuji read de la Blache and Febvre, but their influence on him was limited since, as he notes in the postface added to Fūdo in 1948, he read both of them after writing this text. Moreover, while he approves of de la Blache and Febvre's criticism of Friedrich Ratzel's approach as a form of environmental determinism, he decided against making any major revisions to the manuscript of *Fūdo* because his study of *fūdo* (*fūdogaku* 風土学) is not to be simply identified with the human geography of these two scholars.

It is difficult to think of a Western commentator who has done more than Berque to direct our attention to the important distinction to be made between human geography and Watsuji's *fūdoron*, or to the singular character and intellectual significance Watsuji's *fūdogaku*. By way of conclusion I would hence like to repeat, though in a somewhat different key, the admiration I expressed for Prof. Berque's work in the acknowledgements section of *Watsuji on Nature*. It is precisely because I have benefitted in large and small ways from his scholarly and insightful examination of the concepts of *fūdo* and *fūdosei* that I regret the missed opportunity here for a genuine encounter between our approaches to Watsuji's work, especially given the manner in which the imaginative and theoretical power of Berque's version of *fūdogaku* has done so much to further the philosophical discussion of these topics.

嶺 秀樹 Mine Hideki
和辻はハイデガーから何を継承し、何を継承しなかったか

　本書のテーマである和辻の風土論は、最近欧米でも取り上げられることが少なくないが、本書の特色は、自己と自然の関係性を間柄としての人間存在の関係性と絡み合わせて考察するところにある。自己の関係性の自然的次元（風土性）と社会的次元（間柄存在）が自己をどのような仕方で自己たらしめているかに着目し、そこから和辻の風土論の主要な論点である自己と自然の連続性、共属性を明らかにしようとしている。著者の関心は、和辻がその風土論において「言い得なかったこと」、「まだ考えられずにとどまっていること」を明確にすることにある。「事実と価値の関係、経験の構造、現象学や環境倫理学の諸問題に対して風土論の及ぼしうる影響」という現代哲学にとっても重要なテーマを視野に入れつつ、和辻の風土論の現代的意義を取り出そうとする著者の仕事は、日本の一哲学者の紹介をはるか超えた読みごたえのある書物となっている。具体的な事象分析をまじえて風土論の理論的核心と思われる部分に切り込んでいく手口は、和辻解釈としても説得力があり、とりわけ実践的行為、言語、情動性のもつ「開示の能力」（faculty of disclosure）に焦点を定めて、和辻の風土論がもつ哲学的可能性を追求するさまは、大変刺激的でもある。

　この書評で取り上げたい論点は、和辻とハイデガーの「関係」（"Japanese Philosophy in the Wake of Heidegger"という副題にもあるように、本書の重要な視点）である。著者ジョンソン氏は、現象学や解釈学を思索の地盤とする哲学者らしく、両者の関係をバランスよく取り扱い、ハイデガーの解釈学的現象学を批判的に継承した和辻の風土論や倫理学の哲学的射程を、和辻に影響を与えた東西の思想的伝統や哲学者たちの文脈に十分留意しながら、粘り強く考察している。しかし、すべて問題が解消したわけではない。たとえば著者は、個人であると共に社会的存在である「自己」の動的弁証法的構造を風土性の問題と結びつけて理解してこそ、和辻の風土論の本来の射程が見えてくると考えている。実際その通りかもしれない。それはまさに和辻自身の立場から見ても正しいだろう。だが、そもそもハイデガーの解釈学的現象学が弁証法的思考と相容れないものをもっていることを顧みるだけでも、和辻におけるハイデガーの継承と批判の問題は、それほど単純ではないことがわかる。

　周知のように、和辻の風土論の構想は、彼がハイデガーの『存在と時間』を読み、「世界内存在」（In-der-Welt-sein）としての「現存在」（Dasein）を現象学的に分析する

手法にふれたことに始まる。しかし和辻はハイデガーの分析が時間性に偏っていること、空間性が背景に退いていることを批判し、その理由をハイデガーの「現存在」が個人的であることに求めた。空間性を重視するならば、人間存在の間柄としてのあり方が際立ってくる。その際、人間存在の根本原理とされたのが、個人性と全体性の間の弁証法的運動であり、それを貫く「絶対否定性」の「空」であった。人倫のこうした根本原理に基づいて間柄としての人間存在の独自な「倫理学」が展開されることになるのである。しかし、和辻の風土論の経験的基盤に注目してみると、「間柄としての人間存在論」と「風土論」とがいったいどのように連関しているかが、やはり問題となる。『倫理学』の第四章「人間存在の歴史的風土的構造」におけるように、和辻が両者を一つの事柄として追求しようとしたことは明らかだが、事象への接近の仕方としての方法論の観点から言えば、自己の関係性の自然的次元と社会的次元の間には連続性よりもむしろ非連続性が顕著になってくる。自己の間柄としての関係性を自己と自然の関係性に絡めて考えることは、そう簡単なことではないのである。

こうした困難は、著者も言及している坂部恵の和辻評、すなわち、和辻には「個と共同体全体との関係を排他的部分とその総和という人格的ないしより正確には間人格的世界の表層でのみ妥当する論理ないし図式に従って考える傾向」がある[1]、という指摘に関連しているように思われる。そこから、「ヨーロッパの主観性を克服しようとした和辻自身がはたしてそこから完全に自由であったかどうか」という疑問も出てくるのだろう。そうした意味で、和辻におけるハイデガーの批判的継承の意味を今一度俎上に載せ、方法論の観点から両者の「自己」理解の内実を検討してみることは無駄ではない。評者としては、特に「開示の出来事」(an event of disclosure) としての「風土の生きた経験」の問題に制限しつつ、次の二つの観点から著者ジョンソン氏に問いを投げかけてみたい。これらの論点は、あくまで著者の和辻解釈の意図をより明確にしていただくための「きっかけ」となることを願って提示したものであることを、あらかじめ断っておく。

（1）「実在の知覚」の「一人称的観点」(the first-person standpoint, p. 207) について。著者は、風土の開示性のありかたをより明確にするために、実在としての一人称的経験に言及している。メルロ＝ポンティやマクダウェルを援用して展開される「自己と自然の連続性」、「相互帰属性」の問題は、和辻が風土論や人間の学としての倫理学を展開した際に、ハイデガーの現象学的解釈学から何を継承し、何を継承しなかったかということにも関わっている。周知のように、和辻は、倫理学の体系を展開

---

1. 坂部恵『ペルソナの詩学』（岩波書店、1989年）、114 ページ。

するに先立って、方法論としてハイデガーの現象学よりはむしろ解釈学を優先し、ハイデガーの「現象学的還元」を「人間存在への解釈学的還元」に転釈した[2]。その意味を十分に検討してみるとよく分かるように、和辻は一人称的観点をつねに保持していたとは言えないのである。この疑念は、和辻の風土論や倫理学の具体的な叙述に立ち入って見てみれば、一層強くなる。たしかに、ハイデガーの「現存在」（Dasein）の「現」（Da）の「開示性」（Erschlossenheit）を主観性克服の契機と捉え、自己の自己性を「開示の出来事」の視点から考えるべきだという著者の方向は正しい。「人間存在と自然の相互浸透性」（和辻の風土性やベルクの通態性）という自己の関係性を、間柄としての人間存在の二重性と重ねて考えるべきだという主張も、和辻の意図に沿うものであり、十分に頷ける。しかし、和辻の風土論の枠組みを決定する思考法に、主観と客観の分離以前の原経験とも言うべき「一人称的観点」から外れるような傾向が含まれているとすれば、どうであろうか。またそれが和辻の風土論における一種の環境決定論的な傾向を生み出す機縁ともなっていたとすれば、どうであろうか。この問題は、ハイデガーの『存在と時間』の現存在分析の基本的視点である「各自性」（Jemeinigkeit）を、単に「個人性」として批判した和辻の主張と関わるだけに、慎重に考えるべき問題であろう。

　（2）ハイデガーの「存在論的差異」や「超越」についての和辻の理解について。和辻はハイデガーの「現存在」を個人的なものにすぎないと批判し、現存在の時間性に基づいたハイデガーの超越概念を、間柄としての人間存在の絶対否定性の構造に転化して理解すべきだとした。和辻のこうした歩みは、ハイデガーの存在論的差異や超越の問題の発展的解消と見なすべきだろうか。それともむしろハイデガーの思索の核心を見逃し、「存在論的次元」（ontologische Dimension）を単に「人間学的存在的次元」に平板化したと見るべきではないか。著者は、和辻が存在論的差異の問題をきちんと捉えていたとし、それを風土論に含まれる「開示」（disclosure）の事柄に認めようとしている。しかし、周知のように、ハイデガーの「存在論的差異」は「超越」と一つの事柄である。そうだとすると、和辻がハイデガーの意味での「超越」を認めようとしないならば、「存在論的差異」についてもハイデガーと違った理解をしていることになる。「存在論的差異」や「超越」の思想をめぐるハイデガーと和辻の違いが、和辻自身の風土論のもつ困難にもその影を落としていると思われるだけに、（1）の問題とも連関させて、和辻の風土論や倫理学の基盤を「存在論的差異」や「超越」の問題の光のもとで

---

2. 和辻全集第 9 巻 176 ページ以下参照（以下 9: 176 のように記す）。

再検討する必要があるのではないか。その際、一つの重要な視点として、和辻が（そして西田や田辺などの当時の他の日本の哲学者たちも同様に）、ハイデガーの「存在論の歴史の現象学的破壊」(eine phänomenologische Destruktion der Geschichte der Ontologie) の課題を十分理解していないことに着目すべきであろう。

　まず第一の問題に関して、補足しつつ質問の意図をもうすこし明確にしてみよう。「一人称的観点」を説明する具体例としては、著者も言及している「寒さ」や「花の美しさ」の経験が挙げられるだろう。和辻によると、我々が寒さを感じるとき、「寒気」というような独立した物理的実在があって、それが我々に影響し、その結果、我々が寒さを感じるのではなく、我々は直接に「外気の冷たさ」を感じている。我々と寒さは、それぞれ別々に存していて関係し合うのではなく、我々ははじめから「寒さの内へ出て」いて、「寒さ自身の内に自己を見いだす」のである。寒さを感じるということと寒さそのものは一つの出来事である。この事態を、我々は寒さが現出する「場所」であり、我々において外の「寒さ」が露わになっている、と言い表すこともできよう[3]。「花の美しさ」についても同様のことが言える。「花の美しさ」は、我々が「花」に投射した主観的な性質や価値ではない。また我々人間存在から引き離した花の客観的性質でもない。和辻によると、「人間は花の美しさを観ずることにおいて、花のもとに出ているおのれの存在を受け取っている」。同じ事態を、我々は「花の美しさ」が露わになる「場」であると言い表してもよいだろう[4]。詩人や画家が描いた作品が、「花の真の生命を露わにしているように感ぜられる」のもそのためである。

　このように、「一人称的観点」が物事が現出する原初的経験、いわゆる主観・客観の区別以前の出来事を言い表す言葉であるとすると、この「一人称的」な観点を他者と区別された「私」の観点とか「個人的」な観点と見なすことは、原初的な「開示性」の出来事にそぐわないことになる。「個人」とか「間柄」ということは、「原初的」で「一人称的」な観点を、つまり実在が露わになる経験の「現場」をいったん離れて、それをいわば外から反省して初めて可能になる「三人称的」規定である。ハイデガーの「現存在の実存論的分析」(die existenziale Analytik des Daseins) の拠って立つ「各自性」(Jemeinigkeit) も同じように理解すべきだろう。

　以上のことが正しいとすると、和辻が「風土の基礎理論」において寒さの志向的経験を根本的には「間柄」の経験であるとし、「寒さにおいて己れを見いだすのは、根源的には間柄としての我々なのである」と述べるとき、「私」の寒さの知覚的直接

---

3. 和辻 8: 8 以下参照。
4. 和辻 11: 106 参照。

的経験が言語や他者との共同性に媒介されているという意味では正鵠を得ているが、経験の構造を分析し解釈する立場としては、すでに「三人称的」観点に立っているといわざるをえないのではないか。ここには、一人称的現象学的開示性の経験に立脚するということと、それを記述し、分析し、解釈するという三人称的立場との微妙な関係が伏在しており、現象学的解釈学に共通の課題となっている。「経験において出会われる風土性」、すなわち「実践的活動性や情動や言語を通して開示される出来事」を言い表すために、著者が「我々としての私、私としての我々」（I-as-we and we-as-I）という言い方をするのは、間柄としての「共同的振る舞い」（shared comportment）を言い表す表現としては適切だと思うが、一人称的な開示性としての原初的の経験の次元には当てはまらないのではないか。

　こうした指摘は、実は和辻のハイデガー批判、すなわち「彼（ハイデガー）においては存在への通路は我れと物との係わり」であり、「人」ははじめから「我れ」として規定されているという主張の正否を検討したいがためである。ハイデガーの現存在の「存在的内容」は「我れ」としての「ひと」であり、ハイデガーの実存論は個人の立場に立っているという和辻の主張は、間柄としての人間存在論の立場から当然出てくることである。しかし、それがハイデガーの基本的出発点（これを括弧付きで「一人称的立場」と呼んでも大過ないと思う）を正しく捉えているかとなると、そうではないと言わざるをえない。というのも、「各自性」としての「現存在」の「開示性」の出来事、言い換えれば「現存在」の「超越」の行き先としての「存在」の「真性（Wahrheit）＝隠れのなさ（Unverborgenheit）」は、「存在者」としての「個人」とは次元を異にするからである。ハイデガーの「各自性」としての「自己」の次元は、本来的実存であれ非本来的実存であれ、現存在の「真性」（および「非真性」）に根ざしたものである。このように、ハイデガーの現存在の「自己性」が「各自性」として、そもそも私と汝、個人と他者、我々と事物などの諸関係が露わになるところの「超越」の「場」（これを後期のハイデガーは「存在の明け開け」（Lichtung des Seins）と呼んだ）であるとすると、和辻のように、『存在と時間』の現象学的立場が「個人の立場」であると断定するのは行き過ぎであり、ハイデガーの曲解であるとさえ言える。和辻の「人間の学としての倫理学」が現象学ではなく、むしろディルタイ的な生、表現・了解の連関に立脚した解釈学の道を辿ろうとするのも、こうした誤解に端を発しているのではなかろうか。それがもし日常性における表現とその了解を通じて人間存在の構造を把握しようとする倫理学の必然の成り行きだとすれば、自然の根源的開示性の経験に基づいた現象学的洞察から出発する「風土論」と、実践的行為的連関に立脚した解釈学としての「倫理学」の絡み合った関係は、より注意深く解きほぐしていく必要

がある。そのための手がかりとして第二の超越と存在論的差異の問題に少し立ち入って考えてみたい[5]。

ハイデガーの「超越」や「存在論的差異」を取り上げる際にまず念頭に置いておかねばならないことは、密接に関連した両概念が『存在と時間』におけるハイデガーの基礎的存在論の構想に従って理解されるべき形而上学的事柄だということである。和辻はこの両概念について形の上ではそれなりの理解を示しているが、ハイデガーの「基礎的存在論」の構想および「超越」や「存在論的差異」の真意については、きちんと把握していたとは言えない。その理由として、彼が当時読むことができたハイデガーのテクストが限られており、しかもその主たるテクストである『存在と時間』が第一部の途中で挫折しており、第二部の「存在論の歴史の現象学的破壊」が発表されずに未完にとどまったことなどが挙げられるかもしれない。周知のように、『存在と時間』の公刊された内容の大部分は、「現存在の実存論的分析」に関わるものであり、『存在と時間』は当時から「実存哲学」や「人間存在論」として受け止められる危険性があった。和辻は『人間の学としての倫理学』において、『存在と時間』公刊の後すぐに行われた1927年夏学期の講義『現象学の根本問題』に触れており[6]、超越や存在論的差異の問題について理解を深める機会があったはずである。だが彼は「超越」の概念を、世界内存在としての現存在が時間性の構造に基づいて「外に出て行くこと」としてしか理解しておらず、現存在の形而上学的生起としての「存在論的差異」との連関において捉えることはほとんどなかった。それはとりわけ、『風土』の基礎理論における「超越」の理解からも窺うことができる[7]。

和辻によると、超越は、第一に、人間存在の超越として、時間性と空間性の相即によって成り立っているところの、全体から個へ、個から全体へという絶対否定性の運動と重ね合わせて理解すべき事柄である。第二に、こうした意味での超越が、間柄の時間的構造として、歴史性の意義を帯びていることに注意すべきである。最後に、超越は「風土的に外に出ること」であり、風土において「自らを見いだすこと」、つまり、個人の立場では「身体の自覚」になり、人間存在にとっては共同体の形成の仕方、意識の仕方、言語の作り方、生産や家屋の作り方などに現れてくるものである。和辻は、超越はこれらすべてを含まなければならないが、ハイデガーの超越概念にはそれが

---

5. この問題についてはかつて拙著『ハイデッガーと日本の哲学』（ミネルヴァ書房、2002年）でくわしく論じたことがある（第2章および第3章を参照）。この書評では「開示性」に焦点を当てて、少し別の観点から検討してみたい。
6. 当時日本では『現象学の根本問題』の講義録の速記に基づいたコピーが出回っていたことはよく知られている。和辻もおそらくその一部を手に入れ読んでいたのであろう。
7. 和辻 8: 18 以下参照。

ないと批判するのである。和辻のこうした指摘は、ハイデガーから見れば、基礎的存在論の基本構想を理解することなく、哲学的人間学のontischな立場に由来すると思えたことだろう。

　ハイデガーにとって「現存在」の「超越」とは、基本的には、「存在者」全体を超えて、「存在者」の「存在理解」を可能にするアプリオリの地平を開くことであり、存在者と存在を明確に区別することとしての「存在論的差異」を遂行することである。その意味で「超越」は、存在者との関わりに没入し、自己の存在を世界の方から理解する傾向にある現存在の素朴なまなざしを、存在者から存在へと向け変えること、そうして存在者との関わりを可能にする存在理解のアプリオリの地平を開示することという、ハイデガーの現象学的還元と構成の明確な遂行にほかならない。「超越」と「存在論的差異」は、「存在理解」の可能的地平に向けた現存在の自己企投という同じ出来事を、二つの側面から見たものだとも言えよう。

　超越や存在論的差異の概念をめぐるもうひとつ重要な観点は、ハイデガーの現存在の実存論的分析が、伝承された存在概念をその作られた源泉に返し、批判的に掘り起こすことによって、既成の存在理解・世界理解の自明性を打ち破り、根源的な存在理解の地平を獲得しようという「形而上学の基礎づけ」への意図を含んでいることである。「存在論的差異」という「存在者」と「存在」の明確な区別の遂行は、存在理解の自己企投の真正さを確かめるために、伝統的概念の批判的解体の作業を必ず必要とする。存在概念の現象学的構成の作業は、「存在論の歴史の現象学的解体」という課題と切り離すことができないのである。基礎的存在論をめぐるこうした方法的課題は、ハイデガーの「存在の問い」（Seinsfrage）を導く現存在の被投性・事実性の自覚に基づいており、伝統の掘り起こしと存在論の革新という、一見相反する事柄を一つに結びつけようという構想に由来している。カントやデカルト、アリストテレスなどの存在論の伝統の現象学的解体というある意味では非常に学的な課題を、「不安」、「死への存在」、「先駆的覚悟性」（vorlaufende Entschlossenheit）という、ある意味できわめて実存哲学的な経験と結びつけ、本来的実存における「存在」や「世界」開示の根源的出来事を、歴史的伝統による存在理解の支配の問題と絡めて展開しようしたところに、我々はハイデガーの思索の大きな魅力を感じるのであるが、同時に安易な理解をはねつけるような困難にもぶつかるのである。

　ハイデガーの思索をさらなる問いへと強制する問題構制の複雑さを、和辻がどこまで把握し受け止めようとしていたかは定かではない。いずれにせよここで重要なことは、現存在の事実性・歴史性の根本経験が「超越」や「存在論的差異」の概念構成の契機となっていたこと、存在理解の実存論的な根源的開示と存在理解の歴史的

規定性とを、どのようにすれば一つの問題連関として展開できるかというハイデガーの「存在と時間」の問いに含まれている困難を、和辻が一体どこまできちんと捉えた上でハイデガーを批判していたか、ということである。「世界内存在」としての「現存在」に本質的に属しているとされる「超越」の出来事を、人間存在の否定性の運動と重ね合わせたり、「風土的に外へ出ること」というように人間存在と世界とのいわば ontisch な関わりとして捉えるのは、ハイデガー解釈としてとても首肯できるものではない。「超越」思想のこうした転釈を導く和辻の風土論の理論的構想そのものに、ある種の「欠陥」があるのではないかという疑念さえ生じるゆえんでもある。

　和辻が風土論を構想するに至ったのは、自らの証言にもあるように、ドイツに留学すべくヨーロッパに渡航した際にさまざまな「風土」に直接触れたことと、ベルリンで『存在と時間』を読んで、ハイデガーにおいて時間性が「主体的存在構造」として活かされたときに、なぜ空間性も活かされないのかと疑問に思ったことに発する。これはハイデガーの「存在と時間」の構想に対する単なる批判の表明ではなく、世界内存在としての現存在の時間性に向けられた解釈学的現象学の手法に対する賛辞でもあり、ハイデガーの手法を風土性の分析に応用すれば、人間存在の「主体的構造」を時間性のみならず空間性としても解明できるという見通しを得たことの告白である。事実、和辻の『人間の学としての倫理学』や『倫理学』の言説は、ハイデガーの「実存」を間柄としての「人間存在」に換骨奪胎しているとはいえ、形式的には驚くほどハイデガーの思考の枠組みをそのまま借用している。根本的に両者の違いを感じるのは、ハイデガーの事象へのまなざしと思索の歩みがつねに緊張関係を保ち、常に「問いを仕上げる」という「開かれた」あり方をしているのに対し、和辻の場合、思考そのものがかなり図式的であり、事象の経験から絶えずインパクトを受けつつ自らの思索そのものを問い直すという開かれた批判的思考が欠如していることである。和辻の風土論が、その理論的構想の部分ではそれなりの説得力をもち、人間存在と自然との「連続的相互帰属関係」についての独創的な発想となっているという印象を与える反面、いざ具体的な分析に取りかかると風土のタイプ論に終始し、一種の自然環境決定論の様相を帯びるのはいったいなぜだろうか。

　ジョンソン氏はこうした和辻の風土論のもつ危険に対して、自然を開示する我々の能力が時代により、あるいは文化間で様々であることを具体的に示すことで応えようとしている。氏は、「自然として現れるものを媒介する開示の文化的様式が強調されすぎると、我々の自然経験を我々の文化形式に還元してしまう危険がある。そして自然を開示するのが我々であることになると、ある種の主観主義ないし相対主義になる」という風土論一般の危険を回避すべく、仏教哲学や現象学の「非二元論」を引き合

いに出すことで、和辻の風土概念の豊かさを明らかにしようとしている。そうするためにも、しかし、著者は和辻の風土論の危険が一体どこに由来するのかを、その思考のあり方の現場に立ち返ってもう少し問題にしてもよかったのではないか。

　和辻の風土論が、たとえ彼一流の優れた洞察に満ちているとしても、結局、一旅行者の体験に基づいたエッセー風の論文であるという印象を我々に与えるのは偶然ではない。和辻の風土論のように現象学的解釈学的な事象分析を遂行するためには、現象の開示の場となる一人称的な直接的経験に基づくことはまず必要なことである。しかし、それだけでは不十分で、例えば旅行中に自らがその場に置かれた風土の具体相を解釈するに当たって、自らの「一人称的直接的経験」を支える「解釈学的状況」（hermeneutische Situation）、すなわち、自らの「先理解」（Vorverständnis）の枠組み的地平についてあらかじめ反省する必要がある。言語的、情動的、文化的に媒介された自然との関わりの中で、その具体的連関を露わにできるのは、まずは一人称的直接的体験であるが、その体験において露わになった事象を解釈するためには、体験を自覚化し反省する三人称的立場に立つ必要がある。旅行者の場合のように、この一人称的体験がその風土のもとにある生活世界に根ざしていない場合、直接的体験は知らず知らずのうちに外部的枠組みをかぶせることによって歪んだ解釈に導きやすい。和辻自身、風土理解を可能にする自らの先構造についての洞察が十分にあれば、旅行中の風土体験における一人称的直接性と外からの三人称的立場との錯綜した関係について、もう少し自覚的でありえたであろうし、現象の開示の場となる一人称的な直接経験と、このコンテクストを支える歴史的文化的規定性との絡み合いに目を向け、自らの理解の先構造についての反省を通して、自らの解釈学的地平をたえず開かれたものにしておくことができたかもしれない。そのためにも、自らの直接的経験と、他者や他文化の風土性についての自らの解釈の枠組みを行きつ戻りつ自己批判的に反省すべきであった。そうすることができば、和辻の風土論が単なるタイプ論に終わることもなかったのではないか。異なった風土における間文化的状況の中で、自己固有のものと異他的なものとの相互浸透に絶えず目配せすることによってのみ、自らの体験や理解の被拘束性について自覚する可能性も開かれる。それは旅行者や一時外国で生活世界を体験する機会を与えられた者の特権的可能性でもある。こうした人たちは、間文化的な緊張関係に置き入れられることによって、間柄としての人間存在の特定の生活世界における存在者の連関を他の異質な生活世界における連関と対比せざるをえなくなり、自らの存在理解を拘束する自明性を異化し、解放された地平に自らを置き直す機会を与えられる。それは自己経験を深めることでもあり、自らの歴史的文化的規定性に対して透明性を確保することでもある。

しかし、これは決して簡単なことではない。本来的実存や人間存在の本来の面目が問われる理由でもある。しかし、ハイデガーの不安や「死への存在」を契機とする「先駆的覚悟性」としての本来的実存にせよ、和辻の「自他不二」的な人間存在の絶対否定性としての「本来の面目」にせよ、その否定的動性の内に「自己の閉鎖性」を解き放つ機能を含んでいるとはいえ、歴史的伝統に支配された自文化の拘束性から自己を一挙に自由にするものではなかった。むしろ、そうした最終的に自己を解放する根拠を求めようとすることこそ、自己の歴史的文化的規定性を排除することにつながりかねない。

『存在と時間』の時期における基礎的存在論の構想そのものに「根拠づけへの意志」が働いていたことは、ハイデガー自身が後に反省することになる。和辻がこうした基本的洞察に導かれることなく、ハイデガーの「超越」や「存在論的差異」を誤解したこと、否、両概念の拠って立つ現存在の基盤に亀裂が存することに十分目配りできなかったこと、そこにおそらく、風土論の様々な困難の一つの理由があるのではないか。歴史的伝承の拘束性と存在論の形而上学的基礎づけの間に、橋渡しすることができない亀裂が存していることは、存在論的差異を現存在の超越の方からのみ考えることを許さない事態であり、ハイデガーを「基礎的存在論」から「存在史的思索」へと転回せしめる動機となったことはよく知られている。こうしたハイデガーの「存在の思索」の困難と途上性格こそ、それを真剣に受け止めることができれば、直接体験の歴史的文化的拘束性に対してより敏感に応答し、歴史的環境的被拘束性と自由の弁証法的関係についても、より注意深く考える道が開かれたであろう。少なくとも風土論のもつ環境決定論的な一面性に対して、和辻は自己批判的姿勢を維持できたのではないか。その意味で、超越や存在論的差異の思想は、換骨奪胎して利用すべきものではなく、それらが拠って立つ「解釈学的状況」の問い直しを通して、風土論の事象分析を遂行する和辻自身の「解釈学的状況」を自覚化するきっかけとすべきものであった。和辻がハイデガーの思想を継承する際に主に注目したのは、思索の主題や方法、そこから帰結する人間存在の基礎的構造であった。しかし我々がハイデガーから学びうるのは、むしろハイデガーの思索の課題の困難であり、彼がこの困難を自覚しつつ思索の不安定な動性を耐え抜き、まさに自らの「存在の問い」を問い続けたことである。彼の思索のこうした徹底したあり方が広い意味での「解釈学的空間」を開かれたものとしていたことを思えば、和辻はハイデガーからやはり大事なことを学び損ねたのである。

David W. Johnson
Reply to Mine Hideki

Prof. Mine rightly observes that *Watsuji on Nature* attempts to uncover the theoretical core and philosophical potential of *fūdoron* through concrete event analysis and an investigation into the disclosive capacity of practical action, language, and emotions. His review approaches this core by focusing on the relationship between Watsuji and Heidegger, noting that the subtitle of the book is "Japanese Philosophy in the Wake of Heidegger." He restricts the scope of his inquiry to two aspects of the question of what I have called "the lived experience of *fūdo* as an event of disclosure." The first involves methodological and philosophical issues in the first-person standpoint of disclosedness, and the second reconsiders Watsuji's understanding of Heidegger's concepts of the ontological difference and transcendence. Mine notes that he presents these issues in the hope that reflection on them will serve as an opportunity for clarifying my intentions in interpreting Watsuji.

Because these matters are interrelated in ways that are difficult to pry apart, in what follows I take up the most salient points more or less in the order in which they appear in the original essay. Mine begins by suggesting that the deterministic drift of Watsuji's theory of *fūdo* is linked to his tendency to misunderstand the function and significance of the first-person standpoint in phenomenology. This tendency can be seen in Watsuji's criticism of Heidegger's notion of *mineness* (*Jemeinigkeit*) as too individualistic. But in (illegitimately) undermining *mineness*, Watsuji also undermines the first-person point of view that is the basic starting point of Heidegger in *Being and Time*, and loses a proper understanding of the phenomena of disclosure and transcendence that belong to this standpoint. The misunderstanding of these concepts, in turn, are a source of the geographical determinism that appears in Watsuji's *fūdoron*.

There are at least two dimensions of the first-person standpoint in Heidegger's work that Mine thinks Watsuji has misunderstood. In discussing the first issue, he cites Watsuji's examples of our experience of feeling cold as well as our experience of perceiving a flower as beautiful. These examples are meant to illustrate the way that this viewpoint is that of the original experience of the appearance of things; it is the event before the bifurcation of subject and object. But if this is the case, Watsuji cannot characterize the first-person perspective of Heideggerean phenomenology as an *individual* one, since this is already the stance of a (single) subject divided from the objects of experience.

Notwithstanding this point, Watsuji claims, moreover, that rather than being the standpoint of an individual, the first-person stance is actually that of *aidagara* 間柄, or being-in-relation to others. Regarding this claim, Mine acknowledges that while it is true that the direct perceptual experience of the "I" is mediated by language and co-existence with others, "being-in-relation to others," is, like "individuality," a determination from the third-person standpoint that analyzes and interprets the structure of experience. Since I, too, follow Watsuji here in expanding on this idea with the claim that things and events are disclosed through the shared comportment practical action, emotions, and language, my account appears to face the same difficulty.

Mine maintains that the first-person standpoint is not that of *aidagara* but rather that of the "mineness" of Dasein, and, as such, one that constitutes the field of appearances in which the relationship between self and other, and we and things, are disclosed in the first place, a disclosure (in the sense of *Wahrheit* as *Unverborgenheit*) which already belongs to the transcendence of Dasein. His further observation that we can identify this field with what Heidegger in his later period calls the *Lichtung des Seins* also serves to reinforce the conclusion that the *Jemeinigkeit* of Dasein is different in dimension from that of the *individual* as an *entity* such that these must not be conflated with one another.

Mine's criticisms about Watsuji's misreading of Dasein as too "individualistic" are well placed, and seem in important ways to be right. What Watsuji should perhaps have criticized more clearly was the overly *subjective* cast of Dasein as being "there" and being the "there." Insofar as this original field of appearing was intended by Heidegger to subvert the subject-object dichotomy, identifying it with the mineness or *Jemeinigkeit* of Dasein (namely, the "I" of direct personal involvement in something, such that it is "I" in each case who, e.g., is making a confession of his sins, or who loves his wife, or who is dying of cancer) serves to reify the subjective dimension of this field rather than pass beyond it. Mine's allusion to the *Kehre* here bolsters this point, as it is in part precisely because the later Heidegger viewed his early iteration of Dasein as too subjective that he began to turn to a different kind of language.

But this does not really obviate the other claim at stake, namely, that the field of disclosure is constitutively linked to others. Mine is right to point out the distinction between how I experience the first-person standpoint, on the one hand, and an explicit understanding of *what* this standpoint is—which is something that is grasped only in the third-person standpoint of reflection. I may experience this standpoint (at times) as a form of what Nishida calls pure experience and so one in which I am fully absorbed in my activity such that there is no explicit distinction between subject and object; I may experience this standpoint at other times as an individual facing off against a world of others who do not understand me; I may also experience this standpoint as a consciousness wholly distinct from the objects which it encounters. One of the tasks that phenomenological reflection has is to distinguish in these experiences between those in which the natural attitude reads into experience what a more careful phenomenological description does not find (such as the latter notion that I experience the first-person standpoint as a consciousness sealed off from objects that it subsequently encounters, rather than as always already being determined by the objects of awareness, and so a consciousness "of" something). Such phenomenological descriptions, along with other forms of reflection in the third-person, can contribute to the development of philosophical claims about what this first-person standpoint *is*.

In the case of Watsuji's claims about the nature of the first-person standpoint there is a similar gap between how we generally experience this stance and what he maintains is actually involved in it. Let's begin with the question of how we experience the first-person stance. Even if we jettison with Watsuji the notion of *Jemeinigkeit* as too subjective in describing how we experience this viewpoint, it nevertheless can be said that we experience this standpoint in terms of what phenomenologists call *pre-reflective self-awareness*, namely the (usually unattended) background awareness I have in any activity that *I* am the one engaged in it. Moreover, as it is virtually impossible to be mistaken about this implicit sense that it is I rather than someone else who is having this experience (except in certain rare cases such as that of schizophrenia, in which this feeling can be missing), I always experience this first-person stance as belonging to me.

Now, as I have tried to show, an important result of Watsuji's own phenomenological descriptions is that it disrupts or puts into question the assumption that this stance is reducible to our experience of it in terms of the subjectivity of pre-reflective self-awareness. Watsuji shows that essential modes of consciousness, activity, and embodiment, which are indispensable for the first-person standpoint, always already depend on our being in relation to others in order to be what they are, just as in transcendental phenomenology consciousness depends on its objects to be what it is. However, it must be granted that this relation is not as robust as that between consciousness and object, since it appears to be possible to uncover moments or aspects of the first-person standpoint that escape the constitutive relation to others. Nevertheless, Watsuji's broader aim and its rationale remain valid: to move away from *Jemeinigkeit* as too subjective a construal of the structure of the first-person standpoint. In short, inasmuch as the original field in and through which experience unfolds moves beyond a form of subjectivism in being an event before the distinction between subject and object, it must also move beyond subjectivism in being a standpoint before the distinction between self and other.

The challenge here is articulating just what this standpoint entails—a challenge that admittedly still has not been fully met by Watsuji. I have explored a possible further step in this direction in a recent article about Kimura Bin's work in this area.[1] Drawing on long clinical experience and observation, Kimura posits a form of impersonal subjectivity that underlies and precedes our experience of ourselves as individuated subjects. His analysis uncovers two structural features relevant to our discussion that characterize the impersonal subject. First, this subject can be identified as the subject of basic and impersonal forms of sensation and perception, and so must be understood as the source of an experience that precedes the individual self. Kimura draws in this regard on the work of Viktor von Weizsäcker, who has uncovered a form of subjectivity that underlies even pre-reflective self-awareness. Second, this impersonal subject functions as a constituent ele-

---

1. David W. Johnson, "The Anonymous Subject of Life: Some Philosophical, Psychological, and Religious Considerations," *Research in Phenomenology* 49/3 (2019).

ment in the collective subjectivity of the group (as when, e.g., a group of musicians plays a piece of music together).

Kimura's concept of the impersonal subject can in this way open up a path toward understanding the first-person stance in both a less subjective and less individualistic manner. Notwithstanding these points, Mine thinks that there is also a second important issue at stake in Watsuji's approach to the first-person standpoint, namely, a link between his misinterpretation of the Heideggerean concept of transcendence and the geographical determinism that makes its appearance in his theory of *fūdo*. He suggests that Watsuji's problems here may have their source in the (admittedly) confused and confusing relationship between the phenomenological character of his *fūdoron* (which thematizes the first-person standpoint of the experience of the geo-cultural environment) and the reflective standpoint of his *Ethics as the Study of the Human* (人間の学としての倫理学), which attempts to grasp the structure of human existence via an understanding of its expressions (objectifications of lived experience) in the manner of Dilthey's hermeneutics, a philosophical method which, of course, does not take a phenomenological approach. Thus, rather than keeping at the center of his approach the first-person standpoint of the Heideggerean phenomenology of *Being and Time* and so with it the site in which beings are transcended by their being, Watsuji instead explicitly develops his ethical theory by prioritizing hermeneutics, translating Heidegger's "phenomenological reduction" into a "hermeneutic reduction to human existence."

One of the most important consequences of this is that Watsuji fails to grasp Heidegger's concept of transcendence as Dasein's openness to the horizon that enables the understanding of the being of an entity in a manner that transcends the entity. If this is the case, this will also mean that when Watsuji criticizes Heidegger's concept of transcendence, he does so without an understanding of the ontological difference between being and beings. Mine observes that for Watsuji, transcendence (in the sense that is relevant here) has its source in the unified spatio-temporal structure of Dasein as being-in-the-world-in-relation-to-others. For this conception of human existence, *fūdo* is the context through which we come to see ourselves in cultural structures, processes, and products, one that both constitutes and reflects our self-understanding and mediates our experience of nature. Via this mirroring process we are able to grasp both the ways that we are determined by and the ways that we are capable of transcending our limitations in relation to the natural world in which we have our ground. Watsuji's criticism of Heidegger in this regard is that his concept of transcendence fails to include all of these things.

Mine points out that Watsuji does not in this instance treat the concept of transcendence in the context of or in relation to the question of the ontological difference, and that he rarely does so. In addition, at the time he wrote this Watsuji did not fully understand the problem of Heidegger's phenomenological deconstruction of the history of ontology. Mine thus contends that the relationship here between human existence and the world is grasped ontically rather than ontologically. Watsuji's viewpoint, he suggests, has likely come from the ontical standpoint of philosophical anthropology. Hence while transcendence for Watsuji has historical significance as the temporal structure of *aidagara*, one might draw the conclusion that this is the temporality of what Heidegger calls *Historie* rather than *Geschichte*. All of these factors can help us understand why, as Mine notes, when the time comes to perform a concrete analysis of *fūdo*, Watsuji turns the typology of climate into a kind of environmental determinism of nature.

Prof. Mine wonders whether it might not have been appropriate for me to have paid somewhat more attention to the concrete conditions of Watsuji's way of thinking here, and disentangled the phenomenology of Watsuji's *fūdoron* from the Diltheyean thrust of his hermeneutic "study of the human" (人間の学). This, in turn, would have enabled me to more effectively locate the source of the determinism in Watsuji's theory of *fūdo*. This seems to me to be a valid point. A clearer and more readily identifiable contrast between the phenomenological approach taken in 風土：人間学的考察 and Watsuji's self-proclaimed hermeneutics of human existence as this is set out in 人間の学としての倫理学 would probably have allowed me to more effectively make two points which may not have come across as clearly as I would have liked.

The first point is that my account of Watsuji's construal of transcendence in terms of a certain form of freedom was meant to show how important elements in Watsuji's own thinking work against its deterministic tendencies. That is, I tried to show that on his reading of transcendence, nature has a history, and that this appears as the historicality (歴史性) of *fūdo*— historicality understood as *Geschichtlichkeit* in Heidegger's sense (see, e.g., WTZ 8: 119–20). While Watsuji may have struggled to articulate a proper understanding of Heidegger's concept of transcendence, he appears to have had an implicit grasp of the ontological difference that is required for this understanding. For this reason, I felt justified in giving an ontological reading of his construal of the relationship between human existence and nature as it appears in and through the phenomenon of world. Perhaps I should have been more explicit about the fact that this understanding of the difference between being and beings is implicitly present, even if this difference is not something that Watsuji himself was always able to see. This, I maintain—and this is my second point—becomes evident upon close inspection of Watsuji's hermeneutic theory. I won't rehearse here the evidence I lay out in Chapter 7, noting only that it ranges from a consideration of Watsuji's ultimate intentions and aim in turning to a hermeneutic of human existence (158–9), to an overview of the overlaps and parallels between Heidegger's and Watsuji's conceptions of the ontological relationship between "having" and "being," one that forces a reconsideration of the true meaning and significance of the term *expression* (表現; see, e.g., WTZ 9: 176–7) as it is used in Watsuji's hermeneutics, to the implicitly disclosive character of linguistic, affective, and practical comportments as these are treated in Watsuji's work. What I did not say, but probably should have, is that as confused as Watsuji himself might have been, all of this goes to show that his hermeneutic procedure was far closer to a thinker such as Gadamer than to Dilthey, and so was an approach that can be reconciled—however unintentionally—with the phenomenological path Watsuji pursued in his theory of *fūdo*.

If this is so, one can ask: how then to account for the determinism that is widely acknowledged to be present throughout much of the text of *Fūdo*? Here I would appeal to the publication history of *Fūdo*. As I point out (41), there is evidence to suggest that Watsuji only realized the philosophical significance of existential spatiality for Heidegger's phenomenology sometime after his return to Japan, and even perhaps as late as 1933. This realization would have come after the body of the text from the second chapter forward—which was based on informal observations he made during his journey by sea from Japan to Europe in 1927, and which tends toward a kind of geographical determinism—was written. Nevertheless, it remains a mystery as to why Watsuji allowed these statements and claims to remain in the text if they were not reflective of his fully considered views or of his newfound appreciation of Heidegger.

The atmosphere of puzzlement begins to fade if we take seriously Mine's criticism of Watsuji's failure to establish the requisite self-critical and reflective distance in relation to his direct experience of the various geographical locales he visited. It is indeed true that Watsuji's personal experience of the geographical regions of the world which he described was not rooted in a lived understanding of these areas, but instead reflected the more superficial experience of a traveler passing through them. And while it is not disqualifying in itself that this was the hermeneutic situation that supported Watsuji's first-hand experience, what was required of him in this instance, as Mine points out, was a to-and-fro movement between his direct experience of other people and their geo-cultural milieu and the framework belonging to his own history and culture through which he interpreted this experience. Only this kind of alertness to the historical and cultural constraints of our own direct experience of what is alien can enable us to avoid a distorted interpretation of what we encounter. This problem demonstrates, too, that despite the overlap between Watsuji and Gadamer alluded to above, there is still an important distance and difference between their renditions of philosophical hermeneutics.

While Watsuji might be forgiven for not having read Gadamer, one wonders about the inexplicable failure later in his career to continue to engage more fully and deeply with Heidegger's work, since Heidegger's own philosophy at this time was developing apace. Much of my own book was intended to show what a Heideggerean philosophy of *fūdo* might offer us had he done so. Prof. Mine is to be thanked for showing us just how difficult that task actually is.

Hans Peter Liederbach

Disclosure without Normative Background?
David Johnson's Watsuji

Only when no longer knowing what's what in one's own domain, one turns to "the other" in search for advice. In this sense, the recently growing interest in non-Western, particularly Japanese philosophy bears witness to a feeling of disorientation among some philosophers in the West. This feeling harks back to the dissatisfactions with philosophical modernism, influentially articulated by Nietzsche and Heidegger. The suspicion that Western philosophy has reached an impasse motivates those philosophers to cast their eyes to the East in the hope to find solutions for problems the West has generated but is no longer capable of solving. Preparing the stage for "world philosophy" is the latest attempt in this strand of thought; changing the rules of the language game "philosophy" figures prominently on its agenda.[1]

I

With his book on Watsuji Tetsurō, David Johnson has given a brilliant example for engaging Japanese philosophy in a way that does not depend on a philosophical narrative of the alleged end of Western metaphysics. Johnson's take on "Japanese Philosophy in the Wake of Heidegger" (as the subtitle of the book reads) renders Watsuji's thought in strictly problem-oriented (*sachlich*) terms. Since Johnson restricts his juxtaposition of Heidegger's *Being and Time* and Watsuji's writings of the 1930s (mainly *Fūdo*, *Ningen no gaku toshite no rinrigaku*, and *Rinrigaku*) to a set of philosophical issues that came to the fore with Husserl, Heidegger, and Merleau-Ponty, his study is a creative adaption of John Maraldo's maxim to use Japanese philosophy as "a lens on Greco-European thought."[2] I call his adaption "creative," for he further develops Maraldo's maxim in that

1. Cf. *inter alia* DAVIS 2020. For a critical investigation cf. LIEDERBACH 2019.
2. MARALDO 2017, 21.

he provides a stereoscopic view on the problems under consideration. On one hand, Johnson's interpretation of Watsuji opens novel perspectives on issues that are conspicuously absent in *Being and Time*: nature, space, and body, which, on Johnson's view, are grounded in *fūdo*; on the other hand, the Heideggerian lens he applies on Watsuji puts into focus those aspects in *Being and Time* Watsuji had only insufficiently appreciated: particularly the phenomenological method. By exposing the phenomenological structure of how nature is disclosed as *fūdo*, Johnson further develops Watsuji's often "thin and imprecise"[3] descriptions, which, in turn, enables him to articulate the desiderata of *Being and Time*. It is its truly dialogical nature which sets Johnson's book apart from the majority of literature on Japanese philosophy; in short, his take on Japanese philosophy is non-oedipal.

It is, therefore, conclusive that Johnson's book goes beyond an account of Heidegger's effective history (*Wirkungsgeschichte*) in Japan.[4] When Watsuji in his rejoinder to Heidegger insisted on the significance concrete human spatiality as *fūdo-sei* has for a comprehensive account of being-in-the-world, he, as Johnson holds, ultimately pointed at the possibility of a "partial reenchantment of nature,"[5] which is part of a larger project of Johnson's, that is "overcoming subjectivism."[6] For making his claim, Johnson highlights the phenomenological implications of Watsuji's theory of *fūdo* which Watsuji himself only insufficiently had spelled out. Watsuji was, in fact, highly critical towards phenomenology, particularly in a Husserlian vein, which he found ill-suited for dealing with the structure of human existence, i.e. "betweenness" (*aidagara*).[7] Moreover, in that Johnson links the reenchant-

---

3. JOHNSON 2019, 104.
4. Pre-eminent in this regard is MINE 2002.
5. JOHNSON 2019, 49.
6. JOHNSON 2019, 192. In this paper, I will mainly focus on this wider aspect of Johnson's take on Watsuji; on the problem of reenchantment I will touch only in passing.
7. On Watsuji's view, Husserl shares with Descartes and Kant a certain kind of foundational subjectivism; moreover, as he holds, the danger of "letting the study of ethics fall victim to the study of subjective consciousness" has "to be admitted" also for phenomenological research in the line of Scheler and Heidegger; WTZ 10: 35–6; WATSUJI 1996, 33; translation altered; cf. WTZ 9: 140–2; see also WTZ 10: 72; WATSUJI 1996, 68: "Even in contemporary philosophy, whether it be phenomenology or fundamental ontology, the central question is, in the final analysis, the consciousness of ego"; translation altered. Similarly, in a paper on Theodor Lipps dating from 1935, Watsuji draws a line from "the Cartesian tradition" to the phenomenologi-

ment of nature to the "return to *Lebenswelt*" and the "reconciliation with the world,"[8] he considerably enlarges Watsuji's notion of *fūdo*, and at the same time contributes to further developing the problem of being-in-the-world as exposed in *Being and Time*. So the lens on Greco-European thought Johnson applies, goes well beyond the fulfilling of desiderata of both Heidegger and Watsuji; it provides the optic for a philosophical investigation in its own right. However, for all its productive novelty, in that Johnson accepts the interpretative framework that, since Tosaka Jun's critique of Watsuji's hermeneutical method,[9] has proven useful for making sense of Watsuji's theories of *ningen* and *fūdo* by contrasting them with *Being and Time*, he also accepts the limits inherent to this framework. As we shall see, going beyond these limits is vital for getting into sharper focus some of the long-standing problems in Watsuji's dialectical account of *ningen*, which, in turn, will allow us to fully appreciate Johnson's account of the conceptual possibilities of *fūdo*.

II

As is well known, Watsuji came across *Being and Time* during his sojourn in Berlin in 1927. This encounter was catalytic in that it provided the conceptual tools Watsuji needed for coming to grips with problems he had been engaged with prior to his departure to Germany, namely those of "Japanese culture" and "history of ethics."[10] That is, *Being and Time* allowed Watsuji to reframe these problems in their interrelatedness with the phenomenon of *fūdo*. In fact, after his return to Japan in 1929, Watsuji immediately began drafting "Notes on 'Investigation into National Character'"[11]

---

cal method of "departing from the phenomenon of the self"; WTZ 9: 392. While Watsuji uses a much too broad brush in his characterization of phenomenology, he has a point in that his notion of *aidagara* is non-foundational and therefore meant to designate a form of being-in-the-world that cannot be methodically reduced to any kind of individual consciousness or individual existence, including Heidegger's notion of *Dasein*. In contrast, Watsuji sets out to determine the possibility of any encounter with beings/entities as actualization of a hermeneutical activity within *aidagara*, he calls "formation" (*keisei*).

8. JOHNSON 2019, 209.
9. TOSAKA 1965, 299–308.
10. Cf. WTZ Bekkan 1, 369–70.
11. Cf. WTZ Bekkan 1, 378ff.

where he employed the conceptual framework of Division One of *Being and Time*, in particular the notions of "disposition" (Befindlichkeit), "involvement" (Bewandtnis), and "spatiality" (Räumlichkeit) for sketching out a theory of historical life forms in relation to their natural environment.[12] These notes form the initial stage of Watsuji's philosophical project that materialized in the Iwanami Kōza article *Rinrigaku* (1931), the books on *Ningen no gaku toshite no rinrigaku* (1934) and *Fūdo* (1935), and eventually his opus magnum, the three-volume *Rinrigaku* (1937–1949). In the light of the itinerary of Watsuji's thought, the strategy of reading Watsuji through a Heideggerian lens and thus putting *Rinrigaku* and *Fūdo* into the systematical framework laid out in *Being and Time*, suggests itself.

While, in the foreword of *Fūdo*, Watsuji emphatically expressed his appreciation for Heidegger's project, he was also explicit in maintaining that the description of *Dasein* was one-sided since it failed to account in full for the implications existential spatiality has for ethical life. Therefore, as Watsuji concludes, Heidegger had not been able to arrive at a notion of authentic being with others (Mitsein), which in turn was responsible for the lack of concreteness of his notion of historicity (Geschichtlichkeit).[13] While Watsuji can be given credit for having anticipated an objection that was introduced to Heidegger scholarship by Villela-Petit more than half a century after *Fūdo*, namely that, in *Being and Time*, Heidegger had not recognized the problem of spatiality of Being-with,[14] his own notion of *ningen* is far from being unproblematic. There are good reasons to believe that Watsuji's notion of *ningen* is dangerously one-sided—not only, as has been often pointed out, with regard to its political implications.[15] As has been indicated, Watsuji's notion of authenticity (Eigentlichkeit) bears witness to his limited understanding of the ontic-ontological difference, without which the exposition of this notion wouldn't have been possible in the first place.[16] Along these lines, it has been maintained that the way the problem

12. Cf. WTZ Bekkan 1, 378.
13. Cf. WTZ 10: 183; 233; WATSUJI 1996, 173–4; 219–20.
14. VILLELA-PETIT 1996, 142.
15. Arguably the most comprehensive and judicious account of the political implications of Watsuji's ethical thought so far is to be found in MARALDO 2019, 78–96.
16. Cf. MINE 2002, 97.

of death is dealt with in *Rinrigaku* misses the mark,[17] as does Watsuji's treatment of the I-Thou-relation.[18] On this view, Watsuji's insufficient acknowledgement of the possible negation of *ningen*'s totality-aspect results from his poor understanding of Heidegger's fundamental ontology. The dialectic of absolute negation, so the story goes, was burdened with that mishap from the very start. While it was meant to reveal absolute negativity as the ontological grounds for a notion of human existence that would be free from any Cartesian residue, the dialectic lacked a standpoint of transcendence that would account for its absoluteness. Therefore, in Watsuji's treatment, the dual structure of *ningen* appears as a constant, iridescent movement between *ningen*'s ontological and ontic dimensions, which, ultimately, is responsible for the excessive emphasis Watsuji put on the totality-aspect at the cost of the aspect of individuality. From the one-sidedness of the dialectic follows the one-sidedness of the notion of *ningen*. Therefore, from the point of view adopted by those who sympathize with Heidegger's overall approach but, at the same time, are aware of the problematic implications that surface in Division Two of *Being and Time*, fixing the one-sidedness of *ningen* means abandoning Watsuji's dialectical thinking in favor of a notion of transcendence similar to the one which had been introduced in Division Two, while avoiding Heidegger's existentialist rigorism. There is a curious dialectical twist to this reading, since for appreciating Watsuji's critique of *Being and Time*, his dialectic of *aidagara* has first to be sent to the purgatory of Heideggerian transcendentalism.

In that applying an Heideggerian lens on *Rinrigaku* proved useful to uncover certain shortcomings in Watsuji's ethical thinking, it prepared the ground for appealing to *Fūdo* as some last resort for making good of Watsuji's objections to the notion of *Dasein*.[19] In this optic, with the phenomenon of *fūdo* figuring as the place of transcendence Watsuji would need to bring home his point about the dual nature of the notion of *ningen*. However, this solution comes at a price, that is the abandoning of the dialectical interconnectedness of individuality and totality and, ultimately, the dynamism Watsuji thought to be the centerpiece of the structure of *ningen*,

---

17. Cf. YUASA 1995, 352.
18. Cf. FURUSHŌ 2006.
19. Cf. MINE 2002, 112–7; LIEDERBACH 2001, 181–4.

which he, after all, characterized as "practical subject" (*shutai*). While, on the basis of an Heideggerian reading of Watsuji's ethical thought, the move from *Rinrigaku* to *Fūdo* could be justified with respect to the problem of transcendence, the fact that, thereby, the issues of human agency and its implicit normativity are getting out of focus cannot go unnoticed.

In any case, from a hermeneutical point of view it is perfectly legitimate to read *Rinrigaku* as Watsuji's confrontation (*Auseinandersetzung*) with Heidegger. Watsuji, so it can be argued, is taking part in a genuine philosophical dialogue with Heidegger, and if we take the notion of dialogue seriously, in order to raise those critical objections with regard to Watsuji's notions of *ningen* and *honraisei*, the Heideggerian lens is indispensable. However, from the point of view of the *Sache* (subject-matter) both are investigating, the situation is more complex. Instead of assuming that Heidegger's existential ontology of being-in-the-World has to be the blueprint for addressing Watsuji's shortcomings on this plane, it might be worthwhile contemplating whether Heidegger's enterprise did not fail in a way that makes *Being and Time* a not so convincing candidate for amending the problematic aspects of *Rinrigaku*. This is not to say that, since what Watsuji pursues is an ethics and not a fundamental ontology, *Rinrigaku* ought to be decoupled from the fundamental issues underlying the project of *Being and Time*, first and foremost the problems of authenticity and existential wholeness. My point is rather that, to further develop the dialogue between Watsuji and Heidegger, the particular interpretation of *Being and Time* that, for so long, has informed the critical objections against *Rinrigaku* has to be revised. It can be doubted that, by pitting the radical transcendence of death and the "metaphysical ego-ness" (*metaphysische Egoität*) against the immanentism of Watsuji's account of authenticity,[20] the deeper connections between Watsuji and Heidegger can be brought into relief. The reason for being skeptical in this regard lies in Heidegger's failure to account for the normativity inherent in any inner-worldly practice of *Dasein*, its being and acting both individually and commonly within a network of involvements and purposes[21]—a failure that can be traced back to the explications

---

20. Cf. MINE 2002, 96–9; HGA 26, 240 sqq.

21. This point has been made by PIPPIN 1997. I have drawn from Pippin's account to discuss the relationship between Watsuji and Heidegger with regard to the normativity-issue in LIE-

in Division Two of *Being and Time*. In that Johnson mainly operates with the phenomenological toolkit laid out in Division One of *Being and Time*, his reading of *Fūdo* has opened a novel perspective on this dialogue and its significance for today's philosophizing. However, in that he sidelines the problems of authenticity and existential wholeness, Johnson has trouble to articulate with sufficient clarity the normativity issue which, nevertheless, surfaces at crucial stations of his argument.

III

While the problem of normativity hardly surfaces in *Being and Time*,[22] it figures prominently in *Rinrigaku*. After Watsuji has laid out the basic structure of the dialectic of dual negation, he explicates the normative implications of this structure as follows: "When the basic principle of ethical life (*jinrin*) is grasped in this way [i.e. dialectically / HPL], it also becomes clear that the basic issues of ethics (*rinrigaku*), such as conscience, freedom, good and evil, and so on are all included in this principle."[23] To grasp the basic principle of ethical life is to clarify the dialectical structure of *ningen*, and since this principle is nothing else than the authentic realization of the dialectically mediated interconnectedness of *ningen*, the normativity of ethical life as comprised in "the basic issues of ethics" is tied to the ontological structure of *ningen* itself. Says Watsuji: "The fundamental law of human existence is the movement of the negation of absolute negativity" and "this movement, understood as human *action*, signifies the sublation of individuality, the realization of ethical (*jinrin-teki*) unity, and the return to one's own foundation."[24]

While Watsuji's descriptions are overly schematic and abstract, it is evident that, for him, the "return to one's own foundation" is not so much

---

DERBACH 2020. Johnson's book has done much to further clarify what is involved here.

22. However, as Pippin points out, terms like "Freigabe für" or "Bewendenlassen" hint at the problem of the possible normative justifiability of *Daseins*'s "letting beings involved" or "freeing something for its involvements," respectively; cf. PIPPIN 1997, 381–2. On this basis, the issue of "authenticity" in contrast to "falling" can be recasted with regard to its normative implications; cf. PIPPIN 1997, 383–7.

23. WTZ 10: 27; WATSUJI 1996, 23; translation altered.

24. WTZ 10: 140–1; WATSUJI 1996, 133–4; translation altered.

an ontological necessity (as it might seem if the dialectical movement were reduced to only represent *ningen*'s fundamental principle) but rather depends on the continuous actualization of the structure of human existence by means of the dialectical movement of dual negation in concrete actions, which, in turn, leads to the formation of ethical unity.[25] For it is only when this movement "comes to a standstill"[26] that *ningen* "falls into an inauthentic mode of existence,"[27] while, on the other hand, maintaining the continuity of the movement means to realize authenticity by fully actualizing the ontological structure of *ningen sonzai*—all of which "is closely tied to the active and practical spheres of human beings"[28]: "An action counts as good because of its being directed to the return to its foundation."[29] Posed in this generality, this is a rather ambitious claim; trying to make good of it will lead us to the very heart of the normativity issue in *Rinrigaku* and *Fūdo*.

For now, to grasp the core of Watsuji's confrontation with Heidegger, however, it suffices to confirm that, according to Watsuji, Heidegger's notion of authenticity represents *Dasein*'s insistence on its subjective individuality; it stops short at the second aspect of *ningen*'s movement of dual negation, that is the return to totality. Put differently, on Watsuji's view, in *Dasein*'s forerunning resoluteness, the movement of dual negation has come to a standstill. Therefore: "What Heidegger calls *authenticity* is, in reality, inauthenticity."[30] That is to say, Heidegger has painted himself into the cor-

---

25. As Watsuji admits, the exposition of the basic principle of human existence alone does not suffice to account for the normative concreteness of ethical life. "Within the purview of this principle, however, these issues [i.e. conscience, freedom, good and evil] cannot yet come to be dealt with concretely, for attention is paid only to the double character of individuality and totality peculiar to *ningen*, and we have not yet embarked upon a study of the structure of a totality inclusive of numerous individuals"; WTZ 10: 27; WATSUJI 1996, 23. Ultimately, without clarifying the structure of *ningen*'s agency, the concept of totality remains abstract, and only on the basis of a concrete understanding of totality, the normativity issue can be dealt with appropriately.

26. WTZ 10: 142; WATSUJI 1996, 135.

27. WTZ 10: 143; WATSUJI 1996, 135; translation altered.

28. WTZ 10: 126; WATSUJI 1996, 120.

29. WTZ 10: 141; WATSUJI 1996, 134; translation altered.

30. WTZ 10: 237; WATSUJI 1996, 225. In fact, since authenticity in *Being and Time* represents a radical break not only with the everyday practices of "the They" (*das Man*), but with any involvement in the world, Watsuji has a point in insisting on the abstractness of that notion. That only in refraining from any involvement, authenticity should be realizable is indeed, as Watsuji

ner of fundamental-ontological individualism: While *Dasein*, by negating its involvements in everyday practices, can realize its authenticity, it cannot actualize it without immediately returning to the state of falling from which the movement of forerunning resoluteness was meant to break free. Succinctly put, from what Watsuji calls Heidegger's "individualistic" notion of authenticity necessarily follows the standstill of the dialectic movement of dual negation. And since Heidegger failed to grasp the dialectical structure of human existence, he was not prepared to give a normatively robust account of authenticity. In transcending the world in the attunement of anxiety and being-towards-death, *Dasein* is catapulted into a space that, since it is normatively void, cannot be connected to a specific place and a historical time. This is what Watsuji means when he claims that Heidegger's insistence on the superiority of temporality over spatiality prevented him not only from grasping the concrete totality of *Dasein*, but also from spelling out a concrete notion of historicity.[31] After *Being and Time*, this conceptual flaw led Heidegger to develop a notion of history that goes beyond the framework of fundamental ontology and terminates in the concept of "History of Being" (*Seinsgeschichte*). To be sure, Watsuji did not take notice of the philosophical development of Heidegger in the 1930s, also known as the *Kehre*. However, when he presses Heidegger on giving the spatiality of *Dasein* its proper place within the analytics of being-in-the-world, he is well aware of the limits of *Being and Time* on that plane. Therefore, with his account of *ningen*, Watsuji does not wish to balance a one-sidedness of fundamental ontology while maintaining its systematical framework. Since, in *Being and Time*, *Dasein* exists temporally and not historically,[32] and since the dialectical movement of *ningen*'s dual negation always concretizes itself in a norma-

---

holds, a "totally inverted viewpoint"; WTZ 10: 236; WATSUJI 1996, 225; translation altered. Recent interpretations of *Being and Time* are pressing Heidegger on this point and suggest a different determination of the relation between *Dasein*'s disclosing, its falling and resoluteness that would allow for a more concrete reading of authenticity; cf. FIGAL 2013, 131–3.

31. "As a result, his [i.e., Heidegger's] temporality fails to concretize itself in the form of historicity. Instead, it only plays the role of fundamentally grounding 'beings' as the object of an individual consciousness. That Heidegger's main theme was concerned with 'being and time', but not with *ningen sonzai* and time, reflects this from the very beginning." WTZ 10: 233; WATSUJI 1996, 220; translation altered.

32. Cf. FIGAL 1992, 101.

tively structured determinate history and place, his take on the problem of being-in-the-world points beyond the exposition of the ontological structure of *Dasein* in *Being and Time*.³³

Even without going any further into the details of Watsuji's confrontation with Heidegger on the issues of authenticity and totality, it is fair to say that what both are aiming at is to articulate the horizon that makes possible *Dasein*'s and *ningen*'s everyday practices. Although they differ in determining that horizon, the common problem they are trying to come to grips with is "the very possibility of intelligibility at all."³⁴ When Heidegger and Watsuji touch on ontological problems like that of being and nothingness, or emptiness (*kū*), respectively, they are aiming at determining the ultimate horizon for any possible sense-making of the world and how human agency is possible within this world. What Johnson's phenomenological reading of Watsuji deserves credit for is nothing less than having highlighted these problems as being indispensable for coming to grips with Watsuji's theory of *fūdo*.³⁵

IV

If one were to give a common denominator for characterizing Johnson's multifaceted interpretative approach to Watsuji, one would most likely choose his attempt to translate the structure of the ontological difference in *Being and Time* into Watsuji's account of *ningen sonzai*. This appears

---

33. Ultimately, Watsuji and Heidegger offer radically different possibilities for opening up a perspective on Being-in-the-world that articulates the difference between existence in its everydayness and its authentic mode. With regard to *Being and Time*, this is obvious, since *Dasein*'s fore-running resoluteness marks a break in the inevitable movement of falling. While Watsuji is not that explicit, he, too, determines *ningen*'s totality as "possibility" and concedes that "in its everydayness, human existence is not concerned with its authentic countenance (*honrai no menmoku*)"; WTZ 10: 196–7; WATSUJI 1996, 188; translation altered.

34. PIPPIN 2005, 59. Again, with regard to *Being and Time*, this is obvious, while pinning down Watsuji's take on this problem is more difficult. I will expand on this in the last section.

35. However, as I will try to show, carving out the intelligibility problem in *Fūdo* is possible only by taking into account the issues of wholeness and authenticity. Not that *Fūdo* is the last resort for making good of Watsuji's dialectical ethics; it is rather the other way round: Watsuji's theory of *fūdo* is truncated if the issues of human agency and its inherent normativity are sidestepped.

to be necessary for him to lead back Watsuji's notion of subjective spatiality to a realistic (in Johnson's parlance: "physical") notion of space that would figure as the key for not only solving the problem of how Watsuji's notoriously imprecise remarks about the unity in difference in *ningen*'s ontological structure (*jita-funi*; "self-other-not-two") are to be made sense of, but also, and more importantly, how a realistic notion of space undergirds any possible account of being-in-the-world and the intelligibility of entities. In this regard, Johnson obviously wishes to go beyond both Heidegger (who, in *Being and Time*, did not arrive at a notion of space at all) and Watsuji (whose notion of space remains by and large hermeneutical); this makes for much of the novelty of his interpretation. For getting an idea of how Johnson's translational approach plays itself out, we will have to look at some examples.

In his "attempt to reconstruct"[36] the dialectic of *ningen*, Johnson addresses the difference between "the metaphysical structure of non-dualism and the basic movement underlying human life"[37]—a move which is obviously inspired by a Buddhist reading of certain concepts in *Rinrigaku*, particularly the concept of *ningen* itself. Having instigated this differentiation, Johnson goes on to maintain "that Watsuji's confused and confusing attempt to identify the movement of the self between individuation and community with the metaphysical structure of the nondual whole of human existence *as such*"[38] leads to all kind of problems.

It is not clear at all in what respect Johnson calls the non-dual structure of *ningen* metaphysical, but it is evident that, for Watsuji, it is neither a pre-critical entity like, for instance, monads or Platonic ideas,[39] nor could it be a transcendental structure in a Kantian sense that would provide the condition of the possibility of human agency. After all, according to Watsuji's self-understanding, the method of *Rinrigaku* is hermeneutics, not transcendental philosophy. In fact, Watsuji himself never maintained that difference with the clarity expressed in Johnson's claim. Instead, he renders what he calls "the Absolute" as intelligible only in and through its actualization in a

36. JOHNSON 2019, 111.
37. JOHNSON 2019, 110.
38. JOHNSON 2019, 111.
39. Cf. WTZ 10: 125–6.

finite ethical totality, such as family, company, society, and the state.[40] Therefore, when he introduces the four areas of problems he wishes to address in *Rinrigaku*—(1) the dual structure of *ningen sonzai*, (2) the concrete analysis of this structure, (3) the problem of solidarity within ethical organizations, and (4) the climatic-historical structure of *ningen sonzai*[41]—Watsuji exposes them as interconnected in that they are to be investigated on the same level of analysis; no methodological shift can be observed throughout the first three chapters of *Rinrigaku* that make up volume ten of Watsuji's Collected Works.[42] Watsuji's critique of the absence of a notion of concrete historicity in *Being and Time* would be incomprehensible if he were to introduce an equally abstract concept of non-dualism to expound the notion of *ningen*. This would inevitably raise the question how out of that concept the historical concreteness of human existence would have to be derived. Rather, in the discussion of Nāgārjuna, which Johnson draws on,[43] Watsuji maintains that the problem of how out of a state of non-differentiation (*kū-mu-sabetsu*), difference (*fu-kū*, i.e. *sabetsu*) arises, could be discussed in a meaningful way only if one understands the principle of *kū* as activity of "emptying itself": "If one says that the essence of 'emptying' (*kūzuru*) means to realize itself in such an Other [i.e. *sabetsu* / HPL], then *kū* necessarily is nothing else but 'giv-

---

40. Cf. WTZ 10: 129–30; WATSUJI 1996, 123: "Without the formation of ethical (*jinrin-teki*) wholes, the movement of returning to the Absolute could not occur;" translation altered. Similarly, cf. WTZ 10: 126–7; WATSUJI 1996, 120: "Due to their negative structure, practical and active human beings are finite beings. The absoluteness of absolute negativity lies in its being in accordance with this finitude." These remarks surely are not suitable to give evidence to an "effort" on Watsuji's side "to directly correlate the processes of individuation and communion with the multiplicity of the one, that is with the nondual totality;" JOHNSON 1996, 111.

41. Cf. WTZ 10: 26–30; WATSUJI 1996, 22–6.

42. If the above-mentioned list were to substantiate Johnson's claim, I suggest that (1) and (2) would equal the "metaphysical structure of non-dualism," whereas (3) and (4) would cover the "basic movement underlying human life." However, Watsuji neither discriminates ontologically between these four areas, nor does he discuss them as relative to some higher level of investigation. To be sure, there is a different level of analysis involved, but only as an extension of problem (4), which leads to the issue of "national morality discourse" (*kokumin dōtoku ron*). Watsuji expounds on this as follows: "This topic has two aspects: as the study of principles and of history.... These two must not be confounded. Still, even the study of principle cannot be completely separated from the problem of history;" WTZ 10: 30; WATSUJI 1996, 26. While this last remark is meant to characterize the proper approach to the topic of national morality, it accurately depicts also the nature of inquiry into problems (1) to (4). More on this below.

43. Cf. JOHNSON 2019, 115–16.

ing birth to difference."[44] The intricacies of Buddhist ontological discourse aside, this view is reflected in *Rinrigaku*. As we have seen, Watsuji claims that the "fundamental law of human existence" (that is, the return to absolute totality via the movement of dual negation) reveals itself and is realized only in and through the "context of common practices" (実践的行為的連関). However, the practices of *ningen* can never become identical with absolute totality, since the latter only provides the direction in which the practical movement of *ningen* has to be carried out. In this respect, says Watsuji, is the "self-return of the absolute… the direction of its infinite realization."[45]

If my understanding of Johnson is correct, by differentiating between metaphysical principle and concrete practical movement he sets the stage for applying Heidegger's notion of ontological difference to the systematic framework of *Rinrigaku*.[46] The problem raised by introducing that differentiation is how to phenomenologically describe *ningen*'s constant movement of individuation and return to the whole, and Johnson seeks to solve it by further differentiating four phenomenologically distinct layers of subjective space which, in their totality, are contained in the "world space."

These sketchy remarks can impossibly do justice to the hermeneutical boldness and phenomenological richness of Johnson's reconstruction. However, for the purpose of this paper, it is more important to note that Johnson, despite his careful reading of Watsuji's texts, never loses sight of his own philosophical project, that is the overcoming of subjectivism. It is for this reason that he claims that Watsuji, since his concept of subjective space owes much to the notion of spatiality in *Being and Time*, "runs squarely into a problem that Heidegger's account generates but never resolves."[47] Like Heidegger, Watsuji "has difficulty in unambiguously incorporating the spatiality of containment into his overall account of subjective space."[48] Only a realistic notion of space, as I read Johnson, "can function as a receptacle

---

44. WTZ 9: 475.
45. WTZ 10: 127; WATSUJI 1996, 121; translation altered.
46. Strictly speaking, this differentiation is already prepared in Johnson's suggestion to distinguish two different meanings of *aidagara*: (1) "relational contact" and (2) "direct interactional exchange;" JOHNSON 2019, 85. For him, (1) is more foundational than (2), since it is tied to the realistic notion of space I will refer to in the following.
47. JOHNSON 2019, 127.
48. JOHNSON 2019, 129.

within which we find both ourselves and the assemblages of equipment that help to compose the internal structure of the world. This space, in turn, must be rooted in a particular kind of location or place it is to be capable of surrounding and containing human beings and the objects produced by them in this way. It is this dimension of space that Watsuji appears to suppress in his account of the hierarchy of forms of space."[49]

Johnson's point is that the dialectical movement of separation and unification can take place only within a space that separates and at the same time connects a multitude of individuals. Watsuji addresses this problem under the heading of "subjective spatiality." Since this is to signify a symbolically charged space of shared meaning and understanding, it provides the hermeneutical underpinning for the dialectical movement to materialize in concrete, normatively informed actions. In that Johnson reduces this movement to a realistic notion of space, his inquiry is, *sensu stricto*, no longer a reconstruction of Watsuji's intentions. That is, Johnson' s introduction of the notion of world space leads him to a reading of *ningen*'s practices, its involvement with entities and with others that is normatively void; he reduces Watsuji' s hermeneutically complex analysis of common practices, how they are mutually understood, and more importantly, Watsuji' s rather unusual claim that *ningen* "has" the entities it deals with (including herself), to the phenomenon of "disclosure." It is at this stage of the inquiry that the truly challenging part of Johnson's endeavor is brought front and center.

V

Making explicit the connection between dialectic and normativity in *Rinrigaku* has revealed that, according to Watsuji, in her everyday practices, *ningen* can get it right or not. Not any attempt to actualize the structure of dual negation will do; *aidagara* can, in fact, fail. To stress this point, Watsuji seems to have felt the need to borrow from Heidegger the notion of authenticity. It can be doubted that, with this move, he did himself a service; it can be asked whether relying on Heidegger didn't force him to expound an ethical ideal that is difficult (if not impossible) to substantiate in *ningen*'s everyday practices. It is, therefore, not surprising that Watsuji

49. JOHNSON 2019, 128–9.

failed to show how the formal account of authenticity is linked to a normatively determined horizon of common practices within a specific place and time, i.e. a concrete context of common practices. However, there are, in fact, good reasons to argue that, for the sake of argumentative consistency in *Rinrigaku,* the formation of *aidagara* cannot but be guided by some normative yardstick; otherwise Watsuji's discussion of authenticity and the possible wholeness of *ningen* would become obsolete. The question Watsuji doesn't develop himself but which, nevertheless, makes itself unmistakably heard, is this: "How is *aidagara* brought into existence so that the normative orientation the dialectical movement of dual negation received from the fundamental law of *ningen sonzai* can be translated into a historically and climatically concrete context of common practices?"

Johnson repeatedly claims (and rightly so) that Watsuji's explications often lack conceptual precision. This is also true for his account of the inherent normativity of *aidagara*; therefore, it needs to be unpacked. However, in that Johnson heavily stresses the bodily aspect of *ningen sonzai* and its spatial containment, he absents himself from attending to this task. This is particularly obvious in his reading of what Watsuji treats as "expressions" (*hyōgen*) of *ningen sonzai*. By carrying out a shrewd deconstruction of Watsuji's usage of this term, Johnson aims at reducing what I would call Watsuji's hermeneutical space of meaning and understanding to a space of atmospheres and affordances. For this purpose, he (again) introduces a differentiation that Watsuji himself did not make, but which, from Johnson's phenomenological point of view, suggests itself.

Drawing on a linguistic ambiguity of the term *ningen sonzai* which could be translated as both "human being" and "human existence," Johnson distinguishes two kinds of expressive function of inner-worldly entities, particularly artifacts and tools; according to him, they express (1) "their practical significance" for human existence, or (2) "the self-externalization of human beings [that is] forms of *aidagara*."[50] While for Watsuji the crucial point about expressions is that they are understood by *ningen* within a context of shared meaning, and therefore provide a methodological access to the hermeneutical space of *ningen sonzai*, Johnson maintains that expressions allow also for opening up a space of affordances that is disclosed prior to

50. JOHNSON 2019, 135–6.

any hermeneutical act of interpretation on the side of *ningen*. That is to say, on Johnson's view, *ningen* (her actions and her mood) is determined by the atmospheres generated by the artifacts and tools that are part of the world space, and we understand the practical significance of these entities "in terms of what [they] afford and do not afford."[51]

While all this is coherent in a phenomenological sense, it leaves open how the issue of normativity, which is, as we saw, central to Watsuji's project, can be accommodated within this account. To be sure, Johnson's distinction of "the social, artifactual, and natural dimensions"[52] of space is illuminating in that it helps to structure the different fields in which entities are understood. However, in that he situates understanding within "the physical spatiality of containment,"[53] the question of how an understanding of entities is shaped by the normative demands that pervade *aidagara* gets out of focus. That, for Watsuji, there are such demands is beyond doubt. His constant reference to the forms (*kata*), "ways" (*shikata*) and "manners" (*sahō*) that determine *ningen*'s involvements with entities and others points in this direction. Therefore, I would qualify the interpretation Johnson applies to Watsuji's example of waking up and having breakfast in a family home. The fact that this situation requires other forms of comportment than, for example, waking up and having breakfast in an inn or a boardinghouse,[54] has nothing to do with the dining room's furniture or the flavor of the food Johnson puts emphasis on, but with the normative horizon, the understanding of which goes along with living in these different kinds of dwellings. What is at issue here is first and foremost an understanding of these normative horizons, and not so much "a shared palate and a communal set of preferences;"[55] and even these are accompanied by "manners of eating"[56] which point at the emphasis Watsuji puts on the normative claims that are pervading the various kinds of comportment within *aidagara*, and which, in the example under consideration, also determine the "exchange of words and gestures within a family"[57]

51. JOHNSON 2019, 139.
52. JOHNSON 2019, 130.
53. Ibid.
54. Cf. WTZ 9, 163, where Watsuji explicitly draws these comparisons.
55. Johnson, 137.
56. WTZ 9, 164.
57. Ibid.

during breakfast. So, what is communal here is, of course, a shared palate and other common culinary preferences—Johnson gets this point perfectly right. But what escapes his attention is the fact that these commonalities can only be actualized and understood within a normatively determined horizon of a shared understanding of what kind of comportment is required by a specific context, be it boardinghouse or family home. It can be doubted whether Harold Garfinkel's subjects did really enjoy their breakfast.[58]

So, waking up and having breakfast can go wrong. And getting it right is different from merely being solicited by affordances. If a wife serves her husband who is holding out to her his rice bowl in his usual demanding way, she is responding to what the rice bowl affords to her in a material sense; and yet, for her getting it right depends on whether she serves her husband with the appropriate *sahō*, that is a norm of comportment which is part of the shared understanding in a typical Japanese family of the early Shōwa period. Serving him, for instance, in a careless or defiant manner would constitute a violation of that norm. There is, in fact, a wide range of possible modifications inherent to any comportment or action within *aidagara* that stretches beyond what can be explained by referring to affordances or atmospheres. Getting it right implies an awareness for these possibilities. Therefore, I would hold with Watsuji that also artifacts like rice bowls give expression to *ningen sonzai* in both senses, and that actions and comportments within *aidagara* virtually "contain a limitless amount of understanding."[59] This is not to deny the importance of atmospheres created by artifacts and spaces for a comprehensive description of *ningen sonzai*, and Johnson deserves credit not only for making this explicit but also for disclosing the descriptive potential hidden in Watsuji's texts. The problem is how to get from atmosphere to normativity. The fact that, in Johnson's account, the question of how to differentiate between success and failure of such everyday comportments and actions does not surface, affects also his reading of Watsuji's characterization of *ningen*'s relation to entities in terms of "having" them.

---

58. Cf. GARFINKEL 1967. In one of Garfinkel's ethnomethodological experiments, students who were living with their parents had to comport themselves as if they were living in a boarding house. The result was a total breakdown of the mutual understanding between the family members.

59. WTZ 9, 142.

VI

In a truly masterful interpretative tour de force, Johnson unearths behind Watsuji's claim that entities are because *ningen* "has" them the structure of disclosure. One cannot but admire the philosophical rigor of Johnson's "speculative reconstruction,"[60] which sets out to transfer Heidegger's notion of "clearance" (*Lichtung*) into Watsuji theory of *ningen*, and I am perfectly comfortable with his contention that "the larger philosophical point that Watsuji wishes to establish amounts to a claim about the human capacity to disclose the world."[61] However, everything depends upon how "disclosure" is to be interpreted in the context of Watsuji's theory of *ningen*, and it is in this regard I wish to add some clarifications.

Similar to Heidegger, Johnson maintains that the clearance is the site of *ningen*'s disclosure of the world; and like Heidegger, he avoids the question of how the clearance is held open, which would be essential if *ningen* were to go on with her common practices of disclosing entities. Translated into Watsuji's parlance, the continuous movement of dual negation within a context of common practices would have to depend on a shared understanding of the normative horizon that is carrying *ningen*'s common disclosure of entities. For Watsuji, only within such a horizon can entities be disclosed. Hence, he is unambiguous in maintaining that there is no entity *ningen* can encounter that does not belong to the structure of *aidagara* and, therefore, depend on the fundamental law of human existence:

> Such things as the historical world, the natural world, and logic can all be discovered (*mi-idasaruru*) in human existence.... The subjective human existence is the basis on which all objective beings are brought into existence (*nari-tatashimeru*). If so, then we have to say that what obviously follows from this is that the historical world, the natural world, and so forth, all take in their respective and specific ways the fundamental law of human beings as their fundamental principle.[62]

This is arguably the most comprehensive of Watsuji's various claims about

60. JOHNSON 2019, 170.
61. JOHNSON 2019, 163.
62. WTZ 10: 125–6; WATSUJI 1996, 119; translation altered. Needless to say that, with these remarks, Watsuji does not espouse subjective idealism or some Neo-platonic theory of entities emanating from a supreme, metaphysical principle; cf. WTZ 10: 126.

ningen's "having" of entities in that here, the discovering of entities is tied to the normatively determined structure of *ningen sonzai*. This is to say that, for Watsuji, the discovery of entities is something that, similar to comportments and acts in a specific *aidagara*, can fail. Now, Watsuji does not elaborate on the conditions for success or failure in this regard, but when he claims that not only entities but whole worlds (history, nature, logic) are brought into existence by *ningen*'s subjectivity, he seems to espouse the view that the conditions for any intelligibility of entities in general depends on some kind of sense-making activity.

Therefore, Johnson is right in maintaining that "the objectivity of objects is always contaminated with (and made possible by) the subjectivities of subjects."[63] But what he has offered here with one hand, he takes back with the other when he adds that "an entity is what it is because we are 'there' for and present to it; we have it in or it enters to our awareness.… This openness to being is an openness that we *are* rather than one that we *have*."[64] It seems as if Johnson holds (with Heidegger, from whom he quotes) that, within the context of Watsuji's comprehensive claim, the objectivity of objects is something that simply "occurs" or "happens." Similar to the case of affordances, Johnson wishes to reduce *ningen*'s sense-making activity to something more fundamental, in this context: "disclosure." And the question which arises now is how to get from disclosure to the formation of normative horizons. These remarks hardly suffice for coming to grips with what is at stake here; even giving an in-depth interpretation of Watsuji's claim and how it connects with Johnson's contention about *ningen*'s disclosure is beyond the scope of this paper.

Therefore, my claim that Watsuji touches on a fundamental layer of *ningen*'s sense-making practices in that he maintains that the way in which *ningen* discloses entities is normatively structured by virtue of "*ningen sonzai*'s constant creation,"[65] must remain undefended. However, in turning to *Fūdo*, I will try, at least provisionally, to corroborate my claim.

63. JOHNSON 2019, 161.
64. Cf. JOHNSON 2019, 161. Immediately after having made this claim, he refers to Heidegger.
65. WTZ 10: 126; WATSUJI 1996, 120; translation altered.

VII

"Is" *ningen* its openness or does *ningen* "have" it? Breaking down the normativity issue in Watsuji ultimately leads us to this very question. While it is not clear how, on the basis of a notion of *ningen* being its openness, the normative demands that are pervading *aidagara* can be thematized, Watsuji's claim about *ningen* having its openness, although lacking conceptual underpinning, allows for addressing this problem.

All the same, the problem of normativity in Watsuji cannot be avoided; even Johnson concedes that *ningen*'s "shared understanding… or the lack of one, is determined largely on the basis of a shared background of values, ideas, and norms."[66] Now the philosophical interesting question is how these values, ideas, and norms come into being, how they are established, actualized, acknowledged, justified, transformed, and so forth. Johnson gets very close to this question, when he discusses the issue of "dialectic of freedom and determination"[67] in Watsuji. His remark deserves to be given in full:

> While the past, based in *fūdo* and carried into the present in the form of tradition, is experienced as determinative for us, we are able to transcend this determination to some extent, not by leaving behind our culture of *fūdo*—since these are part of the very setting that makes possible human life and activity—but through the production of new equipment and artifacts and the creation of new ways of thinking, and so of speaking, acting, and feeling, all of which, in turn, open up nature in novel ways and thus also furnish new modes of self-understanding.[68]

I am in full agreement with the overall thrust of Johnson's contention, but I also wish to ask for an explanation of why and how all this production and creation, which, by borrowing from Watsuji, can be summarized as "development" of *aidagara* and its expressions,[69] is carried out in the first place. Why not simply stick to one's tradition? As Watsuji maintains, "*aidagara* as such moves forward into the future," and, thereby, "forms of how communities are shaped, forms of consciousness, and, hence, ways

---

66. Johnson 2019, 131.
67. Johnson 2019, 188.
68. Johnson 2019, 189.
69. Cf. WTZ 10: 38.

of creating language, furthermore, forms of production, ways of building houses, and so forth"[70] are developed. Bringing into being these kinds of entities depends on "our own freedom" as well as on "phenomena of *fūdo*," while at the same time, "we have appropriated the understanding that has been accumulated since the times of our ancestors,"[71] which accounts for the "climatic load"[72] *ningen* has to carry. That is, the freedom of bringing into being various entities, which, as expressions, function as the horizon for *ningen*'s self-understanding, depends on the interconnectedness of *fūdo* and history/tradition. Says Watsuji: "We saw ourselves in *fūdo*, and, in this self-understanding, we turned towards our own free self-formation."[73] In my rendering, *ningen* does not simply "encounter" her free self-formation, as Johnson translates this passage,[74] but purposefully attends to it. In other words, against the backdrop of Watsuji's comprehensive claim above, the formation (*keisei*) of *aidagara* (like the discovery of entities) is a normative enterprise; it, therefore, can fail. Moreover, this normative enterprise has a historical dimension. Therefore, to get it right, a normative yardstick beyond the sense-making activities mentioned so far is indispensable. Neither in *Rinrigaku* nor in *Fūdo* does Watsuji provide any suggestion of how to render this problem, although it makes itself heard. Only in volume three of *Rinrigaku*, where he ties the development of *aidagara* to a progressive history of human freedom, Watsuji offers a solution to this problem.[75]

VIII

To bring this review to a close: With his inquiry into the significance the phenomena of subjective spatiality, physical space, and natural

70. WTZ 8: 18.
71. Ibid.
72. WTZ 8: 20.
73. WTZ 8: 12.
74. JOHNSON 2019, 187. Besides the context of this sentence, it is the past tense of the verb *mukatta* that indicates that it is meant to clarify the sentence before, which ends, also in past tense, on the verb *tsukuri-dashita*, "created," "produced." So, in my reading, Watsuji writes in retrospect that, when *ningen* created those entities, she saw herself in *fūdo* and turned towards / attended to her own free self-formation.
75. Cf. WTZ 11, 59–67.

place have for Watsuji's concept of *ningen*, David Johnson has pushed the established interpretative paradigm "Watsuji and Heidegger" to its limits. Moreover, in doing so, he has also helped to bring into sharper relief the problems this paradigm has generated but cannot solve. Particularly the issue of normativity in Watsuji can be pursued only in going beyond the "Watsuji and Heidegger" paradigm. That is to say, overcoming subjectivism (understood as Cartesianism) not necessarily depends on a phenomenology in the line of Heidegger, Merleau-Ponty, and Dreyfus. By acknowledging the aspect of normatively determined formation in *ningen*'s self- and world-relation without relapsing into subjectivism, Watsuji has given us much to think about other, equally viable possibilities of anti-Cartesianism. What we can learn from Watsuji is that these possibilities do not exclude each other but overlap. There is, in fact, abundant textual evidence for both a phenomenological and dialectical reading of Watsuji. Johnson, by maintaining that *ningen* is the site for disclosure, has succeeded in carving out the phenomenological Watsuji, while, in my emphasis on *ningen*'s making intelligible what she encounters, insisted on taking into account the dialectical aspects of his thought. These two readings are no strict alternatives; they rather complement each other. Only a stereoscopic view that embraces both problems of space and normativity can do justice to Watsuji's ethical and *fūdoic* thought. Having opened our eyes for this stereoscopic view, is, in my light, Johnson's greatest achievement.

References

Abbreviations

HGA   Martin Heidegger Gesamtausgabe. Frankfurt am Main: Klostermann 1975-.
WTZ   『和辻哲郎全集』[Complete Works of Watsuji Tetsurō] (Tokyo: Iwanami Shoten, 1961).

Literature

DAVIS, Bret W.
    2020   "Introduction: What is Japanese Philosophy?" in Bret W. Davis, ed., *The Oxford Handbook of Japanese Philosophy* (New York: Oxford University Press), 1–79.

FIGAL, Günther
    2013   *Martin Heidegger: Phänomenologie der Freiheit*. Neuausgabe (Tübingen: Mohr Siebeck).

Furushō Masataka 古莊真敬]
 2006 「和辻哲郎、九鬼周造：〈他者〉との共同性をめぐって」[Watsuji Tetsurō, Kuki Shūzō: On Commonality with "the Other"] in 秋富克哉・安倍浩・古莊真敬・森一郎編『続・ハイデガー読本』(Tokyo: Hōsei Daigaku Shuppankyoku) 321–8.

Garfinkel, Harold
 1967 "Studies of the Routine Grounds of Everyday Activities," in: *Studies in Ethnomethodology* (Englewood Cliffs, New Jersey: Prentice-Hall).

Johnson, David W.
 2019 *Watsuji on Nature: Japanese Philosophy in the Wake of Heidegger*. (Evanston: Northwestern University).

Liederbach, Hans Peter
 2001 *Martin Heidegger im Denken Watsuji Tetsurōs: Ein japanischer Beitrag zur Philosophie der Lebenswelt* (München: Iudicium).
 2019 "Ex Oriente Lux? The Kyoto School and the Problem of Philosophical Modernism," *Tetsugaku* 3: 89–106.
 2020 「徹底的な有限性：ハイデガーと京都学派の哲学」[Radical finitude: Heidegger and the Philosophy of the Kyoto School], *Heidegger-Forum* 14: 82–100.

Maraldo, John C.
 2017 "Japanese Philosophy as a Lens on Greco-European Thought," in John C. Maraldo, *Japanese Philosophy in the Making 1: Crossing Paths with Nishida* (Nagoya: Chisokudō Publications), 21–56.
 2020 "The Perils of Watsuji's Ethics: An Attempt at Balanced Critique," in John C. Maraldo, *Japanese Philosophy in the Making 2: Borderline Interrogations* (Nagoya: Chisokudō Publications), 78–96.

Mine Hideki 嶺 秀樹
 2002 『ハイデッガーと日本の哲学』[Heidegger and Philosophy in Japan] (Kyoto: Mineruba Shobō).

Pippin, Robert B.
 1997 "On Being Anti-Cartesian: Hegel, Heidegger, Subjectivity, Sociality," in Robert B. Pippin, *Idealism as Modernism: Hegelian Variations* (Cambridge: Cambridge University Press), 375–94.
 2005 "Necessary Conditions for the Possibility of What Isn't: Heidegger on Failed Meaning," in Robert B. Pippin, *The Persistence of Subjectivity: On the Kantian Aftermath* (Cambridge: Cambridge University Press), 57–78.

Tosaka, Jun 戸坂 潤
 1965 『日本イデオロギー論』[Japanese Ideology], in 『戸坂潤全集』[Collected Works of Tosaka Jun] (Tokyo: Keisō Shobō), vol 2.

VILLELA-PETIT, Maria
    1996   "Heidegger's Conception of Space," in Christopher Macann, ed., *Critical Heidegger* (London/New York: Routledge), 134–57.

WATSUJI Tetsurō 和辻哲郎
    1996   *Watsuji Tetsuro's Rinrigaku: Ethics in Japan*, trans. by Seisaku Yamamoto and Robert E. Carter (Albany: SUNY Press).

YUASA Yasuo 湯浅泰雄
    1995   『和辻哲郎：近代日本哲学の運命』[Watsuji Tetsurō: The Fate of Modern Japanese Philosophy] (Tokyo: Chikuma Gakugei Bunkō).

David W. Johnson

Reply to Hans Peter Liederbach

Prof. Liederbach's rich and wide-ranging analysis offered much to reflect on and learn from. I note with special appreciation his observation that by juxtaposing Watsuji's work and Heidegger's, I furnish "a stereoscopic view of the problems under consideration" and provide "the optic for a philosophical investigation in its own right." In fact, one of my central aims in bringing these thinkers together was—to borrow a felicitous phrase from Tom Kasulis's description of his own approach to comparative studies—"to help us perceive a dimension that neither alone could fully access."[1]

There is unfortunately not space enough here to address all of the issues that were opened up by Liederbach's expert account of the relation between Watsuji's thought and *Being and Time*. I will instead focus my remarks on what appears to be the central matter in question, namely, that I leave unaddressed the issue of normativity in relation to *aidagara*. Although the normative center of gravity of my study was located in the task of recovering a reenchanted conception of nature through the concept of *fūdo*, it is also true that, as Liederbach observes, "Watsuji's theory of *fūdo* is truncated if the issues of human agency and its inherent normativity are sidestepped." This point shows the difficulty of giving a full account of *fūdo* without also providing an account of *aidagara*, and vice-versa. Indeed, this book as originally conceived proposed to examine in full both of these dimensions of what I called the "topological self." Such a project, however, turns out to be too substantial and unwieldly to be contained in a single volume.

Perhaps the first thing to be said about these issues is something that Prof. Leiderbach could not have known, namely, that rather than it being the case (as he puts it) that I overlooked or absented myself from attending to the task of presenting an account of the inherent normativity of *aidagara*, there was not sufficient space to do so due to restrictions the publisher placed on the length of the manuscript. It is now clear to me that I should have signaled more directly in the book itself what had been left aside for reasons of

---

1. Kasulis, *Engaging Japanese Philosophy*, 110.

space. And because this study was explicitly centered on the concept of *fūdo*, and since, as Liederbach acknowledges, Watsuji himself did not manage to address this problem in a substantive manner, my own forays into the question of the normative dimensions of *aidagara* remain just that, forays. But I note that this means that I did not ignore or overlook the problem of the normative aspects of being-in-relation *tout court*. For example, in Chapter 5, Sec. III "Between Individual and Communal: Oscillation and Dialectic" I explain why and in what sense the formation of *aidagara* must be understood "as nothing less than the unfolding and development of ethical life" and give a range of examples that show the sense in which "the social and individual poles that structure our existence are sites of moral danger as well as of moral self-realization." Liederbach does not comment on this section of the text, but it may be the case that this analysis is too brief. In this regard I am happy to have the opportunity to include here some of what was cut from the original manuscript, since I think these passages offer an example of one way of responding to the pressing question which Liederbach raises of how *aidagara* is "brought into existence" such that its "normative orientation, the dialectical movement of dual negation" "can be translated into a historically and climactically concrete context of common practices." Just before Sec. III, the excised passages read:

> We need not only speak and act with others "as" a strict mother, or genial uncle, or concerned teacher—we can also adverbially modify our actions in ways that are not directly linked to our social roles, and conduct ourselves in a fashion which expresses a specific manner of existence.
>
> One of the most sensitive and acute accounts of the way in which this dimension of the self emerges from our styles of interaction can be found in the work of Michael Oakeshott. I want to briefly consider Oakeshott's view of the self in order to augment Watsuji's pivotal—but underdeveloped— claim that one becomes an individual in relation to others. The self for Oakeshott is best understood—just as it is for Watsuji—as an activity rather than as a substance or thing.[2] The self is never in a state of rest or passivity out of which, to use Oakeshott's examples, activities such as perceiving, feeling, desiring, thinking, laughing, crying, dancing, and so on, emerge. We are active from the moment we are born, since not to be active is not to be alive.

---

2. See Michael Oakeshott, *Rationalism in Politics and Other Essays*, Timothy Fuller, ed. (Indianapolis: Liberty Fund, 1991), 496.

Oakeshott maintains that activity is constitutive of the self insofar as the self discloses itself through goal-oriented action and through transactions with other selves. Such self-disclosure brings an identity into existence, but this identity lacks a substantial core or essence: an agent "has a 'history', but no 'nature', he is what in conduct he becomes."[3]

If action is the source of the self, it is also the source of much of the contingency and frustration in human life. Our actions in relation to other selves are subject to what they think and do and as such can be thwarted or foiled by them. Further, even if an actor were to achieve his or her desired aim, this creates circumstances with new problems and needs which will in due course necessitate another response, so that every achievement is at the same time a frustration. The desiring self that inhabits this world is caught up in an endless round of satisfying wants and needs, so that from this standpoint, human activity can come to seem futile.

While the self viewed as a collection of actions directed towards particular goals is subject to frustration, failure and defeat, self-disclosure is only one aspect of the self. The self consists not only of those actions related to the ends that we seek to accomplish in doing what we do, it can also be seen in terms of *how* we do what we do. This is "an agent's sentiment in choosing and performing the actions he chooses and performs."[4] Agents or actors are able to qualify their actions adverbially, to do this or that in a particular manner. An agent may perform the same act in a different sentiment: "grudgingly, charitably, maliciously, obligingly, magnanimously, piously, spitefully, gratefully, avariciously."[5] The sentiments or adverbial modifications with which Oakeshott is concerned above all are those that enhance the quality of an action in a non-instrumental way. These sentiments are chosen based on who we understand ourselves to be, as well as who we are trying to become. Insofar as through these choices we cultivate specific virtues and motives in aspiring to become a particular sort of person, we enact ourselves as we wish to be and acquire a distinctive self.

This aspect of the self, moreover, is more fully sheltered from contingency than self-disclosure. Self-enactment does not seek or depend on the responses of others. Nor does the value and integrity of the self from this point of view come from the successful or unsuccessful consequences of choices. Oakeshott illustrates this point with the example of a battle. Even

---

3. Michael Oakeshott, *On Human Conduct* (Oxford: Oxford University Press, 2003), 41.
4. Ibid., 71.
5. Ibid., 72.

when a battle is lost, the loyalty and fortitude of the actors is an achievement that cannot be defeated in the same way. This thought, too, lies behind his observation that "Cervantes created a character in whom the disaster of each encounter with the world was powerless to impugn it as a self-enactment."[6]

Like other philosophers in the twentieth century, Oakeshott worried about the triumph in our era of utility as the master value by which to measure all others. He was especially concerned with the way in which the pragmatic standpoint reduced all meaningful and worthwhile action to instrumental action, so that the significance and value of our activities depends on outcomes such as the satisfaction of our desires and the achievement of our purposes. Since for this view the value and meaning of what we undertake to do is fragile, fleeting, and finally elusive, this way of understanding human activity threatens to close off the possibility of a certain kind of autonomy and even of a certain kind of happiness. Oakeshott, who had a keen sense of the limits and risks of action, was alert to the danger. Like Aristotle, he took a tragic view of action and understood that the complexity, obscurity, and fragility of human action meant that suffering and failure are ever-present possibilities in the nature of action itself. Human finitude and human blindness mean that we can fail to see where our actions will finally lead, that we can be overwhelmed by the complexity of events, and that we are in important ways powerless in the face of contingent events and circumstances. And even where we manage in the face of all of this to attain our ends and so achieve something of value, the instrumental logic of getting and achieving tends to subvert what has been accomplished, since this attainment only results in a situation with new problems and conditions that will eventually call for a further response, leading to a never-ending pursuit of satisfactions.

Oakeshott hence ties the question of individuation to the problem of how to live in the face of the contingency and sense of futility that characterize large areas of human life and action. His view is that although neither the vulnerability of action nor what he calls the "deadliness" or endlessness of doing can ever be completely overcome—so that our basic situation is a predicament to be contended with and not a problem to be solved—this predicament can be abated, and even escaped to some extent, through a particular mode of self-fashioning. So that while for Oakeshott as for Watsuji, we disclose who we are and construct who we are becoming only in interactions with others, Oakeshott also wants to show that my transactions with others

---

6. Ibid., 241.

allow me to be a certain way for them not only in terms of what my social roles prescribe, but also in terms of *how* I do what I do with, for, or against them. Insofar as these adverbial modifications of actions and behavior express my singular way of being in speaking, walking, acting, and so forth, they amount to the enactment of a distinctive self.

Oakeshott's approach thus shows how a normative orientation can be established through an ideal of dialectical self-formation understood in terms of intrinsic value, and so in relation to a value that escapes the pragmatic assessments and instrumental logic that structures so much of contemporary life.

Liederbach also contends that I reduce Watsuji's hermeneutical space of meaning and understanding to a space of atmospheres and affordances. As a result, I focus too exclusively on the dimension of practical intelligibility at the expense of the normative aspects of our activity of sense-making. But I wonder if the claims about reductivism are not somewhat overstated. I describe and investigate Watsuji's hermeneutical space of meaning in ways that reach substantially beyond the phenomenon of practical intelligibility at various stages throughout the study, notably in Chapter 4, "The Relational Self: A New Conception" (esp. Sections I and III), Chapter 6, Sec. II "World Space and Social Tenor," and Chapter 7, Sec. V, "Shared Intentionality as Disclosive Comportment." These portions of the book are peppered with examples of the normative demands that pervade *aidagara* (and even of how an understanding of entities is shaped by such demands, as for instance in how a stage, kitchen, horse farm landscape, field, or seascape shows up is dependent on comportments that are inherently normative), so the complaint here must not be the lack of such descriptions, but something else.

If I have understood Liederbach correctly, this something else is that "the question of how to differentiate between success and failure of such everyday comportments and actions does not surface," as well as that "the philosophically interesting question is how these values, ideas, and norms come into being, how they are established, actualized, acknowledged, justified, transformed, and so forth." Each of these questions represent distinct and formidable philosophical problems in their own right; to even begin to address them would have required—at the very least—an additional chapter. Although it was not possible to include such a chapter for reasons of space, these kinds of issues were indeed on my mind; in another now excised section I began to explore the question of how social relations can be normatively grounded beyond the sheer fact of *our* having established this ground—which is where Watsuji leaves these questions (see, for example, WTZ 10: 246–8, 252, 254–6). And while Watsuji does not really provide an account of how the normative demands that pervade *aidagara* come to be "established, actualized, acknowledged," or address the problem of justifying norms (both their success conditions and their transformation), I indicated in Chapter 8 what a "realism" about values as properties and qualities in our lived experience of nature might look like in a way that comports well with Watsuji's own philosophical commitments. The now excised passages extended these indications into an exploration of the form a viable moral realism might take within a hermeneutic and phenomenological framework. In what follows I provide a summary of what was set out there. I realize that these ideas are by no means uncontroversial and not without some daunting obstacles still to be overcome; I intended only to sketch what one robust response to these issues might look like. While these all too brief remarks will not address every point that was made, I hope that they will be viewed as supplementing and enlarging Liederbach's own focus on the normative dimension of sense-making in Watsuji.

I began with an examination of the ways in which the phenomenology of our moral experience resists external, objective accounts of what happens in such experiences. My claim is that the best explanations are those that are formulated from within the experience itself. And if, as I try to show, these are the best accounts that we have, we will be justified in positing the existence of whatever is entailed by such explanations. Here this will mean the existence of moral (and aesthetic) facts as irreducible configurations in what appears that warrant our evaluative judgments, or merit a response in the form of an action or in the taking up of an affective attitude.

One of the main objections to a view such as this is that we cannot know when our responses are the right ones, and that this is reflected in the not uncommon failure to reach agreement about ethical questions. These problems, in turn, casts doubt on the truth of moral realism itself. To address the question of how it is that we can come to know that our judgments about normative facts (i.e., detectible properties or qualities of an object, action, or situation that require us to take a specific action, or that merit a particular affective attitude) are true judgments, I turn to Gadamer's hermeneutic conception of truth. Gadamer shows how a judgment which is finite, which functions within a particular historical and cultural horizon, and which is linguistically mediated and so always made from a context of prejudices, can nevertheless make a claim to truth. In doing so, he provides us with a plausible and attractive alternative to that form of truth characterized by certainty and objectivity and reached through method that has monopolized the modern sense of truth.

In considering the problem posed by the existence of moral disagreement, especially as evinced by extreme moral variation between people and cultures, I hold that we can account for much of this by attending to the distinctions to be made between different kinds of disagreement. If we are careful about such distinctions, we will see that some moral disagreements can be traced to the phenomenon of what Isaiah Berlin calls value pluralism, other disagreements can be reduced to disagreements about the interpretation of the non-moral facts, and yet other disagreements can be attributed to the inadequate or distorted apprehension of the normative landscape by one party to the dispute. This misapprehension, in turn, can be accounted for if we are willing to accept that there are some aspects of the world that are only revealed by exercising a certain kind of sensitivity (analogous to a perceptual capacity) that is affective as well as cognitive, and that some are exemplary in their sensitivity, while others misperceive, misapprehend, or simply miss, the relevant facts.

In short, once we have accepted the existence of moral qualities and values as properties of things, persons, situations, and actions, there seems to be no reason why there could not be better and worse apprehensions of such properties, much in the same way that we acknowledge that there is better and worse in visual perception, or in textual interpretations, or skill in everything from flying airplanes to playing chess—since all of these activities involve the ability to pick out what is salient, or important, or normative in a situation. In the same manner, it may be that we can explain some disagreements over what is right as attributable to the superior perceptual capacities of a moral exemplar.

To modern ears this kind of moral realism sounds hopelessly subjective. What reasons could we have for deferring to the perceptual judgments of an exemplar, who has somehow "seen" something in the world that others have not? A satisfactory response to this might begin with the seemingly uncontroversial point that perception is always interpretive—the same people notice different things or see the same things differently—but not every interpretation is as good as any other; some interpretations are better than others because they are richer or more penetrating, because they are more accurate or encompass a wider range of phenomena, that is, because they do justice to what is perceived. This, in turn, is a consequence of the fact that the overall orientation and sensibility of the experiencing subject can determine what appears, such that some people are able to perceive things that others miss. My suggestion is that the appearance of what is good can sometimes depend on the exercise of a sensibility that accurately deploys affectivity as a form of cognition, that is oriented by a specific set of interests, and that has been formed by experience and training.

This does not mean that an exemplar is an infallible standard for what is right in every case. Her judgments are always human judgments, that is, they are made within a community of interpreters with whom she is in dialogue and by whom she can be corrected about the matter at hand, and they are made from a particular historical and cultural perspective and so open to future revision. We may also have to acknowledge that human finitude and human limits, in the form of the inherent and intractable complexity of human experience and the multifarious character of the larger linguistic, cultural, and historical reality within which it is situated, suggest that there will always be disagreements about the meaning of experience, such that reaching the completeness of truth will always remain, to borrow Gadamer's phrase, "an infinite task."[7]

---

7. Hans-Georg Gadamer, "The Ideal of Practical Philosophy," in *Praise of Theory: Speeches and Essays*, trans. by Chris Dawson (New Haven: Yale University Press), 58. This final paragraph can be found in David W. Johnson, "The Experience of Truth: Gadamer on the Belonging Together of Self, World, and Language," *Graduate Faculty Philosophy Journal* 36/2 (2015): 394. I thank the publisher for permission to reprint this here.

Rossa Ó Muireartaigh
Aichi Prefectural University

On Historical Consciousness

Tanabe Hajime 田辺 元

ORIGINAL TITLE:「歴史の認識に就いて」『田辺元全集』[Complete works of Tanabe Hajime] (Tokyo: Chikuma Shobō, 1964), 1: 413–22.

KEYWORDS: history—historical consciousness—scientific method—early essays of Tanabe—Kyoto School

On Historical Consciousness
Translated by Rossa Ó Muireartaigh

History seeks to describe the individuality of an object, whereas the natural sciences aim to establish universal laws. Of course, when we start splitting up those objects of history we have made, we do quickly find common characteristics between them and this can be taken as examples of actual universal laws. But if all we do is simply seek to detect and analyze cases of universal laws, and find explanations of their origin, we have given history a methodology that is no different to the natural sciences. Indeed, history's object must be that which cannot be reduced to one more element of a universal law presenting itself for analysis. Instead, it should be something that requires individual expression as an event occurring one time and never to be repeated within the unified all. What is special about historical consciousness is its individualized descriptions of a historical totality that develops inside a particular circumstance. Upon what can these various historical totalities be grounded? By what principle do the various parts of history's object unite in the whole? And how does this principle of unity differ to the unifying principles to be found in the natural sciences? The fundamental aim of the natural sciences is to unify, through a few basic universal theories, the totality of nature, and to construct what can be called *world configurations* to understand, through these theories, natural phenomena as particular determinants of the universal. If we believe that the essence of ordinary actual experience is exhausted by the various concepts we can extract from such experience then we will never be able to construct various world configurations from these concepts.

Perhaps we should think of the concepts of sciences as being akin to "functional numbers" where the universal acts as the location for the differentiation of particulars in relationship with other particulars. The particular parts are unified in a synthesis following a few universal principles and an overall configuration is constructed with the functional numbers differentiating the concepts. In fact, this is how it is done in the world configuration of physics—theoretical physics—that field which claims the methodological crown of natural science. Particular individual events, then, are the specific values for functional numbers which are universalized in terms of quantity. There is a particular reciprocity between numbers that is a completely external relationship devoid of any internal development of meaning going on in-between. Any individual value can convert to one by means of another value. The interiority here is like the cause-effect relationship that exists between phenomena that appear successively in time. The value relationship between functional numbers involves small values and large values matching in time as parameters of differential equations acting to combine nature's continuous situations. At the extreme of what we might call Bergson's geometrization, the development of all internal meaning is removed, all is externalized and impersonalized, and making ultimate the unity of the particular all in the differentiation of functional number concepts becomes the goal for the systematic construction of universal consciousness in the methodology of natural science. However, we must distinguish between individual consciousness of history and its appearance. In history, the part stands mutually against the all of the object when aligned in a relationship that is completely external. There is no internal meaning in between, and the all cannot be synthesized in this way.

Any totality endowed with individuality must be a living and creative thing. Through this creativity, real value unifies the parts from inside through a relationship of internal significance. Of course, in the natural sciences, even physics cannot be reduced to mathematics. In the physical world, there are concepts, such as force, which can be sorted into simple numbers, and unified internally within this world. However, methodologically, physics organizes this kind of special internal unity into an external numerical unity, and the guiding idea is to restrict all within the special limits of mathematics. The ideal methodology for the natural sciences is externalization in the form of a functional relationship of numbers. A system—as in the whole becoming an external combination of the parts—becomes the ultimate goal.

By contrast, in history the whole sustains the parts from within. It penetrates them and combines them in a relationship of meaningful development. The parts, as separate from the whole, are to be understood as similar to one another and to be true examples of a universal law. They only acquire the individual life of the whole when they are combined within the whole. They have their own individuality as expressions of this. Unity of overall form in history is aimed towards an internalizing unity. Even though in general history looks at the development and progress of individuals and nationalities as subjects, environments are seen to be extremely important. When we look for an overall unity of form in history we are looking towards an internalizing unity. History books, in general, do ponder the development and progress of individuals and nationalities as subjects. But environment is seen to be of essential importance. However, is the environment something internal, something separate to the spiritual life of individuals and nationalities, something with its own meaning when set apart? No, not at all. Even when environments are considered identical when examined externally with the eyes of natural science, they will still have completely individual meanings for the subjects experiencing them from within. Environment here is not meant to mean something that encircles the subject from the outside as in the original meaning of the word. Rather, it is something internal, that individualizes through meanings changing from within through the experiences of the subject. It is impossible to have a historical environment without this internal unity.

When we consider the form of the unity which is essential to the formation of the historical totality, the historical cause and effect here is seen as a successive relationship in time through the combination of internal self-expression in the experience of the historical subject. Cause and effect is not, though, simply a relationship of succession in time. It always involves a necessary synthesis between phenomena occurring in succession. Furthermore, the essentialness of this synthesis is determined as that which does not permit change due to the overall unity which includes the synthesis of this essentialness. In the case of cause and effect in natural science, the system of universal law and theory that unites the particular in the whole as its binding limit becomes the necessary grounds for this binding. As against this, in the case of history, the formation of the whole comes from nothing other than the subject's individual development. The changing of the grounds of the necessary binding in historical cause and effect can only be the totality developing within the subject which attributes individual meaning to events through experience. It is impossible to think of historical cause and effect without this. To be aware of the cause-effect relationship in regard to those contents that are separate to the unity emerging internally in the historical subject means that a necessary successive relationship based on universal law has been established that is externalizing from the standpoint of nature. If we extract those factors that shape actual historical totality from the totality, it means that we are employing just one particular law and this can of course be bound to natural cause-effect relationships from the standpoint of nature. However, the abstract standpoint of awareness uses the means of a concrete standpoint, so sure enough it becomes a factor in the totality that is unified through the objectives of this concrete standpoint. And so we do not need to doubt that concrete historical awareness is included in abstract natural cause-effect as this factor. Thus, cause and effect is either historical cause and effect based on the development of subjective individuality or natural cause and effect based on the universality of laws.

If we think of the two types of cause-effect other than in terms of being natural or historical, we will be mistaking conventional gradations for theoretically autonomous objects within the world, leaving both types of cause-effect methodology confused and undistinguished. Either way, historical cause-effect, creating the particularity of history, cannot be separated from the historical subject that is united experientially with the total phenomenon from the standpoint of internal meaning. With natural science, the subject is fused with the totality of natural phenomena, it too reduced to a functional concept in an external unity—its unique characteristics taken to be self-differentiation. The subject, that which creates new meaning from within itself, ultimately cannot be recognized in the methodology of natural science. But in history, this creative subject developing internally has a particular historical meaning. When this is abstracted we completely lose that which is history.

In history we will always find a personality. I mean this in the wide sense of an individual or ethnic group incorporated in that subject which unifies the totality. Human development, and history in its basic meaning, begins with this. We must not, of course, overlook completely the important question of which should be emphasized: the individual or the group. Historical research is divided over this question but it does not really concern us here. Whether it be the individual or the group, either way, the essential point I am making is that there would be no history without this underlying unifying personality conforming from within to the meaning of experienced events. So how can we become aware of this personality that unites events from within through experience? I have already mentioned, of course, how the personality can be known through its external links to universal laws. We know the personality of another through our common empathy with it deriving from within our own selves. Knowing the personality of another is *Verstehen*, not *Begreifen*. We enter into the object through *Verständnis* and attain direct knowledge through the experiences of the self. This unity in the internal development of the personality is known directly through the experience of the self from such a standpoint. Historical consciousness, as I have pointed out, gives shape to the totality creating the unity from within through the personality in the broadest sense. As such, historical consciousness is clearly, then, the essence of the direct understanding that psychologists would call empathy. It is the special characteristic of historical consciousness that it can be seen as an action. But to think of it another way, it is a part of the unsolvable puzzle of how the subject, limited as it is to our individuality, can understand from within the personality of the other. We need to recognize basic facts that do not conform to the action or advancement of empathy as in the explanations of psychologists theorizing about the mental phenomena of individual experience. To explain how one limited personality can understand the personality of another is to ask the impossible. When understanding the personality of another we do so from the standpoint of one limited personality. The ability of one absolutely limited personality to know the personality of another is a contradiction. In so far as we can understand the personality of another, it is from the standpoint of one personality.

Each experience of pure activity that emerges from within us is free activity with no particular limits in itself. Whether any kind of unified personality develops through the contents of experience depends on its freedom in that situation. A real personality is limited by the particularizations of a personality with limitless potential. Each development of this is borne by a universal personality of infinite potentiality, and this determination limits freedom and becomes realized. The real personality is limited by the infinite universal personality. In general, the determination of particularities can first commence on the basis of the universal. What is determined absolutely as particular from the beginning cannot even have the meaning of a particular. There will be universality and freedom already to be expected on the reverse side of any determination of such particularity. Individuality too must be determined by the universal totality. To say that a personality has individuality is to say that there is a particular determination of the universal which creatively develops from limitless possibilities. Of course, the universal here is not that universal that is extracted from the particular, as in when we think of the universal in logic. It is not this kind of abstract universal but the universal all that includes every particularity within, and which has infinitely abundant content. A particular personality is determined upon the surface of the underlying universal which lurks as the infinite potential all. As such, our personality is always linked to the universal all of infinite possibility looming behind. We remove the limits of the particular personality that is the reality of our self, and return to the universal all behind it. At this standpoint, the inner unity of another personality can be understood from within. Understanding the personality of another has nothing to do with the standpoint of one's own determined self. Removing these limits and occupying the standpoint of the universal totalized personality looming behind, means the contents of any personality can be freely experienced from within. Empathy, which from the perspective of empirical psychology is seen as a primordial fact and, which cannot be explained further, must be understood exclusively from such a metaphysical basis. Moving away from this type of understanding lets us finally solve this puzzle. Historical consciousness is only possible on this philosophical basis. However, from the point of view of pure theory, what is possible is not necessarily always completely reality. What I am saying here is that each human has a path towards common mutual understanding with the universal totalizing personality that is behind them. However, the actual range of this common understanding varies. It is us who don the halo of the universal totalized personality lit in the surrounding dimness as that light honing in on where lurks the inner particular personality. The intensity of light from the halo and the width of its brightness will be of a diverse multitude depending on each person. But however weak the intensity of light, no matter how big or small the halo, it is never zero. Such a person would find it completely impossible to understand, or have common feeling with, or empathize with another. But at the same time there are a great many variations, and we must recognize the considerable difference in wideness or narrowness in ranges of understanding. What is necessary for historical consciousness is that the light of understanding is truly wide.

The complete and free realization and attainment of the universal totalized personality lurking behind the subject must be the ideal of the historian. To empathize with the minds of heroes, and understand the special spirit of an era or the mind of a people, a historically conscious subjectivity is required. In this way, the function of a historian is to freely occupy the standpoint of the universal totalized personality, and to understand from within the internal development of the personality transforming into a unity the historical all as an object, and through this, molding the individualized form. This is never like natural science with its constant conceptualization seeking to configure and pattern that which is external. Only those forms derived from the unity of inner experience are to be harnessed for history. With history, intuition and inner understanding is the essence of its consciousness. On that point, history is remarkably similar to the creations of art, in particular, that of literature. The creation of a novel or drama is the same as in history, where the most important requirement is that the subject freely enters and exits the infinite universal all-embracing mind. The literary person will be a man inhabiting a woman's mind, an old person taking on the thoughts of a younger heart, so as to describe persons imbued with individuality. Shakespeare was *myriad-minded* in having this ability. The only difference between literature and history is that literature is unrestrained by reality. It follows the dictates of the free self-expression of the author to create a new world through imagination, in contrast to history which is always shaped by reality. This shaping is imposed and is not delegated to subjective freedom. In this sense, history is not about creativity through imagination but involves consciousness of reality. But even so, looking at the overall shaping process going on in history, there is artfulness through literary creation in the sense of the formation of the individual centering on the unity of internal experience through the personal. If I can be forgiven for using the concept of "*historischer Sinn*" (historical sense), I wish to employ it to indicate the potential for shaping the whole through this common understanding. Historical consciousness as well as being the basis for this kind of intuition is a way of very simply outlining my thinking upon historical consciousness, without my daring to conjecture from my own extremely poor understanding of the experiences of historians. It would be an unexpected pleasure should I have an opportunity to have my ignorance enlightened by the teaching of such well-informed people.

Morten E. Jelby
Ecole Normale Supérieure, PSL, Paris

Urai Satoshi
Ōtani University

Quentin Blaevoet
University of Strasbourg

On Thetic Judgment

Tanabe Hajime 田辺 元

ORIGINAL TITLE: 「措定判断に就て」『田辺元全集』[Complete works of Tanabe Hajime] (Tokyo: Chikuma Shobō, 1964), 1: 3–10; first published in 『哲学雑誌』[Journal of philosophy], 1910.

KEYWORDS: pure experience—judgment—representation—content of consciousness—perception—object—negation—psychology—epistemology—Wundt—Brentano—Sigwart—Kyoto school

Tanabe Hajime

On Thetic Judgment

Translated by Morten E. Jelby, Urai Satoshi, and Quentin Blaevoet

It occurs that we forget the distinction between the things and ourselves, and follow down the "stream of consciousness." This is the case, for instance, when we gaze absentmindedly (無心に) at the blue skies, lying on the grass on a spring day. In this situation, there is no consciousness of the blue sky separate from me nor of me perceiving it. The distinction between the things and ourselves disappears, and in consciousness only the clear blue sky remains. We cannot call this clear sky an object since only that which stands opposed (*gegenüberstehen*)[1] to us can be called an "object" (*Gegenstand*). Here, however, there is nothing of the kind, but only content of consciousness. Of course, we cannot call this state "knowledge"[2] either. Knowledge is only established when there is a subject that knows and an object that is known, but what we find in the case of our example is a state of unification entirely devoid of any such distinction. Many scholars call this "pure experience." This means that [the fact] is experienced purely and as is, in consciousness, and that it has not yet undergone any act of processing (*Bearbeitung*),[3] such as abstraction or distinction. Pure experience of this kind is in a certain sense the original form of all mental acts. Insofar as our mental acts become

---

1. [The German term figures directly in the text, following 対立する.]
2. [The term 認識, translated here as "knowledge," corresponds to the German "*Erkenntnis*," sometimes rendered in English as "cognition." Cf. for instance THZ 2: 180, where Tanabe himself offers both "*Erkenntnis*" and "knowledge" as translations.]
3. [加工作用, with the German term indicated in *furigana* (ベアルバイツング).]

conscious to us, they all appear in this form. Whether we claim that we recall a past consciousness by transcending the present consciousness or think of an object independent of consciousness, we can only do so in present consciousness; in this respect, all our mental acts are pure experience. But in accordance with the meanings contained in [pure experience], various different mental phenomena are produced. Now, I use this word exclusively to designate an experience which—regardless of the aspect considered—is purely unified and truly has no other meaning than itself. In other words, this is identical with what can be called a "self-sufficient experience" (自全経験).

Let us return to our previous example. The state of being absorbed in gazing at the sky, while lying on our backs on a warm spring day, is clearly a pure experience. But after a moment, I return to myself from this state where I had been forgotten. At that moment, my soul is already no longer in a state where it has melted away in the spring light; I am *here* as an *ego* (自我) and the sky is *there* as an object independent of me. In other words, the pure and unified state of experience is broken, and I enter the state of discriminating and dualistic knowledge that is perception. Generally, even if different types of sensations and representations[4] become conscious, they do not necessarily become perceptions. When we do not particularly turn our attention towards them, we are simply in a state of pure experience, but when we do turn our consciousness [towards them], this state of pure experience splits, and the sensible representations are distinguished from the *ego* and posited (*gesetzt*)[5] as objective objects.[6] Following Riehl, I call this act "thetic judgment" (*Das thetische oder setzende Urteil*).[7] (Strictly speaking, pure experience is not entirely devoid of any act of attention. It is simply that since [the attention] advances while continuing to face a certain con-

---

4. [Up until 1916, Tanabe used the term rendered here as "representation" (写象) as the equivalent of *Vorstellung* (sometimes rendered in English as "presentation"). After that, he preferred 表象.]

5. [措定せられる. Tanabe adds the *furigana* ゼツツエン to the first term, ie. the German *setzen*. The Japanese *suru* allows Tanabe to dispense with German conjugations, a luxury the English language does not afford us.]

6. [Objective object : 客観的対象.]

7. Riehl 1879, 2: 43.

tent, it does not break the state of pure experience. What causes it to break is the turning about of attention.)

If we define thetic judgment simply, we might say that it is the judgment which posits the sensible representation (the content of consciousness) as an object of the *ego*. "Content" thus designates all that becomes conscious in the state of pure experience, already explained, when the *ego* and the object are not yet distinguished. It must be noted here that consciousness and content do not exist separately; generally, consciousness is nothing but the term for that which binds together the individual contents. As opposed to [the content], the object is *Dasjenige, das ich mir, oder dem ich mich innerlich gegenüber gestellt habe* [that which, internally, I have put before myself, or before which I have placed myself][8]; in consciousness, it is that which stands before the *ego,* independent of the *ego*. In other words, in this case, consciousness is no longer one, but contains a distinction. Here the following problem arises: how do such objects appear, in opposition to the *ego,* from within the unified state where they were included as content of consciousness?

When the object appears from the content of consciousness, as we have said in the above, we turn towards the content which is to become an object for us. This turn is thus an act of attention, and as Wundt says, attention is an internal activity of volition and establishes itself from the element of feeling (*Gefühlelement*).[9] Here, the representational side, founded on sensation, and the emotional and volitional[10] side of attention come to appear in the content of consciousness.[11] The representational side is not something that is originally produced as content of consciousness by our will; it is the given (*das Gegebene*)[12] which cannot be freely modified by will. Thus, this side demands to be distinguished from the emotional and volitional side.[13] The act by which, acknowledging this demand, the emotional and volitional

---

8. Lipps 1907, 21.
9. [感情の要素. ゲフュール and エレメント accompany 感情 and 要素 respectively in *furigana*.]
10. [情意的. The term 情意 is sometimes seen translated as *Gemüt* or "mind," sometimes as "feeling and will." The pages by Wundt to which Tanabe is referring allow us to disambiguate.]
11. Wundt 1902, 266–70.
12. [所与, with the German term indicated in *furigana*: ダスゲゲーベネ.]
13. Wundt 1897, 94–7.

side (i.e. the *ego*) posits the representational side as an object facing it, is precisely thetic judgment.

This judgment is something very fundamental and the process mentioned in the above is clearly not conscious, but is established almost instantaneously. For this reason, many people do not admit this type of judgement. However, I consider it an important judgment which constitutes the foundation of knowledge. Considered simply—from the standpoint of pure experience as previously discussed—as content of consciousness, all sensations and representations in general are nothing but mere facts entirely devoid of the distinction between truth and falsehood. However, once they are no longer simply facts of consciousness, but are posited as objects for the *ego* through objective perception, the distinction between truth and falsehood arises. For instance, in the case of "hallucinations," the representation posited as an objective object is subsequently falsified, since it contradicts the general system of knowledge, and it then becomes clear that it is nothing more than a subjective representation. And as this type of distinction between true and false has been recognized as a characteristic of judgment since Plato and Aristotle,[14] I think it is appropriate to consider the thetic act as a type of judgment.

The thetic act should be recognized as a judgment not only due to its consequences (as we have just argued), but furthermore, if we consider the act itself psychologically, it includes elements which are absent from simple acts of representation. If we compare, for example, the moment we call to mind a certain representation through imagination, and actual (実際の) perception, then we notice, in the latter, a type of demand and an emotional and volitional attitude of acknowledging[15] this demand, which are absent in the former. This is what the Stoics named συγκατάθεσις [assent], and it is the critical element which is recognized by Brentano—who is known for having provided an innovation to modern logic[16]—as the sole property of judgment.[17] His thought certainly contains errors, as has been

14. PLATO 1871, 338–9; ARISTOTLE 1873, 52.
15. [The term for "acknowledge" (承認する) corresponds to the German "*anerkennen.*" Cf. for instance THZ 1: 46, where Tanabe explicitly uses the term for "*Anerkennung*" in quoting Rickert.]
16. SCHALLY 1899, 28.
17. BRENTANO, 1874, 1:, 266–7.

shown by Sigwart,[18] Jerusalem[19] and others, but it is nevertheless generally accepted that judgment is characterized by this critical attitude.[20] In other words, in thetic judgment there is a demand that the perceptual representation be distinguished from the *ego* and posited as an objective object, and the *ego* acknowledges and attests to (確立) this demand. Consequently, "thetic judgment" clearly possesses this [critical] element. Accordingly, even from a psychological standpoint, we have sufficient grounds for calling it a "judgment."

What calls for attention, regarding this critical element, is negation as opposed to acknowledgment. Ordinarily, in logic, affirmation and negation are considered as two types of qualities (*Qualität*)[21] of judgment opposed to one another. This distinction has existed since Aristotle[22] and is pertinent in a logical perspective. But when the motives of negative judgement are examined in a psychological perspective, we discover some subtle differences with regard to the case of affirmation. First, as Wundt claims, at the foundation of the formation of judgment, there is a collective representation (*Gesamtvorstellung*),[23] which we analyze into S and P, i.e., subject and predicate.[24] At the same time, the content of judgment is established through the synthesis of the two elements thus distinguished.[25] For this reason, "to speak of a transition from *S* to *P* is wholly false [since][26] we never have an *S* first, and then tack a *P* onto it"[27]; rather, from the start, the foundation of judgment is the collective representation which includes the S-P relation. Consequently, as long as it does not contradict the pre-established system of knowledge, the connection S-P is naturally established as an affirmation. Negation emerges when the content of the collective representation

---

18. SIGWART 1873, 1: 79.
19. JERUSALEM 1895, 83.
20. JAMES 1890, 1: 283–6; WINDELBAND 1904,1: 170; MILL 1878, 421; RICKERT 1904, 101; HÖFFDING 1887, 174; JERUSALEM 1895, 82.
21. [質, with the German term indicated in *furigana*: クワリテート.]
22. ARISTOTLE 1873, 53.
23. [集合写像, with the German term indicated in *furigana*: ゲザムトフォルシュテルング.]
24. WUNDT 1903, 3: 575.
25. SIGWART 1873, 1: 71.
26. [This logical connection, implicit in Bosanquet's text, is made explicit in Tanabe's translation of the quote.]
27. BOSANQUET 1888, 1: 86.

is clarified through analysis and synthesis, and is subsequently rejected and abolished for contradicting the existing system of knowledge. In the case of "thought judgments" which Wundt calls "secondary forms of thought" (*sekundäre Gedankenformen*),[28] the collective representation is produced by our thinking; this connection [S-P] is therefore loosened, and negation and affirmation tend to oppose each other. But in the collective representation based on intuition, which precedes thinking (i.e., the "primary forms of thought" (*primäre Gedankenformen*)[29]), the demand of this connection is considered as coercive and as a necessary connection which cannot be influenced by our will; consequently, only in certain cases (e.g. when impressions are ambiguous) can judgments become negations, but normally all judgments are affirmative. This is why Sigwart does not consider negation to be as fundamental a class as the affirmation to which it is opposed.[30] Now, if we consider the case of thetic judgment, it is the most primordial judgment objectively positing sensation and representation, and it precedes acts of reflexive thinking. Since we are necessarily forced, in every case, to posit sensations and representations as objective objects, there is no negation in thetic judgment. If this demand is negated, [this negation] already contains an act of reflexive thought, and once thetic judgment reaches this stage, it is called an "existential judgment" (*das existentiale Urteil*).[31] Lipps speaks of the first in terms of "*Denkakt*" [thought act],[32] and of the second, i.e. what he calls *Wirklichkeitsurteile* [judgments of reality], in terms of *Denktätigkeit* [activity of thought].[33] In existential judgment, that which has already been posited as object through thetic judgment is further reflected on, and depending on its concordance with or contradiction of the existing system of knowledge, [the object] is either affirmed or negated; this is why these

---

28. WUNDT 1907, 1: 43–4. [Tanabe writes 第二次的思想形式, indicating the original German in *furigana*: ゼクンデレゲダンケンフォルメン.]

29. [第一次的思想形式, with the German term indicated in *furigana*: プリメレゲダンケンフォルメン.]

30. Sigwart 1873, 1: 150.

31. [In German in the text, following 存在判断.]

32. ["*Denkart*" (i.e., type of thought or way of thinking) in the original text, but this is no doubt a typographical error, as attested by the reference in question; furthermore, in a text of a slightly later date, Tanabe again mentions the Lippsian *Denkakt* in a passage dealing with the very same issue as here. Cf. THZ 1: 111; translation, TANABE 2013, 142.]

33. LIPPS 1907, 53.

two directions [i.e. negation and affirmation] can be considered as mutually opposed. Even so, for the reasons stated above, I do not maintain that only existential judgment is to be recognized [as a judgment] to the exclusion of thetic judgment. They only differ in terms of stages of development, but they are the same in terms of their being judgments. (Opinions concerning existential judgment differ among thinkers, but this is my understanding of the matter. Cf. Sigwart, *op. cit.*, I: 79; Jerusalem, *op. cit.*, 83; Brentano, *op. cit.*, 266–7; for further details, please refer to our discussion in the following.)

Since ancient times, it is generally admitted that judgment contains a subject, "S," and a predicate, "P"; and *as* judgments, both thetic judgment and existential judgment involve these elements. That is, "S" is the very sensation or representation of which we are conscious in the present; or in other words, from the point of view of pure experience, "S" is a sensation or representation as content of consciousness. On the other hand, "P" is the meaning of this content, i.e. its being an object independent of the *ego*. In fact, as we have shown, thetic judgment is established so instantaneously and so inevitably that its process does not become sufficiently and clearly conscious, and its elements subsequently become known as the result of an analysis; S and P are thus not clearly distinguished, and they do not always become conscious. However, from the perspective of the content of this judgment, I believe this interpretation is valid. Since existential judgment is realized on the level of reflexive thinking, both elements are here clearly distinguished; the representation "S" is normally subsumed under the concept to which it pertains; its being an objective object is also established in a concept of *Sein,* and takes the form "A is" ("*A ist*").[34] There is, however, a certain school of thought (Marty, Höfler, Meinong, among others), represented first and foremost by Brentano, which defends the idiogenetic theory (*[die] idiogenetische Theorie*).[35] Negating the necessity of subject and predicate in judgment, these thinkers claim that existential judgment merely contains the conceptual element "A," whereas "*ist*" is not an element that is to become predicate. According to Brentano, "when we say 'A is,' this sentence is not, as many have believed and still do believe, a predication (*Prädikation*)[36] in

34. [The German figures directly in the text, following the Japanese 「Aあり」.]
35. JERUSALEM 1895, 67. [The German expression figures in parenthesis, specifying 一元説.]
36. [説定, with the German term indicated in *furigana*: プレデカチヨン.]

which being (*Sein*)³⁷ is connected as a predicate to the subject A. It is not the connection of the characteristic (*Merkmal*)³⁸ "being" with A; rather, A itself is the object of our acknowledgement."³⁹ However, we would have to say that this argument is insufficient. As represented content, A "is discovered. It is *there*⁴⁰; and we cannot say that I acknowledge it,⁴¹ and even if one were to try to reject it, I do not know how one is to do so."⁴² As Sigwart says,

> If we were forced to acknowledge "A," we would only be capable of acknowledging that we actually make a representation. But this acknowledgment is not the affirmation of the existence of A. Because this affirmation has to do with the fact that A is part of the real world which surrounds me, that it is perceived by me and that it can act upon me and upon other things.⁴³

It is certainly true that Brentano's view does not recognize "A" as this type of representation, but as an object independent of the *ego*; nevertheless, we can grasp the object nowhere else than in its representation. What we acknowledge is nothing but "A" as a representation to which the predi-

---

37. [Even though Brentano's text reads "Existenz," Tanabe writes 存在, indicating *Sein* in *furigana* (ザイン).]

38. [徴表, with the German term indicated in *furigana*: メルクマール.]

39. BRENTANO 1874, 276: [Differing slightly from Tanabe's rendering, Brentano's text reads as follows: "Wenn wir sagen, "A ist," so ist dieser Satz nicht, wie Viele geglaubt haben und noch jetzt glauben, eine Prädikation, in welcher die Existenz als Prädikat mit A als Subjekt verbunden wird. Nicht die Verbindung eines Merkmals "Existenz" mit "A," sondern A selbst ist der Gegenstand den wir anerkennen."]

40. [Tanabe's italics. そこにあるものである.]

41. [Tanabe's translation here differs from Jerusalem's text, which rather says "whether I acknowledge it or not" (cf. note 39).]

42. JERUSALEM 1895, 68. [The original German text translated here by Tanabe reads: "Der vorgestellte Inhalt ist Gegenstand meines Bewußtseins, ich finde ihn vor, er ist da, mag ich ihn anerkennen oder nicht, und ich weiß nicht, wie man es anstellen soll, ihn zu verwerfen."]

43. SIGWART 1888, 50. [We have been unable to find any passage corresponding to Tanabe's quote. On the page in question, Sigwart affirms, in short, perception as the ground of the affirmation of the existence of a given thing, but there is no mention of the acknowledgment of representations. The lines that most adequately correspond to Tanabe's "quote" are the following: "Ohne auf die schwierige metaphysische Frage nach dem Begriffe des Seins überhaupt einzugehen..., können wir in dem vorliegenden Gebiete als allgemein zugestanden voraussetzen, dass der Grund, die Existenz von irgend einem Ding oder einem Vorgang zu behaupten, die Wahrnehmung, in der äusseren Welt die unmittelbare sinnliche Wahrnehmung ist.... wer in diesem Sinne behauptet, dass etwas in der Welt existire, behauptet, dass es irgendwie an irgend einem Orte und zu irgend einer Zeit wahrnehmbar sei."]

cate of its being an independent object is affixed. Both existential judgment and, naturally, thetic judgment, which serves as its foundation, contain the abovementioned S and P and are established through their synthesis. However, as the content of [thetic judgment] differs slightly from that of ordinary judgments (namely, this process is instantaneous and necessary in thetic judgment, and its content is clarified analytically only after the fact), it has either been misunderstood or entirely rejected as a judgment.

As I believe that by now the formation and the content of thetic judgment are almost clear, I would like, in the following, to briefly consider its significance for epistemology. As we have seen in the above, in the state of pure experience there is no room for talking about knowledge. It is merely the unified state in which subject and object are not yet separate. However, when we engage in an act of attention, this unified state is broken up, and what up until now had been the content of consciousness as pure experience, appears with the demand of being posited as an objective object. It is not something new that emerges due to the internal volition (i.e. due to the act of attention). What was originally in the content of consciousness, enters into a new type of relation with the act of attention. Consequently, as internal volition, the act of attention comes to form a type of experience which can be unified under the term "*ego*." For this reason, what we call "object" is not produced by the *ego*; on the contrary, both (i.e. the *ego* and the object) are only meaningful insofar as they are mutually opposed and co-dependent (相互相俟ちて). That is indeed not to say that their distinction becomes conceptually clear to a sufficient degree in thetic judgment. Rather, considering its significance, this is how I understand it. If this [distinction] becomes clear, we are already in existential judgment. Since this judgment emerges following an adequate (相応) development of the concepts of *ego* and object, a thetic judgment with the same meaning has already taken place. In fact, this [thetic] judgment is the most fundamental knowledge, the foundation of all objective knowledge. However abstract a thought (思想) is, insofar as it relates to objective objects, it cannot but presuppose the being of these objects. And the being of these objects is precisely established by this thetic judgment. In the end, from the standpoint of empiricism, being is nothing but "to be perceptible." In other words, being originates in pure experience and is established through thetic judgment. In this sense, [the thesis] *esse est percipi* is valid. But the reason why until now many empiricists have fallen into subjective idealism is that, having failed to acknowledge thetic judgment, they dogmatically determined sensations and representations to be subjective in essence (本来). If, in order to explain objective knowledge, one were to seek a characteristic (*Merkmal*)[44] objectivizing the something of the sensations and representations[45] which one has thus considered as subjective, this approach flips the facts upside down and makes the goal entirely unattainable. As there is no reason why being (有) should emerge from nothing, nothing objective can come from inside what is subjective in essence. Subjective idealism is a natural consequence of this [reversal of the facts].[46] Rather, the content of consciousness, which appears in pure experience, originally transcends the subject–object [distinction], and from within it, the objective object appears in opposition to the subjective element of the *ego*. Subject and object (客観), *ego* and object (対象),[47] are after all the names given to two different systems that are parallel to each other in pure experience, and one cannot be said to follow nor precede the other.

The object which thus appears in opposition to the subject is itself governed by laws and is not influenced by subjective will. Knowledge is always established when this object makes the subject acknowledge a certain aspect which the object has developed according to its own laws. The point of unification of these two sides is none other than pure experience. We call the feeling which emerges when the subject is forced to make this acknowledgement "necessity" (*Notwendigkeit*)[48] of knowledge. Furthermore, among the objective objects posited by perception, there is something which has a particularly intimate and inseparable type of relation to the emotional and volitional element that is our *ego*: namely, our body. This concept is established where there is a certain parallel relation between the emotion and volition [on the one hand] and sensations and representations [on the other], which form this concept; further, parting from the bodies of the others—posited

---

44. [徴表, with "*Merkmal*" indicated in *furigana*: メルクマール.]
45. [感覚写象の或もの.]
46. Cf. the section on knowledge in WUNDT 1897.
47. [Tanabe distinguishes between two terms for "object": 客観 and 対象, corresponding respectively to *Objekt* and *Gegenstand*.]
48. [必然性, with the German term indicated in *furigana*: ノートウェンデヒカイト (sic).]

as having external shapes similar to the body related to my *ego*—I posit, through an act of analogical inference, the *ego*s of the others in intimate relation to these bodies of the others; and I come to empathize [with them] by projecting onto them the feelings of my *ego*. The previously mentioned feeling of necessity thus extends to the other *ego*s; and the anticipation emerges that, like myself, they are to acknowledge [the object]; this is what we call "universal validity" (*Allgemeingültigkeit*)[49] of knowledge.

We can thus understand that a theory of knowledge that takes its starting point in thetic judgment does not take the standpoint of a subjective idealism, but rather that of an objective idealism. Knowledge is established in consciousness, but this consciousness is not my subjective present consciousness, but rather the eternal present which swallows up past and future; it is the pure and unified experience, beyond the distinction between self and other. After all, reality (実在) should be sought nowhere else.

> * When we had finished the first draft of this translation, it came to our attention that Takeshi Morisato had already translated this very text in collaboration with Timothy Burns, without, however, having published their results. Through the generosity of Mr. Morisato, we were able to compare the two versions, a process which allowed us to improve our translation in numerous places. In a later round of corrections, additional keen observations made by Mr. Morisato further helped establish the present text. For this we wish to express our deep gratitude to Morisato and Burns.

References

Abbreviation

THZ 『田辺元全集』[Complete works of Tanabe Hajime] (Tokyo: Chikuma Shobō, 1963–1964).

Other works cited

ARISTOTLE
    1873 *Das Organon des Aristoteles,* trans. by Hermann Bender (Stuttgart: Hoffmann'sche Verlags-Buchhandlung).

BOSANQUET, Bernard
    1888 *Logic or the Morphology of Knowledge* (Oxford: Clarendon).

49. [普遍妥当性, with the German term in *furigana*: アルゲマインギルチヒカイト.]

BRENTANO, Franz
   1874   *Psychologie vom empirischen Standpunkte* (Leipzig: Duncker und Humblot).

HÖFFDING, Harald
   1887   *Psychologie in Umrissen auf Grundlage der Erfahrung* (Leipzig: Fues's Verlag).

James, William
   1890   *Principles of Psychology* (New York: Henry Holt & Co.).

JERUSALEM, Wilhelm von
   1895   *Die Urteilsfunktion. Eine psychologische und erkenntniskritische Untersuchung* (Wien und Leipzig: Wilhelm Braumüller).

LIPPS, Theodor
   1907   "Bewußtsein und Gegenstände," Theodor Lipps, ed., *Psychologische Untersuchungen* (Leipzig: Wilhelm Engelmann).

MILL, John Stuart
   1878   *Examination of Sir William Hamilton's Philosophy and of the Principal Philosophical Questions Discussed in his Writings* (London: Longmans).

PLATO
   1871   "Theatetus," in *The Dialogues of Plato*, trans. by Benjamin Jowett (Oxford: Oxhord University Press).

RICKERT Heinrich
   1904   *Der Gegenstand der Erkenntnis. Einführung in die Transzendentalphilosophie* (Tübingen und Leipzig: J. C. B. Mohr).

RIEHL, Alois
   1879   *Der philosophische Kritizismus und seine Bedeutung für die positive Wissenschaft* (Leipzig: Wilhelm Engelmann).

SCHALLY, Otto
   1899   "Natur des Urteils: Eine historisch-kritische Darstellung ihrer Lehre," in *Jahresbericht des Communal-Obergymnasiums in Aussig für das Schuljahr 1898–99* (Aussig: Selbstverlag des Communal-Obergymnasiums).

SIGWART, Christoph
   1873   *Logik* (Tübingen: Verlag der H. Lauppschen Buchhandlung).
   1888   *Die Impersonalien. Eine logische Untersuchung* (Freiburg: J. C. B Mohr).

WINDELBAND, Wilhelm
   1904: "Logik," in *Die Philosophie im Beginn des zwanzigsten Jahrhunderts: Festschrift für Kuno Fischer* (Heidelberg: Carl Winter's Universitätsbuchhandlung).

Wundt, Wilhelm
   1897   *System der Philosophie* (Leipzig: Wilhelm Engelmann).
   1902   *Grundriß der Psychologie* (Leipzig: Wilhelm Engelmann).
   1903   *Grundzüge der physiologischen Psychologie* (Leipzig: Wilhelm Engelmann).

1907 *Logik. Eine Untersuchung der Prinzipien der Erkenntnis und der Methoden wissenschaftlicher Forschung* (Stuttgart: Ferdinand Enke).

Tanabe Hajime 田辺 元
2013 "On the Universal," trans. by Takeshi Morisato and Timoty Burns, *Comparative and Continental Philosophy* 5/2: 124–49.

Carlos Barbosa
Universidad Pedagógica Nacional, Bogotá

La ciencia y la religión

Nishitani Keiji 西谷啓治

ORIGINAL TITLE:「科学と宗教」, first delivered as a lecture in 1966 and subsequently published in 1969 in a collection of essays by various authors entitled 『親鸞と現代』. It is included in Nishitani's collected writings, 『西谷啓治著作集』6: 327–51.

KEYWORDS: tecnología—ausencia de lo humano—verdadera apercepción de la realidad

Introducción a la traducción

El ensayo cuya traducción aquí presentamos tuvo su origen en una conferencia que Nishitani Keiji ofreció en junio de 1966. Posteriormente, fue publicada en la colección de ensayos titulada *Shinran y la actualidad* (『親鸞と現代』) en 1969, volumen que además cuenta con contribuciones de figuras como Soga Ryōjin u Ono Seiichirō. En las *Obras de Nishitani Keiji*, es el último artículo del volumen 6, dedicado a varios ensayos escritos por él entre 1941 y 1969.

Uno de los mayores obstáculos para aproximarnos a la filosofía de un pensador como Nishitani es su lenguaje, profundamente permeado por el budismo no menos que por sus lecturas de filosofía occidental. La huella del budismo en su estilo le da a sus palabras una apariencia misteriosa: uno podría pensar que habla de experiencias místicas o esotéricas, o de planos secretos de la realidad inaccesibles a la experiencia ordinaria. Pero si recordamos que su punto de vista de la vacuidad es un punto de vista existencial orientado a un «más allá» que nos termine regresando más firmemente al «más acá» de nuestra vida ordinaria de lo que ordinariamente experimentamos, y si ponemos énfasis en que la cuestión de fondo es siempre esa: retornar a la vida concreta misma en toda su riqueza y concreción, tal «misterización» de su pensamiento se revela completamente fuera de lugar.

En términos de forma, puede imaginarse que un japonés medianamente cultivado tendría no pocos problemas con la prosa de Nishitani. El estilo del autor es repetitivo y quizá hasta errático. Frecuentemente redacta larguísimas oraciones que bien podrían dividirse en partes más pequeñas, utiliza más de un término o frase para referirse al mismo concepto o asunto, es dado a digresiones o rodeos, da vueltas y vueltas sobre el tema central a tal punto que es fácil perder el hilo. Pero si el lector le concede un poco de su paciencia, se encontrará con una manera de pensar sumamente matizada y amplia: capaz de notar numerosos aspectos relevantes de una problemática sin perder de vista el conjunto. Más aún, podrá encontrarse con una inspiradora constelación de imágenes que contribuyen a la indagación de los temas en discusión tanto como los conceptos.

En ese punto hallamos un aspecto del estilo de Nishitani que incide grandemente en el contenido: pone a trabajar la imaginación no como «fábrica» de fantasías, sino como facultad capaz de orientarnos hacia una comprensión más integral y directa de la realidad de lo que los conceptos lograrían por sí solos. Eso es lo que con su estilo apenas aparentemente «mistérico» pretende: remitirnos de vuelta a la plenitud de la existencia concreta tal cual se da en el aquí y ahora, cosa que al concepto siempre se le escapará debido a su intrínseca tendencia a la abstracción. Pues acaso al echar mano del indiscutible poder cognitivo del *abstraer* siempre pagamos el precio de *sustraer* a nuestra atención algo (usualmente mucho) de la plenitud de los hechos concretos.

En todo caso, no intento aquí mejorar la prosa de Nishitani, no trato de corregir o mejorar su estilo, esto por dos motivos. Primero, tal empeño está por encima de mi capacidad, para ser francos. En segundo lugar, no creo que esa deba ser la tarea del traductor. En lo que al estilo respecta, apenas he procurado, pues, limitar las redundancias «a sus justas proporciones» (por así decir), parafrasear en algunos casos puntuales y agregar pequeñísimas frases aclaratorias en otros. Todo esto es con el fin de lograr que el texto suene más natural en español, lo cual no deja de ser difícil toda vez que el texto suena relativamente innatural incluso en japonés. A la vez, he considerado importante, dado lo dicho en el párrafo anterior, mantener en lo posible la fuerza expresiva de las imágenes y ejemplos a los que él recurre.

Dicho lo dicho, el análisis de la situación contemporánea que encontramos en este ensayo sigue vigente. Nishitani piensa que en el trasfondo del pensamiento científico se cierne una amenaza que denomina «ausencia de lo humano». Esta problemática se debe a que la ciencia procede haciéndose una imagen del mundo que supone una forma de abstracción y una forma de reducción. Lo que abstrae es la subjetividad en su sentido más básico, y con ello la experiencia fenoménica. La reducción científica consiste primariamente en que es posible remitir todo lo existente en el universo (humanos incluidos) a átomos y fuerzas, al punto que podría afirmarse que todas las cosas son *nada más que* configuraciones de átomos y fuerzas.

La primera suposición es difícil de cuestionar, pero la segunda resulta mucho más ambigua de lo que parece (y tal ambigüedad es sumamente común a la hora de discutir el reduccionismo). Sea como sea, en conjunto indican una dirección que sigue el proceder de la ciencia, y con ello también el de la tecnología y de todas las acciones que se basen en ellas dos: una tendencia a no dar lugar a lo subjetivo, cualitativo y experiencial de la vida un lugar en nuestra imagen del mundo. Con ello el gran peligro está en que las ineludibles necesidades espirituales humanas quedan desatendidas y en que nuestro potencial para entrar en una conexión empática viva con otros (otros humanos, otros seres sintientes e inclusive con el ambiente en general) se debilita. No es que las cosas estén sucediendo exactamente así, pero sí hay una tendencia en esa dirección. Podríamos aventurarnos a afirmar que grandes problemas de nuestro tiempo son alimentados por esa tendencia: el incremento de la depresión, la cultura de consumo, la depredación ambiental o la objetualización no solo del ambiente sino a veces inclusive de los seres humanos, entre otros.

Así pues, es fácil preguntarse si este pensador sostiene acaso una acre hostilidad hacia la ciencia. Pero no es el caso: desde el principio él insiste en que la ciencia y la tecnología modernas nos han traído grandes bendiciones. Es más, no nos es posible simplemente renunciar a ellas. El camino, pues, no es «combatir» a la ciencia sino ubicarla en un marco desde el cual pueda recuperar el «alma» que se le ha extraviado. Para ello intenta una reinterpretación del ideal científico de objetividad en la dirección del concepto budista de «verdadera apercepción de la realidad» (si bien sugiere que otras religiones, incluso muy diferentes, también posibilitan ese redireccionamiento). Se trata de ampliar nuestra idea moderna de «ver las cosas como son», una objetividad que olvida estar basada en la abstracción, para abrirnos a la plenitud de la existencia de todas las cosas y de nosotros mismos. Si superamos las distancias de estilo, lenguaje y perspectiva (incluso de época) que pueden separarnos de Nishitani, creo que sus palabras tienen todavía mucho que decirnos sobre las grandes problemáticas de nuestro tiempo.

Nishitani Keiji
La ciencia y la religión
Traducción de Carlos Barbosa

Esta charla, que tratará sobre «la ciencia y la religión», resultará vaga. Actualmente la tecnología producida tanto por la ciencia como por el conocimiento científico se ha desarrollado bastante, y por esa razón surgen cambios sumamente grandes en nuestras vidas. La modernidad es ese tipo de era. La fuerza de la ciencia y la tecnología es enorme. No solo eso: además, se expanden a un tempo sumamente rápido. La rapidez de ese tempo llega a tal punto que, visto desde la historia del desarrollo del conocimiento, un año moderno equivale a cientos o miles de años de otros tiempos. A ese rápido tempo las diversas ciencias y tecnologías progresan y se desarrollan. Sin duda, esto es, a grandes rasgos, sumamente espléndido. Por ejemplo, consideremos problemas de la vida como las enfermedades que antiguamente no se podían curar o no podían recibir un fácil tratamiento, o también el problema de la pobreza: como la productividad o la tecnología para fabricar cosas se han desarrollado enormemente, es posible fabricar diversas cosas de manera comparativamente más barata y en cantidades cada vez mayores. Por su parte, enfermedades por las que antiguamente morían muchas personas hoy se hacen fáciles de tratar. Ya casi no se da que masas de gente mueran de golpe por una enfermedad infecciosa o por hambruna.

Antiguamente, existía en Occidente un país sumamente grande conocido como Imperio Romano. Se extendía no solo por casi todo Occidente sino por parte de África y Asia: un país tan colosal que podía ser calificado como un gran mundo. Pero cayó. Si bien hay varias causas de esta caída, puede decirse que una de ellas fue la malaria, que se hizo prevaleciente sin que se hubiera desarrollado la ciencia y tecnología médicas para tratarla. Hoy en día entendemos que se transmite por medio de un mosquito, pero en aquellos tiempos se pensaba que era alguna suerte de mal o fuerza maligna caída del cielo, o bien un castigo divino sentenciado por los dioses, entre otras cosas. A la final, no se entendía el porqué. Los historiadores afirman que, dada la enorme cantidad de personas que murieron, la malaria fue una de las causas de la caída del gran Imperio Romano. Es solo un ejemplo, pero hoy en día no se da algo así.

Desde ese punto, sobra decir que el progreso de la ciencia y la tecnología —por ejemplo el de la ciencia y los tratamientos médicos— es algo muy valioso para la humanidad. Asimismo, la productividad económica se ha incrementado enormemente, con lo cual nuestras vidas se han hecho más prósperas. Con todo y eso, al mismo tiempo viene a surgir aquí un grandísimo problema en tanto problema actual. Como bien se dice hoy en día, en la sociedad moderna lo humano se está desvaneciendo gradualmente. Desde varias facetas lo humano está desapareciendo gradualmente. Es decir, el ser humano no es ya verdaderamente humano. En su verdadero sentido, no hay humanos. Hay muchos seres humanos, pero no viven de manera propiamente humana. Esa es la situación en ciernes, por lo que bien puede ser denominada ausencia de lo humano.

Por el progreso de la tecnología, así como el de la ciencia que le sirve de raíz, el ser humano se hace sumamente próspero y se enriquece, pero por otra parte su naturaleza humana empieza a desvanecerse. El ser humano empieza a perderse de vista. Me parece que nos hallamos aquí ante un problema moderno sumamente difícil. No es posible parar el progreso de la ciencia o la tecnología, mucho menos renunciar a ellas. Renunciar a ellas nos orientaría de vuelta hacia los tiempos primitivos, por tanto no es posible. No obstante, si dejamos las cosas como están no se sabe qué será del ser humano. Lo cual es decir, me parece, que surgirá un enorme problema. El problema está en que aunque el continuo progreso no ha de ser en realidad tan sumamente rápido, el caso es que el ser humano no puede seguirle el paso a la rapidez del progreso de la ciencia. En su veloz y continuo progreso, la ciencia y la tecnología dejan atrás varios asuntos humanos. Su tiempo no se ajusta al nuestro.

En el seno de esta cuestión, destaca sobre todo el problema de la religión, por lo cual el budismo también está implicado. Pienso que el asunto de la religión está imbricado con el fundamento primario del problema consistente en el desajuste entre el tiempo de la ciencia y el tiempo humano. Pensado desde la larga historia de la especie humana, en cualquier época la religión ha sido el sostén básico de los seres humanos: esto no cambia ni en Oriente ni en Occidente. Incluso antes del surgimiento del cristianismo, cada uno de los pueblos no occidentales tenía también alguna forma de religión que constituía el sostén de la vida humana; igualmente en Oriente existían el budismo y otras varias religiones que desempeñaban la misma función. Sin embargo, esta larga vida de la humanidad y el progreso de la ciencia no encajan nada bien. La vida humana a la cual hasta ahora la religión sirvió de base no puede ir al ritmo de la ciencia. Aquí surge en varios sentidos una dislocación. Así, el antes mencionado problema de la ausencia de lo humano se genera en ese lugar de dislocación.

Dicho problema no lo es solamente para cada individuo o en el seno de cada uno, sino un problema para la sociedad entera. Para tomar por caso la familia, pienso que en las relaciones humanas al interior de la familia está surgiendo gradualmente una ausencia de lo humano, una desaparición de los sentimientos humanos. Bien es cierto que al respecto se pueden señalar responsabilidades individuales; pero me parece que, en términos generales, debido al gran vigor con que se mueven la sociedad o la historia, cada individuo humano está involucrado en el problema.

En ese punto la religión se ha convertido gradualmente en algo desconectado de los integrantes de la sociedad en general. Por otra parte, en esa medida el perjuicio causado por el continuo progreso científico que es la ausencia de lo humano se ha agravado. Todo el mundo está pensando en que hay que hacer algo al respecto ahora. Para ello varias cosas parecen ser necesarias: la educación moral o el cultivo de la sensibilidad, por ejemplo. Otras más se mencionan desde diversos puntos de vista. Empero, pienso que en todo caso la más valiosa resulta ser la religión. No obstante, en tanto cuestión práctica, la que mayor daño recibe del progreso de la ciencia es ciertamente la religión. Es en ese punto donde se halla la raíz del problema. Por tanto, aunque considero que el problema es bastante difícil, en todo caso querré referirme a él en términos sencillos.

Problematizar la ciencia y la religión se trata, en una palabra, de clarificar en qué consiste la religión y qué sentido tiene para el ser humano. Este es un asunto al que he dado varias vueltas ya, pero siento que debo pensarlo una vez más desde el seno de la difícil condición moderna. Por eso el título que le he dado al presente texto.

El primer problema al respecto es cómo surge en general esta relación entre lo tecnocientífico y lo humano. Hoy en día, especialmente entre los jóvenes, se confía bastante en la ciencia, con lo cual cabe afirmar que esta se torna muy influyente. Mas aún, en conexión con esta manera científica de pensar, se manifiesta la actitud de racionalizar todo cuanto el ser humano hace y resolverlo de forma claramente definida. Así, en tal actitud se muestra un cierto carácter tecnológico. Me parece que la tecnología no solo se da en terrenos como la manufactura o las obras públicas: se puede pensar de un modo más amplio. Por ejemplo, sea en una empresa o en una oficina gubernamental, el trabajo o los negocios se llevan a cabo lo más prontamente posible. Si se trata de una empresa, su estructura u organización se racionaliza de forma clara, y sus labores o funciones se ejecutan fluida y eficientemente. En un sentido amplio, todo esto también puede ser considerado tecnología.

Más aún, en lo que respecta al trabajo de los seres humanos dentro de tal tipo de estructura, dicho trabajo humano viene a adquirir un carácter tecnológico en tanto parte del movimiento de un mecanismo. Refirámonos a lo tecnológico. En pocas palabras, a la hora de manejar cualquier asunto, el manejo evita los rodeos, evita el desperdicio [de tiempo o recursos], y se ejecuta racionalmente y con prontitud. En ese sentido, pienso que tanto la organización de las empresas como las actividades o labores humanas como tender puentes o construir edificios tienen todas fundamentalmente algo en común. Puede decirse, me parece, que ese algo en común es lo tecnológico. Todo cuanto hace el ser humano se torna gradualmente tecnológico en ese sentido. En ello hay desde luego un lado positivo: uno opera fluidamente, sin quedarse atascado aquí o allá, sin desperdiciar [tiempo o recursos]. No hay duda de que eso es bueno. Dicha actitud tecnológica dedicadamente ingeniosa al hacer cualquier cosa está conectada con la forma científica de pensar. Por tanto, desde la manera como a gran escala se establece la organización de la sociedad entera hasta los diversos pensamientos y acciones de cada persona a pequeña escala, todo ello adopta un carácter tecnocientífico. Así son las cosas.

¿En ese caso, qué será del ser humano? Si el epicentro donde empieza a ocurrir el problema de la ausencia de lo humano en la sociedad moderna es la ciencia y la tecnología, ¿qué pasa con el ser humano en un mundo visto desde la ciencia y la tecnología? En pocas palabras, en ese mundo desde el principio no hay seres humanos, o quizá es mejor decir que no hay cosas humanas. Es un mundo sin humanos. Desde luego, en el mundo real los científicos e igualmente los ingenieros son seres humanos. Estas personas son admirables estrellas de la modernidad, pero si pensamos cómo se figuran en su cabeza el mundo desde el punto de vista de la ciencia y la tecnología, y a partir de ello cómo es el mundo en el que a través de acciones reales diseñan, fabrican y manejan diversas cosas, ese es, a mi parecer, un mundo sin humanos. El mundo como lo piensa la ciencia es desde el principio un mundo sin humanos, y el ser humano que es el científico lleva a cabo diversas investigaciones sobre el mundo de la ciencia mientras se ubica (por decirlo así) fuera de este. En el mismo mundo sin humanos el ingeniero fabrica diversas cosas. O, en fin, va transformando continuamente la naturaleza mediante la tecnología.

Si nos subimos a un Shinkansen[1], entenderemos fácilmente esta transformación. Antiguamente, por ejemplo, se logró construir una vía para cruzar las duramente escarpadas faldas del monte Hakone. En esta época antigua también había tecnología, si bien se procedía buscando un lugar por donde fuera fácil pasar la vía, irla construyendo y así cruzar la montaña. Sin embargo, la tecnología basada en la ciencia moderna es enteramente diferente. Si hay una montaña, se le pasa un túnel por debajo de una de sus laderas. Ya no se da el problema de si la pendiente de la ladera la hace difícil o fácil de cruzar. Por la montaña se pasa un túnel, sobre un río se construye un puente de hierro, y así se cruza rápidamente en línea recta, sin importar que haya montañas y ríos [en el trayecto]. En tal caso la naturaleza no pone grandes problemas, a tal punto que es enteramente subyugada. Sobra decir que de este modo la vida humana se ha hecho sumamente más práctica.

Sin embargo, también cabe decir que al mismo tiempo un mundo sin humanos ha estado infiltrándose brutalmente en el interior del mundo humano. Como antiguamente los viajes se hacían a pie, en el camino había montañas, había ríos, a veces sensaciones penosas. Aun así, cosas como el brotar de las flores o el canto de los pájaros hacían entretenido incluso un viaje penoso, con lo cual ese mismo viaje parecía algo humano de principio a fin. Como puede advertirse al viajar en Shinkansen, incluso cuando está a la vista la hermosa figura del monte Fuji los pasajeros están viendo el magazín en lugar de mirar alrededor. Entre tanto, el tren pasa a toda velocidad. Me parece que en comparación con los antiguos, que contemplaban sin descanso el monte Fuji durante sus viajes, la gente moderna está perdiéndose de mucho. Como se ha hecho difícil tener un viaje en el cual se pueda estar sin prisas en constante contacto con la naturaleza, hoy en día se pasa a toda velo-

---

1. *Shinkansen* (literalmente «nueva línea troncal») es la red de trenes de alta velocidad de Japón. Aunque no es técnicamente apropiado, popularmente los trenes que ruedan por dichas líneas también reciben, por metonimia, dicho nombre.

cidad por en medio de ella mientras se lee el magazín. A cambio de una vida más práctica, se ha llegado al punto de que lo humano ha sido substraído.

Sea como sea, el mundo de la ciencia es desde el principio un mundo sin humanos. Para tomar el caso de la disciplina llamada medicina, esta no incluye en absoluto, en tanto ciencia, una relación con lo humano. Por ejemplo, no se relaciona con la diversidad de sentimientos humanos. O podemos también mencionar lo siguiente. Pienso que hablando desde el punto de vista de los médicos que lidian científicamente con el problema del cáncer, no hay algo así como enfermedad: no hay enfermedad o ausencia de enfermedad en lo que al cáncer respecta. Desde un punto de vista puramente científico, entre el cáncer y las diversas condiciones fisiológicas normales no hay ninguna diferencia. Todos ellos son igualmente fenómenos que ocurren dentro del cuerpo humano. Desde el punto de vista académico de la ciencia, no se da la diferencia entre el primero como enfermedad y las segundas como condiciones saludables. Esa ausencia de diferencia es en general un rasgo del punto de vista de la ciencia. La ciencia es así.

Desde luego, para los seres humanos el cáncer es un gran problema. No solo el cáncer, sino todas las enfermedades. La enfermedad es algo malo, algo que debe ser persistentemente evitado. Por ende, la salud es algo bueno y deseable. Como para los seres humanos dicha diferencia entre bueno y malo siempre existe, lo humano consiste en que ella exista. Sin embargo, visto desde el punto de vista de la medicina en tanto ciencia, entre el fenómeno del cáncer y las así llamadas condiciones saludables no hay, en tanto fenómenos naturales, la menor diferencia. Por lo tanto, cuando se investigan desde el punto de vista de la ciencia, tanto el fenómeno de la enfermedad como el de la salud son igualmente considerados como fenómenos de la naturaleza. Son, pues, hechos investigados en tanto fenómenos fisiológicos en el cuerpo humano.

Desde luego, la muy esmerada investigación del cáncer está conectada con el deseo de superarlo de alguna manera y expulsarlo de la humanidad. No es posible separar la ciencia médica de la tecnología médica, es decir, de la tecnología para curar la enfermedad. Se hace investigación científica a fin de refinar los tratamientos médicos. Sin embargo, la ciencia médica investiga el fenómeno de la enfermedad como un puro fenómeno natural. La ciencia médica tiene que ser así. Por lo tanto, diría, también desde esa perspectiva se concibe que desde el principio lo humano no entra en el mundo de la ciencia. Es más, este punto es sumamente importante para la investigación científica. Que no esté lo humano consiste también en que se intenta ver el objeto de investigación —como el fenómeno del cáncer, para retomar nuestro ejemplo— puramente, tal como es, sin considerar si nos entristece o nos alegra, dejando a un lado los sentimientos. En ese punto radica la razón por la cual la gente confía enormemente en la ciencia y lo científico es sumamente valioso.

En el budismo también se ha expresado la idea de ver las cosas tal como son, en su caso a través del vocablo «verdadera apercepción de la realidad» (如実知見). Ver las cosas tal como son, directamente, dejando a un lado los sentimientos humanos —como el amor y el odio, lo agradable y lo desagradable, lo bueno y lo malo. Esto, que en palabras modernas se llama ver las cosas objetivamente, también ha sido sumamente importante para el budismo. En ese punto, el punto de vista científico se asemeja a la perspectiva budista. Si bien sería muy problemático afirmar que son exactamente lo mismo, aquí tenemos un aspecto en el cual se asemejan bastante en tanto perspectivas de las cosas. Más aún, como acabo de decir, en dicha objetividad se halla uno de los motivos por los cuales la gente confía enormemente en la ciencia. Se cree que decir «científicamente no hay lugar a error» es lo mismo que decir «no hay lugar a error». En otras palabras, el mundo como lo ve la ciencia es un mundo sin humanos, sin seres humanos: un mundo en el cual no existen el agrado o el desagrado humanos, el bien o el mal, el quiero esto o no quiero aquello, es decir, no hay amor u odio ni bien o mal entendidos en un sentido amplio. Es un mundo ajeno a la noción de la enfermedad como un mal o de la salud como un bien. Desde dicho punto de vista se pueden obtener diversos conocimientos por primera vez. Por ende, a partir de dichos conocimientos se da enseguida el desarrollo de la tecnología.

Ese mundo de la tecnología es enteramente el mundo humano. Por ejemplo, la tecnología médica que la ciencia médica desarrolla es la técnica que cura a la gente de enfermedades como el cáncer o la tuberculosis. El médico que utiliza esta técnica también es un ser humano, por lo cual la relación entre médico y paciente viene a ser una relación entre dos seres humanos. Por medio del conocimiento médico, el médico pone todo su esmero en curar al paciente. Desde la antigüedad la medicina es acción benevolente. La benevolencia es lo propiamente humano del ser humano en el mejor sentido del término y en tanto tal es la más elevada «virtud» humana. Por ello en tanto un médico es un ser humano piensa, desde luego, cómo recuperar la salud del ser humano que es su paciente, y entra en una relación humana uno a uno con él. Así, la tecnología presupone lo que se designa con la antigua palabra «virtud», es decir lo ético. O sea que presupone el amor a la humanidad. En efecto, el punto de vista del amor a la humanidad se halla a la base de la intención de salvar al paciente de la enfermedad. He aquí que el punto de vista de la ciencia, que no deja lugar para lo humano, está en realidad, visto desde su motivación, oculto bajo el amor a la humanidad. Es lo que lleva el amor a la humanidad a su verdadero éxito y cumplimiento. Esto es esencialmente así. Por tanto no hay problemas mientras en su esencia funcione bien, pero la verdad es que para nada se detiene en su esencia.

El progreso de la ciencia es sumamente importante. Para volver al ejemplo del principio, si la medicina progresa, enfermedades antiguamente incurables como la malaria se vuelven fácilmente curables. Que miles o decenas de miles de personas mueran rápidamente una tras otra a causa de una enfermedad contagiosa se vuelve cosa del pasado. Así está sucediendo hoy en día, con lo cual es conveniente que la ciencia y la ética o amor a la humanidad armonicen entre sí en el seno de la tecnología. No obstante, como dijimos al principio, en cuanto la perspectiva científica sin humanos se fortalece debido al continuo progreso de la ciencia, esta perspectiva se hace con el dominio de la manera de pensar y actuar de las personas y desde allí gana un enorme impulso. De este modo, el mundo del amor a la humanidad se va contrayendo gradualmente. Tal es, me parece, la condición resultante. Un lugar como un hospital es para curar enfermedades, por tanto no es el caso que allí desaparezcan completamente las relaciones humanas. Sin embargo, en la medida que los hospitales se mecanizan, los tratamientos médicos van perdiendo el factor humano. Pienso que esta tendencia está continuamente presente.

Para volver al ejemplo del mundo de los negocios que mencioné antes, cuando una empresa crece y su organización va siendo racionalizada, en el interior de dicha organización los trabajadores se convierten en engranajes de una máquina. Es decir, a medida que la organización se racionaliza, su operación se hace más eficiente, desparecen los desperdicios [de tiempo o recursos], y la organización de la empresa se mecaniza. Por ende, las personas que trabajan allí se convierten gradualmente en engranajes del mecanismo y el carácter vivo del trabajo de las personas se pierde. Esto se dice a menudo.

Si bien desde luego es sumamente valioso que con su racionalización la organización de la empresa opere en general más fluidamente o —dicho en un sentido amplio— es sumamente valioso que progrese la tecnología, al mismo tiempo surge aquí el problema de la ausencia de lo humano. Tanto en las empresas como en las oficinas gubernamentales pasa lo mismo. En el caso de estas últimas, su organización burocrática se convierte en un gran problema. En cuanto avanza la tecnología de los negocios en la administración pública y la burocracia se fortalece, se torna sumamente difícil que se dé el trabajo vivo de las personas. El mundo sin personas, es decir el antes mencionado mundo pensado por la ciencia, viene a manifestarse realmente de varias formas. Surge de varias formas en los hospitales, en las empresas, en la administración pública y en varios otros lugares. Cabe pensar que desde el principio la tecnología comporta dicha tendencia.

Este problema se puede pensar desde diversos ángulos. Aunque con ello daré un gran rodeo en mi charla, pensaré en el asunto de los nombres y las palabras como una manifestación de la situación de ausencia de lo humano, lo cual encuentro relativamente interesante. O eso espero... En fin, lo que quiero decir es lo siguiente. Lo más claro que hay en el mundo humano es que cada persona tiene un nombre. Cualquier persona tiene su propio nombre. Cierto que como hay tantos seres humanos, puede suceder que varias personas tengan los mismos nombres y apellidos; pero en todo caso fundamentalmente cada persona tiene sus propios nombres y apellidos. Es decir, cada persona es nombrada con un nombre propio. Se llama a una persona dada con un nombre propio. Así, puede decirse a grandes rasgos que el mundo humano es el mundo de los nombres propios.

No obstante, fuera del ámbito humano —por ejemplo en el mundo animal—, no es el caso que cada animal tenga su propio nombre. No es el caso que cada vaca tenga su propio nombre. Así, solo en algún caso especial, es decir cuando hay que dejar muy en claro que cierta vaca es única [por algún motivo], se le da un nombre. En un caso tal, una persona y esa vaca entran en una relación sumamente íntima, tanto como la relación entre dos personas. Por ejemplo, dice una historia que Shiobara Tasuke lloró al separarse de su caballo. En un caso así, a un caballo se le llama Azul si es de color azul. A las mascotas, como los perros y los gatos, también se les da un nombre propio. En esas ocasiones, los animales son incorporados al mundo humano. Para decir aún más, es frecuente que incluso se le dé nombre a cosas inanimadas.

Por ejemplo, hay muchos casos de implementos como una taza de té o una cucharilla, o armas como una espada o una armadura, que reciben un nombre. Los nombres de tales artículos o espadas famosos son literalmente nombres propios. Lo mismo sucede con ciertos instrumentos musicales, a los cuales se les da nombre porque son únicos e irreemplazables. Los nombres de estas cosas son nombres propios.

Dichas cosas, sean animales, plantas o cosas inanimadas, entran en la misma red de relaciones que hay entre los seres humanos. Antes me referí al amor humano: las relaciones humanas son relaciones uno a uno, de individuo a individuo, como la que hay entre un médico y un paciente. En ellas surge lo que llamamos amor en un sentido amplio. El mundo así enlazado por el amor consiste también en relaciones uno a uno con entidades no humanas. Por cierto, la orientación contraria a esto es, tanto como la ausencia de lo humano, la ausencia de vacas u ovejas. Para explicarlo en otros términos, en inglés la carne de vaca o la carne de oveja se dicen *beef* o *mutton*, [respectivamente]. Al hablar de carne de res ya no hay vaca. Cuando nos referimos a esta o aquella vaca particulares, no hace falta darle a cada una un nombre propio: sigue habiendo la cosa llamada vaca, la cosa llamada «vaca» es la cuestión. Sin embargo, cuando hablamos de carne de res, ya no existen esta o aquella vaca. De cuál vaca estemos hablando ya no es la cuestión. Si la ofrecemos como carne de res, cualquiera da igual. Desde luego, cabe decir que también en el caso en que cualquier vaca da igual la cosa llamada «vaca» se vuelve una cuestión. Cuando se habla de esta o aquella vaca, la cosa llamada «vaca» también puede verse como una cuestión. Sin embargo, pensándolo una vez más, aquí hay una diferencia fundamental. Cuando se dice solamente «vaca», este es un nombre común (general). Lo que este nombre común indica es la vaca en general, es decir, el *concepto* de vaca. El *concepto* de «vaca» tiene el sentido del nombre común «vaca».

Más o menos en esto consiste un nombre común, pero aquí están contenidas dos orientaciones fundamentalmente diferentes. Por un lado, la palabra «vaca» está conectada con las vacas en tanto existencias que tienen carácter real. Cada una de ellas puede tener un nombre propio. Aunque en realidad esta o aquella vaca no tengan su propio nombre, siempre es posible ponerles uno. Igualmente pasa con cada gorrión y cada pino. Puesto que cada cosa —por ejemplo cada gorrión— es irreemplazable, es un individuo. Por tanto, los nombres comunes contienen una orientación hacia los nombres propios: los nombres comunes están conectados con la existencia real. Sin embargo, por otro lado, la carne de res comporta una relación con el nombre general vaca, pero no en tanto nombre general conectado con dicha *existencia*. Aquí no hay esta o aquella vaca. Siempre que sea una vaca, cualquiera da igual. La vaca es una cuestión solo en tanto comida, solo como «algo que se puede comer». La cuestión con la vaca no es la vaca en tanto «cosa» (en tanto existencia), sino solamente en tanto «algo» que se puede comer. Cabe decir que es un «algo» sin ser «cosa». Cuando comemos carne de res, es normal que expresamente digamos «comer carne de res» en lugar de decir «comer vacas». Si dijéramos que comemos vacas, nos haríamos animales como un tigre o un leopardo, o bien nos haríamos gente salvaje. Igualmente, al comer pollo no se nos viene a la cabeza el pollo en tanto existencia. Si habláramos tal cual de comer aves, nos haríamos iguales a los zorros. Sea como sea, incluso si al decir carne de res el concepto de «vaca» se vuelve una cuestión, en ese caso el concepto no se orienta hacia la conexión con la *existencia* de la vaca; por el contrario, cabe decir que se orienta a abstraer la *existencia* y hacerse una cuestión tan solo desde el punto de vista de la lógica formal abstracta. En ese sentido, el concepto de «vaca» no es más que un simple concepto abstracto. Estamos hablando del punto de vista de la ausencia de la vaca.

Avanzando un poco más, pasará lo siguiente. ¿Qué es, por ejemplo, la carne de res? Es proteína, proteína animal. Por ende, hay que comer carne de res para tener fuerzas. La proteína animal resulta así ser un nutriente infaltable. Con mayor razón se da la ausencia de la vaca si la carne de res es una fuente de proteína animal. A la vaca se le sustrae su existencia, y así ya no hay una cosa llamada vaca. Ahora bien, al hacer de la proteína un concepto científico, el mundo de la ciencia es completamente diferente del mundo en el que la vaca pasta. Al seguir esta orientación completamente, pasando al mundo de la física, el concepto se hace aún más abstracto: la proteína se vuelve calor, fuerza o energía. Visto así, este es un mundo completamente contrario al de los nombres propios donde hay vacas individuales. El mundo donde se da el amor, en el que la vaca vuelve con el granjero siempre que este le vocea «¡Eh, Clarita!», se desvanece. La orientación científica es ese tipo de orientación, es decir, no es solo la ausencia de humanos, sino también la de vacas, y rastreándola hasta la raíz, también la ausencia de escritorios o tazas de té. Así como la vaca se convierte en carne de res y en proteína animal, también la taza de té se convierte en nada en el mundo de la ausencia de tazas de té. En el fundamento de la perspectiva de la ciencia y tecnología modernas se da esta orientación. Incluso la tecnología para la fabricación de porcelana adopta la ciencia moderna y aplica los resultados del análisis químico a diversos aspectos del proceso. A partir de aquí se piensan distintas soluciones ingeniosas. A la vez, a partir de esta orientación se fabrican diversos materiales sintéticos como plásticos o metales ligeros para reemplazar la porcelana usada hasta ahora. En el caso de cosas como la carne de res, cabe pensar en la comida enlatada. Una empresa que fabrica comida enlatada se automatiza completamente, hace una línea de ensamble, y a final de cuentas la vaca se le entrega al transportador en forma de comida enlatada. Mediante la ciencia y la tecnología, la perspectiva científica de la ausencia de la vaca se hace así real. Por ende, ¿no podría pensarse que el mismo fenómeno se está manifestando en el mundo humano?

Evidentemente, en el verdadero mundo humano cada persona tiene su propio nombre. Por ejemplo, cuando vamos caminando por la calle, no nos preocupa casi en absoluto quiénes son las personas con quienes nos cruzamos en medio del trajín. En las grandes ciudades, todas son personas desconocidas. Nos ignoramos, pues, los unos a los otros. Cuando prestamos atención a alguien es porque lleva puesto un bonito kimono o algo así. Acaso si uno quiere llamar la atención tiene que vestir un bonito kimono o algo por el estilo. Pero en general no nos prestamos atención, al menos no en el sentido de existencias humanas. Cuando estamos dentro de un tren atestado, no prestamos ni un poco de atención a la existencia humana de los otros mientras nos empujamos unos a otros hasta un nivel físicamente desagradable. Pienso que el mundo en el que no existimos realmente en tanto seres humanos se ha vuelto universal en nuestros días. Sin embargo, cuando en un tren atestado o una calle agitada alguien de repente nos llama diciendo «¡eh, Pepe!», en ese instante se manifiesta el mundo humano original. Se despliega el mundo con humanos, aquel en el cual podemos llamarnos y respondernos unos a otros. Así es como pienso el asunto.

Por tanto, que cada persona tenga su propio nombre significa que cada una es una existencia irreemplazable. Cuando nace un niño, se le da un nombre sin falta. Dar un nombre es un importante acto que contiene un profundo significado. Si bien en tiempos recientes se dice que un nombre no es más que un símbolo o código, la verdad es que dar un nombre es el acto que inserta a cada persona en el mundo humano original, por lo cual en la antigüedad se llevaba a cabo como una importante ceremonia. Como un vestigio de ello, hoy en día en Europa se instituye la figura del padrino o madrina. Quienes traen a un niño al mundo de la naturaleza son sus padres de sangre, pero quienes le ponen nombre y con ello lo introducen en el mundo humano son sus padrinos. El sentido de los padrinos parece ser el de otorgarle al niño una existencia en el mundo humano. Cabe considerar que los antiguos aún tenían la capacidad de captar el profundo significado contenido en el dar un nombre, por lo cual este acto era tenido en gran estima. Es decir, aún mantenían la sensibilidad a lo humano y a la existencia humana.

Lo mismo es mucho más claro en el caso de la tierra natal. ¿Qué tipo de mundo es la tierra natal? Dicho en términos simples, pienso que es un mundo en el cual todas las cosas existentes se relacionan con uno mismo en tanto todas tienen su propio nombre, un nombre propio. No tengo tiempo para expresarlo en detalle, pero en todo caso en la tierra natal cada persona sabe quién es y de dónde viene. Si no siempre, sí en la gran mayoría de casos se sabe quién vive en cada casa, quiénes son sus padres y quiénes son los padres de sus padres. No solo los seres humanos: también las montañas o los ríos se presentan ante mí como cosas con nombre propio. Es decir, como decía arriba, tanto los seres humanos como las montañas o los ríos se presentan cada cual en su propia *existencia* ante mí. Desde mi propio punto de vista, me aproximo con un sentimiento real al hecho de que la montaña esté aquí o el río esté allí. La tierra natal es el lugar donde nací, donde llegué a este mundo, por tanto es el lugar de nacimiento de mi propia *existencia* dentro de este mundo. Pero como recién decía, este lugar de nacimiento de la propia existencia es al mismo tiempo el lugar donde siento realmente todas las cosas cada cual en su propia *existencia*. En último término, esta persona, aquella otra, esta montaña, aquel río, incluso cada árbol y cada hoja de hierba sin nombre, mueven mis sentimientos solo por el hecho de *estar* allí. Cada existencia y la existencia de mí mismo entran en contacto; es más, en profundo contacto. En eso, me parece, consiste la tierra natal. En ello radica que despierte profunda tranquilidad y melancolía.

Avancemos un poco más. La propia tierra natal no puede ser separada de la tierra natal de los dioses. La tierra donde uno nació tiene un espíritu protector, de modo que la existencia de uno está conectada con él. Puesto que todas las personas de esa tierra nacieron por la gracia de esta divinidad, los padres llevan ante la estela del dios a los niños recién nacidos para expresarle su gratitud y pedirle su bendición. Las personas han hecho esto por muchas generaciones. La divinidad tutelar de un territorio es la fuente donde se constituyen y existen las montañas o ríos, pájaros o bestias, incluso cada árbol y cada hoja de hierba en dicho territorio; donde se constituyen y existen todas las cosas que hay en la tierra natal. Además, es donde los integrantes de cada familia se ganan la vida que han llevado por generaciones y generaciones. En otras palabras, dado el espacio de la tierra natal, dadas toda la naturaleza y toda la historia de la tierra natal, a la raíz del conjunto de todo esto está el dios tutelar. Tanto la existencia de uno mismo como la de todas las cosas están conectadas con el dios. Inclusive el contacto entre existencia y existencia que se da en la tierra natal es posible fundamentalmente en virtud de la fuerza conectiva del dios. Cabe pensar que la tierra natal es ese tipo de mundo. Cabe también decir que es un mundo donde cada cosa tiene su propio nombre. Es decir, a la raíz (en el fundamento) de la existencia de todas las cosas —los seres humanos, las montañas o ríos, cada árbol y cada hoja de hierba—, en el mundo de la gran armonía, en dicho lugar fundamental puede sentirse la presencia del dios. Este es, pues, el mundo en el que uno ha nacido. Creo que a grandes rasgos eso es lo que significa «tierra natal».

Por cierto, todas la religiones tratan acerca de dicha «tierra natal», del mundo donde todas las cosas se relacionan entre sí en términos de nombres propios, el mundo humano original. No obstante, en lo que respecta a la pregunta por dónde está la verdadera tierra natal, no basta quedarnos con el sentido ordinario de tierra natal como lugar de nacimiento de los seres humanos, como «mundo de los vivos». Aun cuando esta tierra natal es el lugar que de algún modo trae tranquilidad a las personas, al tiempo que es el lugar donde nacen es el lugar donde mueren. Esta sigue siendo una grandísima cuestión, a saber, la inevitabilidad del nacimiento, la enfermedad y la muerte: la presencia de la muerte en la existencia humana es enorme sufrimiento. Más aún, una vez que un recién nacido recibe su nombre, a medida que va creciendo va teniendo experiencia de cosas que le agradan y cosas que le desagradan, y entra así en el mundo del amor y el odio. En el fundamento del agrado y el desagrado se encuentra la distinción entre lo bueno y lo malo. No hay cómo extirpar esta distinción del mundo humano, no hay cómo extirpar el amor y el odio del mundo humano: por ello se convierten en semilla del sufrimiento. No solo la muerte: también la vida humana misma es sufrimiento. A partir de la diferenciación entre lo agradable y lo desagradable, lo bueno y lo malo, el sufrimiento brota todo el tiempo en la vida humana. No solo la muerte, sino también la vida humana misma es sufrimiento.

Así pues, considerando este hecho más fundamentalmente, en el fundamento primario del ser humano se halla la distinción entre yo y otro. Es decir, yo y otro existen separadamente y en mutua oposición, uno frente a otro, de modo que el yo es el yo y el otro es el otro. A partir de esta distinción entre yo y otro, surge la diferenciación entre bueno y malo, amor y odio. Más aún, surge también lo que llamamos temor a la muerte: temor de dejar de existir. Todo esto se encuentra en el mundo humano. Así las cosas, ¿qué sucede entonces con la tierra natal? Es verdad que todas las personas que tienen una tierra natal la añoran y hallan tranquilidad en ella; pero en tanto hecho real la tierra natal no es más que el mundo del amor y el odio en el cual borbotean las opiniones sobre lo bueno y lo malo: el mundo de la vida y la muerte. No es el lugar donde se puede hallar la verdadera tranquilidad: la de librarse de la distinción entre amor y odio, vida y muerte, yo y otro. Siendo así el caso, ¿dónde está, pues, la verdadera tierra natal? No en el mundo humano. Este es, en su fundamento, un mundo de sufrimiento, por tanto no es el mundo de la verdadera tranquilidad. Para tomar como ejemplo la muerte, no se puede solucionar solamente desde el mundo humano el problema del temor a la muerte o la incertidumbre sobre lo que pasará después de la muerte. El mundo humano no es la tierra natal última. Según pienso, el mundo de los humanos no es la *tierra natal* de los mismos.

En este punto, si pensamos en qué puede consistir el problema de la muerte —o del temor a la muerte—, consiste en que por nacer y vivir en este mundo tememos a la muerte. Sobra decirlo. Es natural que a cada persona nacida en este mundo le llegue la muerte. A la existencia que es uno le llegará la hora de esfumarse y desaparecer de este mundo. Así pues, ¿qué es del mundo anterior al nacimiento? Toda vez que hablar aquí de «mundo» resultaría extraño, baste hablar de qué pasa antes del nacimiento. Antes de nacer, no parece haber temor a la muerte. Es a partir del nacimiento que la muerte se vuelve un problema. Toda vez que antes de nacer no hay ni nacimiento ni vida, tampoco hay muerte. Suena extraño hablar de cómo es el yo antes de nacer, pero en todo caso no se trata del yo que nace de sus padres, sino de como es un poco antes.

Sobre este yo como es antes de nacer ha pensado el budismo desde siempre. Por ejemplo, en escuelas como el zen se habla del sí (el «sí-mismo») como es antes de nacer de sus padres mediante expresiones como «el rostro original antes de nacer de los propios padres». El propio rostro original significa el rostro que uno tiene desde el principio: el yo verdadero. No se trata del yo que nace de sus padres, sino del que no nace de los padres: se trata del yo allí donde no hay ni siquiera temor a la muerte. Así, antes de nacer de los propios padres significa antes de que este mundo entero se constituya. Más aún, como el budismo habla también de la transmigración por los seis mundos, puede decirse que un ser humano pudo haber sido anteriormente, por ejemplo, una vaca o un caballo. En ese caso, resultaría que como vaca o caballo temía a la muerte y llevaba una vida de sufrimiento. Por ende, durante ese interminable ciclo de muerte y renacimiento todos los seres sintientes han sido padres o hijos unos de otros. Así las cosas, puede decirse que «antes de nacer de los propios padres» significa antes de la transmigración por los seis mundos, del ciclo de muerte y renacimiento. Sea como sea, se trata del yo *anterior* a todas las cosas de este mundo, *antes* del tiempo y del espacio enteros. Desde su punto de vista, el zen intenta clarificar este sí. A esta clarificación se le llama *kenshō* o *satori*.

Cierto es que puede pensarse el «antes» a la manera de una religión muy diferente del zen; pero, dejando por un momento el cristianismo de lado, en el caso del budismo quizá haya lugar a hablar del llamado del Buda desde ese «antes». En otras palabras, el Buda llama al ser humano desde el mundo anterior a haber nacido de los propios padres. Un poco antes ponía como ejemplo cuando caminamos en medio del trajín de una calle agitada, o cuando nos empujamos unos a otros en un tren lleno. En casos así, con que alguien nos llame diciendo «¡eh, Pepe!», en ese instante y en ese lugar se manifiesta súbitamente el mundo de los humanos que tienen, cada uno, su propio nombre. En medio de la situación de la ausencia de lo humano, el mundo de lo humano se abre realmente. Sin embargo, evidentemente no basta con eso. Tampoco basta con la «tierra natal» en el interior del mundo humano: es el mundo en el que borbotean y se agitan las distinciones, el amor y el odio, la vida y la muerte, el yo y el otro. Si observamos el mundo humano entero desde un punto más elevado, se presenta como el empujarse unos a otros dentro de un tren. En medio de ello, el instante en el que se abre el lugar de la realidad y el campo en el que se manifiesta el sí original, evidentemente, es cuando alguien llama diciendo «¡Eh, Pepe!».

En este caso, ese es el llamado del Buda. O sea, es un llamado desde el mundo anterior al nacimiento donde no hay ni siquiera temor a la muerte. Desde allí uno es llamado por su nombre. O bien puede decirse que uno llama en esa dirección. Es lo mismo. O bien puede decirse también que el Buda llama al Buda por su nombre. Es como cuando dentro un tren una persona A se dirige a una persona B y le llama diciendo «!Eh, B, soy yo, A!». Se trata de lo mismo. En el hecho de ser llamado están siempre incluidos el propio nombre y el nombre del Buda. El propio nombre es un nombre propio, es decir, uno mismo es el significado de dicho nombre. Cuando se profiere, uno mismo está siendo llamado. Que uno sea llamado por su nombre o que el otro invoque el nombre son dos lados de un mismo hecho: ser llamado. Tomemos como ejemplo el «nombre del Buda». Veamos. Cuando se invoca el nombre del Buda, uno es llamado y contesta sí. Tanto esa invocación del Buda como el que uno sea llamado se dan desde un lugar «antes de nacer de los propios padres», anterior a la formación del mundo. Es decir, desde un mundo donde no hay ni nacimiento ni muerte (sin *samsara*, dicho a la manera budista): un mundo más allá de las distinciones, del amor y el odio, la vida y la muerte, yo y otro. Estamos hablando de una invocación y un llamado desde dicho mundo. Por ende, las personas que están en el samsara, es decir que han nacido y por tanto deben temer a la muerte, escuchan y responden: sí.

Yo siento una transmisión en este llamado mutuo de responder al llamado y sentirlo en la invocación, o en lo que en el zen se denomina «el rostro original antes de nacer de los propios padres». A esto también puede aludirse como no dualidad entre samsara y nirvana, o no dualidad entre obstrucciones mentales y despertar. Si bien hay otras varias maneras de decirlo, en todo caso desde el punto de vista fundamental del budismo se puede pensar como un lugar de transmisión. Dígasele ya rostro original, ya unidad del llamado mutuo entre Buda y persona ordinaria, fundamentalmente se trata de un lugar de transmisión que es un aspecto fundamental del budismo. ¿No será que si buscamos el verdadero lugar donde halla su fundamento primario la existencia humana, si buscamos la verdadera «tierra natal» del ser humano, resultar ser ese lugar de transmisión?

Por ende, ¿no será ese el lugar desde el cual inclusive el mundo de la ciencia, el antedicho mundo sin lo humano, puede verdaderamente sostenerse? El mundo sin lo humano es el mundo de las cosas inertes, es decir una suerte de mundo de la muerte. En el mundo como es pensado por la ciencia, no hay amor u odio, ni distinción entre bien y mal, ni temor a la muerte. Así como no hay sufrimiento, no hay dicha. Tampoco se da la distinción entre yo y otro en virtud de la conciencia humana. Es una suerte de mundo de la gran muerte. Cabe afirmar que es un mundo que abandona todas las distinciones entre amor y odio, sufrimiento y dicha, bien y mal, yo y otro. Si bien ese es un mundo sin humanos, la fortaleza del punto de vista de la ciencia se halla en que se separa de todo lo humano en virtud de asentarse sobre dicho mundo de la gran muerte. Es un punto de vista que consiste en captar las cosas desde una mirada objetiva y a distancia de la subjetividad humana. Este saber objetivo de las cosas opera realmente en la tecnología y va transformando así la vida humana. En ese ámbito, pues, la ciencia tiene enorme fuerza.

Sin embargo, como hemos dicho antes, aquí surgen también diversos perjuicios. El fundamento de donde surgen es la ausencia de lo humano. Tomar distancia de las ideas de distinciones como amor y odio, yo y otro es una especie de «deshumanidad» (un separarse o tomar distancia de lo humano) que tiene muchísimos aspectos positivos. Recordemos que el mundo humano es uno en el cual nos empujamos unos a otros dentro de un tren abarrotado: el punto de vista «deshumano» de la ciencia es una vía de escape de ese tren. La ciencia es un campo de escape desde el mundo humano de las distinciones (como el amor y el odio) hacia el vasto mundo de la naturaleza: es un punto de vista de escape hacia el mundo del universo. Aunque esto es algo positivo, esta deshumanidad se está transformando en ausencia de lo humano. No puede sino concluir en la sustracción de los seres humanos. Eso es un problema. Si nos preguntamos por qué sucede eso, hallamos la causa en que la ciencia es el punto de vista que intenta reducir todas las *cosas* del mundo a *materia*. Desde dicho punto de vista, resulta que el ser humano mismo puede ser pensado como cosa material, como cosa inerte. Visto desde la ciencia, el mundo entero es un mundo de cosas inertes, el mundo de la gran muerte. Puesto que escapar del tren del mundo humano es en realidad ver al ser humano como cosa inerte, es natural que el mundo de la ciencia sea el de la ausencia de lo humano. Sin embargo, si nos detenemos en ese punto no será posible resolver el problema humano.

En relación con lo recién dicho, hay otro problema: como el punto de vista científico considera el mundo y todas las cosas solamente como objetos, no puede avanzar un paso más. Los objetos científicos se limitan al mundo de lo visible con los ojos. Más aún, este es visto como el mundo de la materia, el mundo de las cosas inertes. Cabe afirmar que es el mundo de la gran muerte. Es decir, en el punto de vista de la ciencia no hay una vía para escapar de la muerte y superar verdaderamente el temor a la muerte. Lo deshumano solo puede acabar en el mundo sin humanos de la muerte, en el mundo de la ausencia de lo humano. Desde ese lugar, por tanto, no puede surgir la fuerza necesaria para superar verdaderamente la muerte.

La verdadera superación del temor a la muerte se da, como mencionaba arriba, en virtud del llamado desde el lugar anterior a nacer de los padres (es decir, anterior a la formación del mundo) y en virtud de la respuesta a ese llamado. Es a partir de ello que por primera vez se manifiesta la vía hacia la verdadera distanciación tanto de la muerte como de la vida. Se abre al ser humano el punto de vista desde el cual se supera tanto el mundo humano del samsara como el mundo científico de la gran muerte. Se abre así un mundo que no es ni el mundo humano del samsara ni el de la ausencia de lo humano. En el mundo con humanos, estos nacen, viven y mueren con distinciones como la del amor y el odio; pero dicho mundo (donde los seres humanos existen y viven) no se limita simplemente al punto de vista de las distinciones entre amor y odio, o vida y muerte. Es decir, desde la no dualidad entre samsara y nirvana, los seres humanos no solamente viven en el mundo humano, sino que reviven. De ese se puede decir que es el verdadero punto de vista humano. El autodespertar de esto se convierte en la verdadera apercepción de la realidad que mencioné antes. Considero que ello se da en el fundamento del budismo.

Si hacemos de ello el fundamento del punto de vista budista, ¿no revive desde ahí el aspecto positivo que comporta la ciencia? Dicho aspecto positivo es el punto de vista del saber objetivo consistente en ver las cosas tal como son tomando distancia de lo bueno y lo malo o el amor y el odio, y en ver al mundo tal como es tomando distancia de lo humano. Desde este punto de vista, surgen diversas tecnologías y acciones en pro de los seres humanos. Por ejemplo, el progreso de la tecnología industrial saca a la gente de la pobreza, y el progreso de la medicina cura sus enfermedades.

Sin embargo, ¿no está contenido en el budismo el punto de vista desde el cual se da un gran paso más allá de este saber científico y esta actividad tecnológica y se supera la ausencia de lo humano y la deshumanización que provocan, con lo cual el uno y la otra se pueden aprovechar verdaderamente? Si las montañas y los ríos, los animales y las plantas, el sol y la luna y los cuerpos celestes son todos vistos como reducibles a moléculas o átomos de materia, o a su fuerza y energía, el resultado es un mundo en el cual montañas o ríos, plantas o animales, sol o luna están ausentes. Por otro lado, puesto que el de la religión (en nuestro caso el budismo) es un punto de vista basado en el lugar anterior al nacimiento del sí y al surgimiento de todas las cosas del mundo, desde ese ángulo no hay humanos, no hay montañas ni ríos, todas las cosas son vacías; pero al mismo tiempo desde allí se puede concebir que hay personas, montañas y ríos. Es decir, es un punto de vista desde el cual no haber montaña y haber montaña son dos aspectos del mismo hecho: son la misma cosa. Pasa lo mismo con las diversas operaciones humanas (a saber, «sensaciones, percepciones, formaciones mentales y conciencia»): desde el lugar donde no hay tales operaciones, puede concebirse que las hay.

Verlo todo de esa manera es el saber que antes hemos denominado verdadera apercepción de la realidad. Decía antes que el autodespertar consistente en ser revivido es la verdadera apercepción de la realidad, también lo es el ver que hay montaña a partir del lugar anterior al mundo en el cual no hay montaña. Así, puede afirmarse que el autodespertar de la vida de uno mismo (el autodespertar de mi existir) y el saber que hay montaña se conectan y unifican en el seno de la verdadera apercepción de la realidad. En este mundo hay montañas y ríos, sol y luna y cuerpos celestes, plantas y animales, y también humanos. En el interior de este mundo uno también vive y existe, uno ve las montañas y los ríos, uno piensa y siente diversas cosas.

La realidad es de ese modo, pero la realidad entera se constituye desde el lugar anterior a que exista esta totalidad, es decir, desde el lugar del «todos los agregados son vacíos». Es decir, el lugar donde no hay ni montañas ni ríos, ni ver ni sentir ni saber. Conocer ese lugar donde la constitución de la realidad entera halla su fundamento no es otra cosa que conocer la realidad entera tal como es y, más aún, conocerla fundamentalmente. Es conocerla desde el fundamento de su constitución. A esto se refiere el *Sutra del corazón* allí donde dice «ver con intuición iluminadora que todos los agregados son vacíos». Se trata de conocer tal como son la montaña y a mí mismo mediante el retorno al lugar donde no hay montaña visible ni yo que vea. Por tanto, esta verdadera apercepción de la realidad es un saber autodespierto a (autoconsciente de) que mi existir y el existir de todas las cosas en la naturaleza son uno.

El carácter de la talidad que tiene este saber es completamente diferente de la objetividad del saber científico. La talidad no es la objetividad de la ausencia de lo humano, sino más bien el punto de vista del autodespertar de la existencia total de la persona. El saber científico que, mientras considera simplemente como objetos todas las cosas de la naturaleza (los fenómenos psíquicos animales o humanos inclusive), ha abstraído además lo *humano*, no pasa de ser una vista transversal del volumen de la verdadera apercepción de la realidad. Sin embargo, la ciencia natural y la ciencia social, cada una con sus propios métodos, logran descubrir las leyes ocultas de la naturaleza y la sociedad. Como cabe afirmar, toda vez que el conocimiento así captado agrega constantemente nuevos contenidos a una sección de la verdadera apercepción de la realidad, aquel debe revivir desde el punto de vista de esta.

Lo mismo puede decirse, me parece, de la reificación del saber científico: la tecnología. En el *Sutra del corazón* dice, justo después de la cita anterior: «liberar a todos los seres del sufrimiento». Esta frase expresa la compasión de un bodhisattva o gran compasión del Buda. La tecnología médica que mediante el conocimiento médico permite tratar la enfermedad, o la tecnología industrial que mediante el conocimiento de la física y la química permite superar la pobreza, por ejemplo, son una sección de la actividad orientada a salvar a todos los seres del sufrimiento asentada sobre la verdadera apercepción de la realidad. Así pues, debe ser revivida desde el punto de vista budista de la gran compasión.

Me parece que debería clarificar un poco mejor este asunto, pero me permitiré terminar mi intervención aquí.

Kyle Michael James Shuttleworth
Rikkyō Uiversity

Sayaka Shuttleworth

Middle School

Watsuji Tetsurō 和辻哲郎

ORIGINAL TITLE:「自叙伝の試み：中学生」[Attempt at an Autobiography: Middle School]『和辻哲郎全集』[Complete works of Watsuji Tetsurō] (Tokyo: Iwanami Shoten, 1961–1978), 18: 266–332.

KEYWORDS: Byron—Fujimura Misao—Himeji—Keats—Meiji literature—Natsume Sōseki—Russo-Japanese War—Tennyson—Tokutomi Roka—Tokyo exposition—Uozumi Kageo—Watsuji Tetsurō—Yosano Akiko

Watsuji Tetsurō
Middle School

*Translated by Kyle Michael James Shuttleworth
and Sayaka Shuttleworth*

After the summer break of Meiji 33 [1900], my older brother, who was a fourth year student at Himeji Middle School, lodged at Gokan boarding house, which was at Hokujōguchi in Himeji, and my older male cousin Kiyoshi in first year started boarding at the middle school. Therefore, it was only myself that commuted on foot every day for the route of about six kilometers. Although I did not feel especially sad, as I was already accustomed to it, it was quite a burden for an eleven-year-old to make a six kilometer round trip every day. Not only was it a burden physically, in terms of time it was more than three hours return, and on days when I was a little tired, it took about four hours. So there was no time for me to play carefree like a child.

This was quite a significant change for me. It had already been a year since I stopped playing with the children whom I was familiar with from my village; even when I returned after a year and a few months, I did not make any effort to restore these relationships. My old classmates had started helping with work around their houses, doing half a man's work, and as such it was impossible for me to play with children my own age. So, even whilst living in my own village, I was not a member of the village children. In fact, I would leave the house at around 6:30 am, reside in the town of Himeji during the majority of the day, and return home tired close to sunset in the evening, so I did not even have the opportunity to actually meet with the village children.

Nor could I join a group of children from Himeji. Indeed, the class of second year students of Himeji Higher Primary School consisted of children from the city of Himeji. Even the children who were not born in Himeji were city boys, even more so than those from Himeji, since they were the children of the people who were working at a school, regiment, or tribunal, and born in Tokyo, Osaka, and the like. Although I only had contact with such children in the classroom, and spent some time with them inside and out of the temple where the classroom was, I had never been to any of their houses or played with them around Himeji city. That is to say, having spent the day time with the city children, I never really got together with any of them. The burden of having to walk home for close to two hours after school prevented me from doing that. Not only did I not go to my new classmates' houses, but I never even called at Gokan boarding house where my older brother was lodging. The reason why I remember the name of the house is because my older brother frequently told me rumors about it. In this way, I was rarely in the city of Himeji after sunset. This meant that I never became accustomed to city life.

    In this way, I was no longer one of the village children, nor was I able to join the city children. That is to say, the time and energy that would shape friendships with people around my age was instead spent on the daily commute of over six kilometers. Of course, at that time I never thought about the significance this would have for my personality and fate. Firstly, I never expected that kind of situation to last long enough to influence my personality or fate. After all, I intended to take the entrance examination for middle school in March of the following year. The rule that allowed one to enrol in a middle school after finishing the second year in an upper primary school was first implemented around that year, so the people around me and myself were thinking of utilizing it in the following year. I vaguely expected that once I started middle school, I would be staying in a boarding house or lodging like my older brother and older male cousin before me. However, it did not go as I expected, and after I started middle school in the following year the same situation continued. One reason was because it was bothersome to change the arrangement, but another reason was because my mother preferred it that way. It is not that I did not try to tell her that I wanted to join a boarding house, as I could no longer bear all that walking, but my mother answered that she felt reassured by my presence, even if I was home only at night, and desired that I continued commuting from our home. As for the help which my parents employed, in that period both males and females were commuting from their own houses rather than staying at ours. So at night, it was only my grandfather in his seventies, my parents, a younger sister of ten years, another younger sister, and myself. If there was a medical emergency in the middle of the night, and someone would wake my father by knocking on our door, my father would get the person who had called to wake the nearby rickshaw puller, and while the rickshaw puller was getting ready, my father would also prepare to go out. After that, my mother would stay for a while next to my grandfather, the two toddlers, and myself. Of course, my grandfather, the toddlers, and I did not wake in such a situation. We would only listen to those noises while half asleep. But in such a scenario, having a boy of already fourteen or fifteen years of age sleeping nearby, was very reassuring for a mother carrying a baby. I finally realized what my mother meant. For the first time, I felt that I could understand what it meant for my village classmates to already be doing half a man's work so well. So, when I heard my mother's wishes, I readily withdrew my suggestion and resolved to continue walking to school from my home. In this way, for a long period of around five and a half years, until I turned seventeen, I spent three or four hours of time and energy on that route every day.

Then, what kind of route was it that I spent a great amount of time and energy on, and which caused me to abandon the opportunity to become a city kid?

Before reaching the plains where the city of Himeji lies, the valley of the river Ichi, which flows through the middle of Banshū, becomes narrow just like the neck of a *sake* bottle. Hills of roughly two-hundred meters in height close in from the east and west, and at no point is the distance between them more than five or six hundred meters, including the width of the river Ichi. Such a narrow passage only continues for about two kilometers from the north to the south: if one heads north, the valley soon widens to three or four kilometers, and further upstream it becomes six or seven kilometers wide, so this narrow section really looks like the neck of a *sake* bottle. My birth village, Nibuno, is placed just before the neck of the *sake* bottle, therefore, looking from the village, the valley of the river Ichi goes far and wide to the north side while the mountains interrupt the line of sight in the nearby south. In terms of landscape, my village is inside the valley. However, when self-governing villages were created in the Meiji era, my village was connected to the downstream village, not the upstream village. The downstream village is that of Tohori, which lies just on the neck of the *sake* bottle. The south edge of Tohori village was originally extremely close to the town area of Himeji. So now Tohori village is incorporated into Himeji city and the village I was born lies on the north-eastern edge of the city. Therefore, the paths that I walked in the old days are now all within Himeji city. However, this does not mean that the places where fields and forests once spread widely have now become a messy city area, where there is no trace of the old times, as we see in the suburbs of Tokyo. Although it has changed, if one looks for remnants of old times, one can find them.

Speaking of having changed, the main road that was running along the green of the river bank and the foot of the mountains, in order not to waste farming land, has now become a paved road which runs straight through the middle of the fields, and has buses driving along it. The roadside has large factories and hospitals here and there. The number of village houses on the roadside has probably also doubled since the old times. Also the railway, which went into operation when I was a child, and which only did a few round trips each day, is now crossed by trains in both directions, and the number of stations is also increasing. It seems that almost nobody walks, except for short distances.

However, now that I try to remember the scenery of those times, even if the houses on the roadside increased, the countryside scenery of carefully cultivated fields still remains almost the same. Especially from afar, we can say that the change is relatively small. From around my village, looking upstream towards the valley of the river Ichi, you can see several mountains in the distance with Mt Kasagata at their center. Although they are low mountains, of less than one thousand meters, it is still impressive that one can see them from twenty kilometers away. This distant view would disappear once you reach the middle of the above mentioned bottleneck, but before it disappears, from the south entrance of the bottleneck, the outline of White Heron castle [Himeji castle] comes into sight. It became visible around the village of the temple of Takeda Junshin, who was my classmate from Tohori Primary School. Such a distant view cannot be seen when the air is not clear, but perhaps it was the same in the old times too. The shapes of the mountains standing there like a folding screen on the east and west of the bottleneck have not changed at all, I think. In particular, even if a new road has been built, the path that I walked in those days remains the same, so one could still tread on it just like in the old times.

The path that I walked on after going out of the village was the main road along the edge of the river, on the outskirts of the farmland. I walked with the distant view of Mt Kasagata in the background, looking at the rapid current of river Ichi on the left-hand side, and along the stream of irrigated water of Tohori village. I made a round trip on this path every day for the four years I commuted to the common primary school. Cows that were kept by the village were grazing on the grass that grew up to the river bank. My primary school was just one kilometer away, but it felt much further when I was a primary school student. As the commute to Himeji continued for a long time, I began wishing for a shortcut and some kind of change, and therefore when I walked I would look for alternative routes than the main road. I would sometimes go on the railway line, or other times I would go as straight as possible on the ridge between the rice fields. The kinds of canals which irrigated my village farmland would naturally come into sight.

After passing the primary school, one enters the previously mentioned bottleneck, as the main road passes between houses that are at the foot of the mountain on the west side, it curves quite windingly. So, I would stop walking on the main road in most cases and follow the railway line, or take the narrow country road through the village where Takeda Junshin's temple was, and then head out to the main road on the east side. This main road ran parallel with the main road that ran through my village, leading to Himeji from the north between the villages on the east side of the river Ichi, but the river Ichi flows below the cliff of the mountains on the east side at the previously mentioned narrow bottleneck, and it would be unavoidable to cross to the west side of the river running below the weir on the west coast. No matter which path I chose, it was about two kilometers to the outskirts of the bottleneck. I also sometimes tried to follow the ridge between the rice fields here, but I do not think it was much of a short cut.

On the outskirts of the bottleneck, there is a water-intake of the stream from river Senba that goes out to the west of Himeiji castle. This river seems to have played the role of irrigating the farmland on the outer wall of Himeji city, as well as a canal about four kilometers from the castle town of Himeji and the harbor of Shikama. Although it was no longer functioning as a canal when I knew it, it was the largest irrigation channel that took in water from river Ichi. So this river was quite prominent. The main roads on the east and west would come close to the river and were only two or three hundred meters away. Therefore, even if you walk along the main street on the west side, or along the railway track, it was normal to move to the main street on the east to cross river Senba at this point.

I think the main street on the east was a little wider than the main street on the west. Without going into the subunit of the village, if you look at the place where they connect, it might have been a new road after the Meiji era. Although there were no other roads around there than the main road, if you go about one kilometer, you will come across a wide riverbank called Dainichi. At that time, there were no buildings around this riverbank, just some grassy wasteland between the sandy beach and grass plots. As the main road diverts into a large semi-circle over the weir, we would leave the main road and cut straight across the riverbank. Since it was about one kilometer, it was a fairly wide riverbank.

This riverbank was wide in the area where the sandy beach and grass plot were, but the area where cobblestones were lined up was also quite wide. At that time, cow-hide was tanned on the riverbank stones, and I think that tanned hide was a speciality of Himeji. I remember hearing the rumor that during the Russo-Japanese War, they took a Russian troop prisoner there who knew well about tanned skin to teach them. Also, after the war, about half of this riverbank became a pig farm and rubbish from Himeji city was taken there. However, until that happened, this riverbank wasteland was a place that stirred-up children's imaginations. In parts of the wasteland, there were traces from when it had been cultivated into a farm, fragments of the weir which seemed to have been built at that time remained. A few years later, I was practicing a handstand and fractured my leg on such fragments from the weir. In this region, uncultivated land is so rare that its crudeness may have stimulated my imagination. I dreamed of constructing a paradise where boys could get together to play pretend wars and run wild, doing whatever they wanted.

If you cut across this riverbank, you would reach the original main road, which bypassed the weir. About a kilometer from there, the main road led straight through the cultivated land to the side of the middle school.

The scenery of these roads would change depending on the season, such as arable land turning to a paddy field from a wheat field, and from a rice field with waving rice plants back to a wheat field with ridges in orderly lines, but ultimately it is an extremely common road. However, what was worse is that I had no choice but to walk about half of the route on the main road. Although it was of course not paved like it is now, it became solidified by gravel being spread out every few years so the wheels of horse and cattle-led carts would not become stuck. Instead, from the weight of the cartwheels the grey powder of the broken stone and soil covered the surface of the main road with a thickness of several centimeters. If it rained appropriately, it would settle down as a sandy soil, but if the dry weather continued, it emerged on the surface of the road as if it were wheat flower. The powder of the soil seems different only in color to the red clay powder near Tokyo, but the delicate powder grain seemed to be much larger than the red soil powder grain. The proof is that when the wind blows and it soars into the sky, it does not go as high as the powder of the soil in Tokyo. It seems that the powder of red clay of Tokyo is not as small as the yellow grain of China, so compared to the rising cloud of yellow dust of China, the dust of Tokyo might not be special, but even still, when I first came out to Tokyo, I was quite surprised looking at the sky covered in dust from the parade ground of Aoyama and Yoyogi. Although I was used to seeing dust, I had never once experienced it covering the sky. Instead, the leaves of the rice plants in the fields on both sides of the road that were covered with grey dust had become completely white. Of course, our shoes and gaiters became full of dust from walking on the path. Even still, it was pretty easy, as it was the period that bicycles did not initiate dust as now. Additionally, probably because of the size of the dust particles, the nature of the mud when it rained was lighter and easier to deal with than the red clay mud of Tokyo. Not only that, once a little rain falls, the dust on the surface gets washed away, and the gravel and sand starts to show.

 I spent a lot of time and energy walking back and forth on these roads every day, but it was not that there was no means of transportation to reduce time and energy. This route was mostly along the Bantan railway line, and there was a railway station in my village and right beside the middle school. If I had used it, I would have been able to eliminate the waste mentioned above. However, in those days, the manager of the railway did not take commuting students into consideration, and it did not seem that the school was pleased with students using steam trains to commute. This is evident in the construction of the steam trains' timetable. The first train bound for Himeji from Shōno was to arrive at Kyōguchi station near the middle school after school had already began, that is, after 8:00 am. I think it was 8:08 at the earliest. It would not have been much trouble to make it ten or fifteen minutes earlier, but the railway did not make an effort to do so, nor did the school request any such amendment. If I arrived at the station near the middle school at 8:08 am, it would have been easy to arrive at the classroom by 8:10 am with a jog. However, when permission was requested to commute by steam train, the middle school principle, Mr Nagai Michiaki, apparently answered, "That is right, but who can guarantee that the train will arrive on time, and if you are always late, we cannot accept a way of commuting that we must expect you to be late in advance." Principle Nagai was a person who enthusiastically encouraged exercise, so he might have hoped that students would instead walk a route of five or six kilometers.

However, if that was the only reason, even if I could not use the train in the morning, I should have been able to use it on the way home after school, but the reason why I did not do that was because it felt terribly wasteful to use a normal ticket or book of tickets instead of a school commuter pass. Having said wasteful, it was seven *sen* between Himeji and Nibuno in those days, six *sen* between Kyōguchi and Nibuno, and when the price went up later, it was eight *sen* and nine *sen*. Or that might have been the time when the toll was introduced. However, when city trains were built in Tokyo in my third year in middle school, the train fare became the uniform price of three *sen* the following year, so the amount of six *sen* and seven *sen* before that was an incredibly high price. It was after I came to Tokyo that the train fare increased from three *sen* to four *sen*, but that mark-up of one *sen* caused a great deal of commotion. It was like that even in Tokyo, so it is natural that this train fare felt wasteful in the countryside a few years before. In comparison to the price of rice in those days, the transportation fee was much higher than now.

Even if that was not the case, at that time, horse-drawn coaches had been built and trains were starting to be made, but transportation was not developed enough for such vehicles to be used conveniently for commuting to school, and it was not uncommon to walk a route of five or six kilometers to school. Not to mention, it was natural for children to walk to school in the countryside, as riding a vehicle itself was thought to be wasteful. Also, when it comes to walking, five or six kilometers was not out of the ordinary. In a world controlled by such common sense, neither the school nor the guardians sought to bring about the convenience of trains as a means of commuting to school. So I walked silently every day along the dusty main road parallel to the railway or the narrow path in the paddy field. This was my fate.

However, there were exceptions. Namely, when I went to the wholesale store for ingredients for Chinese medicine on my father's request. At that time, medicine was supplied to my house by Sanada's wholesale store, and sometimes the head clerk would visit to ask for our order and deliver the medicine, but in the case of noticing a shortage, or in the case of wanting to quickly order a certain medicine out of necessity, I was told to call at the store on the way back from school to get the medicine. Anyway, the wholesale store was located between Himeji station and Nikaimachi street, which was the busiest street in the city of Himeji. Although it was over one kilometer from school to the wholesaler, it was a short distance from the wholesale store to Himeji station. So, on the day I was ordered to do this task, I was able to take the train home with great pride.

The trains in those days only ran about three times in the afternoon, one passed around the time class was dismissed, and the last train passed after eight o'clock. Thus, I was only able to take the train that left Himeji station around 5:30 pm. So, on that day, I naturally had to hang around the bustling streets of Himeji for one or two hours. At that time, I was attracted to the bookstore in Nikaimachi. Initially, there was only Kimura Bookstore, but later, Nishimura Bookstore appeared in the neighborhood. As there was only one bookstore in Himeji city at that time, we were greatly excited by the opening of a second bookstore. I think one or two hours passed quickly when I went to the bookstore to look at the books and magazines on display.

Although the bookstores of Himeji used an agency in Osaka as an intermediary to order publications from Tokyo around that time, not all of the publications arrived. In my experience, when I entered upper middle school, there were quite a few things which I wanted that did not appear in the shop front of the bookstore. So, I could not necessarily understand the state of the publishing world at that time just from this shop front. However, as it was a quiet period, books which were published one or two years before were still displayed on the shelf as new publications. Older publications may even have been mixed in. So I was able to see relatively many books there. Of course, there was no library to that extent in school. It was natural that the detached classroom, that rented a part of a temple, did not have a library, even the library for students in middle school was extremely poor and there was only one bookcase of two shelves with glass doors. In addition, the main content was an anthology of Japanese literature, which was a letterpress version of pre-middle age Japanese classics, so there was almost nothing that a middle school student wanted to read. I did not even use the library until I was a fourth year student, when I was made a member of the library committee. So as far as publications are concerned in those days, I gained an immeasurable benefit from the two bookstores.

This was the main stimulation that I received from the town of Himeji. Compared to the stimulation that children raised in Tokyo received from the bookstores and shops selling picture books, it was truly nothing significant. In later years, I heard a story that Karino Junkichi saw various books while visiting a shop in Asakura when he was a child, and learned various things from the head of the Asakura shop, which greatly stimulated his interest. This was a long time before I was born, but I was still surprised by the tremendous difference in environment. When I was a middle school student, other students of my age in Tokyo would go to Maruzen from time to time. It seems like a completely different world.

Nevertheless, what did not change in terms of quality was Kōbe beef. Kōbe beef was already popular at that time, but there was a shop that sold Kōbe beef near the above mentioned bookstore. On the days when I was going to the wholesale store, it was a custom to buy a sirloin of Kōbe beef from this shop. In comparison to the sirloin of the beef shop that I experienced since coming out to Tokyo a few years later, this meat was superior. In those days, beef was already popular among villages, and they would constantly come to sell it to our village, but such meat was very tough, though the taste was not bad. So Kōbe beef was completely different in terms of quality. However, I think it was about eighteen *sen* per 0.6 kg.

In those days, Himeji Middle School carried somewhat of an authority as the oldest middle school in Hyōgo prefecture. As we entered in Meiji 34 [1901] and were the seventeenth graduates, it was probably at the end of the first decade of Meiji that it was completed. During our time, Kōbe Middle School was completed in Hyōgo prefecture, but I think it was a new middle school that I had not previously heard of. However, there used to be an old school called Ono Middle School in Hyōgo prefecture and Minobe Tatsukichi was a graduate from there, but for some reason the school was closed by my time. It was a few years after that when Ono Middle was established again alongside the new Tatsuno Middle School. To that degree, Himeji Middle School was still attracting three or four times as many applicants, and the entrance examination was quite competitive. However, I barely remember anything about the entrance examination. Although it is not clear, I think it was at this time that I had to solve four arithmetic problems, such as calculating the values of two unknown quantities from their unit total and the total of one of their attributes, the relation between the ages of parents and children, and other problems that could not be solved by algebra. What I do remember clearly is gathering in front of the school on the day when the results of the examination were announced, as the announcement was at 5 pm. For some reason, the announcement was delayed and it became completely dark. So I started to seriously worry about whether I could catch the last train. At this time, I went to see the announcement by myself, so not even my family, my older brother, or older male cousin were by my side. In the first place, I did everything by myself from the procedure of submitting the application for admittance to the examination and I never had anyone to do it or to accompany me. I felt this was natural. However, if the announcement was delayed and I could not make the last train, I would have to walk back home on the road during the night for about six kilometers on my own. I had never done this before, so it seemed somewhat daunting. I wanted to avoid this if possible. In that case, if the announcement was delayed, I could return home on the last train and come to see the result on the first train the following morning, but I did not have the nerves to calmly wait for a dozen hours until the following morning. I was in two minds about what to do. Having such uneasy feelings, it was probably after 7 pm, when I could still make it to the last train, that I heard the footsteps of the school teachers coming out and whom stuck a piece of horizontally long paper with the examination numbers and names written in a line under the eaves of a corridor on the west side of the school yard. Then the teachers illuminated the results with the light of paper lanterns. Although it is doubtless that I was happy to pass the entrance examination, more than that, I clearly remember feeling relieved to catch the last train.

When I entered the school, Mr Komori Keisuke, who was highly regarded as an excellent principal, was transferred to the Ministry of Education as a school inspector, and the new principal, Mr Nagai Michiaki, had not yet started his new post. I think he was appointed two or three months later, but it seems that the former principal, Mr Komori, also came to Himeji on that occasion. I only once remember seeing the previous principal passing in front of us whilst we were lining up. I heard rumors that he was a very great person, and I can almost recall the previous principal's appearance if I focus my attention. However, I do not know anything specific about how Principal Komori was great. Perhaps he had the ability to calm student' commotions without overdoing it. The year before I entered the school, that is, when my older brother was in fourth year, there was some kind of issue and a union closure of school was about to take place. There is a small hill called Mt Tegara towards the south of Himeji city, and there is some kind of shrine at the top of the hill. It is right in the middle of a branch temple of Amida Buddha's Original Vow called Hontoku temple in Kameyama and Himeji city. Students apparently gathered in front of the shrine on top of the hill to conspire or make a pledge. At that time, a song called Shinonome Strike was popular, and the word "strike" was already well known to the public, but I think what the middle school students did was not referred to as a strike but as a "union closure of school." I think this form of resistance, for students to submit a request for a union closure of school in response to dissatisfaction with treatment by the school authorities, probably occurred after Meiji, but, when I was a middle school student, I already had the impression that it was an old tradition. It was thought to be a splendid masculine act to bravely show the attitude of resistance without being afraid of expulsion from school. Although I do not remember what kind of issue the resistance movement was based on, when my older brother was in fourth year I remember that he was making the following argument: "Is it not a little ridiculous to copy not wearing *tabi* socks with split toes in mid-winter and not to make men's *hakama* longer than one foot below the knees, saying it is 'simplicity and vigor,' as it is a custom in the country of Satsuma where it is warm in winter?" Something like that might have been the issue as Principal Komori was a Satsuma native. Other than that, according to Uozumi Kageo, who was in fifth year in those days, Uozumi, alongside Kiyose Ichirō and Kurosaka Sadaji, attacked the administration of the alumni association and the disorder of public finance, and destroyed the alumni association. Also the same Uozumi apparently urged the principal, with the above companions and also Hunabiki Zenkichi and Igarashi Tomehiko, to punish a classmate who performed a martial arts demonstration at the theatre. This martial art demonstration was probably a sword dance. Just around that time, in Nishiki theatre in Kanda, Tōjō Hideki performed a sword dance and gained acclamation, so there may have been some such trend. Then, such a trend was thought to be connected to Satsuma. To connect such things, the problem seems to become clear to some extent. The former principal, Mr Komori probably did not try to protect the style of simplicity and vigor in regard to such an issue. That would have been the reason why he was said to be an excellent principal.

However, in spite of Uozumi devoting himself to that claim, he hated Himeji and left for Tokyo about three months before Principal Komori. For that reason, he had to delay his middle school education for one year, but he wrote that he felt the world had become brighter from this time. From Uozumi's point of view, Principal Komori was not necessarily an excellent principal.

I do not know if there was any association between the above issues and the personal selection of the new principal, but anyway, the new principal, Mr Nagai Michiaki was apparently famous in his former post at Unebi Middle for being very enthusiastic about gymnastics. This became much more prominent at Himeji Middle, and when we were in fifth year, he was ordered by the Ministry of Education to go to Sweden to study abroad to research gymnastics. After returning from studying abroad, he was appointed as a professor of gymnastics at Tokyo Higher Teacher Training College, and was in office until the beginning of the Shōwa era [1926]. We had initially welcomed someone who was a gymnastics expert as our principal. Additionally, it was a few years before the Russo-Japanese War, so it is natural that my middle school became famous for military type gymnastics.

However, I think that during the first year Principal Nagai was appointed, he compromised a lot of the original ways. One of them was the baseball team. When I was a first year student, there was still a baseball team, and I remember going to the parade ground to the south of White Heron castle as they were going to play a match. The pitcher was a fifth year in the same class as my older brother called Koganei, who later became a military physician. He looked very courageous and like a good pitcher. However, after this fifth year graduated, baseball was banned. One reason might have been that the middle school's sports ground was too small to play baseball. However, the main reason was that Principal Nagai did not like baseball. Instead, the principal encouraged association football and came out on his own during the gymnastics period to explain the rules and let us play a match, with himself acting as the referee, but students were not interested at all. Association football is soccer, which is now popular. It is strange that soccer did not attract the interest of young people at all, but we might be able to say that it is Japanese young people's habit that has changed now, or in the old times that they did not have any feelings towards what was not popular. So what we started doing in school for one or two years instead of baseball was apparatus gymnastics. Principal Nagai personally appeared at the sports ground to enthusiastically instruct students in free-standing exercises, apparatus gymnastics, and military type formation exercise, but of these, only apparatus gymnastics was useful as a game, and as Principal Nagai started to see this tendency he subsequently stopped any encouragement of soccer. As a principle, he received an unexpectedly good result, and must have been pleased with himself.

Another thing is that he abolished the yearly school trip which students very much looked forward to. Until then, when we became higher grade students we were able to travel for one week or even longer. I think my older brother's grade walked from Yamato to Kishū when he was in fourth year. I vaguely remember the figure of my older brother enthusiastically studying the map. Students were expected to go much further in the fifth year, and they must have spent a considerable amount of time planning, but in the autumn of that year, as the first step of abolishing such school trips, Principal Nagai prohibited any trips outside the prefecture for which steam trains were required. Even still, the school trip remained and we went on a two night trip, which mainly consisted of students from first year to fifth year walking together. On the first day, we walked about twenty-eight kilometers and stayed in the town of Miki in Tōban, and on the second day, we went out to Kōbe over Hiyodorigoe. I remember going on a tour of Kōbe's water supplier's purification facility on the way. On the third day, we walked to

Akashi after touring the famous places in Kōbe, but Kōbe Middle, which we visited, was in the middle of a rice field over the forest of Ikuta, and when we crossed over the newly created river Minato towards the west, it was all country paths in the middle of rice fields. It was completely different scenery from now. The only remaining remnant from the old times might just be Ichinotani. We walked in the dust of that coast road quietly assembled in formation. There were fifth year students attached to our formation as squad leaders or platoon leaders. I can recall the two or three fifth year students at that time. These people looked like mature adults. They were all about eighteen or nineteen years old and their bodies had become equivalent to adults, so they might have been about twice our size at that time. Their group also walked with an air of extreme boredom, but since they quietly complied there was no resistance movement, and from the following year in 35 [1902], the regular school trip was completely abolished and they instead did one-day excursions twice or three times per term. Therefore, whilst attending middle school, other than the Kōbe trip, I was only taken on a temporary two night school trip to attend an exposition in Osaka in the spring of Meiji 36 [1903].

There might have been some kind of adverse effect from abolishing the school trips in this way, but I do not remember anything. The Minister of Education intervened regarding a school uproar in Meiji 35 [1902], so it might have been something to do with that. When the interest of baseball changed to the interest of apparatus exercise, and the planning and walking to a different region changed to military style marching, I think the control of Principal Nagai had become quite effective. Even if the way of doing things was different from the past, if physically stronger guys became school heroes and were always placed as commanding officers, so-called campaigners would not take issue or have any hostility towards what the principal was doing. That is to say, that the principal was supported by physical strength. However, not many students were necessarily like that. Military style marching was not very popular, and when it was announced in advance, the number of absences increased dramatically, so the principal thought to announce it suddenly at the starting time on the day, that is, after all the students entered the school gate. Even still, clever students sensed the signs and nimbly hid themselves. In that way, it does not mean there were no complaints at all, but such students did not have enough courage to express their complaints. So on the surface, a great majority of the students went along with the campaigners. Therefore, for the five years that Principal Nagai worked, there was not one resistance movement or union closure. The atmosphere of placing a disproportionate emphasis on gymnastics was unsuitable for fostering interest towards thought and literature. I got into reading those kind of things when I was still at the age when I enjoyed reading exploration novels.

A few months after Principal Nagai, Mr Aida Keinosuke was appointed from September and took charge of Japanese and essays in my class. I think it was thanks to Mr Aida that I first felt the enjoyment of *waka* and classic poetry. As he encouraged us to freely write our impressions in the style of "drawing from nature,"[1] I think free choice of a literary topic, which Mr Aida later became famous for emphasizing, already appeared substantially in practice. As proof of this, what comes to mind is an essay that I wrote after going on an excursion to Mt Shosha in November of that year. In the villages near the foot of Mt Shosha, persimmon fruits grew beautifully. So, I wrote my impression in the essay, with continuous red marks dotted through half a page. The teacher enthusiastically praised it in the classroom, and for a while after that I was referred to as "Persimmon" by my classmates.

The following might have been connected to that episode to some extent. After watching and remembering what my older brother was doing around that time, I did some hectograph printing. In fact, I used vegetable gelatine instead of *konnyaku* [devil's tongue] but in order to print like that, I needed a text to be printed. I do not remember what I wrote, but anyway I think I wrote two or three papers in purple ink for copying. At that time, as there was a little blank space, I vaguely remember writing a poem and a phrase. That is to say, that I learned from the appearance of magazines that was generally done at that time. However, I could not do the printing very well, and I was only able to print three or five copies at most. Moreover, the result was not very good. Still, I made it at great pains, and I think I gave one or two

---

1. The style of "drawing from nature" (写生) was pioneered by Masaoka Shiki, and emphasized describing the subject rather than devising an abstract account. Moreover, Shiki espoused that haiku should be written from direct experience rather than the imagination. In Shiki's account, there are three stages: beginners copy reality as it is, the advanced select carefully from experience, and masters include the internal, psychological reality of what is truthful (*makoto*).

copies to my classmates with whom I was friendly at that time. It was around the end of the first year, and I think it was around when I turned fourteen years old, but most of my classmates were already sixteen or seventeen and their bodies were much bigger. Those like me, who entered after finishing the second year of upper primary school, were only about ten percent of the students, and we were gathered at the end in a row and were treated as children even by our classmates. So, of course, I did not think I would be noticed by students in higher grades. One reason was because I was receiving indirect protection from my older brother in fifth year, but I felt my attitude was extremely childish, and I did not even notice such things in those days.

However, a few months later, shortly after my older brother graduated and I became a second year student, Fujita Naoichi, who had newly became a fifth year student, gave me a warning on the way to school in the morning: "Some of the upcoming fifth year students have been making a fuss, saying they would impose sanctions on the cheeky students in lower grade. You are being watched by them. They said you are very impertinent to make and distribute magazines. You should be careful." This was a great surprise to me. What these sanctions entailed was being punched or kicked by those who are physically strong, that is, so-called "striking with fists" sanctions, but I could not understand however hard I tried how that unsuccessful *konnyaku* printing was worth receiving such a dreadful punishment. When I thought about it later, it was true that I handed over one or two copies of the *konnyaku* printing magazines to friends, and it is possible that people who seen it judged it to be part of a few dozen. A few years before in this middle school, in a circulated magazine that was made by a club called *Kyōkenkai*, Uozumi Kageo had written an essay that criticized the punishment imposed by upper grade students, but even if I had not written such an essay, compared to a circulated magazine, *konnyaku* printing was more dangerous. So, it seems that making such a thing itself was extremely cheeky. However, there was no way that I could have known at that time, and it seemed like a truly mysterious persecution. From this day, I think that the way I looked at upper grade students changed.

Fujita Naoichi later became a professor in the department of pharmaceutics at Tokyo University. When I think about it later, it seems he was being used as a lackey by another student in the same class at this time. What connected to this wave of physical sanctions was the uproar of those targeted students, and regardless of Principal Nagai's new appointment, the encouragement of sanctions remained to the same degree. Shortly after I was surprised by the encouragement of such sanctions, I noticed that a guy appeared from Fujita's class who tried to be my guardian. That boy was small and did not have a good physique or strength like an athlete, but acted very impudently and kept trying to persistently approach me. I somewhat felt fearful, but the sense of hatred towards that boy sprang up from the bottom of my heart and I even avoided speaking to him.

I think the pressure from upper grade students continued until around summer break, but before long I no longer had to endure it. By that time, the prohibition of baseball and abolishment of the school trip had clearly appeared, so Principal Nagai's encouragement of gymnastics and the new way of taming physical strength would have been effective to repress pre-existing abusive practices. When we became upper grade students, "disciplining" lower grade students was no longer something that was even spoken about. The guys with strong physical strength were busy issuing orders and being put to work by the principal. I think it was around the time when we were second year students that this style of schooling finally started to appear.

Just around that time, I read Tokutomi Roka's *Memoir*[2] for the first time, and I felt like my eyes had been opened.

It was my classmate Shimodoi Yoshiaki who introduced me to this novel. I think he was older than I, but of a relatively small build, and in order of height we were both close to the end of the line, and we often played a lot together. Above all, I remember practicing *sumo* wrestling with Shimodoi. He was not so strong, so I was under the impression I could somehow win, but Shimodoi knew all kinds of techniques and always threw me down easily. Later, he taught me the various moves. As I spoke to Shimodoi about various things at every opportunity, the topic of reading materials seems to have arisen. At that time, I enjoyed exploration novels for boys, but I had not reached other kinds of novels. I read *The Tale of Eight Dogs* one or two years before that, but I knew almost nothing about newly published novels

---

2. The Japanese title of the book is 思い出の記, and although I have chosen a more literal translation, this book also exists in English under the title *Footprints in the Snow* (translated by Kenneth Strong, 1970).

at that time.[3] In contrast, Shimodoi knew quite a lot more than me by being one or two years older. This was due to the fact that Shimodoi's brother was at Sankō or Kyoto University at that time and had taught him such things. Shimodoi mentioned how *The Cuckoo* by Tokutomi Roka was very popular, and if you read *The Cuckoo* without crying, you are not human; he also mentioned that Roka recently published a novel called *Memoir*, which was even better and that it was a very useful book for us to read. *Memoir* was published as a paperback in May of Meiji 34 [1901], so it seems that it was about one year after its publication. I am not sure whether Shimodori lent me *Memoir*, or if I bought in it a bookstore, but anyway, shortly after hearing the story, I read *Memoir* and felt a deep emotion which was like having my eyes opened for the first time towards life.

The most memorable part of that novel was the description of the protagonist's hometown that appears at the beginning, the depiction of how his older friend who first introduced him to Christianity later died on top of Mt Hiei after being struck by lightning, and the portrayal of the main character achieving romantic fulfilment at Kugenuma in the end.

First of all, the description of the hometown is a natural depiction of a basin in the middle of Kyūshū, which is four kilometers wide and twelve kilometers long. The main character was born in the village of Tsumagome, which is the capital of this valley, and it is said that "the number of households is less than a thousand," but if there are almost one thousand households, it must be said that it is a fine town in such a countryside. However, what the author strongly described in the beginning was the beauty of nature which surrounds such a rural town. Especially the clear water of this valley and the beautiful rice plants. The transformation of the landscape of rice fields from rice planting until autumn harvest was described in a most vivid manner, and the description of how the water springs from the mountains in the four cardinal directions flowing long and wide and becoming a small stream gave the impression that I could hear the sound of water while reading. These descriptions gave me a very fresh and indescribably good feeling.

3. *The Tale of Eight Dogs* (南総里見八犬伝) was a serialized novel by Kyokutei Bakin about eight children, referred to as the eight dog warriors, who are brought together by fate and united by the Satomi clan. The plot is loosely based on the fourteenth century Chinese novel, *Water Margin* (水滸傳).

It might not have been an especially rare description for those who had read *Nature and Life*, which was published before *Memoir*, but I did not know that such an anthology had been published at that time, and even after finding out, I think it was after I started Ichikō when I read it. Therefore, as I started reading *Memoir* I received the same kind of deep impression that the people who are five or six years older than I received from *Nature and Life*. Looking at it now, it does not seem to be a very clear depiction, but as flowery sentences were common at that time, Roka's composition probably gave a truly clear and refreshing impression in contrast to that.

Secondly, the depiction of the approach to Christianity had the strongest influence on me, but from the content rather than the composition. The main character's passion for success in life and ultimate misfortune did not really leave a strong impression, despite the author's effort; but the figure of a Waseda student called Kanetō, who brought the main character closer to Christianity, not only gave the impression of a very likeable character, but his unexpected death on top of Mt Hiei, and the protagonist's subsequent conversion, caused the reader to sympathise. It may have something to do with the atmosphere present in part of the society at that time. It was just around that time that my older brother entered Sankō and started to be close to the Church, and it was just the year before Uozumi Kageo was baptized in Tokyo. The following year, the incident of Fujimura Misao's suicide occurred. In that kind of atmosphere, I think it had already become clear that the awareness of the problem of faith and the meaning of life were much more important than success in life.

Thirdly, the depiction of romance is not intense at all and extremely innocent, but perhaps that was just right for my age at that time. I was fascinated by it, and felt strongly intrigued by the feeling of longing for that kind of love. Perhaps that pulled me away from interest in fairy tales and exploration novels. In this respect, I can say that I started to shift my attention to the adult world when I read *Memoir*.

Just because it was Roka's novel that opened my eyes, it does not mean that I came to like novels from that time. Even though it was a novel by the same author, I did not really like *The Cuckoo*. I do not remember whether Shimodoi also lent me this novel, but I vaguely remember reading *The Cuckoo* shortly after I read *Memoir*. It is true that I felt sorry for the heroine, but as a work I did not really like it. Also, as a novel at that time, Ozaki Kōyō's *The*

Golden Demon was very popular, but I did not really feel like reading it. Teiji, the older brother of my classmate Kurosaka Tatsuzō, was probably attending Sankō at that time and sent *Yomiuri* newspapers to Kurosaka. As *The Golden Demon* was serialized in it, Kurosaka often told me about the novel. When I went to Kurosaka's house to play, I think I glanced at it. However, I was not enthusiastic enough to borrow and read it. Therefore, I think it was one or two years after that when I read *The Golden Demon* for the first time, when the complete works of Kōyō came out. At that time, the text regarding the scenery of Shiohara in that novel was famous as an excellent composition, but I was not really impressed by it. If somebody asked me what other novels I read at that time, I do not think I could recall anything else.

I was interested in new style poetry rather than novels. At that time, I was subscribing to a magazine called *Book Collection* for some reason, and I read the works of Kawai Suimei, Yokose Yau, and Irako Seihaku with pleasure.[4] In addition to poems, *Book Collection* contained short pieces like word pictures, which unified the written and spoken form of language and gave a very fresh impression. Also, I have a feeling that the Japanese Alps climbing records by the likes of Kojima Usui were already serialized there. So my memory of *Book Collection* is not necessarily focused only on poems, but because I was subscribing to *Book Collection* I soon came to subscribe to *Morning Star*.[5] That is to say, when a monthly contracted reader decided to suddenly unsubscribe, the head of Nishimura bookshop recommended that I take over the subscription. If it was not for such an opportunity, it would have been absolutely impossible to see *Morning Star* in a shop front in the town of Himeji. So, after about three years since *Morning Star* was published, I became a subscriber. I was more attracted to new style poetry than *tanka*. I especially liked the poems by Susukida Kyūkin and Kanbara Ariake.

In terms of ideology, there was nothing that impressed me as much as *Memoir*. Just around that time, Takayama Chogyū was praised extrava-

---

4. *Book Collection* (文庫) was published between 1895 and 1910, and was first edited by the poet Kawai Suimei. As Watsuji acknowledges, the content also included editorials, travelogues, novels, poetry, haiku, waka poetry, and Chinese poetry.

5. *Morning Star* (明星) was published monthly from April 1900 until November 1908. It was formed as the literary output for the New Poetry Society which had been founded by Yosano Tekkan in the previous year. And although it began by focusing exclusively on *tanka* poetry, it eventually came to promote the visual arts and Western style poetry.

gantly among the youth, and I think people a little older than us recited his writings. My classmate who was such a senior recited *An Account of my Sleeve*, and let me hear it. However, my older brother did not do things like that, and I did not have the opportunity to experience that kind of atmosphere, so I never had a love for the writings of Chogyū. I think I read a little of Chogyū's writing in *The Sun* in those days, but no impression remains.[6] What I clearly remember reading at that time was *One Year and a Half* by Nakae Chōmin. I was struck by the attitude of this author calmly writing such a composition after learning he did not have long left to live, but I do not think that I received a strong impression from the content. The impression that remained until later was that this author was severely abusing politicians such as elder statesmen. When I searched for it now, I can find the phrase "Yamagata is a little crafty, Matsukata is foolish, Saigo is a cowardly Confucian, and the other elder statesmen who are worthy of sweating the writing brush study English; if Itō and the others died one day earlier, it could benefit the nation for one day." I think I accepted such criticisms as they were. However, in those days I did not at all notice the meaning of the same author only leaving words of praise here and there regarding Inoue Tsuyoshi.

I was fourteen years old in March of Meiji 36 [1903], and at that time an exposition was held in Osaka. This was the Fifth National Industrial Exposition, and I think it was the last of the national expositions that started in Meiji 10 [1878]. Four years later, in Meiji 40 [1907], an exposition was hosted by Tokyo prefecture in Ueno, and quite a strong impression still remains from both of these expositions. It was not because I was still a child, but I think that Japanese society received strong stimulation from such events in those days. At the end of Roka's *Memoir*, the concluding paragraph is recorded in the form of a letter from the main character, which says, "My parents-in-law said next year without fail they would come to Tokyo to see their grandchild's face and sightsee at the Osaka exposition." Although the parents-in-law were from a town of Kumamoto in Kyūshū, it was naturally expected

---

6. *The Sun* (太陽) was first published by Hakubunkan in January 1895 and continued until February 1928. It mostly contained literary criticism, Japanese literature and translations of famous Western literature. However, it also featured articles on current affairs, including political, military, economic and social commentary.

that spectators would gather from across the nation. However, since Roka wrote this around spring of Meiji 34 [1901], the exposition may have been scheduled to be held at the beginning of 35 [1902]. I do not remember why it was postponed, but anyway it is true that it was talked about two years before the actual opening as above. Regarding the exposition of Tokyo in Meiji 40 [1907], a big deal was made about it in *The Poppy* by Sōseki, who started writing novels for the first time in *Asahi* newspaper in those days. The exposition itself was that stimulating.

I went to see this exposition during the vacation at the end of March, beginning of April. At that time, my older male cousin Inoue's house was still in Nishinomiya, so I got to stay there and we went to see it together. I think we went two days in a row.

When I follow the memory of that time, I only remember a little about the exposition and the phenomenon that is to do with it, but there is no impression of the city of Osaka. I must have been taken to Osaka once before this, but I do not really remember that time. It was probably in the winter of the year when the Inoue family moved to Nishinomiya, I remember feeling very curious upon hearing the sounds of town at night for the first time. Namely, the sound of wooden clappers for fire prevention, and the street vendor's cry of selling *udon* noodles at night. Foreigners often seem to recall the sound of *geta* as the first impression of a Japanese city, I myself felt curious about the sound of *geta* when I read such a description.[7] The sound of *geta* would also be heard in villages, but it is rare to hear them treading busily along a frozen road at night, though we might be able to say that it was a normal occurrence in a city at night. The impression of the night when I stayed in Nishinomiya for the first time like that remained, but in terms of the time when I was taken to the city of Osaka during the day, nothing remains in my mind other than going to Nakanoshima on a rickshaw and eating lunch at Toriya on the street along the moat. At that time, there were no buildings in Nakanoshima that surprised me. I found the hen's eggs in *torinabe* [chicken

---

7. In Watsuji's essay on Professor Koeber (ケーベル先生) he quotes Koeber's first impression of Japan, where it is stated: "What looked strange in Japan at first was the figure of walking wearing *geta*. I thought how they could walk well." K. M. J. Shuttleworth and S. Shuttleworth. "Professor Koeber Watsuji Tetsurō." *Journal of East Asian Philosophy* (https://doi.org/10.1007/s43493-021-00002-9).

cooked in a shallow pan with vegetables], which were starting to cook, to be more curious.

In this way, at the time of the exposition sightseeing I came into contact with the large city Osaka.

Although it was my first time, instead of having any interest in Osaka as a city, I think I only had eyes for the exposition. Of course, there were no trains in Osaka at that time, and the only form of transportation in the city were rickshaws, so what we used was the steam train running to the outer wall of the city. Changing to Jōtō line at Umeda station, going south of the eastern suburbs, where there still continued to be fields in those days, to Tennōji station, and walked through the fields for a few blocks to the venue of the exposition. That is to say, that we did not pass through the city of Osaka at all.

However, I noticed that this exposition gave a kind of mood of excitement in the surroundings of Osaka city. In those days, bogie cars were still not made for passenger cars in steam trains, and passenger cars were small cars with doors on the side with a capacity for about fifty passengers, but that was mainly carrying the sightseers to the exposition, when we got on in Nishinomiya, it was already crowded and there were many people standing inside the car. Of course, having said crowded, it was no comparison for the people who experienced the crowded conditions after the Great Kantō Earthquake and the Pacific War, but it was a rare phenomenon at the time. Especially for country people, the crowd of people itself looked very stimulating. The crowd of people rushed into the same small passenger car on the Jōtō line in Umeda station, so the normally quiet line that goes around the suburb was very crowded. In this way, one train arrives at Tennōji station, and the passengers that it spat out would walk in a line towards the exposition venue on the path in the middle of the field.

There was a large main gate at the venue, and inside it were various buildings like the industry building, agriculture and forestry building, and mechanical building, which were Renaissance-style constructions and looked very fine. There was also an art museum on the top of a small hill at the front of the main gate, it was the only two-story building and it looked like an especially splendid construction. To talk about the design of the whole venue, this was probably the center of it. Beneath the slope and in front of it, there were ponds with fountains on both the left and right, and water came out from a moulded sculpture placed inside. On the left side towards it was a statue of Yōryū Avalokiteshvara, which was sitting on the rock island in the pond. Water was flowing out from the jug that this Avalokiteshvara was holding in its right hand, and falling onto a flower basin that a child playing beneath the stone was carrying. This statue of Yōryū Avalokiteshvara looked very beautiful to me. It may be because it was the first time I had just saw a plaster sculpture, but I do not remember seeing a statue of the dragon god in another pond at all, so I think the statue of Yōryū Avalokiteshvara was itself attractive as a sculpture.

There must have been a very large number of works in the art museum, but there are surprisingly few that I clearly remember. Among them, what strangely made a strong impression in my mind was an oil painting with the title "Tree spirit." A half-naked woman was depicted in a forest with wide open eyes, both hands at the back of her ears, her mouth open a little, and a thick tree trunk at the back. It might have been easy to understand the expression was a concrete representation of a tree spirit, but not only that, but the brightness of this picture as an outsider might have caught my attention. Anyway, I received the impression that a new world opened. For some reason, I associated the name of the painter Okada Saburōsuke with the impression of this painting. However, "Tree spirit" was a work by Wada Hidesaku, and I do not know why I made such a mistake. Perhaps there were also works by Okada Saburōsuke on display at this time and I received a strong impression from these works as well. However, I cannot easily remember what it was. As Okada and Wada had returned from Paris in the previous year, "Portrait of a Woman" was a famous work at that time in Europe, so it is possible that painting was on display.

Other than that, there was something like a theatre, and I think I saw a plump western woman do something, but no impression of that remains. What I also saw there and clearly remember was an experiment displaying the perspective from an x-ray. I could dimly see the skeleton of a person who was participating in the experiment, and also how the silver and copper coins in the purse in their pocket looked black. It was eight years since Roentgen discovered x-ray, so it was reasonable that I felt it was very new.

However, what gave a stronger impression was the lighting of the venue that started in the evening. It was called illumination in those days and was one of the main attractions of the exposition. Having said that, it was just light bulbs which were set up along the contours of the buildings of the exposition and once lit up the outline of the buildings could be seen in the line of light. Moreover, the light bulbs used in the early days were carbon wire, and it can be said that it was at quite a primitive stage in relation to today's standard when the technology of lighting has advanced. However, at that time, electric light was mainly indoors, and people would look at it with the feeling as if they were looking at the palace of the dragon king.

It is not just because I was a child of a rural village who was unaccustomed to electric light. At the exposition of Tokyo, which was held four years after that, this illumination was also the main attraction. At the beginning of *The Poppy*, Sōseki describes a scene in which the main characters go to see this illumination. Young people today might read that depiction and imagine how great the facilities were, but in reality, it was just carbon light bulbs lining the framework of the buildings of the exposition. However, from such illuminations, people at that time received a strong impression as if they were depicted by Sōseki. That's the impression that adults in an urban city like Tokyo received, so, it is not at all amusing if a village child in the countryside felt their spirit was being snatched at the exposition in Osaka four years before that.

When I think about it now, it was also dark at night in cities at that time. The lighting inside houses was normally by oil lamp, and gas lights on the street had finally started. So, even in cities, the distinction between the moon light and dark night was clear, and people in towns did not forget that the moon light was shining. Not to mention in the countryside, we could not walk without lanterns on nights without moon light. To think from that standpoint, the development of the technology of artificial lighting during the succeeding half a century was great. It was apparently the invention of incandescent light bulbs by Edison that marked the development of a new era, but at the time of the exposition, about twenty years after the invention, there was not enough power to exterminate oil lamps and it was in this situation that it was unclear which would win the competition with gas lamps. As I was raised with paper-enclosed oil lanterns, oil lamps felt bright and I was satisfied with the large-mouthed glass oil lamp chimney. So I think that the degree of the light that I was normally used to was in a completely different league from now. Another issue worth considering is how happy people have become because of the advanced lighting technology, but it seems that the technology of lighting has advanced so much that people are eager for it to be bright as a firefly, even if it is only a little bit brighter. This must have something to do with the use of fire as the basis of human cultivation.

Probably as a consequence of things like that, I think my feeling of longing for the city was greatly fuelled by the sightseeing of the exposition.

Shortly after the new academic year began, I went to the exposition of Osaka once more on a field trip with the school. However, I do not remember if I saw it with my classmates. The lodging house was near Osaka castle and a temple facing a parade ground. On the second day, we walked through to the south through the city of Osaka and went to a beach in Sakai via Sumiyoshi shrine. I think there was an aquarium there and we went to see it. On the way back, we went on a small steamship from Sakai beach and saw the construction of Osaka harbor. It was soon after the long breakwater was completed. An Asama cruiser was anchoring not so far from the entrance of the breakwater. I remember being surprised because it was unexpectedly small. Other than that, what remains in my memory is that we were all making noise from being in high spirits on the ferry. The face of Mr Aida, who was dealing with the noise by adopting a smile, also arises. However, I do not think the field trip left a stronger impression than the first time because of the collective mood.

I was able to be in high spirits and make noise together with my classmates, but that was just during the seven or eight hours in the day time, and I had a lot of time to be alone before and after that, so I felt my mind was gradually being eclipsed by the feeling of longing like above. It directly appeared as a feeling of bottomless dissatisfaction towards the reality of my life. It was not based on a certain cause, such as discontent, which could be satisfied if I did something, but felt like something desirable was always at a distance and lay beyond my grasp, it was like an emotion which was infinitely unfulfilled. I think it was also related to various demands, such as those which were awakened by *Memoir*. I remember walking in the middle of fields with bright wheat and skylarks singing with an indescribably lonely feeling.

At the end of the May, the incident of Fujimura Misao's suicide occurred.[8]

---

8. Fujimura was a student at Ichikō, and interestingly, Natsume Sōseki who taught at Ichikō also wrote about Fujimura's suicide. In chapter 12 of *Grass Pillow*, Sōseki refers to Fujimura's death as heroic, claiming, "That youth gave his life—a life which should not be surrendered—

At that time, Fujimura Misao was eighteen years old, and I was already fifteen, so the age difference was only three years. (To be specific, it was two years and seven months.) Having said that, Fujimura was a prematurely talented person raised in Tokyo and was hanging out with Uozumi Kageo and Abe Yoshishige, who were six years older than I, I think that our mental age difference was more than three years, even if our actual age difference was no more than two years and seven months, so it is not especially mysterious if I received a strong shock from the suicide of Fujimura Misao. I knew this incident only by newspaper report but the composition "Feelings at the Precipice" instantly left a strong impression in my mind:

> The boundlessness of heaven and earth, the remoteness of past and present, I want to measure these with my mere five-foot body. What authority does Horatio's philosophy have? The true nature of creation, is in one word— "incomprehensible." With resentment in my chest, I have arrived at the decision to die. Standing on a rock on the top of a waterfall, I have no anxiety. I recognize for the first time, great sorrow is the same as great happiness.[9]

This writing might feel a little too pretentious now, but at that time, the writing of Chogyū was praised extravagantly, so we can say it is quite simple for a youth of eighteen years old who wrote in that kind of time. In the *Tribute* of Uozumi, which was written at that time, he mentioned this writing and says, "True feelings are plaintive, brevity of words from sudden thought, if people cried it would not stop. Singing for a long time about a poet's feeling of weakness in society, you gained the true character of bravery," but I think there were many people who read this with such a deep emotion at that time. Uozumi was twenty-one years old when he wrote this, but focusing on youths around that age and about ten years older and younger, there were many people who read this with deep emotion and recited it.

I belonged to the youngest among that age group. I think I learned the words "Horatio's philosophy" and "authority" for the first time from Fujimura's composition. Because of that, the idea that Horatio's philosophy did not have authority felt profound and mysterious. Then an interest in the drama *Hamlet*, in which Horatio appears, became strongly planted for all that is implicit in the one word 'poetry.'"

9. Before committing suicide at Kegon Falls in Nikkō, Fujimura removed a piece of bark from a nearby tree and engraved this poem on the tree trunk.

in my mind. I think an interest in the study of philosophy also occurred through "Horatio's philosophy." It was the writing of Fujimura Misao that awoke reflection about the meaning of life in my immature mind. During the summer vacation of that year, I remembered that composition as I lay on the outdoor table every night, looking up at the stars in the sky. Words like "incomprehensible" and "anxiety" repeatedly appeared on the surface of my consciousness. That feeling of dissatisfaction that appeared in spring and the bottomless feeling of dissatisfaction towards reality were both connected to reflection on the meaning of life.

However, this kind of feeling is not suffering or misfortune because of something specific, so it was very incoherent. So I do not think I discussed such feelings with anyone. On the summer break, my older brother, who had finished his first year at Sankō returned, but I do not have any memory of discussing such things with him. It was my older brother who gave me *An Outline of the History of Western Philosophy* by Professor Hatano Seiichi, but I feel like it was one or two years after this time. The impression that my older brother gave me during this summer was that he was very much enjoying high school life in Kyoto. He entered Sankō together with four or five classmates from middle school and also made new friends there, so I think it was in fact fun. I remember one such friend, Iwamura Kinzaburō who came to play that summer. He was a nephew or younger male cousin of Iwamura Tōru, who was famous for his art criticism at that time, and later succeeded the family of Dr Hirai Ikutarō of Kyoto University School of Medicine. He was very cheerful and good at watercolor painting. I think I just watched aimlessly on the side, not able to speak much.

However, in the atmosphere of Sankō that my older brother brought about, what impressed me the most was the translation of Keats' *Lamia* that was in the Sankō alumni association magazine. I do not remember who the translator was, but it was prose translation. It was a work that you would not understand unless you know at least a little about Greek mythology or Greek epic poetry, but I do not clearly remember the degree of background knowledge I had. Anyway, I felt a very strong attraction reading this prose translation. What especially felt indescribably charming was the depiction of Lamia's nymph standing on a mountain road, which leads to Corinth from the harbor of Cenchreas on the side of the Aegina bay, in the evening after being changed from a snake back to the figure of a woman, waiting for their beloved youth Lycius to return, and the depiction of going into the castle gate of Corinth with this youth after capturing the mind of Lycius. In this way, I felt like my eyes were opened for the first time to the beauty of Western poems, which stand on a Greek foundation.

At that time, a series for getting boys closer to world literature was published and Masamune Shiratori wrote a simple translation of Homer's *Iliad* and Nakashima Kotō translated Dante's *Divine Comedy*. Other than that, I think *Shakespeare's Tales* was published by Lamb's Books as a source book. I cannot clearly remember if I read them before Keats' *Lamia* or after that. That is to say, it is unclear whether I was attracted to *Lamia* with those books as background knowledge, or whether being attracted by *Lamia* inspired me to start reading those books. However, it is certain that both of these things were after I started worrying about the meaning of life.

Among the series of introductions to world literature, the introduction to *Divine Comedy* by Nakashima Kotō left an especially strong impression. This work should not be understood by a boy of that age, but apart from the ideological content of that work, if we only follow the fantasy tour of hell or the world of cleansing sin, we can say that it is unexpectedly easy to understand, even for children. The scene of listening to a memory about Francesca's unrequited love of is one of them. Dante, who was listening to it falls off saying "amen" out of pity. This word is not in the original poem, but I remember for some reason that the word "amen" was used and at that time it felt very effective.

As Meiji 36 [1903] was the year before the Russo-Japanese War, warmongering and pacifism were already rampant before Fujimura Misao's suicide, but I think the debate began to heat up just after that incident. It was not until June that Kōtoku Shūsui, Sakai Kosen, and Uchimura Kanzō actively advocated pacifism within *Yorozuchōhō* newspaper, it was also in June when the seven professors of Tokyo Imperial University's Department of Law united to propose their opinion to the government that war was inevitable. At this time, pacifism was not oppressed as anti-war ideology. Rather, we even received the impression that the government had a weak attitude and looked at warmongers as trouble. So, the proposal of the seven professors seemed to represent the general public's opinion. I think this kind of feeling was even higher when the Russian army invaded Korea in autumn. In

October, the *Yorozuchōhō*, which was a vanguard of pacifism, abandoned its standpoint. Pacifists such as Kōtoku, Sakai, and Uchimura resigned. It was at this time when Kōtoku and Sakai started publishing the weekly *Heimin* newspaper.

For some reason, I started subscribing to *Heimin* newspaper and continued until it was discontinued in October of the following year. The position of socialism was clear, but the tone was not so radical. I remember reading about universal suffrage and the family life of English labourers in this newspaper. The author was Sakai Kosen, if I remember correctly. At the time of the first issue, it proclaimed its position of pacifism, but I did not start subscribing to this newspaper because I sympathized with pacifism. On that point, I think I sympathized with the belief that war was inevitable. However, this was not from the feeling of desire for war or liking wars. My juvenile mind was very concerned about what would happen to Japan if we were to fight against a powerful nation such as Russia. However, Russia's aggressive attitude since the Triple Intervention, after the First Sino-Japanese War, gave the feeling of oppression to my juvenile mind. I felt that we had to resist this at any cost. I remember writing an essay of such enmity in school. It was close to one year since the war started when the feeling of pacifism started to occur.

Just as I was pulled in the direction of the theory of war, which was the prevailing attitude of society, I began to adapt to the feeling at school under the influence of my classmates and became engrossed in apparatus gymnastics. After lunch, when all of the students were gathered at the sports ground, the senior students who were good at apparatus gymnastics would show off on the horizontal bar. Looking at this display, the desire to participate arose. To do that, you had to be able to do handstands very well. So, I started practicing handstands as if I was possessed. I became able to do a handstand on a shelf and jump off the shelf by leaping with my hands, or go down drawing a semicircle with my legs while using my hands, but I was still too scared to do a handstand on a beam.

One day in such a situation, I think it was at the beginning of December, if I am not mistaken, together with my primary school classmate Takeda Junshin, I approached Dainichi Kawara Park. There was an embankment about thirty centimeters high, which seems to have been originally a weir and fragments of which still remained. When I saw it, I immediately felt like doing a handstand, so, asking Takeda to wait, I climbed up on the embankment. For the first handstand I jumped off, leaping with my hands. At the time of the second handstand, I went under the embankment drawing a semicircle with my legs, but in the moment before my legs touched the ground, I somehow felt "Ouch." In the next moment, I felt a severe pain in my right ankle as if I was biting into the ground and was shouting, "It hurts! It hurts!" It hurts!" The root of the embankment was on a little bit of a slope, and I must have thrust my ankle into it. Although it was just the one bone on the outside that had fractured, the pain was the most severe I had experienced. I have never experienced such pain after that either. I might have fainted if it was more than that. Fortunately, I was with Takeda who went to a town quite far from the embankment to get a rickshaw. By that time, the severe pain had subsided. I returned home instead of going to a doctor in town. As my family were doctors, we both thought it was natural.

When I returned home, my father treated me. Since he did not have materials for a plaster cast, he just stuck a bandage on a board like a *kamaboko* board. Probably because of that, my right ankle was bent outwards a little, but there was no other damage, and I was able to go to school limping after about fifty days. At this time, I was allowed to commute by steam train as an exception.

Not only had I given up on the horizontal bar because of this fracture, but I became accustomed to engrossing myself in reading poetry and novels while recovering for almost two months. Even so, I hardly remember what I read whilst recovering. Just around that time, people such as Maeda Ringai, Iwano Hōmei, and Sōma Gyofū separated from *Morning Star* and started a new magazine called *White Lily*, as I remember the first issue gave me a very fresh feeling, I might have been reading that kind of magazine. At that time, I think poetry was more attractive than novels.

It was about two months, from December of Meiji 36 [1903] to January of 37 [1904], when I was recuperating after fracturing my leg, during that time I have a memory of feeling that I was suddenly changing. Before long, at the beginning of March, I turned fifteen years old, so it might be because of the apparent age or the particular phenomenon of the recovery period from the injury, but anyway, around this time, I think my interest in literature and ideology suddenly increased. It may have helped that I was permitted to commute by steam train for three months after being able to finally walk.

It was at the beginning of February when my father bought me commuter tickets for the steam train, after obtaining permission from the school. This was probably the only case when he took care of something related to school. As it was rare, I can remember my father's facial expression at that time. However, I do not think he went to school to negotiate. He probably asked Mr Hagiwara Tsunekichi, who was teaching mathematics at my school. Mr Hagiwara's house was in a village across the river called Shigekuni, and he was commuting to school from there, or lodging in Himeji, but at that time he was commuting from home. He would go out to the station passing near my house. In addition, my father constantly visited Shigekuni village for house calls. So, it was easy for my father to get in touch with Mr Hagiwara. I did not necessarily confirm that, or remember something about those things, but we probably asked Mr Hagiwara to deal with various things.

What I can remember clearly about that time is a scene on the morning of Empire Day on the 11th of February, a few days after starting to commute to school. I met Mr Hagiwara at the station and heard about the outbreak of the Russo-Japanese War. I think the imperial edict outbreak and sinking of a Russian warship in Incheon were reported together. At that time, many people feared the outbreak of war with the mighty Russian Empire, but the report that the Russian warship was easily sunk helped to calm people's feelings. I vaguely remember the expression when Mr Hagiwara, who does not normally get excited, was constantly talking about such things.

I was taught maths from first year until the end of fifth year by Mr Hagiwara. I was never once troubled by maths as it was very clear and easy to understand. Geometry was especially clear and I think it was easy to memorise. Mr Hagiwara was apparently very fond of me, and my friend told me his words which conveyed such a meaning. However, I think it was only once, around the spring of the year when I fractured my leg, that another teacher took charge of algebra. He was a tall lieutenant with a handlebar moustache, who just came out of the military. I did not necessarily think the teacher's explanation was hard to understand, and I seemed to have understood just as well as with Mr Hagiwara, but for some reason, I made mistakes in the examinations. After that, I revised much more than when I was being taught by Mr Hagiwara, but I still made mistakes in the examination.

I did not have any idea why. I thought it was shameful that I always gained full marks in examinations of teachers who favoured me, and always made mistakes in those of teachers who did not, but it was hopeless. Fortunately, this teacher soon disappeared, probably due to the war, and Mr Hagiwara returned to being in charge of algebra as before. Then I stopped making mistakes in examinations. In the end, I think Mr Hagiwara's way of teaching was good. Thanks to that, when I took the entrance examination for high school a few years later, although I made mistakes in English, I did not make any mistakes in maths. So I passed comfortably.

After that, when I returned home during the summer break after finishing my first year in Ichikō, I told Mr Hagiwara about Mr Sudō Onosaburō's lecture on the "concept of irrational numbers." Mr Hagiwara became very interested in it and asked me to show him my notebook and took it home. I received the impression that he was a studious person. In the next academic year, I heard a lecture on non-Euclidean geometry by Mr Sudō but it was so difficult that I could not digest enough. So I do not think I could report to Mr Hagiwara either.

However, this was fifty years ago. Mr Hagiwara has had a long life and is still in good health, but in the later years he was devoted to Dōgen and apparently grasped something very deep both in terms of religion and the understanding of ideology. When I saw him a long time after the war and heard that kind of story from the mouth of my eighty year old teacher, I was very surprised at first. However, if I think about it calmly it was not mysterious at all. The temple in his village, which I think was called Endō-ji, was a branch of the Sōtō sect, and his family supported that temple. So it was a natural course of events that he gradually started to have a deep interest in Dōgen, the founder of the sect, as he grew older.

Since I was a child, I was constantly looking over the river at the outline of this temple and felt a certain feeling. The temple was probably fourteen or fifteen blocks north east from my village, but I could see a white-walled fence on the terrace that was somewhat higher than the paddy field that stretched across the river. It was my father who taught me that it was a Zen temple. My father was rather apathetic about religious things and was never sympathetic towards my grandfather's enthusiastic faith in Shin-Buddhism, but he sometimes talked in a respectful tone and with interest about the chief priest of the Zen temple. I think he told me some stories of the chief priest, saying he called at the temple and was deep in discussion. However, I did not learn that the temple belonged to the Sōtō sect in Zen Buddhism and it was Dōgen that developed the Sōtō sect in Japan at that time. Or maybe I was taught, but it did not remain in my head. It was fifteen or sixteen years later, and by an extremely coincidental opportunity, that such a name started to become important to me. However, Mr Hagiwara was born into a family that supported the temple. Even if he did not say a word about Dōgen or the Sōtō sect at the time when I was taught maths, it would not have been because he did not have that kind of thing in his mind. For Mr Hagiwara, he had a connection with Dōgen without having to wait for a coincidental opportunity. It must have become a subject of deep interest which gradually came to mature with age. In comparison to that, I only glanced from outside the gate on a chance occasion. It might have been a little funny that I felt surprised hearing the name of Dōgen from the mouth of Mr Hagiwara for the first time.[10]

As I write about maths teachers, I also remember many other teachers. I was taught English by Mr Waki Toyokura and Mr Fukazawa Yūjuro; Mr Waki served as a principal of Himeji Middle for a long time after that, and Mr Fukazawa became a professor of Waseda University after being a lecturer at Sixth Higher School. Among them, Mr Waki taught me English basics and Japanese-English translation. Mr Waki, who was a small, extremely gentle person, enthusiastically made an effort to teach us English pronunciation. I feel like I can still hear the repeated voice of "It is not A, not E, but æ" while trying to teach us pronunciation that we do not have in Japanese. However, in the countryside, where we did not have an opportunity to hear such pronunciation outside of the classroom, I did not feel the importance of such memorization, lacked the natural enthusiasm, and was not able to master it. In that respect, I think it is completely different from people who

---

10. Watsuji's surprise undoubtedly came from the fact that he was unaware that the teacher he admired had devoted himself to Dōgen, whom Watsuji himself had composed an influential text on in 1923 (沙門道元). Indeed, Dōgen's writings had previously been privy to Zen practitioners and practically unknown outside of these inner circles. As Thomas Kasulis makes explicit "[Watsuji's] *Shamon Dōgen* radically altered Dōgen's status in Japanese intellectual history, transforming him from being a revered and little-read patriarch of Sōtō Zen Buddhism into one of the major philosophers of East Asian Buddhism." *Purifying Zen: Watsuji Tetsuro's Shamon Dōgen*, translated by Steve Bein (Honolulu: University of Hawai'i Press. 2011), x.

learned a foreign language by being in contact with foreigners from childhood in Tokyo.

Mr Fukazawa was always dressed in Japanese clothes and was almost always sitting in the chair at the podium and rarely used chalk. Instead, I think he told various interesting stories related to the contents of the textbook. Using a Tokyo dialect that stood out, mixing in puns and sarcasm he sometimes raised my spirit. I borrowed an English novel from him and read it, but I do not remember what led to this. Perhaps I went to ask about reading materials. The first book which I borrowed was an American detective novel. This was also the first book that I read in English, but I do not remember the title or the name of the author at all. What I remember is the use of "revolver" instead of "pistol," and the main character was a detective who tracked down a criminal, pointed a revolver, and said, "*Hold up, or I'll shoot you*" (I think). At that time I did not yet know of the noun "hold up" meaning to forcibly stop someone. However, I was able to finish reading it in one go, so I gained courage from it and read *Jane Ayer* by Charlotte Bronte that Mr Fukazawa loaned to me. This was very interesting and I think I read it through, thrilled until the end. I think it was the summer break of 37 [1904].

I do not remember what other books I borrowed from Mr Fukazawa or what kind of things I learned about British literature at all, but it was probably after Mr Fukazawa taught me when I subscribed to English magazines published by Tsuda English study cram school by Sakurai Ōson, and bought and read books on the history of British literature published by Waseda University Press around that time. The editorial office of Sakurai Ōson's magazines sold English books as an agent for the convenience of local readers. Having said English literature, they were cheap editions such as a series of poetry by Routledge, the *Albion* series by Macmillan, and the *Aster* series by Crowell, which were popular in Japan. For those of us who did not have any other convenient way of buying English literature, we were very pleased with this agency sale. However, there must have been something which led to the choice of obtaining the collection of poems by Byron, Keats, and Rosetti in this kind of way. However, I do not remember hearing about such poets or collection of poems directly from Mr Fukazawa. I think that such knowledge was gained from Horiuchi's *History of British Literature*. It was quite a thick book with a chrysanthemum label on the thin brown cloth cover. I have a feeling that Shōyō was not used as the name of the author, but it was Tsubouchi Yūzō. As I read this book with great interest, I have the impression that this was the best of all the Shōyō books that I read after that. As there were no other literary works of this type, I might have valued it in that sense, but it can also be said that the scholarly passion in the younger days of Shōyō actually brought vitality to this. At least I received a very strong impression from this book. It was not only that I roughly learned about Shakespeare for the first time, who wrote *Hamlet*, which was the object of my interest since I learned the phrase "Horatio's philosophy." Other than that, *Canterbury Tales* by Chaucer, *Pilgrim's Progress* by Bunyan, *Paradise Lost* by Milton and various other things came into my range of vision and started to strongly stimulate my interest. The eighteenth century did not much appeal to my interest, but Romanticism of the nineteenth century appealed strongly to me. Poets such as Wordsworth, Coleridge, Byron, Shelley, and Keats started to reflect in my eyes as great writers. I wrote before that I was strongly enchanted reading the translation of Keats' *Lamia*, but I think that I came to like Byron, not by attraction to his work, but based on the description in Horiuchi's *History of British Literature*, who described this poet's wild life rebelling against convention with a sympathetic style of literature, especially the last action of this poet who participated in the Greek War of Independence. Later, when I acquired the collection of poetry by Byron, in the series of poets by Routledge, I got to like it more by looking at the portrait of Byron that was placed on the opening page and which had a sidelong glance showing the whites of his eyes. Anyway, the most important works such as *Childe Harold's Pilgrimage* and *Don Juan* were very difficult and hard to digest, but I was somehow attracted and bit into it without knowing the flavour. Around that time, Kimura Takatarō started translating Byron, and I remember worrying about not being motivated. Then, at the end of 37 [1904] or beginning of 38 [1905], I ended up translating Byron's poem *The Prisoner of Chillon* and published it in the middle school alumni association magazine. Chillon is the name of a castle on a rock placed at the east edge of a lake in Geneva and it was François Bonivard, who disobeyed Prince Savoy in an attempt to protect the freedom of Geneva, who was held captive there for six years. I was not particularly interested in Geneva's annals or the roles served in the Reformation, but I chose this poem based on it being easy to understand and not so long. Moreover, I thought that seven-seven style would be good for translating Byron's poem into Japanese.

Although I did not particularly like Tennyson as a poet, poems that are understandable are certainly better than poems that I could not comprehend, so, in the end, I think I spent the most time reading Tennyson's poems. In particular, I read the poem about King Arthur's Knights of the Round Table with great pleasure. I was attracted by this tale of the middle ages, but the main reason was that it was easy to read and understand. It was not only short poems such as *Princess Charlotte*, but it was the same for a longer pieces such as *King's Pastoral Poem*. Not only that, but I think the beauty of Tennyson's short poems captured my mind quite strongly. For example, I do not know how many times I repeated the lullaby that begins with "sweet and low" that comes at the beginning of the third chapter of *Princess*.

I think I started reading Tennyson in the *Handbook of the History of British Literature*, but it might be connected to my prior interest in Dante Gabriel Rossetti and the feeling of adoration towards long poems such as those by Susukida Kyukin and Kambara Ariake. In particular, Ariake was a poet who adored Rossetti, so there would have been stimulation from that direction as well. In this way, I was constantly absorbed in reading Byron, Tennyson and Rossetti around the autumn of Meiji 37 [1904], but the memory that reminded me that it was just in the middle of the Russo-Japanese War remains as well.

Around that time, other than the magazines such as *Book Collection*, *Morning Star*, *White Lily*, and *New Voice*, I subscribed to *Imperial Literature*, which was stimulated by the outbreak of the Russo-Japanese War and published poems and writings about the war by professors of Teikoku University. I think it was around May before the summer break. Before long, Natsume Sōseki's *Military Service* was mixed in. It was a long poem of seven clauses of six lines each, with the tones of "I have an enemy, battleships roar, do not forgive the enemy, the spirit of man." For me, who felt charm for the poems of Kyūkin and Ariake in those days, this poem was very unsatisfactory. However, it is not clear why I only remember this poem and not anything written by the other professors. I remember it was half a year later, when I read *The Tower of London* in *Imperial Literature* in the following new year of 38 [1905], that the existence of Natsume Sōseki started to reflect clearly in my eyes, but thinking about *Military Service*, I was supposed to already have looked at Sōseki with a certain expectation. Perhaps I got to know about Natsume Sōseki, who newly returned to Japan, and had some kind of expectation.

What was that expectation? I wonder if I was seeking something that would solve the problem of the meaning of life which was smouldering in the darkness since the previous year. Anesaki Masaharu, who also returned to Japan in the previous year, similarly published *Resurrection of Dawn* at the beginning of this year. I clung to this book enthusiastically with a very high expectation, but I felt disappointed from not being able to understand the content very well. The only thing I remember about this book was a picture of Burne-Jones's painting of *King Cophetua and the Beggar Maid*, which was inside the book and the discussion of the looks of such people. Burne-Jones was a disciple of Rossetti and an influential member of the Pre-Raphaelite School, and this painting was also very Pre-Raphaelite, which covers the tales of knights in the Middle Ages. Judging from this painting being in a book of someone newly returned from abroad, it seems that the Pre-Raphaelite School must have been at the center of attention at the beginning of the twentieth century. The longing for the Middle Ages which is shown there had appeal for those who seek the meaning of life.

Sōseki's *Military Service* did not answer this kind of expectation, but I think *The Tower of London*, half a year later, strongly fulfilled that demand. When I read that work, I experienced a very strong feeling of ecstasy. It was like directly realizing the meaning of life, rather than making us hear it. It is not unrelated to the fact that Sōseki's creative power exploded there and that work had such power. Furthermore, Sōseki began writing *I Am a Cat* around the same time. That is to say, that the creative power of Sōseki exploded in the autumn of Meiji 37 [1904]. Why did that happen in the middle of the Russo-Japanese War, moreover during the general offensive of Lüshunkou? Why was Sōseki, who sang, "if you swear to heaven, you can even pass through rocks, listen for one meter, the sound of running scabbards" in *Military Service* able to create something like *The Tower of London* a few months after that?

I cannot help but recall how different the period of the Russo-Japanese War was to the recent period of the Pacific War. There was a large number of people killed in the Siege of Port Arthur, but even at that time, people's freedom and energy were never deprived due to the pressure of the war. A good proof of this is Yosano Akiko's *Thou Shalt Not Die*, which was published in *Morning Star* in September within a few months of Sōseki's *Military Service*. This poem was written when Ms. Akiko's younger brother, who was an Imperial Bachelor of Engineering, or a Doctor of Engineering, was called up as a reserve officer to go to war. I think it frankly declared feminine emotion, and was a very pleasant poem. In those days, soldiers did not apply pressure to others by declaring such free expression to be anti-military ideology. Instead, nationalists among scholars and journalists spoke out. Ms. Akiko received attacks from such people, if I remember correctly, and was called an unpatriotic individual. However, Ms. Akiko did not flinch from it at all and I think she stood firmly on the firing line of such patriotism.

When I read this poem, I did not yet feel sympathetic towards pacifism. It might have been because this poem came out around the time when the spirit of enmity towards the Russian Empire reached its climax. That is to say, I heard the history teacher Mr Takatani Zenkichi very efficiently summarize the history from the beginning of the Russian Empire's Siberia invasion to building a naval port at Lüshunkou, and I remember receiving a very strong impression. I thought the lecture was somehow Mr Takatani's "inaugural speech," but Mr Takatani was called up to go to war that September and there was a farewell ceremony, so the above speech was most likely his "farewell speech." The excitement that comes from going to war might have awakened such eloquence. I vividly remember the flashy moving face of Mr Takatani who was talking at the lectern at that time. Around when he advocated that the Russian Empire's invasion gradually approached Japan through the construction of the military port at Lüshunkou, his face gradually started to shine with an increasing redness. I listened to it as if I was drunk. Then I felt the spirit of enmity spring out from the bottom of my heart towards the Russian Empire's strong colonialism invasion. That feeling might have been the same as Sōseki wrote about in *Military Service*. However, I have never felt that feeling expressed in *Military Service* before or after. As a poem, I rather sympathized with Ms. Akiko's *Thou Shalt Not Die*. This seems somewhat contradictory, but it is a feeling that I can understand. It is extremely natural that a woman would possess the emotion which Ms. Akiko expressed at the time of her family member going to war, and also, even if such natural emotions were expressed as they were, the spirit of enmity which sprang up from the bottom of my heart was not necessarily erased. More than that, praying silently, "thou shalt not die" and saying you are prepared for your death in battle on the surface is unnatural and contradictory. At the time of the Russo-Japanese War, the military authorities did not force the nation to adopt such an unnatural contradiction. Rather, there were scholars or journalists who forced this line and tried to welcome the idea of military authority. In comparison to that, the attitude of Ms. Akiko can be said to be loyal to oneself. I think that made a good impression on me.

When Akiko's anthology *Dishevelled Hair* came out, I was still an admirer of exploration novels and I was not interested in new poems. After that, I started subscribing to *Morning Star* where I learnt about the existence of *Dishevelled Hair* and wanted to acquire it, but there was no way of obtaining it in the countryside. Also, no one had this anthology within my range of contacts. Even still, as it was quoted in various other people's writings, I knew the kinds of poems such as "You who speak of morality, do you not long to feel the hot blood of this soft skin?" and "Two stars deep in heaven, the whisper of love behind the curtain of night, those of this world lie with their hair in gentle disarray." Also, I think I read somewhere and knew around the time when Akiko got married to Tekkan. I remember reading somewhere that the poem "Tekkan" was from during their romantic period, which goes like "The collected poems in hand, two people's intimacy, Kii's haze is darker than Izumi." As I was interested in Akiko in this way, I acquired the second anthology *Little Fan* as soon as it came out, but I did not really receive any deep impression from this book. It might have been because I was more enthusiastic about *tanka* than *waka*. All the more, the long poem of *Thou Shalt Not Die* gave me a strong impression.

I did not discuss such a thing with anyone at that time. I do not even remember discussing Byron or Tennyson with my closest friend, Kurosaka Tatsuzō. At that time, there was a newspaper-sized magazine called *Success*, which encouraged young people to be successful in life, and the two of us talked about that magazine. Also, I do not know if I knew it from this magazine, but we took the popular book called *The Strenuous Life* by American president Theodore Roosevelt as an issue between the two of us. However, the tale of The Knights of the Round Table probably did not attract Kurosaka's interest at all. What captured Kurosaka's heart at that time seemed to be the more pressured issue of a life plan. Whenever I had free time, I was reading Byron and Tennyson, and Kurosaka was reading books on English grammar and asking Mr Waki to look at the practice questions which he had carefully written. I did not know that he was doing this for a particular purpose, as he was such a studious person, but around the end of 37 [1904], if I remember it correctly, he confessed that he was in fact planning to go to Tokyo to take an entrance examination to transfer to the fifth year of middle school at the beginning of the following school term. He said that he had to finish school even one year earlier and cannot leisurely attend school due to his family circumstances. I finally understood how important this was for Kurosaka a few years later, though I did not really feel any significance at that point. At that time, it was popular to enter a higher school without graduating from middle school, cutting short for one year, and my older male cousin Kiyoshi had taken an examination for Kōshō in Hitotsubashi during the first school term in the fifth year about half a year before that, and quickly entered the school. I thought Kurosaka was doing the same kind of thing.

At that time, I was a committee member of the library club at the alumni association, so I was close to Matsuzaki Tatsurō, a fifth year committee member who later became a soldier, and was kind to me in various ways, but I do not remember discussing poems, songs, or ideology. The job of the library committee was to distribute the *Nihon* newspaper of Tokyo, which the school received in the corridor of the student waiting area every morning, to keep watch of the library after school a few times in a week, and to edit the alumni association magazine once a year, but I think I was mostly entrusted with such things. Since I entered the middle school, *A Drop of Black Ink*, *Random Comments whilst Reclining*, and *Six Foot Sick Leave* by Masaoka Shiki were published in *Nihon* newspaper, and I remember reading them, but it was more than one year since Shiki's death that I displayed it every morning. I do not remember what was in the paper at all. The best I could do was to quickly paste the newspaper on the wooden wall, I do not think I even had time to read it. Compared to that, keeping watch of the library was easy. It was a small room on the second floor of the main building which was at the end of the school gate, though having said a library, there was just one bookcase of two shelves which had a fitted glass door. Moreover, the only books that were inside there were the complete set of Japanese literature by Hakubunkan, and no other outstanding books. So there were few visitors and the library was like my own private reading room. The editing of the alumni association magazine was also entrusted to me, which was easy because I did not need to consult with anyone. For that reason, I translated *The Prisoner of Chillon* and put it there. I do not have any memory of discussing the translation of this poem with anyone. I do not think that it was even on my mind that there would be people among my classmates who might read it.

In this kind of situation, I read *The Tower of London* by Sōseki in the New Year when Lüshunkou fell, and felt a strange fascination. However, I do not have any memory of discussing it with anyone at all. Thus, I never had the opportunity to learn about Sōseki from my friends. Sōseki had written the novel *I Am a Cat* in the February or March edition of *Morning Star* and which I learned about became interested in from the essay Ōtani Masanobu wrote. So I made an effort to acquire the magazine *The Cuckoo*, which had Sōseki's work in it, but not one copy had arrived in Nishimura Bookstore. I asked the head of the bookstore to order the magazine, but it was apparently not easy to obtain because the order had to go through an agency in Osaka. The magazine probably sold out because *I am a Cat* was popular and they did not have enough stock to satisfy the order. Because of that, I could not read *I Am a Cat* until it was published as a book. I think *Shield of Illusion* was the same. I was only able to read *Imitation Cry of the Koto* when it was in the magazine. That was because I was subscribing to a magazine called *Seven People* which was published in the autumn of the previous year.

It was not long before my classmate Kurosaka Tatsuzō, who went to Tokyo in the third semester of the fourth year, let me know that he graduated from Ikubunkan Middle School in Hongō, the Battle of Mukden ended in victory on the 10th of March, and I think it was at the end of the month. In the letter, I strangely remember that he used the expression "Footprint of *geta* on the first snow" referring to his result at the time of the graduation. Even though I have an extremely dull intuition for such expressions, I was able to understand the meaning, so perhaps I was taught the phrase by someone that goes, "The first snow, two figures, two figures, the trace of *geta*" before that, but what surprised me was not that Kurosaka was freely using such an expression, but that my fellow fourth year middle school student from the country, suddenly jumped into the fifth year of middle school in Tokyo, and graduated with a good result of second place. This somewhat gave me the impression of a fairy tale.

I found out later that the top student was Sugita Naoki, and once entering Ichikō in the following year he was one grade above me in group three. Haruyama Takematsu, who also graduated from Ikubunkan in the same grade, became the same grade as I in Ichikō, and I started to keep close company with Sugita, but Sugita also continued to be a top student in Ichikō. In fact, he was a person with an unprecedented talent. If I had known those kind of things a year and a half ago and saw Kurosaka suddenly catch up from one grade below to Sugita, my surprise might have been ever greater. However, even without knowing those things, it is true that I received the feeling that it was somewhat like a fairy tale.

Another thing I found out later was that Ikubunkan backed onto Sōseki's villa. I received a very deep impression reading *The Tower of London* by Sōseki in that New Year, and around February or March I knew the same Sōseki had written *I Am a Cat* in *The Cuckoo* and was troubled to somehow acquire a copy of the magazine. Around that time, there was a vacant lot facing the school yard of Ikubunkan that had seven or eight camphor trees in a row which surrounded the north side of Sōseki's villa, where students of Ikubunkan freely entered to eat *bentō* or to gossip. If I was a student at Ikubunkan at that time, I would probably have entered the vacant lot to try to take a peep at Sōseki's villa. I did not check if Kurosaka and Sugita did such things, but we can almost guess that the number of students who entered there gradually increased as *I Am a Cat* became popular. In September of that year, Sugita entered Ichikō and Kurosaka entered a foreign language school, so they were not in the group of people causing an uproar, but Haruyama remained in the Repair Department or something, and apparently ended up in the middle of a scandal. The uproar eventually came to be described as the "Hall of the Descending Cloud incident" in chapter eight of *I Am a Cat* that appeared on New Year's Day the following year.[11]

---

11. In chapter eight of *I Am a Cat*, there is one scene which involves an individual student from "Hall of the Descending Cloud." In this scene, Sōseki "captures" a student for invading his garden to retrieve a baseball without permission, and demands that a representative from the school come to resolve the issue. It is highly likely that Haruyama is the student in question whom Sōseki reprimanded.

The officials at Ikubunkan would have frowned upon such an incident, but the bad students seemed to have applauded this wildly. Due to that, Haruyama was reading *I Am a Cat* very intently. He memorised almost entirely what Waverhouse did here or what kind of pun he said, or what Mr Sneaze did there. In the autumn of that year, when I first met Haruyama in the dormitory of Ichikō, he showed me around not only Sōseki's villa and Ikubunkan, but the various places depicted in the novel as if it was his territory. Kurosaka was probably not that much interested, but he would have known the situation. So, if I had asked Kurosaka about *I Am a Cat*, or to ask to acquire the magazine, I would have learnt a lot immediately. But, I do not have any memory of discussing such issues with Kurosaka at that time. So in the end, I could not read *I Am a Cat* until it was published as a book in the following year.

I do not remember clearly if Kurosaka's move to Tokyo stimulated my desire to travel, but I went to Kyoto for spring break that year. It was the first time when I saw Kyoto. My older brother was a third year student at Sankō, and my uncle had just become a professor of medicine after returning from Germany in the previous year. I stayed at that uncle's house and went around famous places in Kyoto every day with my older brother as a guide. However, not many of my first impressions seem to clearly remain. What I can somewhat specifically remember was after walking up to Mt Hiei from the river Kitashira, and looking at Shimeigatake and Konpon-chūdō, and that we went down towards Sakamoto on a canal boat from Ōtsu, passing north of Yamashina going in and out of tunnels and returned to the incline by Nanzan temple. The experience of using a canal was only at this time, so it is certain that my memory is from then. At that time, it was common to use steam trains to go to Kyoto from Ōtsu, as the Kyoto train was of course not constructed, the railway track diverted from Yamashina to the south to go out to Kyoto basin around the south of Inari shrine, so it was a lot further in distance than the current railway track, and so the canal was in fact a shortcut. In addition, I think going through tunnels and going down the canal by boat itself excited my interest. So, there were an incredibly large number of passengers on the canal boat.

As for the impression of Kyoto at that time, we can say that the canal and train were more memorable than the famous places. As trains were operating from earlier than in Tokyo, what I came in contact with for the first time coming to Kyoto was this rare train. I think it was called Shichijō station, but as we got off the steam train there, we were able to get on the train in front of the station. I think it went up towards the north of the town of Kawara before the town street widened, and through to the Shimogamo bridge, passing the east side of the old Imperial Palace. I have a feeling it took almost one hour to reach the final destination. The body of the car was very small, but even still where the town width was narrow, the train passed almost touching houses. However, around that time, that kind of width for a road felt normal, so I did not necessarily receive the impression that it was particularly narrow. My sense of speed and the width of roads was completely different from now. More than that, the train itself was rare.

Around that time, my uncle's house was placed in the town of Tōnodan Sakuragi, so I think I was on the train on the first day until the final destination or until one station before that. Then, I forget if it was that day or the next day, I got to know that my older brother was interested in Dōshisha and he took me to the front of it, and while we were there we entered Shōkoku temple through the back between the school buildings and turning to the right from around the front of Hondō, if I remember it correctly, and guided me towards Tōnodan on the road in the middle of a wide bamboo grove. My uncle's house was placed on the north of Futasujime near the bamboo grove. I think it was perhaps a newly opened area from the exposed bamboo grove. When I went to look around at the end of the Taishō era, after I started living in Kyoto, it had become quite far from the bamboo grove. Most of the original bamboo grove would have been cut down to become a town. When the story came out at Mr Konishi Shigenao's house around there, Mr Konishi talked about how a bamboo shoot sprang up from under the floor of his study and broke through the floor.

In the previous year, shortly after the Russo-Japanese War began, a military transport ship called Hitachimaru was sank in the open sea of Genkai. Just before that, my uncle had returned from Germany on a ferry that passed by the Hitachimaru. So it had been more than a year since he returned from abroad during this spring break. In the garden of the house in Sakuragi, a small two-story western-style house was newly constructed and downstairs was used as a reception room and upstairs as a study. A sofa, armchair, and large desk were set up there, but such western furniture was very curious to me.

At that time, my younger male cousin Haruki had just entered second year in middle school in April, and three of my younger female cousins were all in primary school. The youngest boy, Hiroki had not yet been born, but his mother was in her last month of pregnancy. So my uncle bought a book of fairy tales with pictures as a souvenir, and my younger female cousins explained various things whilst on the sofa. It was a story of "Max did this" or "Hans did that." My younger female cousins who talked about that story had very beautiful Edo dialects. During the time when my aunt was alive, who was the daughter of a lower ranking vassal, the children did not pick up a Kyoto dialect even though they lived in Kyoto. Although the children became familiar with regional words, I think their mother was constantly correcting them. During the few days when I was staying, I remember my aunt taking something out from a small cabinet whilst saying to the children in a joking tone, "Look. Tetsurō uses the proper words that way. Children, if you use strange words, one by one you will fault…. No, that's not right, fault-will-be-found-with-your-words" and laughed very openheartedly. I do not clearly remember what kind of wording I used at that time, but it was probably in contrast to the beautiful Edo dialect that my aunt and younger female cousins were using, so I would have made an effort to use Tokyo dialect that I read and knew so as to adapt the style as much as possible. My aunt probably sympathized with my consideration like that. Even though I only saw them once when I was an infant, I think it was because of my aunt's attitude that I felt very comfortable in my uncle's house at this time.

I do not remember what I talked about with my older brother during the few days when he showed me around the famous places of Kyoto, but I remember asking why he was boarding instead of staying at my uncle's house. My older brother explained that as they have many children it would be very difficult to look after one extra person. However, I could not really understand it well. I think I was still immature regarding things in society to that extent. Although I forgot most other things, and especially remember this question, the atmosphere of my uncle's house which I came in contact with was probably very comfortable for me. Having said that, the only memory I have of coming into contact with my uncle at this time was when we had dinner together surrounding a pot of beef *sukiyaki*, other than that, I only remember repeatedly looking at various albums that he brought home from Germany without being bored. This leaves a deeper impression than the sightseeing of famous places.

I think that the reason I went to Kyoto for spring vacation was because of the stimulation of my classmate Kurosaka leaving for Tokyo, and to make up my mind about going onto higher school, but at this time the main issue was how to prepare for the entrance examination for high school after graduating from middle school, though I did not really think specifically about that. My older brother had aimed for Sankō from the beginning, but I think he went to Tokyo for the examination preparation and also took the examination in Tokyo. There were no facilities for preparing for examination in Kyoto. So, it was decided that I would similarly go out to Tokyo at the end of March of the following year and study in some school until the entrance examination in July.

So, I had not yet arranged the consultation during spring break, but I think the desire to enter to humanities instead of medicine in the future was already present at this time. It was about half a year later in the autumn when I made up my mind to write a letter of consultation to my older brother, but during that time I thought and worried about various things. One of them was the problem of school expenses that Kurosaka threw at me. We cannot say that it was a problem unrelated to me. I probably heard from my mother that my grandfather said that they would let my older brother go to university so the younger brother would be fine with Okayama, where there was a medical college at that time. I knew my parents did not have that idea, so I thought I would naturally be able to proceed to a senior high school, but because it seemed that my grandfather said things like that due to the issue of school expenses, and as my mother never forgot to warn me to be modest every time she complained to me, I felt like seriously reflecting upon the extent that my future school expenses would cause trouble for my parents. In that respect, I think the situation is very different in the city, where they were used to monetary economy, but in the countryside, which was terribly troubled with the cash payment of land tax, things circulated more actively than money. Even though there was plenty of food to eat, there were many cases where there was no money. In that regard, they would feel the payment of only twenty *sen* or thirty *sen* was a great pain. From the perspective of life in an agricultural village, the monthly school tuition of fifteen *yen* (that is to say, the amount of money that I was sent as a monthly expense when I entered Ichikō, and I think it was the price of a year's supply of unpolished rice) was an incredible burden to send to the son. So, I became concerned and wanted to know the financial situation of my house, but I could not ask such a thing directly, so I secretly estimated various incomes. What I could see clearly was the rice paid as rent, which was brought in every January and stored in the rice granary, and various products that people brought every season. It was enough for the family to eat, but I did not know how much cash was coming in. In the end, I gave up trying to determine the financial situation and was satisfied with the conclusion that as long as we do not live in luxury we would have enough for my school expenses. Then, during the six months after that, my desire to enter the humanities in Ichikō in the following year began to increase.

It was of course the stimulation from *Memoir*, the suicide of Fujimura Misao, poetry of Byron and Tennyson, and recently Sōseki's *The Tower of London* that caused my desire for the humanities, but another reason was seeing my father's work as a doctor, I deeply felt that I could not do such a thing. My father mostly abounded his own enjoyment and was fighting illness silently. I truly admired his attitude, so whatever I was asked to do, I tried to accomplish it as well as possible. Not only did I go to the pharmacy to collect medicine, but I also did the work of processing medicine in various ways. What I thought was particularly useful was the stool examination, which we do with a microscope to find hookworm eggs. In the agricultural village at that time, there were many of these parasites, so there were many people who had a yellow face with anaemia. My father had poor eyesight, so he asked me to do the job of looking into the microscope as I was young and with good vision. I can still vividly remember the shape of the eggs under that microscope, but when I took a specimen and looked in, it was usually pinworm eggs that were noticeable at first. There were not so many hookworm eggs, and I could not find them unless I took an incredibly long time to search. Probably because of that, in comparison to pinworm eggs, the shape of hookworms felt very slim. However, even in the case of a patient's initial medical examination, it could be found in the first specimen. What was painstaking was the stool examination of patients in recovery, and the work of estimating that there would be no more hookworm. For that, I looked carefully using many specimens. Even when I reported that there were none, there were many cases that I was told to search again. Although I did such work enthusiastically, it was not because I liked the work of medical science. It was just from the feeling that I wanted to help my father. So, while helping with such jobs, I gradually solidified my desire to enter humanities at Ichikō in the following year.

The Battle of Tsushima occurred at the end of May of that year, and a victory was achieved that can only be considered as "God's blessing," but a little before that, my aunt in Kyoto passed away from typhoid fever after delivering her son Hiroki. This news was very hard to endure, as I had been in contact with my aunt for a few days during spring break when she was in good spirits. After the funeral, I clearly remember the scene of my uncle Inoue coming with my aunt's ashes for the burial. I silently looked on from the side, but my mood was melancholic. It seemed that something very ominous was starting to occur. When I think about it now, the sudden death of my aunt had a huge impact upon the life of my uncle and my younger cousins, especially the life of my younger male cousin. The impact was unexpectedly big.

Baby Hiroki, who was born soon after, was taken as a foster child to a neighboring village with the assistance of my father. So I remember the figure of Hiroki well, being held by a nursing mother and drinking breast milk. Fortunately, Hiroki grew up safely and joined Asahi newspaper after finishing university, but he passed away at the same age as his mother at thirty-three years old. However, among the siblings, it was only Hiroki who did not have any memory of his birth mother, in that respect he might have been rather happy.

During the summer vacation of this year, I lodged close to the harbor of Shikama with five or six classmates and did *kankairyū* swimming, which was an extracurricular activity at middle school. This lodging was a rare experience for me.

It was Principle Nagai who instigated the *kankairyū* swimming, and I think it started when I was in third year. That year, I attended by commuting via steam train, but I discontinued after about three days due to being stung and a stomach pain, which was an inconvenient and unpleasant experience. In that year, if we did not like it we were allowed to wilfully withdraw. In the following year, I think participation or non-participation was free as well. However, when I was in fifth year, everyone had to join in this extracurricular activity. In this circumstance, we were allowed to lodge.

It was my classmate Ishikawa, who was commuting to school from the town of Shikama, who found the lodging house. It was an old house near Shikama harbor of two elderly women for whom the large house was too much. They apparently said they would look after young people with pleasure. So five or six students soon arrived. I think Fukuda Tokujirō and Iwasaki Eiji were in the group. Both of them later became doctors. Fukuda is still in good health, but Iwasaki passed away early on. He was a good person with a particular personality.

Minato was the name of the old harbor, which was of a geometric shape with a rectangular shaped inlet, and the beach was enclosed by stones. Then, a tea house and a brothel were lined-up on the north and west sides. Going through there, on the south side was a wide field with a strip of pine trees and a shallow-sea spread below the cliff. We would do preparation exercises in the pine grove and then go into the sea, but as I could swim from the start, I was able to memorise the frog swimming style of *kankairyū* quickly and I passed examinations for three blocks, five blocks or ten blocks with ease; however, I felt empathetic towards the old teachers who could not master swimming as easily as the young students, and were struggling to swim only three blocks, but had to attend because the principal was enthusiastic. However, those people might have been doing it with the desire to learn how to swim, even though it was late in life, or they were doing it with students because swimming in the ocean, which was newly popular in those days, was good for one's health; but I could not help but somehow think that the despotic pressure of the principal was creating the unusual swimming style of those people. This way of feeling might have been an indication of my antipathy towards Principal Nagai's first doctrine of physical education.

We were very cheerful at the lodge. One evening, when we had went out together for a walk after dinner, we had passed in front of the brothel in Minato without compunction; however, someone had noticed us there and created a rumor, and we received a warning from the teacher in charge, but we did not do anything and we did not quarrel either. One of the reasons why the lodging went well was probably because both of the elderly women in the lodge, who had apparently lost children, were very kind and looked after us very well.

In this way, days passed quickly and soon the day of examination for first rank in the senior class of *kankairyū* arrived. The examination was a long distance swim of fifty blocks. Unfortunately, it was cloudy on that day, the clouds were low, and there were a great many jellyfish floating on the surface of the sea which annoyed us with stinging. Even still, I was able to continue swimming without too much difficulty. It is probably like that for long distance swimming, but it is especially so for *kankairyū*, it was very easy because all I had to do is to float while doing a frog swim slowly. However, on that day, perhaps due to the bad weather, everyone had to go up onto the boat once on the way and we were made to drink hot sugar water. At that time, I tried to go up as usual, by holding the side of the boat with my hand, but my body was so heavy that I could not climb up on my own no matter how hard I tried. Only then did I realize that long distance swimming is in fact very tiring.

The long-distance swim was completed safely, and I passed the first rank, so I think the dinner on that day was very satisfying. However, in the middle of the night I was attacked by a violent gastrospasm. The pain was severe and I could not put up with it and continued moaning loudly. I remember Fukuda and Iwasaki worried terribly and looked after me for a long time, but I do not remember clearly if a doctor came and calmed the pain. Anyway, thanks to that, I was left alone in the lodge to sleep on the following day. When the spasm was gone I was completely fine as if nothing had happened, and I felt like I was able to go into the sea in the afternoon, but the old women in the lodge stopped me and said that there were various books piled up in the storehouse and I could freely pull out anything I liked and read them, so I sneaked inside the storehouse and spent my time looking at various works written in the Edo era. There were books with pictures which were very rare for me. Compared to the long-distance swimming on the day before, the situation became completely different.

Due to things like that, I naturally gave up long-distance swimming above the first rank, but it was not at all regrettable for me. I think there were fourteen kilometer and twenty kilometer long-distance swims that year, if I remember it correctly, but I think I was rather pleased with no longer having to do it, thanks to the illness. What was regrettable was that I did not have enough time to search through all the books in the storehouse. The regret remained until the distant future.

This lodging was very pleasant for me, but I think it was probably due to reflection, in the autumn of that year, Iwasaki Eiji invited me for a one night trip with the five or six students from the boarding house. River Ibo, near the town of Tatsuno, was twelve or sixteen kilometers and flowed towards west Himeji; on the upstream of the river, which is about four kilometers deep in the mountains from Tatsuno, there is a mountain village that is said to be where the soldiers of Heike fled. We went to see that. On Saturday afternoon, we went upstream to the valley of the river Yumesaki, which is immediately west of Himeji, and on that night we slept in a shrine in the middle of the mountain, or on straw in a barn and went out to the village on the following day. It was a village which felt detached from the world.

As it was the first time for me to do this kind of trip, it was very interesting, but everything, such as the plan to go and see that kind of village, researching of the route, and the schedule of time and food, was left to others and I only tagged along. I think the leader was Iwasaki. On the way back from the village, we walked lively for about forty kilometers to Tatsuno along the river Kiho, but when we arrived at Tatsuno in the evening, I remember Iwasaki said we had walked about forty-eight kilometers.

Lodging and participating in this kind of trip was a new trend when I became fifth year, and just as an indication of that, I was made a company commander during firing practice at school that summer. As it was an opposition practice of the troops, both company commanders were supposed to get to the prime location. Matsuzaki Tatsurō, with whom I was a committee member of the library club, was the other company commander, but he was an athlete and a person who later became a soldier, so I thought it was very suitable, but I felt somewhat unsuitable to be made a company commander as I was not an athlete. I could not help but guess that there was some other kind of consideration of the principal and teachers in charge.

Since I was a child, I have never wanted to be a general or a cabinet minister. In the case of thinking about the future, I aimlessly thought I would be a doctor, as I am the child of a doctor. Finally, in recent years, I started to hope to proceed to humanities instead of medical science, but I had never specifically thought about what kind of profession I would like to do. Therefore, I think that the desire to be in the position of controlling people never crossed my mind. Probably because of that, I felt annoyed that I was made to be a company commander, but I never spoke out to decline, and eventually came to accept the role and gave commands with my sabre on the day of practice.

In middle school, there were not enough Murata rifles, so I think it was only those over third year who carried rifles. In total, there were about two-hundred who had rifles and two-hundred without. The company commanders each took half and spread them out among their troops, the physical education teacher lead one platoon as the advance guard, and all the company commander had to do was just take the main unit to a certain region. The gymnastic teacher instructed me in advance, that the region was a weir of a pond at the foot of whichever mountain. Thinking that it would not be so difficult, I began with a relatively carefree feeling.

However, the difficulty occurred at an unexpected place. The two or three year older athletes were not pleased with the mediocre practice of just walking to the weir of the pond calmly carrying a rifle, and instead wanted to run around between fields and hills. Then, when we came close to the mountain after doing a little marching, subordinate platoon officers and squad leaders raised various requests to let them patrol towards that mountain or let a squad deploy on the mountain ridge. Refusing their requests, I marched on the main road quietly, but such requests were persistently repeated. The platoon officer Mitsumata Sōnoshin, who was close to six foot tall was especially persistent. While such a condition continued for about one hour, the weir of the bank that the gymnastics teacher described started to come into view. Then, I probably felt relaxed and finally could no longer refuse their requests, so I said they could advance towards the mountain ridge, but that they should come down towards the weir of the pond from there, and attached one squad to Mitsumata, the tall platoon officer. This was the beginning of disorder. After that, there was no control and platoon officers and squad leaders started to act, leading their subordinates one after another. When I stood on the weir of the pond as planned, I was alone, and I felt disappointed.

I felt very embarrassed about this failure, and the gymnastic teacher apparently thought it was quite unpleasant, but I did not explain why I failed and the teacher did not seem to notice at which point I had trouble. So, he did not give a warning to platoon officers or squad leaders. Then, at the return exercise in the afternoon, he similarly advised me to withdraw to whichever river, take a position of attack at the weir there, and not to release the subordinates as in the morning. On the way back, I was determined not to compromise this time, but because the platoon officers and squad leaders did not think they failed in the morning practice, they hung on to the company commander much more persistently. In the end, I submitted just the same as in the morning. By the time when the gymnastic teacher pulled up to the weir leading the rear guard force, Mitsumata's platoon was still on the other ridge.

From the experience at this time, I fully realized how unsuitable command or control was to my nature. I think this experience had a considerable influence when I decided my future aspirations. It was after that when I sent a letter of consultation to my older brother, stating that I wanted to study humanities. My older brother agreed and encouraged me, so when I proposed that to my father, he approved extremely easily. In that period, parents disliked the idea of their children becoming scholars of literature, indeed in other families there were disputes between the parents and children, but I did not experience any such unpleasant feelings.

Just around that time, Principal Nagai decided to go to Sweden to study abroad in order to research gymnastics, and started attending our English period to constantly study the language. He was the sort of person who could do such a thing extremely innocently. Whether it was the influence of such a change in the principal's circumstances, or making me a company commander was done under such a pretence, at the end of the school term in that December, my result for physical education became unusually high. Although the principal changed to Mr Hirasawa Kanenosuke from the following year, my gymnastics score was still high at the time of graduation in March. It was something that had never happened until I was in fourth year. However, because I felt my role as a company commander was a terrible failure, I remained unconvinced about my physical ability.

Nakamura Norihito
Kyoto University

Fernando Wirtz
University of Tübingen

Two Texts on Technology
The Ideal of Technology, Technology and the New Culture

Miki Kiyoshi 三木 清

> ORIGINAL TITLES:「技術学の理念」(October 1941);「技術と新文化」(January 1942), first published in 『科学主義工業』 [Scientistic industry], reprinted as an appendix to 『技術哲学』 [The philosophy of technology] (1942). The essays are included in Miki's *Complete Works* 『三木清全集』(Tokyo: Iwanami Shoten, 1966–1968), 7: 300–16; 7: 317–29.
>
> KEYWORDS: Miki Kiyoshi—technology—the New Culture—organism—tool—machine—the New Order in East Asia—self-teleology—worldview—poiēsis

Translators' Introduction

One of the most prominent philosophers in prewar Japan, Miki Kiyoshi (1897–1945) left us with reflections on technology that are noteworthy for their philosophical and historical value. His *Philosophy of Technology* 『技術哲学』 first appeared in the collection *Ethics* 『倫理学』 published by Iwanami Shoten in October 1941. It was reprinted again as a book in September 1942, at which time Miki included the two short texts presented here, summarizing the main points of his theory succinctly. The following pages contain the first English translation of these texts:[1] "The Ideal of Technology" 「技術学の理念」(October 1941) and "Technology and the New Culture" 「技術と新文化」(January 1942). Both papers were originally contributions to *Scientistic Industry* 『科学主義工業』, a journal edited by Masatoshi Ōkochi (大河内正敏, 1878–1952), who had been the director of RIKEN,[2] the largest comprehensive research institution in modern Japan, during the prewar period. The social influence of Miki's philosophy, which lies beyond the scope of this brief introduction, suggests that his philosophy was not simply directed at other philosophers but played an important role in the construction of the ideological technocracy of the interwar era as well as during wartime.[3]

---

1. Miki's philosophy of technology has been largely overlook outside of Japan. Exceptions are FEENBERG 2010, 120–3, STROMBACK 2021, HUI 2021 and the forthcoming essay of ARISAKA and FEENBERG. See also TOWNSEND 2009, 220–2.

2. RIKEN is an abbreviation for the 国立研究開発法人理化学研究所 or Institute of Physical and Chemical Research.

3. Analyzing the writings of Japanese technocrats and engineers in the 1930s and 1940s, some authors have pointed out the existence of a certain techno-fascism, in which technology co-exists with its irrational and anti-modernist side. Miki's philosophy may also be regarded as more

Attracted by the figure of Nishida Kitarō, Miki studied at the University of Kyoto and graduated in 1920. Between 1922 and 1925, he studied in Germany and France. At this point, technology was not his main preoccupation, but it is worth noting that his references to technology were strongly influenced by German authors like Werner Sombart, Friedrich Dessauer, Max Eyth, Manfred Schröter, Franz Mataré, Eugen Diesel, and Eduard von Mayer. In 1930, he was briefly incarcerated for allegedly giving financial aid to the Communist Party. After this experience, he distanced himself from the terminology of materialism, although he continued to engage in political activities as a public commentator and journalist. He is best known for heading the Culture Committee of the Shōwa Research Association and his philosophy of technology was strongly connected with his role as an official ideologist (more about this below). After the dissolution of the Association, Miki served as a political advisor and journalist in the Philippines in 1942. These episodes make Miki a complex and polemical figure in the history of Japanese philosophy. Given to the many places where Miki criticizes fascism and authoritarianism, it is hard to understand other texts where he clearly supports military action in the Japanese colonies. The texts translated here will certainly serve to show the dark side of Miki's philosophy. In the end, despite having collaborated to some extent with the government, Miki was imprisoned for a second time and accused of protecting a communist activist. He died in prison in September 1945, just one month after Japan's surrender.

Also of note is the fact that Miki's interest in technology only surfaces during the final period of his philosophical career. In addition to with *A Philosophy of Technology* (1941), this subject is taken up explicitly in two other works: *The Logic of Imagination* (1937–1943) and *Introduction to Philosophy* (『哲学入門』, 1941, but based on lectures from 1938).[4] The first three chapters of *The Logic of Imagination*—entitled "Myth," "Institutions," and "Technology"—offer a useful scheme for understanding the place of technology in Miki's thought. For example, rather than assume a clear discontinuity

---

or less falling within this scope. For the general context of this debate, see MOORE 2013. For an introduction to the philosophy of technology in Japan, see KOSAKA 1986, MURATA 2009, and INUTSUKA 2020.

4. See also TOWNSEND 2009, 221.

among these three subjects, Miki sees technology as a kind of extension of myth in the sense that myth and technology are already products of the imagination and, therefore, may be considered poietic. From another perspective, *Introduction to Philosophy*, a book directed at a general audience, attempts to rehabilitate the importance of common sense (常識) for philosophy, demonstrating how technology serves to incorporate science into the daily life of society. In this sense, technology may be said to function as a mediator between science and common sense.

The two essays translated here were not directed chiefly at philosophers and were written in an accessible tone. This does not mean that they are free of terminological and philosophical difficulties. The term for technology itself, 技術, presents us with the first problem.[5] Since Miki was strongly inspired by German authors (and to some extent his writing style resembles that of German philosophical works), like many of his time, he uses the word in the sense of *Technik*. Depending on the context, the term can be translated either "technique" or "technology." In the expression "new technology," for example, *Technik* refers to some particular new device or method. Insofar as technology includes the Greek concept of *logos*, it may also refer to the knowledge that deals with the whole range of objects, processes, and skills that figure in technical relationships. Properly speaking, this would be what Miki terms 技術学—literally, the study of technique. Here, however, we have decided to render it as "technology," since it is clear that Miki uses the term to refer to the totality of technical activities.

An other problematic aspect of these texts (particularly in the case of *Technology and the New Culture*) is their political overtones. As noted above, between 1938 and 1940 Miki was a member of the Shōwa Research Association, usually described as a group of intellectuals that joined forces to promote the official discourse and interests of Imperial Japan.[6] Some of the ideas in these texts can be read as extensions of official government discourse. For example, while the West is characterized as prioritizing the material dimension of the world, Miki argues for the historical priority of

---

5. For the history of this term in Japan, see INUTSUKA 2020, 239.

6. HARRINGTON (2009, 68) and KIM (2007) are among those who highlight the tension between Miki's philosophy and these political interventions. In this regard, STROMBACK defines Miki's late philosophy as a quasi-idealism (2020, 133–8).

spirit over matter in the case of Japanese culture. Although he saw this as determinative in shaping Japan's singular national character, he went on to stress the importance of developing a machine technology, that is to say, heavy industry and high-level technology capable of competing with the West. The important thing was that such industry and technology be pursued in a manner consistent with the Japanese spirit. Miki also singles out land planning as an example of social technology in the sense that it represents a holistic form of technology that encompasses not only the production of material objects but also the administration of social resources. Set in the context of Japanese militarism and nationalism, this aspect of Miki's writing is clearly problematic. In the words of Aaron Moore:

> Technology in war time Japan meant much more than simply advanced machinery and infrastructure; it included a subjective, ethical, and visionary dimension. As in Europe and elsewhere, from the early twentieth century, technology in Japan began to represent certain forms of creative thinking, acting, or being, as well as values of rationality, cooperation, and efficiency. Technology also lent itself easily to utopian visions of an egalitarian society without ethnic or class conflict. Particularly during the 1930s, as Japan was shifting from a light to a heavy industrial wartime economy, elites developed a more subjective view of technology as increasingly permeating and altering every aspect of life.[7]

Under these conditions, it is hard to separate Miki's philosophy of technology from its political context. Nevertheless, there are elements of his theory worth noting for their own merits.

The main theses underlying Miki's philosophy of technology may be set out as follows: (1) technology is simultaneously a means and an end, and therefore autotelic (自己目的的); (2) technology is subjective-objective, and therefore historical; (3) the Japanese worldview already implies a certain technical conception of the world that may be rehabilitated to create a new, organic technology designed to respond to the historical needs of society. Thinking of technology only as a set of instruments leads to an idea of the world as a place in which things stand opposed to the subject in order to serve as a means to an end. For this reason, technology needs to be understood not only as objective and external, as is the case with the tools and

7. MOORE 2013, 6.

machines we use in daily life. Likely inspired by the philosophy of his mentor Nishida Kitarō (in particular, through the notion of active-intuition, 行為的直観), Miki argued that the self is not abstractly opposed to things but co-exists and with them and interacts with them. From a more macroscopic perspective, technology is not an instrument of economic growth but an autonomous sphere of human agency. In other words, technology is an expression of human intentionality, not merely as a means but as a purpose purpose (or *telos*) constructed through interaction with the surrounding world. This is what Miki means by "subjective-objective" in the texts that follow.

In these texts, Miki also anticipates current debates regarding technodiversity. According to Yuk Hui, the history of philosophy has been dominated by the assumption that technology is universal.[8] In this sense, technology has functioned as one of the main criteria to measure the level of development of a given society. The problem with this way of thinking is that it focuses *de facto* on the Western concept of technology, reducing other techniques (such as traditional medicine) to inferior forms of rationality. Thus, for Hui, Miki's call "to return to tradition is a call for appropriating modern technology into a new frame."[9] Miki also expressed an urgency for reincorporating the moral and spiritual dimensions into the discussion surrounding technology, but without disregarding the importance of investing more resources in the development of new technologies. Feenberg summarizes Miki's position this way:

> Technology must be imbued with the forms of the culture that created it. And in fact Miki argued that the technology Japan has received from the West is an expression of Western culture and must be reshaped to conform to the Japanese "spirit." A new culture must be created that combines the best of both East and West. Like Nishida, Miki believed the solution to this problem to be of world-historical importance. The West had reached a dead end that Japan could surpass.[10]

Thus a critical awareness of the opposition between technology in the West and in the East—the one seeking seeks to dominate nature by objecti-

8. See HUI 2016.
9. See HUI 2021, 225.
10. FEENBERG 2010, 121.

fying its environment and focusing on a materialistic understanding of the world, the aimed at unifying the moral and spiritual spheres with materiality—offers a fruitful starting point for an attempt at reconstructing the history of technology in Japan. In this sense, it is our hope that Miki's texts will bring a wider perspective to Japanese philosophy's inquiry into the role of technology and to draw attention to of other authors who have written on the matter, among them Nakai Masakazu, Tosaka Jun, Oka Kunio, and Saigusa Hiroto.

In the current translations, we have tried to remain as close to the original as possible. Miki's style is often repetitive and redundant, which tends to make the flow of his prose sound somewhat unnatural in translation. This was not entirely avoidable, but at certain points, we paraphrased his wording, broke up long sentences, and added words in brackets to make the text read more smoothly.

Miki Kiyoshi

The Ideal of Technology

Translated and annotated by
Nakamura Norihito & Fernando Wirtz

I

There are many today who preach about the need for technological development. But no matter how much the need is emphasized, it will not in fact be enough. The development of technology is an urgent issue for our country at present. Particularly in these days, the problem of technology is closely linked to the problem of worldview (世界観).[11] The new technologist's spirit (技術家精神)[12] will have to be based on a grasp of that problem

In the first place , the opposition to technology in general, which was once very popular, has been overshadowed today. Science and technology were not only disregarded but even rejected as [an aspect of] so-called "material civilization (物質文明)." This was not only the case in Japan; the anti-technological philosophy of Spengler, Jaspers, and others had become popular in Germany and other countries. Without the establishment of a new worldview to overcome these kinds of anti-technological philosophy, today's theories of technology would not have a stable foundation. It is not enough to say that the war going on at present requires the development of technology; there is a need [now] for the establishment of a new philosophy of technology.

Secondly, and especially in the current context, the [problem of] worldview is becoming the fundamental problem at this turning point in world history. There must be a new worldview to undergird the construc-

---

11. According to the text "The Theory of Worldview-Construction" (MKZ 5: 53–77), this term 世界観 (*Weltanschauung*) comes from Dilthey. However, Miki criticizes his usage. He argues that Dilthey's understanding of worldview is conditioned by his preference for German Romanticism and *Lebensphilosophie*. While Dilthey focuses relatively on the pathetic consciousness (パトス的意識) of worldview, Miki argues for a "dialectical" relationship between the pathetic and logical consciousness.

12. 技術家 could also be translated as "technician." We opted for the less common expression of "technologist" to highlight that Miki is not only talking about those persons who work directly with technical devices.

tion of a New Order (新秩序) and the creation of a New Culture (新文化).[13] If this is true, what significance does technology have in such a worldview? Today's technologists cannot afford to be indifferent to the problem of worldview. It may be said that the characteristic of our age is that every person is required to be aware of their own worldview (世界観的自覚). The technologist must not remain a mere technologist but needs to be armed with a worldview. What, then, is the relationship between worldview and technology? It is here, for example, that the question of ethnic groups (民族)[14] and technology appear.

Thirdly, and more specifically, the problem of a new worldview today is thought to be connected to the problem of tradition. Although we speak of a New Order or a New Culture, we are always referring to the Japanese Spirit (日本精神) or Eastern Culture. What, then, is the relationship between such [issues] and technology? This question is all the more important, given that many Japanists[15] and Asianists have shown contempt towards or taken a dismissive attitude to science and technology—even if such views are not as common now as they once were. The connection between the Japanese Spirit and technology must not be seen as mere opportunism. Simple opportunism is not only harmful to technological development; it would end up harming the Japanese Spirit itself.

In this way, then, the problem of technology includes the problem of a worldview. The topics most actively discussed today have to do with technological policy, which has to be grounded on a correct grasp of the philosophical problems of technology.

---

13. At that time, in the 1930s and 40s, the words 新秩序 and 新文化 were two concepts closely related to the rhetoric of Japanese Imperialism.

14. Miki uses here the word 民族, a word that hard to translate in English due to its problematic connotations. One possible translation would be "race." However, Miki was also aware of the concepts of race promoted by National Socialism in Germany. For this reason some authors render *minzoku* as *Volk*, avoiding softer alternatives such as "people" or "nation." Nevertheless, for Miki, "ethnicity" (民族性) is not something biological or essentialist. For example, in a text from 1940 Miki wrote that "Of course, it is certain that each nation has its own ethnicity. But this ethnicity is by no means just natural, it is the result of longstanding politics" (MKZ 16, 473). That is, Miki understands *minzoku* as something not purely natural but also historical.

15. Japanism or 日本主義 was a form of Japanese nationalism particularly popular during the 1930's which stressed the figure of the emperor and its mythology.

ii

There is also the issue of what technology is, given the various theories of technology. The answer may seem simple, but this is not necessarily the case. Rather, it is fair to say that we have not yet come to a agreement on the [subject]. Indeed, the very manner in which we examine the essence of technology is of fundamental importance for all [aspects] of a theory of technology.

Asked what technology is, it is generally spoken of as a means to an end. Those who try to be more precise would say that technology is the sum total or system of such means. The answer sounds altogether normal, but in fact it is incomplete. First of all, if technology were simply a means to an end, it would have to be said to lack uniqueness (独自性). Something that is unique cannot be simply a means [to an end] and that which is merely a means cannot be considered unique. As a result, technology has been considered nothing more than a means to an end, which is one of the reasons that the problem of technology has been ignored or dismissed in philosophy to date. In fact, if technology were simply a means, there would be no such thing as a philosophy of technology. To establish a philosophy of technology requires technology be seen as unique, and therefore as something that can be considered an end in itself.

Technology is [also] regarded as occupying a middle ground as it were between science and economics. If so, considering technology as merely a means to an end would, on the one hand, deny its uniqueness vis-à-vis science. In that case, technology would be seen as nothing more than the utilization or application of science. On the other hand, from such an approach, the view that seems to assert a close relationship between science and technology would set technology apart from science and have it simply serve the economy, which would lead scientists to be indifferent to technology. If [a scientist] were to ask to what purpose science is utilized as technology, the usual answer would be "for the economy," or in other words, that such purpose would seem irrelevant to the scientist. It is unsurprising that those who fail to recognize the uniqueness of technology cannot truly esteem it. Such scientists would not be willing to cooperate fully in the advance of technology. At the same time, it is hardly desirable for the development of science itself that technology be considered nothing more than an application of science. Scientific developments are often stimulated by technology, and this is inherently possible because technology is something unique. The generally accepted view that technology is influenced by science, and vice versa, is made possible, both logically and effectively, by the fact that both can be both unique and also interconnected. If technology is said to be an application of science, then one could also say that science is a transformation (変形) of technology. According to Scheler, scientific knowledge is "knowledge of work."[16] That is, it is technical in its essence, unlike religious or metaphysical (philosophical) knowledge. It may be said that science not only originated from some technical demand for working on nature and changing it, but that it is also technical in its methods. This is illustrated by the experimental method characteristic of modern science. To experiment is not to observe a given phenomenon as it is but to observe a phenomenon by generating it. In other words, knowing by creating is characteristic of the modern scientific method. We may think of an experiment as technology on a small scale, and of technology as an experiment on a large scale. It goes without saying that science and technology differ from each other. Indeed, science comes about only by rejecting its position as technology. Each is unique and yet they two are interconnected. Understanding this relationship must be the basis of any policy regarding science and technology.

Those who view technology as a means to an end would also see it as principally a means for the economy. But technology is not merely a means for the economy. If this were so, technology would be unequivocally subordinate to the economy and bound to it. Thus, as we have seen in the past, technology can be used simply for commercial purposes, just as there are [situations] in which its development has been limited or hindered by commercial use. It is true, on the one hand, that technology does play a role as a means for the economy. On the other hand, [technology] is not merely a means, but is also something unique, an end in itself. Therefore, it is not surprising that for technology to advance it must be emancipated from the economy. Emancipation from the economic [interests] of commercialism is necessary for technological development. By recognizing its uniqueness in this way, technology can advance and, in turn, the economy can also develop

---

16. This idea could be found, for example, in *Erkenntnis und Arbeit. Eine Studie über Wert und Grenzen des pragmatischen Motivs in der Erkenntnis der Welt* (1926).

as a result. Thinking of technology merely as a means for the economy and restricting its free development would become all the more disadvantageous for the economy as well. While technology and the economy are each unique, they stand in a close relationship to each other. The development of technology influences the mode of economy and vice versa. Although technology has a unique place in the economy, it is not simply an end in itself but rather a means for the economy.

For these reasons, we would have to say that technology is both a means, and also end unto itself. Grasping this relationship as a whole is important whenever we consider the question of technology. Moreover, whereas the common view until now has been biased toward considering technology merely as a means, what must be emphasized today is rather that [technology] contains something unique and self-teleological (自己目的的).

III

Therefore, it needs to be made clear from within that technology is not just something that should be seen as a means. Where this is the case, technology is always thought of as a tool or machine. A tool is indeed a means. Still, tools are not technology. Technology is the action of using tools to make things. Generally speaking, technology takes the form of action (行為の形). Because of this essential characteristic, the tool is included as a an element of this action. Thus, if we define technology as a whole as a form of action, it becomes clear that it is not possible to view it as a mere means.

As an action that includes tools as one of its elements, technology distinguishes itself as something mediated (媒介的). First, to say that something is mediated means that it is not immediate (直接). Technology is always both processional and methodical. Secondly, mediation means that something mediates between a subject and its environment, that is, between a subject and an object. Technology mediates between the subject and its environment and enables an active adaptation to that subject's environment. As such, technology is simultaneously determined subjectively and objectively. Technology is originally subjective-objective (主観的・客観的). It contains both a subjective moment and an objective moment. Technology demands a synthesis between human will and objective natural laws. Yet [in this sense] the subjective-objective cannot be simply regarded as a means.

Anything viewed as a means is objective. For this reason, those who think about technology as a means are generally prejudiced by the objectivist view of technology. Although technology is a purely objective process, its end, the subjective, does not lie outside of it. Technology is originally a synthesis of the ends of human beings and objective natural laws; [therefore] the subjective dimension is included within technology. From the start, the synthesis that occurs in technology between the subjective and the objective is not something that happens only inside one's head, but rather something that actualizes itself in the realm of things through their transformation. Simply put, technology is making things. What we call production is the fundamental determination of technology. If so, can technology be thought of as a means for the end of production? The so-called means of production are tools and machines. Technology and tools are not the same. [Therefore,] tools are nothing but one element of technology. Aristotle did distinguish between praxis and poiēsis: for praxis, the end is not to be [found] in an external activity but in the activity itself, which works as the end, whereas in contrast, the end within poiēsis is not the activity itself but is regarded as work generated outside of it.

It should be noted, however, that practice as defined by Aristotle is actually contemplation rather than practice [as understood] today, and that contemplation was actually considered to be the highest [form of] practice. We would rather have to say that every action is poietic and therefore technical. If "thing" is understood in a broad sense, then all our actions have to do with producing things. What is made technically is not merely objective but subjective-objective. Within the sphere of technology, the subjective is objectified and the objective is subjectified. What is made technically as subjective-objective is also something independent. Thus, the technology that makes independent things cannot be viewed simply as a means.

Yet, it may be thought that technology is only subjective-objective when it comes to tool-based technology. We may also say that this is not the case with mechanical technology, which is distinct from tools. Tool-based technology is tied to human beings. In contrast, mechanical technology, which, as Sombart has said, is characterized by "being freed from the organic," works on its own, apart from human beings.[17] Machines move towards autonomy.

17. This expression actually belongs to Marx's *Capital* (see MARX and ENGELS 1962,

Should this kind of activity of machines as a purely objective process be seen as a means? In that case, the first thing to consider is that even for machine activities, a corresponding subjective aspect to this [dimension to the objective process] is to be expected. Human intelligence or technical skill (技能) is technological. Or rather, it is sometimes called technology within the human [sphere]. The machine, so to speak, is the objective moment of technology; technical skill, so to speak, is its subjective moment, and both taken together determine as a whole what is called technology. Next, [we should also say that] since they are themselves technical products, machines are not themselves purely objective. This shows us that their end is not merely subjective and arbitrary but must possess some objectivity. Machines are also inventions, since they are a synthesis of subjective ends and objective laws of nature. Here we may distinguish between a technical end and a technical means. In this sense, inventions can relate to both. An invention can at the same time be an invention of a means and also of an end. A truly new invention is not just new in terms of the means but also in terms of the end. The technician cannot be thought of solely as an inventor of means. Invention also aims at the invention of new technical ends. In this regard, too, machines do not simply follow causal laws. Of course, from one side, [invention] inevitably follows the law of causality, [and for this reason] science is the basis of technology. However, at the same time, invention includes teleology. The machine, in both structure and application, is teleological. Its teleology, logically speaking, is comprised of an inner, organic relation between the whole and the parts. The machine expresses this relation. [Thus,] technology can be thought as the unification of causality and teleology. Also the "mechanism" (メカニズム) of machines is itself not merely causal but the unification of causality and teleology. Hence, in this sense, whatever contains teleology within itself cannot be considered a mere means. The synthesis of the subjective and the objective is given in the form that emerges from technology, and the unification of causality and teleology can be regarded as a morphology (形態論). In short, what has become clear by seeking an overall definition of technology is that technology should not be seen only as a means.

23: 394).

IV

From the outset, technology is not simply autotelic. It is in all respects a means. Yet, something that uses one technology as a means can only be another technology. Something that actually capable of using one technology is in fact another technology. If [for example] technology functions as a means for the economy, and therefore the economy functions as the end of this technology, the economy must itself be a kind of technology. In this case, what we call technology is not the technology of natural sciences but, on the contrary, a [kind of] social technology. Just as there is a technology based on the natural sciences, so, too, there is another kind of technology based on the social sciences. Social technology also needs to stand on a scientific ground, a sociological ground. Technology is not limited to nature; there is also technology for society. Since these different forms of technology exist, we can conceive of a connection between them with regard to means and ends. Aristotle believed that harness-making technology served military technology, and military technology served politics.[18] Politics itself is also a [kind of] technology. Thus it is possible to posit a hierarchical relationship among various technologies based on the means-end relationship. As a result, we can conceive of a technology that controls all technology in a comprehensive manner. For Aristotle, this is politics. In other words, for politics all technologies may be thought of as a means.

Normally, when speaking about technology, one thinks of material production and hence the natural sciences. But this is meaningless for the idea of technology. What is needed today is to expand that way of thinking. The confusion this is thought to cause comes from our way of considering various form of technology in isolation from one another, without taking into consideration the connections among them in terms of the relationship of ends to means. Thus, to think of the individual forms of technology in isolation is the result of thinking of technology as merely a means. Even when technology is a means, that is only another form of technology. Obviously, the development of technology is necessary for natural science. But that is not the only problem; the development of social technologies is also extremely important. What is now referred to as technological regulation or

---

18. Miki refers to Aristotle's *Nicomachean Ethics*, 1094a.

planning implies the control of social technology, in particular, the politics of technology in natural science. That this is in fact the case is clearly important if we are to grasp the proper connection among the varieties of technology. The first thing to pay attention to here is that something capable of truly using one technology is itself another technology. In other words, a true technology enables politics to work effectively on other technologies. Furthermore, even if a means-end relationship is recognized between one technology and another, this does not mean that one technology is a one-sided means, but that every technology is at the same time both a means and independent. For this reason, we need to understand the fundamental determinations of the end [of that technology] in itself. Furthermore, as in the case with politics, we should not think of other technologies merely as a means. We must rather recognize at the same time their uniqueness and their autotelic nature (自己目的性). This will be important when considering the problem of technological regulation. If it is further understood that there is are connections among technologies, it is also clear that no technologist should be indifferent to politics.

In addition, f we grant a relation between the end and the means in all things technological, what might we say is the ultimate end? To be ultimate, an end has to be its own end and a means for something else. When Kant discussed the teleology of nature—at the time, he thought that there was also technology in nature—he proposed that we take as the ultimate end in the teleological connections of nature the human being as a free subject, in other words, the human being as a moral subject rather than as a natural thing. That said, the moral action of a human must also be technological. To be free actually means to dominate things by technology. It may imply autonomy, but such autonomy should not be considered in the abstract sense. True autonomy lies in the fact that even if human beings are completely embedded in technology, they themselves are beyond technology and can use it as a means. Human beings are not purely autotelic. The human being itself is produced technically. Just as machines created by humans work independently on their own, humans who are made by society work independently in their technical creation of things. As independent and autonomous beings, human beings are autotelic. At the same time, they are only a means to the society that created them. Like other technological things, human beings are simultaneously autotelic and a means.

In our search for a general determination of technology, we have found it in the form of action. So to define technology is to define it in a subjective (主体的) manner, as opposed to the traditional objectivist tendency to consider technology merely as a means. Technology is not purely objective. It is subjective-objective, and in this sense, it is historical. In the world of history, only what is subjective-objective is truly objective. As an action that produces things, technology is historical. [And] all history is continually being produced technologically. Because humans are producing history technologically, the meaning of technology must be understood as historical action in this sense. Moreover, the authentic subject of history is not the individual but something that transcends the individual; it is society that uses individuals working technically as a means, not the individual. Technology is social and human beings are always tied socially through technology. This fundamental sociality of technology needs to be emphasized. The human, defined as a tool-making animal, must also be defined as a social animal.

Now if we regarded subjective technology as a form of action and society as the authentic subject of history, we may then understand the link between technology and ethnic groups. By nature, technology is the manner in which a subject works on its environment, but this subject and this environment are always historical. An ahistorical conception of technology is the result of a perspective that thinks of technology as the mere application of the natural sciences, the same kind of perspective that gives us the notion of abstract cosmopolitanism. The philosophy of technology must be grounded in the philosophy of history, and the philosophy of history must in turn be grounded in the philosophy of technology. In reflecting on of technology today, the most important thing is having a philosophical-historical perspective.

I would make one final observation. I believe that what functions as the basis of the Eastern view of nature (東洋的自然観) or society (社会観) is a kind of philosophy of technology, a technological worldview. Morality may also be thought of in a philosophical-technological manner. To separate the Japanese Spirit and technology from each other is to would miss the general characteristic of this Eastern worldview. To investigate the meaning of this technological worldview is not just interesting; it is also extremely important. However, we should add that the Eastern technological worldview is tool-technical, not mechanical-technical. A transition from the tool-technical to the mechanical-technical has been made possible by modern science. What is crucial for us today is to introduce this modern scientific perspective into the Eastern technological worldview.

Miki Kiyoshi
Technology and the New Culture

Translated and annotated by
Nakamura Norihito & Fernando Wirtz

I

Whatever we think of the creation of a New Culture that needs to accompany the construction of a New Order in East Asia, it is clear that technology must occupy a very important place in the process. At present, the Imperial Army is carrying out remarkable military achievements on all sides. Not be overlooked in our joy at this victory is Japan's technological development. Such success would not be possible without the development of technology. Given that technology comprises such a major element of this New Order War, it is clear that technology must also be of fundamental importance in the New Culture. What is needed above all to keep this war effort going is to develop and use the resources that have been secured. The final victory in this long conflict can only be achieved by actively benefiting from those resources. And for that, technology is clearly indispensable. The war must be both war and construction. Construction is, first and foremost technological. The aim of this war is the construction of a New Order in East Asia or the establishment of an East-Asian Co-Prosperity Sphere.[19] One of the main roles that Japan has to play in making the East Asia Co-Prosperity Sphere a reality is to provide technological guidance in making use of the resources of East Asia. Merely to assert that we possess resources does not mean that we actually do. Fish are in the sea, but we cannot say we actually have fish until they are set on the table. To have them in nature does not yet mean to possess them economically. Natural resources become economically significant through their technological development and use. What

---

19. As other concepts that we find in these texts, the so-called Greater East Asia Co-Prosperity Sphere is a political concept coined around 1940 that expresses the hegemonic and imperialist intentions of Japan. This "sphere" included not only Japan, Manchukuo, and China, but also Southeast Asia, Eastern Siberia, and possibly the outer regions of Australia, India, and the Pacific Islands. While the concept promises an ideal of "co-prosperity," it was certainly built around the idea of strong Japanese leadership.

Japan has to do is to make use of the resources of East Asia. Only then we can establish an East Asia Co-Prosperity Sphere. The first requirement for its establishment is that we acquire advanced technology. Without it, there can be neither a New Order nor a New Culture.

In this sense, the importance of technology in the New Culture of East Asia is obvious. Those who despise technology can only be said not to have understood how a New Order, and therefore also a New Culture, can come about. At the same time, it is wrong to overemphasize technology as if it were the only important element. We also need to gain a much stronger and wider perspective. Technology is just one domain or element in culture. There are others, such as art, morals, religion, and philosophy. In this context, what is commonly referred to as technology—namely, the technology of material production—is directly related to the economy. Thus, to emphasize only technology leads us to an overemphasis on material culture, which runs the risk of falling into economism or materialism. Economism is a characteristic of modern culture, but the New Culture must go beyond modern culture. Its position cannot be a kind of "techno-centrism" (技術主義).[20] This is why the value of spiritual culture need to be emphasized in opposition to material, economic and technological culture. In particular, from a historical viewpoint, what we now today technology was developed in the West. A position of spiritual culture characteristic of Eastern tradition needs to emerge in contrast to the Western material culture. This position has its own reasons as well. The culture of the New Order that is to take shape in East Asia must be connected to the traditions of Eastern culture. Insofar as this is the case, the value of spiritual culture will be emphasized in the New Culture as a matter of course. Even the glorious military successes of the Imperial Army are not only due to the superiority of weapons and technology; they are fruits of the spirit. That said, it would be a mistake to respect the spirit to excess and fall into a "spiritualism" (精神主義) that would exclude or look down on technological culture. As already mentioned, there can be no doubt about the importance of technology. It is only common sense to think that the New Culture should be able to unite technology and spiritual culture without despising technology or holding it only partly in esteem. This is a crucial issue for the creation of the

20. Lit. "technologism."

New Culture that is to accompany the construction of a New Order in East Asia. New Culture must, on the one hand, be connected to Eastern traditions with it own distinct features as a spiritual culture, and on the other hand, it must respect modern technology established in the West and based on modern science. The problem is how to combine and harmonize technology and spiritual culture.

It should be noted that this is not only a problem for East Asia but actually also for world history. It is not only Japanese or Eastern culture that are faced with the question, but it [confronts] Western culture as well. One remarkable feature of modern culture in the West—which in our country is referred to simply as "Western culture"—is the rapid development of technology. But the development of material culture brought about a crisis of spiritual culture, as [in the case of] morality. The development of machines has made us think of human beings as incomplete, which then brought about of a sense of depersonalization (非人格化). It also left in its wake masses of people (大衆) without spiritual personality. The development of material culture made all human beings materialistic. As a result, a pessimism towards technology grew out of the critique of modern culture. As the problem of technology became important for our culture, a so-called "philosophy of technology" has emerged. The fact of the matter is, as long as technology is simply seen as technology [technique], no one doubts its utility. [Technology] becomes problematic when we view it in relation to other forms of culture, especially to spiritual culture. The protest against mechanical technology was not only raised by Gandhi in the East but can be found in many philosophies of technology in the West as well. To be sure, we can defend technology against such pessimism. The development of machines has alleviated the pain of physical labor for human workers. Without any foundation in material culture, spiritual culture would not be able to develop. At the same time, unconditional optimism towards technology is as one-sided as an opposing pessimism. The relationship between technology and humans cannot be viewed merely optimistically. The essence of modern technology lies in what Sombart has called liberation from the organic (有機的なものからの解放). In this sense, modern technology stands as opposed to humans as it is to organic life. Although machines are human products, they maintain an independence from humans and can actually come to restrict and oppress them. The risk here is that something that has proved useful for the development of human culture can eventually promote its destruction. Technology, which develops autonomously by its own power, cannot be left unattended. This is where a "taming of technology" (技術の馴化), as Sombart puts it, becomes necessary.[21] Modern culture, through the development of technology, has brought spiritual culture to the brink. To unite or harmonize technology with spiritual culture has become a fundamental problem for Western culture. An possible answer may lie in the attempt to tame it rather than simply exclude it. This is the task of the New Culture, and it is a world-historical task. The New Culture of East Asia would take on worldwide significance by solving this world-historical problem. That said, we must work towards a technology superior in all respects. The need for this is obvious. In addition, many of the negative cultural effects previously assumed to belong to the essence of technology are actually based on a technological immaturity that can remedied by technological development. On this point in particular, we need to must pay attention to our response to naive technophobes. Nevertheless, so long as there is a fundamental opposition between technology and spiritual culture, it we need to overcome it by developing a high-level spiritual culture across the board.

The problem with technology faced by the New Culture lies in how to reorganicize (有機化) technology [i.e., make technology organic]. The defining mark of modern technology is that it disentangles us from the organic. This, in turn, runs the risk of oppressing humans and acting destructively towards spiritual culture. Modern technology is a mechanical technology. In contrast, the technology of the past can be defined as tool-based technology. There is a fundamental difference here between machines and tools. While mechanical technology is indeed mechanical, tool-based technology is characterized by its organic nature. Contrary to machines, which have the autonomy to work independently of humans, tools are, so to speak, an extension of human hands. Insofar as tools are organically connected to humans, tool-based technology is humanized. The relationship between tool-based technology and human beings is organic. The two are connected organically. Thus, in the case of tools, there is no conflict between humans and technology, and such technology has never been a serious cultural and

21. Miki refers to the title of Werner Sombart's book *Die Zähmung der Technik* (1935).

spiritual problem. Modern technology made a breakthrough with the invention of machinery that work automatically and independently of humans. With time, the organic connection with humans came to be dissolved and machines began to oppress humans. This is where the serious cultural and spiritual problem of technology arises. Alarmed at the harm brought about by mechanical technology, attempts have been made to eliminate machines and return to the simple technology of an earlier time, but this is nothing more than a simple reflex reaction. The development of mechanical technology has [in fact] made an infinitely large contribution to human culture, and may be expected to make more and more contributions in the future.

The problem is how to bring this modern technology into an organic relationship with human life. Originally, technology was linked to humans in the form of tools. Later, in the form of mechanical technology, it came to stand into opposition to human beings. The challenge of the New Culture is to make this technology that has stood against us into something that is somehow once again organically related to human life. Let me add a brief word about the relation between the Japanese spirit and science, which is a matter of frequent discussion today. As long as science is recognized as the ground of tool-based technology (in all its forms, technology must be grounded on the objective laws of nature), it is possible to speak of science as belonging to the traditional Japanese spirit. But there is a dramatic difference between tool-based and mechanical technologies. The science of the present day, which has become the basis for the development of mechanical technology, is also something fundamentally novel. The relationship between the two is by no means a one of simple continuity. For science to develop and technology to advance in accord with the traditional spirit of Japan, there must be new breakthroughs in the Japanese spirit. In fact, as an ethnic group the Japanese have done just that from the end of the Edo period up until the present. This does not imply, however, that the Japanese spirit has a need to be westernized. There is simply no truth to the claim that it is impossible for one ethnic group to become something altogether different. As already explained, the problem for today's world-historical culture is how a technology that, historical speaking, arose in the West, can be harmonized and unified with spiritual culture, how it can be restored to an organic relationship with human life. Obviously, we cannot follow Western culture here, because Western culture has yet to solve the problem. On the contrary, it has shown the tragic side of the problem. We need rather to rely on the creative forces characteristic of the Japanese spirit. The world historical problem facing us today is that, along with our ongoing adoption of so-called Western science and technology, we must go further to create a new and higher culture by solving the problems that Western culture has left unsolved. On this point, the deepening and refinement of the Japanese spirit becomes a necessity.

In this connection, we may ask how it is possible for present-day technology be enter into an organic relation with human beings. This [answer] is not to be found in the methods of tool-based technologies. It is wrong to think that such a thing [as an organic relation] is possible without taking into consideration the fundamental differences between tools and machines. A technology of the mind-heart (心の技術) is certainly necessary. What I mean by that is a technology that produce humanity or soul, and in particular the kind of technology has evolved considerably in the East. We need to restore this tradition. What matters here is the cultivation of the kind of human beings and souls that are capable of controlling technology rather than being controlled by it. Still and all, it is not possible to overcome the gigantic and powerful organization of today's technology with mere spirit. A more objective, scientific method is called for. This is in itself a technology—a kind of [subjective-objective] technology to control technology. We are not speaking of technology that controls nature but something we should call social technology (社会技術). Just as the technology that controls nature is based on natural science, so social technology must be based on social science. Such socially regulated technology will aid in the advance of technology by altering the social conditions that stand in its way.

What has hitherto been regarded as a harmful aspect of technology turns out not to be a sin of technology itself but to have arisen from the social system in which technology is embedded. We must rely on social technology [itself] to remove these harmful effects. For example, from the viewpoint of national defense, health, morality, and so forth, it has become necessary today to subdivide and disperse industries concentrated in modern cities, and this entails making technology once again organically related to human life. Or again, there is the problem of coordinating urban and rural areas. Here too, technology can take on an organic significance in its relationship to nature. The organicization of technology (技術の有機化) could be applied to many of the general aims of social technology, such as National Land Planning (国土計画).[22] Such technology is not directly organicized for individual bodies the way a tool-based technologies are. In contrast, modern mechanical technology can only be organicized for the "social body" (社会的身体).[23] In this regard, modern technology is social in the highest sense. That is to say, it becomes organic in a social way, in relation to the social body. From that perspective it is possible to understand the importance of National Land Planning. Furthermore, from the point of view of a technology organically related to the social body, it is also possible to rethink the question of technology and ethnic groups. By employing the ideal of the organicization of technology in various social technologies, including national land planning, new cultural patterns can be created. Thus, it is not hard to understand why, in the name of constructing a New Culture, the advancement of not just the natural sciences but also of the social sciences has an important role to play. Just as notion of science extends beyond the natural sciences to include the social sciences, so, too, technology should not be limited to a technology based on natural science, but also need to take the form of a social technology based on the social sciences. For these reasons, we must expand the concept of technology as it has commonly been understood up until now. The task of constructing a new technological science (技術学) or philosophy of technology is to broaden the concept of technology and at the same time to clarify the topological relations among

22. The expression "national land planning" (国土計画) refers to a set of policies (in this case implemented specially during the 1930's and 1940's) inspired by other global examples such as the German *Raumordnung* (spatial order) that aimed to coordinate a comprehensive and efficient use of the land. This included not only measures against urban concentration, but also regarding flood control, hydroelectricity, and other infrastructural issues. These policies gained a new impulse with the re-election of Konoe Fumimaro, who was also supported by the Shōwa Kenkyūkai, which in September 1940 submitted a "statement of opinion on the promotion of national land planning." Within this historical context, the concept of "national land planning" also included the administration of the colonial territories of the Japanese Empire (see also MOORE 2013, for example 122).

23. The concept of "social body" is recurrent in Miki, although he never offers a definition of it. Typically, it is used to designate the most concrete instance of historical subjectivity. It is the manifestation of the embodied dialectic between *pathos* and *logos*. In this sense, it may be thought as the subject of history (see for example MKZ 18: 153). It is also clearly reminiscent of Nishida's concept of the "historical body" (歴史的身体).

technologies. I regard such a task as a matter of great significance for the ideal of a New Culture.

If we must expand the concept of technology, we must also deepen our understanding of the essence of technology. I cannot go into [this matter] here, but I should like to make one observation. Until the present day, the understanding of technology suffered from the one-sided bias of objectivism, which was also related to earlier views of technology as simply a means. As I explained earlier, all technology involves a sense of being simultaneously a means and an end. It is therefore is possible to draw connections between ends and means among different technologies while also recognizing the uniqueness and autonomy of each. In acknowledging these connections, the inner relationship between "technology" and spiritual culture becomes clearer. Spiritual culture, for all its many meanings, is also technological. In Greek philosophy, for example, technology and art were expressed through the same word: *techné*. Art is, of course, technical, but so is morality when considered as a form of instrumental action. Scientific and philosophical thinking have something to do with technology as well. Obviously, when it comes to considering what is technical about spiritual culture, technology is not being understood simply as something objective. True, all technology must have an objective aspect. But it is not merely objective. [On the contrary] it is the unification of the objective and the subjective. The one-sided objective approach to technology may also be related to the idea of technology as something that has to do with only the natural sciences. Social technology cannot be treated as purely objective either. Here, too, technology include the element of human volition as a subjective element, which technology aims to synthesize with objective laws. From another angle, the same applies to natural scientific technology. It is not merely objective but always entails a human *telos*. Setting technology as a form of historical action performed by human beings in the historical world makes this easier to understand. All things are technical insofar as they are created in the historical world. The historical world [itself] comes to be technically. Conversely, the philosophy of history must include a philosophy of technology. Spiritual culture is also technological in the sense that it is a historical construct. Of course, [in the same way,] technology is not simply subjective. The subjective element within technology is not itself only subjective, but must rather be objective as well. Technology is historically objective. But to be truly objective in the historical world does not mean to be only objective. On the contrary, it means to be subjective-objective. In the same way that a one-sided objectivism regarding technology needs to be corrected, so, too, does a one-sided subjectivism regarding spiritual culture. For example, while art was seen as a technology [*techné*] in ancient Greece, today it has come to be thought of as merely a product of subjective emotion or imagination. Nevertheless, given its similarity to technology, art cannot ever be seen as only subjective. As Valéry and Alain[24] have remarked, since art is also a technology [*techné*] that works on concrete material, the artist must be a kind of artisan. The idea (イデー) of art is not something inside the head of the artist: a piece of art is born from the manipulation of matter, like language or marble or what have you. Generally speaking, making is a subjective-objective action. Ideas are also, at bottom, historically objective—that is to say, subjective-objective. It is not only spiritual culture that can be called ideal (イデー的); what is commonly referred to as technology can also be seen as expressing a particular idea. For this reason, we may say that the ideal of a New Culture must be located in a technical-artistic worldview. As explained above, the organicization of technology may also be thought of as the artification (芸術化) of technology.

---

24. Miki refers to the pseudonym of the philosopher Émile-Auguste Chartier (1868–1951), who taught Simone Weil, Georges Canguilhem, and André Maurois, among others.

* The translators would like to thank Daniel Burke and the two anonymous reviewers for their extremely helpful feedback and suggestions. Their comments did, without a doubt, improve the translation. The translators would also like to acknowledge the financial support of the Japanese Society for the Promotion of Science and the Thyssen Foundation during the preparation of these pieces.

References

Abbreviations

MKZ 『三木清全集』[*Complete Works of Miki Kiyoshi*] (Tokyo: Iwanami Shoten, 1966–1968), 20 vols.

Other sources cited

ARISAKA Yōko 有坂陽子 and Andred FEENBERG
   N.D. "Nishida and Miki: the Dialectical World in the Philosophy of Technology." [Forthcoming]

ARISTOTLE
   1990 *The Nicomachean Ethics* (Cambridge, MA: Harvard University Press).

FEENBERG, Andrew
   2010 *Between Reason and Experience: Essays in Technology and Modernity* (Cambridge, MA: MIT Press).

HARRINGTON, Lewis E.
   2009 "Miki Kiyoshi and the Shōwa Kenkyūkai: The Failure of World History," *Positions Asia Critique* 17: 43–72.

HUI, Yuk 許煜
   2016 *The Question Concerning Technology in China: An Essay in Cosmothechnics* (Padstow: Urbanomic).
   2021 *Art and Cosmotechnics* (Minneapolis: University of Minnesota Press).

INUTSUKA Yū 犬塚 悠
   2020 "The Historical Development of the Concept of Technology in Japan," *Mechane*, 235–45.

KAPP, Ernst
   2018 *Elements of a Philosophy of Technology: On the Evolutionary History of Culture* (Minneapolis: University of Minnesota Press).

KIM, John Namjun
   2007 "The Temporality of Empire: the Imperial Cosmopolitanism of Miki Kiyoshi and Tanabe Hajime," in Sven Saaler, ed., *Pan-Asianism in Modern Japanese History. Colonialism, Regionalism and Borders* (London: Routledge), 151–67.

Kosaka Shūhei 小阪修平
　1986　「技術論論争」[The debate on technology], in 松本健一 Matsumoto Ken'ichi, ed., 『論争の同時代史』[*A history of contemporary controversies*] (Tokyo: Shinsensha), 168–73.

Marx, Karl and Friedrich Engels
　1962　*Karl Marx & Friedrich Engels Werke.* Band 23 (Berlin: Dietz).

Moore, Aaron Stephen
　2013　*Constructing East Asia: Technology, Ideology, and Empire in Japan's Wartime Era, 1931–1945* (California: Stanford University of Press).

Murata Jun'ichi 村田純一
　2009　『技術の哲学』[*A philosophy of technology*] (Tokyo: Iwanami Shoten).

Scheler, Max
　1926　*Erkenntnis und Arbeit. Eine Studie über Wert und Grenzen des pragmatischen Motivs in der Erkenntnis der Welt* (Leipzig: Der Neue-Geist Verlag).

Sombart, Werner
　1935　*Die Zähmung der Technik* (Berlin: Buchholz & Weißwange).

Stromback, Dennis
　2020　"Miki Kiyoshi and the Overcoming of German and Japanese Philosophy," *European Journal of Japanese Philosophy* 5: 103–43.
　2021　"Notes on Miki Kiyoshi's Anthropological Humanism and Environmental Ethics," *Environmental Philosophy* 18: 227–57.

Townsend, Susan
　2009　*Miki Kiyoshi 1897–1945: Japan's Itinerant Philosopher* (Leiden: Brill).

Raji C. Steineck
Universität Zürich

Die Produktion der linearen Zeit

Ōmori Shōzō 大森荘蔵

ORIGINAL TITLE: 「線型時間の制作点時刻」, in 『時間と存在』 (Tokyo: Seidosha, 1994), 17–46. Zuerst publiziert als selbständiger Aufsatz in 『現代思想』, März 1993.

Ōmori Shōzō (1921–1997) gehört zu den einflussreichsten japanischen Philosophen des 20. Jahrhunderts und ist besonders bekannt für seine Überlegungen zur Sprache und zur Zeit; er wurde in dieser Zeitschrift zuletzt in einem Beitrag von Pierre Bonneels vorgestellt. Während Bonneels sich jedoch auf eine Frühschrift *Ōmoris* bezog, stammt der hier übersetzte Aufsatz von 1993, also aus den letzten Lebensjahren des Autors. Er dreht sich um die zwei Thesen, dass erstens «Zeit» nicht eine Gegebenheit, sondern ein Produkt der menschlichen Kultur ist; und dass zweitens in diesem Produkt der Begriff des «Zeitpunkts» eine problematische Rolle spielt.

KEYWORDS: Zeit—Bewegung—Zeitpunkt—lineare Zeit—Ōmori Shōzō—Zenons Paradox

Ōmori Shōzō

Die Produktion der linearen Zeit

Übersetzt und kommentiert von Raji C. Steineck

Es ist schon lange her, dass die Zeit das Interesse nicht nur der Philosophie, sondern auch der gewöhnlichen Menschen zu fesseln begann. Dadurch ist die Sache allerdings nicht klarer geworden, im Gegenteil – man hat den Eindruck, dass es die Dunkelheit um sie eher vermehrt. Und es hat sich um sie eine bestimmte mysteriöse Atmosphäre zusammengebraut, als ob sich jenseits dieser Dunkelheit ein tiefes Geheimnis verberge und darauf warte, dass jemand die Tür aufstoße. Um diese schwer lastende Luft zu vertreiben, ist es sinnvoll, zunächst einmal allgemein verständlich zu machen, woher die Zeit überhaupt kommt. Allerdings ist bereits schwer zu fassen, was «Zeit» überhaupt meint, wenn man über ihre Herkunft spricht. Hier sei zunächst einmal auf die öffentliche, ganz unverborgene Zeit verwiesen, wie sie für die Zwecke der gegenwärtigen Gesellschaft allgemein im Umlauf ist. Das ist die Zeit der unzähligen Uhren, die von den Herstellern in grossen Massen produziert werden. Man wird zustimmen, dass diese Zeit von der physikalischen Zeit t abgeleitet ist. Es dürfte sich auch kaum Widerspruch dagegen erheben, diese physikalische Zeit t aufgrund ihrer Linienförmigkeit als lineare Zeit zu bezeichnen. Diese lineare Zeit der Physik wurde ursprünglich, ganz ähnlich wie das System «Familie», nach und nach über eine lange Zeit hinweg im Alltagsleben hervorgebracht. Im Folgenden möchte ich dem nachgehen, wie die einzelnen Phasen ihrer Herausbildung, zum Beispiel die Reihenordnung von Vergangenheit, Gegenwart und Zukunft, der Augenblickscharakter der Gegenwart oder die Kontinuität der Zeit, hervorgebracht wurden. Selbstredend kann niemand jetzt mehr reproduzieren, wie vor mehreren tausend oder zehntausend beziehungsweise im Falle der Affenmenschen und Urmenschen sogar vor mehreren hunderttausend Jahren Zeit hervorgebracht wurde. Aber wie Ingenieure mit Druck und Hitze einen Diamanten synthetisieren können, so kann man diese lange Zeit komprimieren und die über Zehntausende von Jahren hinweg erfolgte Zeitproduktion in kurzen Schritten simulieren, und ebenso wird man die Vorzüge und Schwächen dieser Simulation erörtern können. Ich wünsche mir, dass derartige Simulationen der Produktion der Bedeutung von wichtigen Begriffen der Philosophie, nicht nur jenes der Zeit, sondern zum Beispiel auch jene des Raumes, des Ichs, der Fremd-Ichs, oder der Wahrheit, eines Tages als neue Methode der Philosophie Anerkennung finden.

Als Anfangspunkt für die Simulation der Hervorbringung der linearen Zeit nehme ich das «Sein» der Dinge.

Die Zeitprägnanz[1] des fortdauernden Seins, Zeit und Sein

Wenn man sieht, dass ganz gewöhnliche, unauffällige Dinge, die uns umgeben, wie zum Beispiel ein Tisch, Stühle oder Küchenutensilien, an ihrem Platz «sind» [存在する], dann bedeutet «Sein» [存在] hier zweifellos ein «fortdauerndes Sein» [持続的存在].[2] Der Tisch wie der Topf sind dort in dem Sinne, dass sie «die ganze Zeit fortlaufend da sind». Der Topf ist nicht plötzlich dort aufgetaucht, sondern war schon eine ganze Weile vorher da. «Eine ganze Weile vorher» bezieht sich selbstredend auf die Vergangenheit, folglich enthält die Bedeutung des Topf-Seins offensichtlich auch die Bedeutung der Vergangenheit. Genauso umfasst das Sein des Topfes die Bedeutung «er wird wohl noch für eine Weile weiter dort sein».[3]

---

1. Im Original: 時めき. Die Wortbildung im Deutschen erfolgte analog zu Cassirers Begriff der «symbolischen Prägnanz»: wie dort das einzelne Symbol auf den Kontext einer symbolischen Form verweist, so bei Ōmori das Sein der gewöhnlichen Dinge auf den Horizont der Zeit. Siehe das Folgende.

2. An dieser Stelle habe ich *sonzai* mit Blick auf die folgenden Erörterungen als «Vorhandensein» wiedergegeben, um die dreifache Wiederholung von «Sein» zu vermeiden.

3. Der Text unterscheidet in diesem wie im vorigen Satz nicht zwischen «Sein» [*sonzai*] und «Bedeutung von Sein/des Seins» [*sonzai no imi*].

So, wie er nicht plötzlich einfach auftaucht, wird er nicht plötzlich einfach verschwinden. Das Sein des Topfs enthält die Bedeutung der Zukunft genau wie die der Vergangenheit und meint selbstverständlich auch, dass er «jetzt wirklich hier ist», also die Gegenwart.

So sind im Sein alltäglicher Gebrauchsgegenstände bereits *semantisch* [意味的に] die drei Phasen der Zeit, also Vergangenheit, Gegenwart und Zukunft, enthalten. Mit etwas Übertreibung und Nachdruck kann man sagen, Sein ist schon Zeit, die Zeit ist im Sein enthalten. Aber auch wenn man derartige Ausschmückungen beiseite lässt, steht fest, dass die Bedeutung des Seins der Dinge die Bedeutung von Gegenwart, Zukunft und Vergangenheit mit umfasst. Was diese inhärente Bedeutung zu Tage fördert, möchte ich die «Zeitprägnanz des Seins» nennen. Ich glaube, diese «Zeitprägnanz des Seins» ist genau das, was Dōgen in *Uji*, dem 20. Faszikel des *Shōbō genzō,* als «Sein-Zeit» [有時] bezeichnet hat.

> Besagtes *uji* bedeutet, Zeit ist schon Sein, jedes Sein ist Zeit. Der goldene Körper von sechs *jō* [etwa 4.8 m] ist Zeit, und weil er Zeit ist, darum gibt es das erhabene Leuchten der Zeit (…) Die drei Köpfe und acht Arme sind Zeit…[4]

Mit Blick auf sein Lebensumfeld nimmt Dōgen als Beispiel anstelle etwa von Küchentöpfen Buddhastatuen von sechs *jō* usw., aber das dürfte nicht daran hindern, seine Worte als Ausführung zur Zeitprägnanz des Seins materieller Dinge zu verstehen. Dafür, dass *uji* tatsächlich diese Zeitprägnanz des Seins meint, spricht besonders ein Blick auf seine weiteren Beispiele wie «*eine Zeit/uji* der dritte Sohn von Zhang oder der vierte Sohn von Li, eine Zeit/*uji* die große Erde und der leere Himmel».

Es ist nun wohl ganz natürlich, diese Zeitprägnanz des Seins zum Ausgangspunkt der Produktion linearer Zeit zu nehmen. Die Zeitprägnanz aller Arten der Dinge findet sich überall und lässt allerorts die Zeit anklingen. Es wäre eher überraschend, wenn daraus nicht die lineare Zeit hervorginge.

---

4. Die Übersetzung folgt hier der Lesart von Ōmori. Für die Originalstelle und eine Diskussion ihrer Bedeutung vgl. DZZ I, 169 und ELBERFELD 2004. Elberfeld übersetzt: «Genanntes u-ji heißt: Zeit (*ji, toki*) ist [*immer*] schon [*ein bestimmtes*] Gegebenes (*u*), alles Gegebene (*u*) ist [*bestimmte*] Zeit (*ji, toki*). Dieser vier Meter achtzig [*große*] Goldleib ist Zeit, und weil [*er*] Zeit ist, hat [*er*] Herrlichkeit [*und*] Glanz der Zeit/Zeiten (*ji*). Der dreiköpfig-achtarmige [*Wächtergott*], dies ist Zeit.» (ibd., 386).

Allerdings haftet die Zeitprägnanz des Seins der Dinge noch an diesen selbst und ist daher lokal begrenzt. Dagegen ist die lineare Zeit eine allumfassende Zeit, die das ganze Universum einschliesst. Die lineare Zeit lässt sich deswegen nicht vollständig von ihrem Anfangspunkt in der Zeitprägnanz des Seins her ausbilden. Als nächsten Schritt müssen wir uns daher der eigenen Erfahrung, vor allem der Erfahrung der Erinnerung zuwenden.

Die Gerüstzeit: Zukunft – Gegenwart – Vergangenheit

Die Zeitprägnanz der Dinge lässt sich, wie das oben angeführte Wort Dōgens «Eine Zeit der dritte Sohn von Zhang oder der vierte Sohn von Li» zeigt, auch auf Menschen anwenden. Dann bezieht sie sich auf den Leib als materielles Ding. Davon noch einmal unterschieden tritt im Bewusstsein des Menschen eine eigentümliche Zeitlichkeit zu Tage. In der Erfahrung der Erinnerung wird die Bedeutung «Vergangenheit» erlebt, und genauso die Bedeutung «Zukunft» im Erfahren von Absichten oder Erwartungen.[5] Den Kern der Bedeutung der Gegenwart bildet dabei das Erlebnis «jetzt, während gerade....», also die Erfahrung, jetzt inmitten von etwas [einer Handlung, eines Geschehens] zu sein. Das Entstehen der Reihenordnung von Gegenwart und Vergangenheit sowie Gegenwart und Zukunft wird möglich durch diese Erfahrung, jetzt inmitten von etwas zu sein. Die Vergangenheit, die in der Erinnerung erfahren wird, wird erfahren als Früheres gegenüber diesem Erinnerungserleben selbst. Nun ist die Erinnerungserfahrung selbst eine Unterart der Erfahrung, jetzt inmitten von etwas zu sein, nämlich eben die, «jetzt gerade dabei zu sein, sich zu erinnern». Das Jetzt, das hier erfahren wird, ist eines, das dabei mit der Vergangenheit, an die man sich erinnert, verglichen wird, und dadurch wird die Vergangenheit zu etwas, das vor der jetzigen Gegenwart war. Und genauso wird die Zukunft im Erleben von Absicht und Erwartung als etwas erfahren, was nach der Gegenwart kommt.

Auf diese Weise kommt allererst die Reihenordnung Vergangenheit-

---

5. «Erleben» und «Erfahren» geben hier und im Folgenden beide 経験 wieder. Semantisch ist im Text keine Unterscheidung zu erkennen, ob etwas erlebt oder ob es in den Zusammenhang von Erfahrung (im Kantischen Sinne) eingeordnet wird.

Gegenwart-Zukunft zustande, während die im letzten Abschnitt diskutierte Zeitprägnanz der Dinge nur die Reihenfolge von Zukunft und Vergangenheit hervorzubringen vermag.

Mit anderen Worten, die grundlegende Reihenordnung Vergangenheit-Gegenwart-Zukunft wird in der bewussten menschlichen Erfahrung produziert. Hinzu kommt, dass diese im Bewusstsein produzierte Zeit in beiden Richtungen von Vergangenheit und Zukunft unbegrenzt ist. Zum Beispiel lässt sich nicht denken, dass eine bestimmte Vergangenheit in der Erinnerung die älteste Vergangenheit ist, vor der es keine weitere Vergangenheit mehr geben kann. Die Seinsweise der von uns erfahrenen Erinnerungserlebnisse schliesst diese Möglichkeit aus, und genauso verhält es sich mit der Zukunft. Die beiden Richtungen der Vergangenheit wie Zukunft sind ohne Grenzen. So wird das Zeitgerüst produziert, in dem die Gegenwart sich zwischen einer grenzenlosen Zukunft und einer grenzenlosen Vergangenheit befindet. Ich nenne das die «Gerüstzeit». Während die Zeitprägnanz des Seins noch örtlich begrenzt war, dürfte klar sein, dass diese Gerüstzeit bereits nicht mehr lokal, sondern global ist[6]; denn sie wird nicht durch das Sein einzelner Dinge eingeschränkt. Klar ist aber auch, dass die Grundstruktur der Gerüstzeit und der Zeit der Zeitprägnanz die gleiche Form — Vergangenheit-Gegenwart-Zukunft — haben. Darum kann man die lokale Zeit der Zeitprägnanz gewissermaßen auf die globale Gerüstzeit legen. Die Zeit der Zeitprägnanz jedes beliebigen Dinges lässt sich durch solches Übereinanderlegen gleichsam in die Gerüstzeit absorbieren und mit ihr verschmelzen.

Es bedarf wohl keiner weiteren Worte, dass diese Gerüstzeit die Urform und das Gerüst der linearen Zeit der Physik ist. Wenn man noch ein wenig Fleisch an die Knochen dieser Gerüstzeit bringt, so lässt sich daraus die lineare Zeit produzieren.

Die genese von Vergangenheit, gegenwart und zukunft

Die in einem früheren Abschnitt erläuterte Zeitprägnanz des

---

[6]. Ōmori verwendet an dieser Stelle zusätzlich zu den japanischen Termini 局所的 und 全域的 in Klammern die englischen «local» und «global».

Seins bildet den Ausgangspunkt für die Genese der linearen Zeit t, reicht für diese aber nicht aus. Die lineare Zeit ist lokal gleichförmig mit der Dauer gemäss der Zeitprägnanz des Seins, aber zur Ausbildung einer weitgestreckten, langen Zeit, die unbegrenzt in die Vergangenheit und die Zukunft reicht, ist ein Moment vonnöten, das nicht lokal begrenzt, sondern global umfassend ist. Es besteht in nichts anderem als im Ganzen meiner Erfahrung, die von der Vergangenheit bis in die Zukunft reicht. Man wird nicht übersehen, dass in der Erfahrung die Reihenordnung der Zeit, also von «früher», «später» und «gleichzeitig», ursprünglich vorhanden ist. Sie ist sowohl zwischen zwei beliebigen Ereignissen in der Erfahrung der Erinnerung also auch zwischen zwei beliebigen Ereignissen in der Erfahrung von Absicht oder Erwartung gegeben. Es ist ganz einfach und natürlich, dass durch diese Reihenordnung der Zeit alle Ereignisse in Vergangenheit und Zukunft in eine Reihenfolge gebracht werden.

Damit sind aber nur die zwei einseitig unbegrenzten Halbgeraden gebildet, die jeweils den vergangenen beziehungsweise zukünftigen Teil von t ausmachen, und noch nicht t als eine einzige, unbegrenzte gerade Linie. Zur Ausbildung dieser vollständigen Geraden ist die Verbindung der «jetzigen Gegenwart» mit der Reihenordnung von Vergangenheit, Gegenwart und Zukunft nötig.

Viele Menschen missverstehen den Ausdruck «jetzige Gegenwart» als Namen für eine bestimmte Zeitstelle.[7] In diesem Missverständnis gründen die meisten merkwürdigen Rätsel, welche die Zeit den Menschen aufgibt. Wenn man sich von ihm freimacht, eröffnet sich der Weg, die Bedeutung der «jetzigen Gegenwart» in der Redewendung «jetzt, während gerade...» zu suchen.[8] Mit anderen Worten, «jetzt» bezeichnet das «In einer Handlung Begriffensein» im Sinne von «jetzt, während des Essens» oder «jetzt, während des Badens».[9] Die Reihenordnung der drei Zeitphasen Vergangenheit, Gegenwart und Zukunft kommt genau durch die Bedeutung dieses «jetzt, während gerade» zustande.

---

7. Jap. 時刻. Ich vermeide hier das geläufigere Wort «Zeitpunkt», weil es mit einer bestimmten geometrischen Analogie verbunden ist, die an dieser Stelle noch nicht im Spiel ist.

8. Das Japanische 今最中 könnte man auch als «jetzt inmitten» übersetzen, es enthält also einen Hinweis auf die quasi-räumliche Erstreckung der Gegenwart.

9. Die Anführungszeichen sind Hinzufügungen des Übersetzers.

Nehmen wir an, *jetzt sei ich gerade dabei*, mich an ein beliebiges Ereignis X aus der Vergangenheit zu erinnern. Das Wesen der Erfahrung, sich an X zu erinnern, besteht darin, X als etwas Vergangenes, als Angelegenheit aus der Vergangenheit wachzurufen. Zugleich ist diese Erinnerungserfahrung selbst (die *noesis* im Sinne Husserls), da sie eine jetzt gerade geschehende Erfahrung ist, eben auch jetzt gegenwärtig. Und weil X gegenüber diesem Jetzt vergangen ist, ist es früher als die jetzige Gegenwart. Auf diese Weise wird jedes beliebige X, also jede Vergangenheit, zu etwas, das vor der Gegenwart war. Genauso wird die zeitliche Reihenordnung von Gegenwart und Zukunft bestimmt.

In Erfahrungen wie Absicht, Vorhaben, Erwartung oder Sorge wird ein zukünftiges Ereignis X als etwas Späteres gegenüber der Gegenwart erlebt, die darin besteht, jetzt gerade diese Erfahrung zu machen. Wenn etwa ein Kind sich beim Heimkommen verspätet, dann ist der Verkehrsunfall, den es womöglich hat, ganz offensichtlich ein Späteres gegenüber den übertriebenen Sorgen, die man jetzt gerade dabei ist, sich zu machen.

Indem die «Gegenwart» in dieser Weise mit der Bedeutung von «jetzt, während gerade» versehen wird, wird sie allererst in die Reihenordnung Vergangenheit-Gegenwart-Zukunft gestellt. Diese Ordnung erhält man nicht, wenn man nur eine Zeitstelle als «jetzt» setzt. Wenn man das tut, wird die Reihe in der Folge zu etwas Abgelegenen und Mysteriösem verherrlicht.

Nun ist mit dem Obigen die Genese der linearen Zeit *t* abgeschlossen. Und zwar besteht sie darin, dass in Verbindung mit der linearen Zeitachse Vergangenheit-Gegenwart-Zukunft die Richtung der Vergangenheit als das «Vorherige» und die der Zukunft als das «Spätere» gesetzt werden und so alle Ereignisse in der gesamten Erfahrung auf ihr aneinandergereiht werden.

Allerdings erschöpft sich diese lineare Zeit *t* zunächst, physikalisch gesprochen, in einer Reihe von Zeitstellen. Sie wird zur praktisch anwendbaren Zeit erst, wenn man zusätzlich die Messung ihrer Dauer einführt, ein Vorgehen, das ich im nächsten Abschnitt erläutere.

Ich habe das Muster der Genese der linearen Zeit hier so eingehend erläutert, um zu zeigen, wie natürlich und unmittelbar sie aus unserer Lebenserfahrung hervorgeht. Die lineare Zeit ist weder aus dem Himmel der Physik herabgestiegen oder oktroyiert worden, noch wurde sie als abstraktes begriffliches Konstrukt künstlich zusammengesetzt. Sie ist ganz natürlich–

geradezu wie von selbst – aus unseren einfachsten Erfahrungen geflossen und mit unserer Erfahrung so eng verbunden, dass man sie geradezu als deren Sekret bezeichnen kann.

Physiker, die das nicht verstehen, drängen der Zeit eine verzerrte Interpretation auf und entziehen dieser Errungenschaft ihre Basis. Das klassische Beispiel dafür ist die nachgerade mitleiderregend verdrehte Deutung von Vergangenheit, Gegenwart und Zukunft.

Aufgrund der Gewohnheit, die Zeitachse als Linie der reellen Zahlen darzustellen, zeigt man auf einen Punkt auf dieser Gerade und verkündet, «das ist die Gegenwart». Die Vergangenheit ist dann die Halbgerade links davon und die Zukunft die Halbgerade rechts davon, und damit fertig. Einfach gesagt, besteht dieses Vorgehen darin, die Gegenwart als einen Punkt auf der Zeitachse und Vergangenheit und Zukunft aus ihrer Reihenstellung zu diesem Punkt zu definieren. Aber tatsächlich gibt es zuallererst Erfahrungen wie die, sich jetzt gerade zu erinnern oder etwas vorzuhaben, und aus diesen Erfahrungen gehen die Bedeutungen von Vergangenheit und Zukunft sowie jene der Zeitreihe hervor. Die Interpretation der Physiker, die das nicht begriffen haben, stellt die Abfolge auf den Kopf und verdeckt gerade den wichtigsten Punkt.

Messung von Dauer und Zuteilung von Zeitstellen

Damit die lineare Zeit, wie sie durch die obige Prozedur generiert wurde, nicht nur im praktischen Leben, sondern auch in der wissenschaftlichen Forschung, zum Beispiel in Astronomie oder Dynamik, zum unverzichtbaren begrifflichen Werkzeug werden kann, ist selbstredend eine öffentliche (公共的な) Zeitfeststellung und -messung nötig. Diese bewirkt vor allem zweierlei: zum einen etabliert sie ein Anzeigesystem für die Uhrzeit, und zum anderen legt sie Zeitlängen fest. Diese zwei Leistungen sind nicht voneinander zu trennen. Wie die Festlegungen von Strecken- und Gewichtmassen müssen sie aber mehr oder weniger gleichzeitig erfolgen. Die systematische Einteilung und Benennung von Zeitstellen bedeutet nämlich nichts anderes, als dass auch die «Länge» der Zeit zwischen zwei Zeitstellen festgelegt wird. Nichtsdestoweniger kann man diese beiden nicht voneinander ablösbaren Leistungen begrifflich unterscheiden.

Im Fall, dass man die Zeitlängen ausser Acht lässt und nur die Messung von Zeitstellen anstrebt, muss man einfach alle Ereignisse als gleichzeitig mit einem beliebigen Standardereignis [einer Reihe] markieren. Wenn man zum Beispiel die Grade des Hungrigseins fein abgestuft auszudrücken vermag, dann könnte man ein Ereignis A als gleichzeitig mit dem Grad a des Hungrigseins, ein Ereignis B als gleichzeitig mit dem Grad b markieren. Die Skala des Hungrigseins a, b,… würde dann zur Anzeige der Zeitstellen, selbstredend entsprechend der Bauch-Uhr. Es muss aber eben nicht die Bauch-Uhr sein. Jeder Prozess kontinuierlicher Veränderung kann als Standard dazu dienen, beliebige Ereignisse als gleichzeitig einer seiner Phasen zuzuordnen und so zu einer vollgültigen Anzeige der Zeitstelle zu kommen.

Damit ein solcher Prozess als Standard öffentlich verwendet werden kann, muss er allerdings auch öffentlich beobachtbar sein. Zweitens müssen die Zeitlängen, die durch die Zeitstellenunterschiede angezeigt werden, auch zum praktischen Gebrauch taugen. Damit erstens die öffentliche Beobachtung möglich wird, ist anstelle eines individuellen Vorgangs wie der Grade des Hungrigseins ein überall vorkommendes Naturphänomen wie der Grad des Auslaufens von Wasser (Wasseruhr) oder des Abbrennens von Räucherstäbchen (Räucheruhr) zu bevorzugen. Wenn eine möglichst breite öffentliche Beobachtung gewünscht wird, dann verengt sich die Wahl der Referenzvorgänge in der Regel auf die Bewegungen der Himmelskörper und besonders der Sonne. Es dürfte auch natürlich sein, dass zur letzteren hilfsweise ergänzend die Bewegungen des Mondes und der Sternzeichen hinzutreten. Dazu kommt, dass diese Bewegungen periodisch sind. Dadurch lassen sich die Zeitstellen durch die Kombination zyklischer Ziffern für Jahr, Monat, Tag, Stunde, Minute und Sekunde ausdrücken, was äusserst praktisch ist. Man kann nun die solare Uhr (太陽時計) zwar auch mittels einer Sonnenuhr (日時計) verfolgen, bei der man die Bewegung des Schattens eines undurchsichtigen Gegenstands berechnet. Aber direkt wird dafür die Bewegung der Sonne selbst verwendet. Wenn man sich einen grossen Stab vorstellt, der den eigenen Standort mit der Sonne verbindet, dann kann man diesen Stab als grossen Zeiger einer Uhr ansehen, ganz so, als ob eine Sonnenuhr an den Himmel gemalt sei. Wer immer wann es beliebt zum Himmel aufschaut, kann dort diese solare Uhr (太陽時計)[10] sehen.

10. Hier und im Folgenden verwende ich in weitgehender Übereinstimmung mit Ōmoris Sprachgebrauch «solare Uhr» für 太陽時計, wo immer es um eine Uhr geht, deren Einteilung

Ein weiterer Vorteil der solaren Uhr besteht darin, dass sie die zweite oben genannte Bedingung einer praktisch brauchbaren Zeitlängenmessung erfüllt. Die Länge der Zeit/Stunde, gemessen als Unterschied zwischen zwei Zeitstellen/Uhrzeiten (時刻[11]), wird zum Abgleich mit stetigen Naturphänomenen verwendet, etwa mit der Menge Wassers, das mit konstanter Geschwindigkeit [aus einem Gefäss] abfliesst, oder mit dem menschlichen Herzschlag, aber auch mit menschlicher Tätigkeit, etwa einer gelaufenen Distanz oder der Länge einer Ackerfurche. Einfach gesagt, stimmt sie mit dem Rhythmus der Natur und der menschlichen Tätigkeit überein. Darum war es nur natürlich, dass die solare Uhr dazu verwendet wurde, die Stellen der linearen Zeit zu bezeichnen.

Vollendung durch Geschichte und Naturwissenschaft

Die lineare Zeit, die mit der solaren Uhr gemessen wird, ist durch unzählige Anwendungen in unserem Alltagsleben für unsere alltägliche Erfahrung erprobt. Im Gefolge genießt sie in allen Gesellschaften der Welt unerschütterliches Vertrauen und ist zur anerkannten öffentlichen Zeit geworden. Man darf aber nicht vergessen, dass sie auf dem Weg dahin noch zusätzliche Verstärkung erhalten hat. Zuerst wird die lineare Zeit der Individuen in die Richtungen der Vergangenheit und Zukunft verlängert. Wenn es nur darum ginge, die Ereignisse in Vergangenheit und Zukunft innerhalb eines menschlichen Lebens aufzureihen, dann wäre auch nur eine Zeitachse von Bedeutung, die von der Geburt bis zum Tod reichte. Die Zeitachse würde sich also auf eine Strecke zwischen diesen beiden Enden beschränken. Sobald man aber Ereignisse dieser Aufreihung hinzufügt, die andere Menschen in der menschlichen Gemeinschaft betreffen, dann bedeutet das, dass man zusammen mit dem eigenen Leben Ereignisse vor der eigenen Geburt, wie zum Beispiel die Geburt seiner Eltern, oder voraussichtliche Ereignisse nach dem eigenen Tod, wie die Heirat seiner Kinder und so weiter zusam-

---

sich nach dem Sonnenumlauf richtet, unabhängig von ihrer technischen Ausgestaltung. Für die oben beschriebene «Sonnenuhr» verwendet Ōmori den eingeführten Ausdruck 日時計.

11. Zeitstelle und Uhrzeit sind im Japanischen äquivok, daher kann Ōmori hier den Übergang von beliebigen Einheiten von Zeitstellen zur Stunde sprachlich bruchlos vollziehen.

men mit den Ereignissen des eigenen Lebens zu eine Zeitreihe zusammenfügt. Genau darin besteht die Ausweitung der Zeitachse in Vergangenheit und Zukunft. Und diese Ausweitung schliesst darüber hinaus die Chronik der öffentlichen Geschichte mit ein. Oder umgekehrt: die Zeitachse wird in der Richtung der Vergangenheit verlängert, um die ganze Geschichte der persönlichen und öffentlichen Ereignisse aufreihen zu können. Und sie wird in die Zukunft verlängert, damit die möglichen Ereignisse der noch unbestimmten Zukunft in sie eingeordnet werden können.

Nach den Anforderungen, die aus dem Bestreben resultieren, die historischen Ereignisse einzureihen, muss [die lineare Zeit] auch denen der naturwissenschaftlichen Weltbeschreibung entsprechen. Diese enthält mindestens potenziell eine endlose Vergangenheit wie Zukunft, so dass auch die Zeitachse in beide Richtungen *unbegrenzt* verlängert werden muss.

So wird die unendliche lineare Zeit t, die uns heute so vertraut ist, vollendet.

Aus dem Obigen geht deutlich hervor, dass die Zeit nicht unabhängig von uns Menschen existiert. Sie wird vielmehr von jedem einzelnen von uns Menschen produziert, weil sie für unsere Lebensführung notwendig ist, genau wie wir Menschen auch die Sprache oder den Begriff des Ich produziert haben. Die lineare Zeit hängt in der Reihe von Vergangenheit, Gegenwart und Zukunft zusammen, weil wir sie aus den drei Arten von Erfahrung Absicht, Erinnerung und Wahrnehmung so hervorgebracht haben. Die Verbindung ist gemäss der Reihenfolge vom Früheren zum Späteren angeordnet, weil zwischen den Ereignissen in unserer Erfahrung die Beziehung des Früher und Später besteht. Schliesslich ist die Zeitachse unbegrenzt in Vergangenheit und Zukunft, weil wir sie ins Endlose verlängert haben, um die historischen Chroniken und naturwissenschaftlichen Weltbeschreibungen zu integrieren. So ist die lineare Zeit von Anfang bis Ende unser intentionales Produkt. Das heisst nun allerdings nicht, dass alle sie für sich gemäss dem oben beschriebenen Vorgehen hervorgebracht haben. Die meisten Menschen dürften einfach das schon überlieferte Produkt übernehmen. Mindestens Menschen wie Archimedes, Galileo, Newton und Descartes haben aber die lineare Zeit im Wortsinn produziert, als sie zur Beschreibung der Bewegungen materieller Körper die Zeitkoordinate als unbegrenzte Linie zogen. Sie mögen dabei Verschiedenes gedacht haben, aber das sind nur psychologische Nuancen. Die Zeitkoordinatenlinie, die sie zogen, ist nichts anderes als die lineare Zeit, die gemäss dem oben erläuterten Vorgehen hervorgebracht wurde. Übrigens ist auch die manchmal aus Liebe am Seltsamen erwähnte «zyklische Zeit» ihrem Wesen nach isomorph[12] mit der linearen Zeit und hat darüber hinaus überhaupt keine besondere Bedeutung.

Wenn man akzeptiert, dass die lineare Zeit mit ihrer Produktion durch den Menschen zusammenhängt, dann lösen sich auch zum Beispiel die Fragen mit Bezug auf ihre «Kontinuität» auf. Denn die Kontinuität der Zeit und ähnliche Dinge sind ebenfalls ein menschliches Produkt und nichts, was der linearen Zeit von Anfang an eigen wäre. Die Kontinuität der Zeitachse wird produziert, weil sie für die kontinuierliche Abbildung von Bewegungen und Lageveränderungen materieller Körper nötig ist. Sie ist nicht fest und unangreifbar verbürgt, sondern unterliegt diversen Risiken und Zweifeln (vgl. z. B. das 4. Kapitel meines Buches *Zeit und Ich*, «Die Augenblickshypothese und Achilles und das Beobachtungsproblem»). Es gibt aber auch ein gefährliches Produkt, und das ist der im Begriff der Zeitstelle der linearen Zeit enthaltene Begriff der «punktförmigen Zeitstelle».[13]

Zur Pathologie der «punktförmigen Zeitstelle»

Mit ist nicht klar, auf welchem Wege es zur Hervorbringung des Begriffs der «punktförmigen Zeitstelle» mit der Dauer Null gekommen ist. Vermutlich ist er das Ergebnis des Zusammenkommens mehrerer Umstände. So dürfte etwa die Forderung nach Steigerung der Genauigkeit in der Auszeichnung von Zeitstellen nach der solaren Uhr und den auf diese abgestimmten Arten von Uhren ein Motiv bei der Herausbildung dieses Begriffs gewesen sein. Sie wurde weiter beschleunigt durch die Reflexion darauf, dass die beiden Enden eines begrenzten Zeitintervalls[14] selbst als punktförmige Zeitstellen zu denken sind. Hinzu wird der Umstand gekommen sein, dass man in Wettkämpfen wie beim Schwimmen oder dem Schlittschuhlaufen darauf abzielte, den «Augenblick» des Eintreffens im Ziel möglichst genau festzustellen. Auf einer tieferen Ebene kommt hinzu, dass im Verhältnis der

---

12. Im Original in Klammern nach dem japanischen Term 同型 angeführt.
13. Im Original: 点時刻, wörtlich «Punktzeitstelle». Der Term ist im Japanischen nicht gebräuchlich und wohl eine Wortbildung von Ōmori.
14. Im Original: 時間間隔 (time interval).

objektiven Welt zum Bewusstsein zum Beispiel bei der Betrachtung einer Landschaft die Erfahrung des Bewusstseins den Charakter eines «Augenblicks» hat und man im Bemühen, die Zeitstelle dieses Augenblicks festzuhalten, unvermeidlich zum Begriff des Zeitpunkts gelangte.

Unabhängig von den verschiedenen Umständen, die zu seiner Ausbildung geführt haben, wirkt dieser Begriff jedoch wie eine Droge, von der die Menschen abhängig werden, eine Droge, die sie lähmt und ihren Verstand trübt. Erstaunlicherweise gab es schon in alter Zeit, vor mehr als zweitausend Jahren, Menschen, denen das sehr schnell auffiel. Damit sind selbstredend die als Eleaten bezeichneten Gruppe im alten Griechenland gemeint. Deren Einsicht ist am geschliffensten in den zwei Paradoxen zum Ausdruck gebracht, die mit dem Namen Zenons verbunden sind: Das Paradox des fliegenden Pfeils und jenes des Wettlaufs zwischen Achilles und der Schildkröte.

Das erste Paradox des fliegenden Pfeils ist zwar weithin bekannt, aber zur Sicherheit sei hier noch einmal der Aufbau seines Arguments beschrieben.

Wenn es einen fliegenden Pfeil gibt, dann durchquert dieser an jeder Zeitstelle (punktförmigen Zeitstelle!) einen Ort und muss also dort sein (erster Schritt). An einem Ort zu sein bedeutet, an diesem Ort zu verharren (zweiter Schritt). Der Pfeil verharrt daher an allen Orten [seiner Flugbahn], und es ist nicht anzunehmen, dass ein Pfeil fliegt, der an allen Orten verharrt (dritter Schritt). Also fliegt der Pfeil nicht (Schluss). Wie aus diesem Aufbau des Arguments leicht ersichtlich, stellt Zenon nicht im Widerspruch zur Erfahrungsregel die Behauptung auf, dass ein Pfeil nicht fliegt, auch wenn man ihn mit dem Bogen abschiesst. Vielmehr weist er darauf hin, dass der Aussage, der Pfeil fliege, von ihrer Bedeutung her einen Widerspruch anhaftet. Aus diesem semantischen Hinweis kann unmittelbar geschlossen werden, dass es auch in der Erfahrung unmöglich ist, dass der Pfeil fliegt. Es verhält sich genauso wie mit dem «runden Viereck», das einen semantischen Widerspruch aufweist, weshalb es auch in der Erfahrung unmöglich ist, dass es ein physisches Objekt in der Form eines runden Vierecks gibt.

Nun gibt es aber empirisch eine Fülle fliegender Objekte von Pfeilen bis zu Kanonenkugeln. Es sollte also irgendwo einen Ansatzpunkt geben, von dem aus sich Zenons Behauptung widerlegen lässt. Ich denke, er ist gerade im besagten Begriff der punktförmigen Zeitstelle zu finden. Ich habe zwei Argumente gegen Zenon vorzubringen, ein grosses und ein kleines, und beginne mit dem kleinen. Es richtet sich gegen den dritten [sic] Schritt in Zenons Argument. Es ist nicht statthaft, daraus, dass der Pfeil an einem Ort ist, zu folgern, dass er dort verharrt. Es ist selbstverständlich möglich, zu sagen, dass der Pfeil an einem Ort ist und ein bestimmtes Mass an Bewegung aufweist, das heisst, eine bestimmte Geschwindigkeit besitzt. Darum kann man den Übergang von Schritt 2 zu Schritt 3 zurückweisen. Damit ist auch die Schlussfolgerung blockiert.

Dieses kleine Gegenargument nutzt, wie man sieht, eine einfache Schwachstelle aus und ist ohne grössere Bedeutung. Mein grosses Gegenargument richtet sich dagegen auf [den Begriff der] punktförmigen Zeitstelle und reicht wesentlich weiter. Der Kern des Gegenarguments ist, dass man das Sein oder den Zustand eines Dings an einer punktförmigen Zeitstelle gar nicht denken oder sich vorstellen kann. Es besagt also, dass deswegen [die Rede vom] Sein oder dem Zustand an einer punktförmigen Zeitstelle sinnlos ist.

Machen wir uns zum Beispiel die Mühe, uns vorzustellen, dass eine Wand zu einer gewissen punktförmigen Zeitstelle rot sei. Ist denn so etwas denkbar wie, dass eine Wand, die bis unmittelbar vor diesem Zeitpunkt weiss war, nun zu diesem Zeitpunkt für einen Augenblick rot wird und sofort wieder zum ursprünglichen Weiss zurückkehrt? Oder können wir uns etwa denken, dass ein Proton oder Elektron oder anderes Elementarteilchen in einem Augenblick an einer punktförmigen Zeitstelle plötzlich da ist und sofort wieder verlischt? Nein, das können wir nicht. Genauso, wie wir auch nicht denken können, dass genau da, wo man ein *yōkan*[15] geschnitten hat, etwas davon wäre, das man essen könnte. Eine gewisse begrenzte Dauer, wie klein auch immer, ist unfehlbar notwendig, damit etwas ist oder ein Zustand entsteht. Wenn man trotzdem aufgefordert wird, diese Dauer auf Null zu bringen, dann fehlen einem also die Mittel dazu. Das ist nur natürlich. Und was man in keiner Weise denken kann, das muss man als sinnlos bezeichnen. Das Sein oder der Zustand eines Dings an einer punktförmigen Zeitstelle ist undenkbar und sinnlos.

Aber Zenons Paradox des fliegenden Pfeils hat dieses Sinnlose zur Voraussetzung, es spricht nämlich vom Ort, an dem der fliegende Pfeil an einer

---

15. 羊羹. Eine Süssigkeit aus Bohnenmus, Zucker und Agar-Agar (manchmal ersetzt durch Pfeilwurz oder Mehl) mit glatter Textur.

punktförmigen Zeitstelle ist, und seinem Bewegungszustand darin. Bezüglich einer punktförmigen Zeitstelle ist aber jede Rede davon, dass der Pfeil existiert, nicht existiert, dass er stillsteht oder sich bewegt, ganz sinnlos. Die ganze diesbezügliche Erörterung Zenons ist daher aufgebaut aus einer Reihe von sinnlosen Behauptungen, weshalb man hier gar nicht in eine sinnvolle Diskussion eintreten kann.

Diese meine Einrede steht aber unter der Befürchtung, sie würde das Kind mit dem Bade ausschütten. Zwar habe ich so Zenons Schlussfolgerung, der Pfeil fliege nicht, mit einem Handstreich aus dem Weg räumen können. Aber ist dabei nicht auch die vernünftige Behauptung, dass der Pfeil fliege, für sinnlos erklärt worden, da ich doch erklärt habe, auch die Aussage sei sinnlos, der Pfeil fliege an jeder punktförmigen Zeitstelle? Das Problem ist tatsächlich noch viel grösser. Dass sich alle physikalischen Grössen als Funktionen der linearen Zeit t ausdrücken lassen, gehört zu den Grundlagen der gegenwärtigen Naturwissenschaften. Das entspricht jedoch einer Aussage über die Veränderung der jeweiligen Grösse zu jeder punktförmigen Zeitstelle auf der Achse von t. Wenn nun Aussagen über Existenz und Zustand von Dingen an einer punktförmigen Zeitstelle sinnlos sind, dann ist die gegenwärtige Naturwissenschaft aus sinnlosen Ausdrücken aufgebaut.

Ich kann mir hier keine eindeutigen Gründe vergegenwärtigen, um dieses Problem zu klären und muss mich damit begnügen, eine behelfsmässige Überlegung anzuführen.

Sie besteht darin, dass die aus punktförmigen Zeitstellen bestehende lineare Zeit eine idealisierte Zeit ist (ganz entsprechend dem idealen Gas[16]), die von der in Experiment und Beobachtung tatsächlich verwendeten Zeit zu unterscheiden ist. Die reale, praktisch zu diesem Zweck verwendete Zeit, zum Beispiel in der Messung der Fallhöhe im freien Fall oder des Zielein-

---

16. «Ideales Gas» ist ein gegenüber der Realität stark vereinfachtes Modell, das bestimmte Grundeigenschaften von Gasen erklärt. Es setzt voraus, dass Gase aus kugelförmigen Teilchen bestehen, die a) unendlich klein und b) vollkommen elastisch sowie c) elektrisch neutral sind, so dass d) bei Zusammenstössen keine Energie verloren geht und e) sie keine Wechselwirkung miteinander haben. Weiterhin bewegen sie sich f) in einem unbegrenzten Raum, wo das Gas sich also ungehindert ausdehnen kann. Ōmori stellt hier also darauf ab, dass bestimmte Ausdrücke/Begriffe physikalisch sinnvoll sein können, obwohl ihnen kein physisch realer Gegenstand gegenübersteht.

laufs bei einem Schlittschuhrennen, kann niemals die Präzision erreichen, eine echte punktförmige Zeitstelle zu messen. Auch wenn die physikalischen Grössen als Funktionen der idealen Zeit daher keinen Sinn haben, lassen sich die unscharfen Funktionswerte der praktisch anwendbaren Zeit doch messen und haben ihren guten Sinn. Ich wiederhole, das ist nur eine Überlegung zur vorläufigen Abhilfe, bis eine zum Kern vordringende Klärung des Problems eingreifen kann.

Zur Vereinfachung des Paradoxons von Achilles und der Schildkröte kann man eine Koordinate mit der Letzteren als Ursprung nehmen. In diesem Koordinatensystem läuft Achilles von einem beliebigen Anfangspunkt aus auf den Ursprung O [die Schildkröte] zu, kann sie aber nicht einholen, also O nicht erreichen. Das Paradox besagt demnach, dass man von keinem Punkt aus zu O kommen kann. Es verdeutlicht damit die These, dass Bewegung unmöglich ist. Zenons als Dichotomie bezeichnete Fassung des Paradoxons behauptet ebenfalls schlicht die Unmöglichkeit von Bewegung. Die gemeinsame ursprüngliche Grundlage dieser beiden Thesen liegt im Begriff der Unendlichkeit: Es ist unmöglich, das schrittweise Durchlaufen einer unendlichen Reihe diskreter Zahlpunkte zu vollenden. Es geht also nicht, wie manchmal fälschlich angenommen wird, darum, dass dazu unendlich viel Zeit benötigt würde.

Um diesen Punkt zu verdeutlichen, will ich im Folgenden einen Beweis aus Cantors Gruppentheorie auf das Achilles-Paradox anwenden. Er besagt, dass die Dichte von Punkten auf einer Strecke berechenbar unendlich ist. In der Grafik 1 ist [vertikal] eine Bewegung von A nach O dargestellt. Nun ziehe man von einem festen Punkt P aus Linien durch die Durchgangspunkte $x_1, x_2, x_3 \ldots$. Die Punkte, an der sie sich in der Verlängerung mit der [durch O verlaufenden] horizontalen Geraden L kreuzen, seien mit $y_1, y_2, y_3 \ldots$ bezeichnet. Auf diese Weise zeigt Cantor, dass es zur Gruppe der Punkte auf der Strecke AO eine eineindeutig entsprechende Gruppe von Punkten auf der Geraden L gibt, und dass ihre Dichte gleich ist.[17]

Für unser Beispiel bedeutet die Anwendung der Entsprechungsregel aber, dass die Bewegung $x_1, x_2, x_3 \ldots$ eine entsprechende Bewegung $y_1, y_2, y_3 \ldots$

---

17. Anm. im Original: Es heisst, Pascal habe in seiner Schrift «Der Geist der Geometrie» genau die gleiche Zeichnung analysiert.

Grafik 1

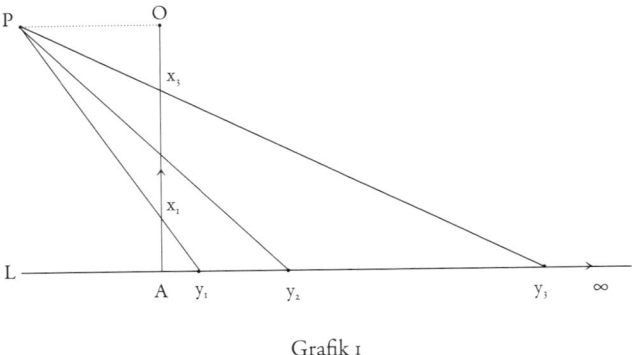

konstituiert. Man kann x_i und y_i durch ein Seil verbinden, oder eben einfach durch eine Regel. In jedem Fall gilt: wenn die Bewegung $x_1, x_2, x_3, \ldots$ möglich ist, dann demgegenüber auch die Bewegung $y_1, y_2, y_3 \ldots$ auf L. Weil die letztere eine einseitig unbegrenzte Halbgerade durchläuft, ist sie unmöglich. Dann ist auch die Bewegung über die begrenzte Distanz von A nach O [also durch x_1, x_2, x_3] unmöglich. So ist deutlich, dass der Grund für die Unmöglichkeit der Bewegung in [der Unmöglichkeit] der «Vollendung des Durchlaufens einer unendlichen Anzahl von Punkten» liegt.

Den Kern des Paradoxons von Achilles und der Schildkröte liegt also darin, dass der Begriff des Unendlichen herangezogen wird, um die Unmöglichkeit von Bewegung zu behaupten.

Man kann aber auch unabhängig von diesem Begriff zeigen, dass Bewegung, wie sie das geometrische Diagramm darstellt, einen Widerspruch enthält. Dieser lässt sich als Widerspruch der Bewegungen geometrischer Punkte bezeichnen, weil die geometrische Darstellung von Bewegung notwendig mit eben solchen Bewegungen von Punkten korreliert ist.

Stellen wir uns vor, ein Punkt P würde sich vom Punkt A nach Punkt B bewegen. Wenn aber der Punkt P sich am Ort des Punkts A befindet, dann sind beide identisch. Die Definition des ausdehnungslosen geometrischen Punkts macht das unvermeidlich. Genauso ist P am Ende der Bewegung mit B identisch. Die Punkte A und B sind verschieden, aber der Punkt P ist sowohl mit Punkt A als auch mit Punkt B identisch. Das ist ein offensichtlicher Widerspruch. Wenn die Bewegung des geometrischen Punktes widersprüchlich ist, dann gilt das auch für das geometrische Diagramm der

Bewegung. Geometrische Darstellungen wie jene der Ortslinie oder die Deckung, die durch Verschiebung von Dreiecken entsteht, sind alles nur Schein. In der Geometrie gibt es keine Bewegung (vgl. das 2. Kapitel dieses Buches).

Es dürfte für alle Augen offensichtlich sein, dass Bewegung und Zeit wie Zwillinge verschwistert sind. Aristoteles identifizierte die Zeit geradezu mit Bewegung. Sobald daher einmal der Begriff der «punktförmigen Zeitstelle» ausgebildet war, musste man auch Bewegung als Bewegung zu einer punktförmigen Zeitstelle denken. Damit ging man aber, wie oben dargestellt, direkt einem Widerspruch in die Falle. Diese Falle hat noch dazu einen doppelten Boden: den oberen Teil bildet die Bewegung von Punkten, den unteren das Paradox von Achilles und der Schildkröte. Wenn man nämlich die Bewegung über einen begrenzten Abstand so denkt, dass zu einer Reihe von Zeitpunkten $t_1, t_2, t_3, \ldots$ die Bewegung durch die Orte $x_1, x_2, x_3 \ldots$ verläuft, dann muss man auch denken, dass die unendliche Reihe $x_1, x_2, x_3 \ldots$ nach und nach in $t_1, t_2, t_3 \ldots$ durchlaufen wird. Und damit wird man unweigerlich zum Widerspruch geführt, der in der «Vollendung einer unendlichen Schrittfolge» – das heisst, dem «Ende einer endlosen Zahl von Schritten» – liegt, der zu den Widersprüchen im Begriff des Unendlichen gehört. Und weiter führt der Begriff des Zeitpunkts auf ein naturwissenschaftliches Grundschema, nämlich die Angabe physikalischer Grössen zu einem Zeitpunkt, beziehungsweise als Funktion davon – und dieses Schema trifft wiederum auf das Paradox des fliegenden Pfeils. Die Eleaten und ganz besonders Zenon haben das schon in ferner Vergangenheit mit scharfem Auge gesehen und die passenden Paradoxa geformt, damit unsere Augen nicht blind darüber hinweggleiten. Noch erstaunlicher als dieser scharfsichtige Weitblick ist, wie Zenons Botschaft über mehr als zweitausend Jahre hinweg unverstanden und unbeachtet blieb. Was ich oben diesbezüglich gesagt habe, ist allererst der Anfang, ihre definitive Entschlüsselung würde das Bemühen zahlreicher Menschen erfordern.

Jedenfalls dürfen wir aber festhalten, dass die Ursache für die Paradoxien und Widersprüche im Begriff der punktförmigen Zeitstelle liegt.

Und doch gehört dieser Begriff zu den Fundamenten der modernen Naturwissenschaften und ist ihr tief ins Herz gedrungen. Aber warum sind dann in den letzten Jahrhunderten ihrer Entwicklung nicht die Schwierigkeiten aufgetreten, die angesichts der in ihm liegenden Widersprüche und

Paradoxien zu erwarten gewesen wären? Habe ich nur Geister gesehen, Probleme, wo keine existieren?

Nein, vielmehr denke ich, dass die moderne Naturwissenschaft es glücklich verstanden hat, den schädlichen Auswirkungen des Begriffs der punktförmigen Zeitstelle zu entkommen, ohne die besagten Widersprüche überhaupt zu bemerken. Wenn dem so ist, was hat sie befähigt, sich so zu immunisieren? Erstens hat sie es vermieden, das geometrische Diagramm bzw. die Bewegung von Punkten in Gänze zur Anwendung zu bringen. Zum Beispiel stellt man die Orbitalbewegungen der Planeten dar, indem man um den Sonnenpunkt im Zentrum elliptische Bahnen zeichnet, welche die Bewegung der Planetenpunkte bezeichnen. Aber diese Ellipsen stellen eben die Umlaufbahn dar und nicht die Bewegung selbst. Für die Darstellung der Bewegung sind Formen nötig, die selbst bewegt sind, wie Filme, Videos oder Modelle. Mit der statischen Zeichnung einer Ellipse kann man keine Bewegung ausdrücken. Bergson identifizierte als Grundfehler im Paradox von Achilles und der Schildkröte, dort würden Bewegungsbahn und Bewegung verwechselt, aber die Naturwissenschaft hat eine solche Verwechslung (nach Bergsons Worten: die Verräumlichung der Zeit) tunlichst vermieden. Über die Bewegung des Planetenpunktes auf der Ellipse sagt die Wissenschaft in Worten nur, sie verlaufe auf ihr; alles weitere mathematisiert[18] sie. Die Widersprüche der Bewegung von Punkten *treten deshalb nicht an die Oberfläche*. So wird die begrenzt bogenförmige Bewegung auf der Ellipsenbahn nicht als Durchlaufen einer unendlichen Reihe von Schritten durch $x_1, x_2, x_3, \ldots$ beschrieben, sondern direkt mit dem Funktionsausdruck $x = f(t)$. Das Achilles-Paradoxon bricht deshalb gewissermassen nicht aus, es zeigen sich keine Symptome. Die Naturwissenschaft vermeidet es, das Innere der Bewegung von/an Punkten bzw. nach geometrischen Diagrammen zu berühren. Sie benutzt nur sacht und vorsichtig ihre Aussenseite und schafft es damit, die verborgenen Minen nicht loszutreten.

Dennoch ist nicht abzustreiten, dass die Wissenschaftler/innen in der Formel $x=f(t)$, also im Ausdruck einer physikalische Grösse als Variable der Zeit *t*, diese als punktförmige Zeitstelle denken. Doch greift hier die oben

---

18. Anm. im Original: Die von Bergson als Fehler identifizierte «Verwechslung der unteilbaren Bewegung selbst mit den Teilen der durchlaufenen Bewegungsbahn» ist dadurch ganz von selbst vermieden.

bezüglich des Paradoxons vom fliegenden Pfeil erwähnte Hilfsmassnahme: denn die im Labor oder Feld zur Anwendung kommende Zeit ist jene, die von massengefertigten Uhren angezeigt wird, und auch wenn man Verbesserungen und Verfeinerungen wie bei der Atomuhr hinzunimmt, erreicht man niemals einen solchen Grad der Genauigkeit, dass eine punktförmige Zeitstelle mit der Dauer 0 gemessen würde. Die Zeit, als deren Funktion physikalische Grössen ausgedrückt werden, ist eine Idealisierung der praktisch zur Anwendung kommenden Zeit, beziehungsweise dieselbe auf die Spitze gebracht (genau wie die Punktskalen der Länge oder des Gewichts Idealisierungen der wirklich gebrauchten Lineale und Waagen sind). Wie das ideale Gas, das elektromagnetische Feld oder die verschiedenen Elementarteilchen ist diese idealisierte Zeit, oder genauer, die idealisierte Zeitpunktfeststellung, als [rein] theoretischer Begriff [ohne korrespondierendes Reales] zu denken. Und damit muss auch die physikalische Grösse zu einem solchen Zeitpunkt als [rein] theoretischer Begriff gedacht werden.

Dass die Bestimmung der punktförmigen Zeitstelle ein solcher theoretischer Begriff ist, lässt sich auch daran sehen, wie die lineare Zeit t in die Physik eingeführt wird. In ihren Anfängen rekurrierte die Physik auf die lineare Zeit der Sonnenuhr, des Herzschlags, oder von Pendeluhren wie dem Leuchter, der in einer von Galilei überlieferten Anekdote vorkommt. Allerdings wurde die mangelnde Genauigkeit dieser Uhren zum Problem, und inzwischen ist, wie allgemein bekannt, die Atomuhr zum Standard geworden. Wie wird dabei aber die «richtige Uhrzeit» oder die «richtige Sekunde» bestimmt, wenn weiterhin unter Berufung auf Genauigkeit weltweit die Uhren um eine Sekunde korrigiert werden? Ich denke, dies geschieht durch die Grundgleichungen der Physik (vgl. das Kapitel «Ist der Beobachter ein Hindernis?» in meinem Buch *Zeit und Ich*[19]). In der klassischen Physik wurde die Zeit t so bestimmt, dass Newtons Bewegungsgleichungen erfüllt wurden, also etwa das aus diesen Gleichungen abgeleitete Gesetz, dass gleich lange Pendel gleich lang schwingen. So wurde dann die Pendeluhr als «richtige Zeit» bestimmt. Und in der Gegenwart ist die Atomuhr zum Standard geworden, weil sie die Zeit so misst, dass die Gesetze der Quantendynamik erfüllt werden und sie zum Beispiel mit den Werten übereinstimmt, die das Spektrum des Cäsiums aufweist. Die Pendel-

19. ŌMORI 1992.

uhr oder die Sonnenuhr gehen aber nicht synchron mit der Atomuhr, und ihre Abweichungen werden dann entsprechend berichtigt. Da die «richtige lineare Zeit» eingeführt wurde, um den grundlegenden Theoremen der Physik zu entsprechen, ist es nur natürlich, dass sie ein theoretischer Begriff ist. Und das verdeutlicht umso mehr, dass die lineare Zeit etwas ist, das die Menschen hervorgebracht haben.

Aber der so produzierten linearen Zeit fehlt es bedauerlicherweise in einigen Punkten an Zuverlässigkeit, und zwar weil eben der Begriff der punktförmigen Zeitstelle in Gefahr steht, auf Widersprüche und Paradoxien wie die von Zenon zu führen, wenn man nicht sehr achtsam mit ihm umgeht. Die Naturwissenschaft hat sich des Begriffs der linearen Zeit nur unter höchst vorsichtigem Umgang mit dem Begriff der punktförmigen Zeitstelle bedient, ganz so, wie man für den Verzehr des Kugelfischs umsichtig darauf achtet, Leber und Eierstöcke nicht anzutasten, und sie wird diese Einstellung wohl auch in Zukunft beibehalten. Und stellvertretend für sie wird [auch] die Philosophie die Aufgabe übernehmen, darüber zu wachen. Die Philosophie, die – ob zum Glück oder zum Unglück – dafür mehr als genug Musse hat, wird gerne dieses von Zenon überlieferte Amt an sich ziehen.

Der Fluss der Zeit und der Zeitpunkte

Der Begriff des Zeitpunkts erweist sich nicht nur auf dem Gebiet der Naturwissenschaft als schädlich, er ruft auch bezüglich der alltäglichen Zeit Verzerrungen hervor. Liegt etwa nicht der Idee vom «Fluss der Zeit», die sich praktisch universell in alter und neuer Zeit in Ost und West vorfindet, das gefährliche Bild einer punktförmigen Zeitstelle zugrunde, der sich auf der Zeitachse bewegt? Das ist aber mit eben den Widersprüchen behaftet, die ich oben bezüglich der Bewegung geometrischer Punkte erläutert habe. Nehmen wir an, die punktförmige Zeitstelle t bewege sich auf der Zeitachse von der Zeitstelle A nach der Zeitstelle B. Wenn t anfangs an A ist, dann ist dieZeitstelle t gleich mit der Zeitstelle A (zum Beispiel fünf nach zwei Uhr). Wenn sie B erreicht, dann ist t gleich mit B (zum Beispiel zehn nach Zwei). Das bedeutet, dass die Zeitstellen A und B gleich sind, dass also zwei Uhr fünf gleich zwei Uhr zehn ist – ein Widerspruch. Dass sich eine punktförmige Zeitstelle bewegt, führt auf den gleichen Widerspruch wie die Bewegung eines geometrischen Punktes. Darum enthält ein einfaches Modell des Zeitflusses, bei dem sich der «Jetzt» genannte Zeitstelle der Gegenwart auf der Zeitachse bewegt, evidenter Weise einen Widerspruch, wie von McTaggart gezeigt.

Was bedeutet dann das Bild vom «Fluss der Zeit», das fast alle Menschen haben? Oder vielmehr, kann es überhaupt etwas bedeuten?

Selbstredend wird niemand denken, dass ein abstraktes Ding wie «Zeit» fliesse oder sich anderweitig bewege. Vermutlich sind es verschiedene Aspekte, die zusammenkommen und die Rede vom «Fluss der Zeit» motivieren. Einer davon dürfte der Wandel der Dinge und Erfahrungen sein, der im Ausdruck «panta rhei / alles fliesst» zur Sprache kommt. Weil die Richtung dieses Wandels vom zeitlich Früheren zum Späteren geht, entsteht das Phantombild von der Bewegung der Zeit. Hinzu kommt die Erfahrung, die ich «das Vergehen der Zeit» nennen möchte. Wenn man auf jemanden wartet, der noch nicht gekommen ist, oder an der Schranke, dass sie sich jeden Augenblick heben wird, oder wenn es in einer Prüfung mit den Antworten nicht vorangeht, während einem der Abgabezeitpunkt bedrohlich vor Augen steht, erlebt man tatsächlich, wie die Zeit verstreicht. Aber besteht diese Erfahrung vom Vergehen der Zeit nicht in Wirklichkeit einfach darin, dass sich ein «zeitlicher Abstand» (eine Länge der Zeit) monoton vermehrt? Handelt es sich nicht um die Erfahrung, dass von da an, wo man zu warten oder die Prüfung zu schreiben begonnen hat, die Zeit Augenblick um Augenblick gleichmäßig zunimmt? Das ruft den falschen Eindruck hervor, dass die Zeitstelle der Gegenwart von Augenblick zu Augenblick voranschreite (tatsächlich schaut man nervös auf die Uhr), dass also die Zeitstelle des «Jetzt» sich von Mal zu Mal bewege, und verführt damit zu der widersprüchlichen Vorstellung von der Bewegung einer punktförmigen Zeitstelle, die einen dazu bringt, das Wort vom «Fluss der Zeit» im Mund zu führen. Und so hält die falsche Vorstellung, dass die Zeit fliesst, die Menschen wohl schon seit der Steinzeit gefangen.[20] Aber auch wenn sie eine uralte Tradition besitzt und von unzähligen Gefühlen und Empfindungen durchtränkt ist, handelt es sich um eine leere und bedeutungslose Vorstellung, die noch dazu mit dem widersprüchlichen Begriff

---

20. Im Original steht hier 縄文以来, was auf die japanische Jungsteinzeit (Jōmon-Zeit) verweist. Ōmori spricht hier aber nicht nur über Japan, wie aus dem Vorigen ersichtlich.

der punktförmigen Zeitstelle verbunden ist. Sich dessen zu vergewissern bedeutet, den fatalen karzinogenen Wirkungen dieses Begriffs vorzubeugen und damit die lineare Zeit zu schützen, die zu den hervorragenden Errungenschaften der Menschheit gehört.

Danksagung

Die Arbeit an dieser Übersetzung erfolgte im Rahmen des Projekts «Time in Medieval Japan (TIMEJ)» und mit Förderung durch den ERC Advanced Grant No. 74116. Der Autor dankt dem Europäischen Forschungsrat für die Förderung und einem anonymen Gutachter für die sorgfältige Prüfung der Erstversion und viele hilfreiche Hinweise.

Literatur

Abkürzungen

DZZ 『道元禪師全集』[Dōgen Zenji: Gesammelte Werke von Dōgen], Bd. 1. Hg. Ōkubo Dōshū Tokyo: Chikuma Shobō, 1969–1970.

Elberfeld, Rolf
 2004 *Phänomenologie der Zeit im Buddhismus: Methoden interkulturellen Philosophierens*. Philosophie interkulturell 1. Stuttgart-Bad Cannstatt: Frommann-Holzboog, 2004.

Ōmori Shōzō 大森荘蔵
 1992 『時間と自我』[Zeit und Ich]. Tokyo: Seidosha.
 1994 『時間と存在』[Zeit und Sein]. Tokyo: Seidosha.

Book Review

杉村靖彦 Sugimura Yasuhiko, 田口 茂 Taguchi Shigeru, 竹花洋佑 Takehana Yōsuke, eds., 『渦動する象徴：田辺哲学のダイナミズム』
[*A Vortex of Symbols: The Dynamism of Tanabe's Philosophy*]
Kyoto: Kōyō Shobō, 2021, 388 pages. ¥12,210.
ISBN: 978-4771034228

　待望の一冊と言ってよいのではないか。いま田辺を研究している人にとってはもちろん、これから田辺を読み、あるいは"使って"みたい人にとっても有益な書物である。

　私見では、田辺哲学は大きく分けて、社会的カテゴリー（社会、国家、個人、民族、法、連帯、宗教等）の「論理」と人間の「生（死）」との関係を分節化する社会存在論と、主に先行学説の吟味を通じた理性批判ないし反省的認識論（数理哲学、科学哲学を含む）の二つの基軸をもつ。だがそれらは体系部門を成すわけでも道具関係にあるわけでもなく、むしろ互いのうちに入り込んで互いを不安定化しながら、絶えず過剰と欠如を産出する思考の運動（「渦動」）をなしている。どこにも落ち着けないこの動性が田辺の複雑さであり、魅力でもあるが、本書は複雑さを捨象することなく様々な切り口から魅力を展示している。

　本書の内容は以下の通り。①田辺の哲学および人物へのイントロダクションとなる、研究者による二回の座談会（参加者一部入れ替え）。②テーマごと5部構成計12本の論文。③初公刊となる二つの資料。(a) 敗戦迫る1945年5月に西田幾多郎に宛てた政治的内容の書簡。(b) 京大講義（1944年12月）の速記録を元にした小冊子『私観　教行信証の哲学』。④この10年余りの間に出た研究文献の包括的なリストを含む「田辺元文献目録 二〇〇九年〜二〇二〇年」。

　①の座談会は田辺の人と思想について、話題ごとに関連する歴史的文脈を接続しながら討議しており、彼の思想の主なトピックと大まかな背景を頭に入れることができる。どの参加者も各々の仕方で田辺に対して慎重な距離を保っており、それは事柄ごとに一定の根拠に基づく批判的距離でもあるが、同時に、袋小路とそこからの転換・

反転そのものをエンジンとする田辺の思考がストレートな同定や肩入れを許さないせいであることも伝わる。この点、複数の視点からツッコミを入れあう座談会形式が功を奏していると思う。

さて②の論文集が本書の主要部であるが、紙幅の都合で詳しい論評は無理なので、全体の構成を示した後、いくつかの論考のさわりを紹介しつつ、主に論考間の連関を書き留めておきたい。

構成は5つのテーマ、I「「種の論理」の意味とその行方」、II〈懺悔道〉としての宗教哲学」、III「死と象徴をめぐる最晩年の思想」、IV「「京都学派」の中の田辺哲学」、V「田辺哲学の今日的可能性」から成り、或る哲学者の全体像をつかむための基本的なテーマ―時期ごとの思想、歴史的布置、アクチュアリティ―が押さえられている。

各論文が補い合うような角度から題材を扱っていることは美徳である。例えば田辺の代名詞である社会存在論「種の論理」に関しては、藤田正勝氏が当時の日本の情況や田辺の経験を踏まえ、時代に対峙する一知識人の社会思想・共同体論としての姿を描き出している一方、村井則夫氏は種の論理とそれを深化した後期の象徴論を、カント図式論解釈（超越論的構想力論）に基づくハイデガーの存在論の限界を見極め、超越論哲学の伝統に連なりつつそれを超克する試み、つまり当時の（そして未だ汲み尽くされざる）西洋哲学の最前線として呈示している。あるいは敗戦迫るなか親鸞の再読から生まれ、哲学（者）の徹底的自己批判―「自己」批判の自己性・固有性にまで達する―を内蔵する「懺悔道としての哲学」に関しては、そもそも田辺自身「哲学ならぬ哲学」と言うこの「哲学」が親鸞の「宗教」とどのように関係する／しないのか、つまり「宗教哲学」の一言では済まない「としての」の複雑さを杉村靖彦氏が解きほぐす一方、ジョン・C・マラルド氏はアウシュヴィッツ生存者の赦しに関する経験ないし証言を手がかりに、懺悔道の鍵となる「絶対他力」を「いわば他力そのものの側から考察する」挑戦的な読解を通じて、懺悔‐責任‐赦し‐他者性の相互関係という緊張を孕んだ問題に取り組んでいる（「一億総懺悔」から臭う「免責」の問題でもある）。

また、こうした焦点的な題材の共通性とは別に、論者の間にモチーフの呼応を聞き取ることもできる。二つだけ取りあげよう。一つは身体である。座談会や藤田論文では、一時期は人間主体の根源的否定性ないし偶然性を担うものとして主題化されていた「身体」が、種の論理の形成に伴って希薄化していく次第が指摘されており、嶺秀樹氏の論文は実際に当該時期の思想たる「絶対弁証法」―田辺の哲学者として自立を印すとも言える―の成立に身体性が果たした重要な役割を論じている。いわば半ばまでしか展開されなかったこの身体論の意義を、宮野真生子氏の論考はさらに遠くまで追求している。宮野氏は、九鬼周造の偶然論に対する田辺の批判の眼目を明確にする中で、身体が過去の「負荷性」を人間に突きつけると共に、負荷性を受け取り直して未来志向的に行為へと踏み出す「転換」の場でもあり、ひいてはその転換の

「力源」をめぐって、「主体」の存在論的な位置づけにも繋がることを明らかにしている（根源的偶然性に否定性・負荷性の主体化（行為的自覚）の契機を見る田辺と、主体不在の現実そのものの動性を見る九鬼、という対比は双方の魅力を見事に引き出しているものと思われる）。

　もう一つは、ある種の関節の外れた時間のモチーフである。田口茂氏は、田辺が懺悔の時間性として語る「時の逆流」、すなわち懺悔が未来の救済への転機になるのではなくむしろその逆であるという信仰行為の「アナクロニズム」を、レヴィナスとデリダへの参照を介して照明している。予期‐充足の目的論的構造に対応する通常の時間秩序の中断・攪乱であるがゆえに、他者としての他者との計算可能性を超えた遭遇の好機となる―したがって同時に最悪のものにさえ開かれていなければならない―この時間の経験としての「希望」が、田辺にあっては、「永遠」ないし「愛としての神」がそれ自身を「滅裂」することが「動く今」の成立の根源にあるという、時間の湧出そのものの核心に見出される。このような時間の断層は、田辺晩年の「死の哲学」における「死者」の位置づけを検討する竹花洋佑氏の論にも呼応する。氏は、生者における死者の「復活」について田辺が一息で語った文章に目を凝らし、そこに複数回出現する「自己」の語の用法が、復活する死者＝自己と、復活を行いによって証する生者＝自己に分裂していることを発見した上で（驚くべき精読！）、この二重性が「死復活」において本質的である所以を論じている。そこで死復活は、我々が「自己の死の向こう側からこの生のあり方を映し出」す、あるいは「生者と不断に格闘することの只中において、生前には知ることのなかった死せる他者に「"生ける"死者」として不意に対面する」出来事であるからには、その時間は死の前／後が斜めにずれ込み合うような関節の外れた「現在」である。加えて、晩年のマラルメ論に「作品が何を象徴しているかではなく、どう象徴しているか」という鋭い問題設定で切り込む立花史氏の論考にも評者はこのモチーフを聞きとる。氏は実際に『賽の一振り』の紙面を掲載して詩の展開を追っていく形で、田辺が着目したタイポグラフィーに焦点を当て、他者の詩に自らの象徴論を象徴させる田辺の遂行的な「象徴」をいわばコメンタリー付きで再演してみせる。そして詩の最終頁の解釈ではまさに、荒海の質料的な動性と静止せる星座の永遠との「媒介転換」、あるいは「終末即始元」をいかにして「象徴」するかが賭けられているのである。なお、座談会では後期田辺が戦後フランス思想に通ずる要素を多くもつことが指摘されているが、これらの論考はそれを陰に陽に示すものと言えよう。

　翻刻の苦労が偲ばれる③の二つの「資料」はいずれも興味深い。特に『私観　教行信証の哲学』は、廖欽彬氏の解題でも示唆されるように、実際には展開されなかった田辺流「固有名の哲学」の片鱗のようなものが見られ、背景への関心や想像が膨らむ。

以上の如く、田辺を"今"読む知的冒険へと読者を誘惑する本書だが、④ の目録のおかげで、とりわけこれから田辺に取り組む者にとって文献へのアクセスがぐっと容易になるだろう。舶来の大物と違って「田辺研究」の存在自体が未だ自明ではないなか、このような研究の土台整備への努力に本書の志の遠大さが感じられた。

INOHARA Jirō 猪ノ原次郎
Hokkaidō University

Contributors

Carlos Barbosa Cepeda teaches philosophy at the Universidad Pedagógica Nacional, Colombia. He received his PhD from Pompeu Fabra University in Barcelona. His main areas of research are the Kyoto School and the philosophy of religion. He is currently interested in potential contributions of Japanese philosophy to cognitive studies and environmental issues, and in the Far-Eastern sources of Kyoto School thought. He is a founding member of the *Asociación Latinoamericana de Filosofía Intercultural* (ALAFI, alafi.org).

Augustin Berque (born 1942), a geographer and orientalist, is a retired director of studies at the Ecole des hautes études en sciences sociales (EHESS, Paris). A member of the Academia europaea, he was the first Westerner to receive the Fukuoka Grand Prize for Asian cultures in 2009. In 2018, he received the International Cosmos Prize. He is the author of many books, including *Poetics of the Earth: Natural History and Human History* (Routledge, 2019).

Quentin Blaevoet is a doctoral student at the University of Strasbourg, France. His interest is in the different receptions of phenomenology in Japan as seen in the works of thinkers from the Kyoto School and more contemporary Japanese phenomenologists, in particular, Nitta Yoshihiro (1929–2020). He is preparing a dissertation on the initial reception of Husserl and Heidegger in Japan and in the works of Tanabe Hajime (1885–1962). He is also part of the ongoing effort to make Tanabe's early works available in French and English.

Inohara Jirō 猪ノ原次郎 is a PhD student at Hokkaidō University. His main area of research is modern Japanese philosophy with a focus on Nishida Kitarō, Tanabe Hajime, and Kuki Shūzō. He is preparing a doctoral dissertation on Nishida's philosophy. He is also currently studying the way in which German idealism has been accepted and interpreted in various modern philosophical traditions, including the Kyoto School and contemporary analytic philosophy.

Morten E. Jelby is a PhD student at the Husserl Archives of the Ecole Normale Supérieure in Paris. His doctoral dissertation deals with being-in-the-world and poetics in Tanabe Hajime and Nishitani Keiji. His primary fields of research are asubjective phenomenology and the Kyoto school, in addition to which he is currently collaborating in translating a number of works by Japanese thinkers. He is a MEXT alumnus (Kyoto University, 2019–2021) and holds Masters degrees in contemporary philosophy (Université Paris 1, Panthéon-Sorbonne) and literary theory (Sorbonne, ENS, EHESS), with theses focusing on perception in Sartre and literature in the philosophy of Jan Patočka.

David W. Johnson is an associate professor of Philosophy at Boston College. He works in the fields of contemporary Japanese philosophy (focusing especially on Watsuji, Kimura Bin, and Nishida), hermeneutics and phenomenology (especially Gadamer, Merleau-Ponty, and Heidegger), and comparative/intercultural philosophy. After a number of years living, working, and studying in Japan and Korea, he returned to the U.S., where he received a PhD in philosophy from The Pennsylvania State University. Professor Johnson has been a visiting researcher at the University of Freiburg (Germany), the Nanzan Institute for Religion and Culture (Japan), the International Research Center for Japanese Studies (Japan), and Pompeu Fabra University (Spain). His current research focuses on integrating the social ontology of the Japanese philosopher and psychiatrist Kimura Bin into the a-subjective phenomenology of Jan Patočka and the phenomenology of life of Merelau-Ponty and Renaud Barbaras.

Kuwano Moe 桑野 萌 is an associate professor at the Department of Intercultural Studies in the faculty of Humanities at Kanazawa Seiryo University. Her main areas of research are philosophical anthropology and comparative religions, with a particular focus on the body-mind theory and the theory of self-cultivation in Yuasa Yasuo's thought. Her principal publications include 「湯浅泰雄の修行論と身体の知をめぐって」 [On Self-cultivation Theory and the Wisdom of the Body in Yuasa Yasuo's Thought] (2015) and 「湯浅泰雄における比較思想研究：超文化哲学のカギとしての身体と超越」[The Methodology of Comparative Thought according to Yuasa Yasuo: The body-mind unity and its Opening towards Transcendence as a Key to Intercultural Philosophy] (2020). Her other interests include the comparative study of identity, culture, and spirituality in modern Spanish and Japanese philosophy

Hans Peter LIEDERBACH received his PhD in philosophy from Eberhard-Karls University Tübingen, Germany. He is professor of Philosophy and German at Kwansei Gakuin University in Nishinomiya, Japan. He has done research on the effective history of Western philosophy in modern Japan (Watsuji, Kuki, Nishitani, Heidegger, and Hegel). He is currently interested in how the philosophical discourse of modernity has been received by Japanese philosophers, and how this reception shapes our understanding of Japanese philosophy and philosophy in general. He is the author of *Martin Heidegger im Denken Watsuji Tetsurōs: Ein japanischer Beitrag zur Philosophie der Lebenswelt* (2001), the co-author of 『ハイデガー「哲学への寄与」解読』[*An Interpretation of Heidegger's "Beiträge zur Philosophie"*] (2006) and various articles. He recently edited the volume *Philosophie im gegenwärtigen Japan* (2017).

MINE Hideki 嶺 秀樹 is professor emeritus of philosophy at the University of Kwanseigakuin, Nishinomiya. He holds a PhD in philosophy from the University of Tübingen and an MA in philosophy from the University of Kyoto. Before retiring, he had been professor in philosophy from 1993 to 2019 and associate professor from 1988 to 1993. His research interests revolve around German idealism, phenomenology, and modern Japanese philosophy. He has published books on Schelling, Heidegger, and Japanese philosophers such as Nishida and Tanabe.

INOHARA Jirō 猪ノ原次郎 is a PhD student at Hokkaidō University, where he is studying modern Japanese philosophy with a focus on Nishida Kitarō, Tanabe Hajime, and Kuki Shūzō. He is preparing a doctoral dissertation on Nishida's thought. His other interests include the acceptance and interpretation of German idealism in various modern philosophical traditions, including the Kyoto School and contemporary analytic philosophy.

Graham MAYEDA is associate professor in the Faculty of Law of the University of Ottawa, Canada. In addition to research on law, he writes on Japanese philosophy, specifically Nishida Kitarō, Watsuji Tetsurō, and Kuki Shūzō, all of whom he treats in his recent book *Japanese Philosophers on Society and Culture* (2021). He also uses the philosophy of Martin Heidegger and Emmanuel Levinas in his writing, which focuses primarily on ethics.

MITSUHARA Takeshi 満原 健 is a part-time lecturer at Nara Prefectural University, Japan. His main areas of research are Kantianism, phenomenology and Japanese philosophy. His publications include "Nishida and Husserl between 1911 and 1917" and 「『善の研究』と心理主義」 [*An Inquiry into the Good* and psychologism] (2018).

Morioka Masahiro 森岡正博 teaches philosophy and ethics at Waseda University. He has published a number of books on bioethics, philosophy of life, and gender issues, mainly in Japanese, which include 『無痛文明論』 [*Painless Civilization*] (2003), and 『感じない男』 (2005), translated as *Confessions of a Frigid Man: A Philosopher's Journey into the Hidden Layers of Men's Sexuality* (2017).

Rossa Ó Muireartaigh is currently an associate professor at Aichi Prefectural University in Japan. He also teaches courses in Japanese philosophy part-time at Nagoya University of Foreign Languages, Meijo University, and Ibaraki University. He is the author of *Begotten, Not Made* (2015), a book dealing with the philosophy of translation, and a forthcoming book on D.T. Suzuki entitled *The Zen Buddhist Philosophy of D. T. Suzuki*. He is an active Japanese to English translator.

Nakamura Norihito 中村徳仁 is a doctoral candidate at Kyoto University, where he is preparing a dissertation on Schelling's political philosophy. His topics of interest cover German idealism, political theology, and the philosophy of technology (Miki Kiyoshi). He is the chief editor of the journal 『夜航』.

Federica Sgarbi teaches Asian philosophy and Western philosophy at Dōshisha University and is a visiting researcher in philosophy at Ristumeikan University (Japan). She received her PhD in philosophy from the Sorbonne in Paris. Her main area of research is Buddhism and its role in developments in spirituality East and West. She is currently interested in D. T. Suzuki's study of Swedenborg's esoteric philosophy and in the contributions of Beatrice Erskine Lane to Buddhist studies.

Kyle Shuttleworth is a JSPS international research fellow at Rikkyō University, where he is researching the interface between environmental ethics and Japanese philosophy. His recent publications include the monograph *The History and Ethics of Authenticity* (2020), the research article "Virtues and Ethics within Watsuji Tetsurō's *Rinrigaku*" (2020), and a translation of Watsuji's controversial essay "America's National Character" (2021).

Raji C. Steineck is professor of Japanology at the University of Zurich (UZH), visiting professor at Yamaguchi University's Research Institute for Time Studies, president of the International Society for the Study of Time (ISST), and principal investigator of the European Research Council's Advanced Grant project on "Time in Medieval Japan" (TIMEJ). His research interests combine Japanese intellectual history, the theory of symbolic forms, and the philosophy of time. Recent publications include *Concepts of Philosophy in Asia and the Islamic World: China and Japan* (co-edited with Ralph Weber, Elena L. Lange, and Robert H. Gassmann, 2018), *Kritik der Kultur: Überlegungen zu Cassirers Konzept der symbolischen Form* (2020), and *The Missing Piece in E. Cassirer's Philosophy of Symbolic Forms: The Economy* (with Georg Blind, 2021).

Bernard Stevens is emeritus professor at the Université Catholique de Louvain. He has been program director at the Collège International de Philosophie (Paris) and guest professor at various Asian universities, among then Fujen (Taiwan), Fudan (Shanghai), and Tokyo, and Dokkyō (Japan). His main books are *L'apprentissage des signes: Lecture de Paul Ricœur* (1990), *Topologie du néant: Une approche de l'école de Kyôto* (2000), *Maruyama Masao: Un regard japonais sur la modernité* (2018), and *Heidegger et l'école de Kyôto* (2020).

Urai Satoshi 浦井 聡 graduated from Ōtani University and completed studies at the graduate school of Kyoto University in 2019. At present he is an assistant professor at Ōtani University. His research has centered on the Kyoto School and Pure Land Buddhism, in particular, Tanabe Hajime, Takeuchi Yoshinori, and Shinran.

Fernando Wirtz holds an MA in Philosophy from the University of Buenos Aires and a PhD in Philosophy from the University of Tübingen. His postdoctoral research project at the University of Tübingen centers on the philosophy of Miki Kiyoshi. Besides Japanese philosophy, he is also interested in German idealism, intercultural philosophy, and the philosophy of myth. He is an active board member of the Gesellschaft für Interkulturelle Philosophie.

EDITORS
Takeshi MORISATO, *KU Leuven*
Leon KRINGS, *Universität Hildesheim*

ASSISTANT EDITORS
Adam LOUGHNANE, *University College Cork*
Alexandra MUSTĂŢEA, *Tōyō University*

ASSOCIATE EDITOR
Pierre BONNEELS, *Université Libre de Bruxelles*

BOOK REVIEW EDITORS
Roman PAȘCA, *Kanda University of International Studies*
Richard STONE, *Hokkaidō University*

EDITORIAL ADVISORY BOARD

AKATSUKA Hiroyuki 赤塚弘之, *University of Hildesheim*
Laurentiu ANDREI, *Université Blaise Pascal*
Thorsten BOTZ-BORNSTEIN, *Gulf University for Science & Technology in Kuwait*
Raquel BOUSO, *Universitat Pompeu Fabra*
Matteo CESTARI, *Università Degli Studi di Torino*
Montserrat CRESPÍN PERALES, *Autonomous University of Barcelona*
Michel DALISSIER, *Université Blaise Pascal*
Dagmar DOTTING, *Univerzita Karlova*
Florencia DI ROCCO, *Université Paris 1–Panthéon-Sorbonne*
Simon EBERSOLT, *Institut National des Langues et Civilisations Orientales*
Alfonso FALERO FOLGOSO, *Universidad de Salamanca*
Felipe FERRARI GONÇALVES, *Nagoya University*
Enrico FONGARO, *Tōhoku University*
Alberto GARCIA SALGADO, *University Michoacana de San Nicolás de Hidalgo*
Marcello GHILARDI, *Università degli Studi di Padova*
Thierry HOQUET, *Université Paris Ouest Nanterre*
GŌDO Wakako, *University of Tokyo*
INUTSUKA Yū 犬塚 悠, *University of Tokyo*
Romaric JANNEL, *École Pratique des Hautes Études*
David W. JOHNSON, *Boston College*
KUWANO Moe 桑野 萌, *Ramon Llull University*
Michael LUCKEN, *Institut National des Langues et Civilisations Orientales*
Hanna McGAUGHEY, *University of Trier*
Rebeca MALDONADO, *Universidad Nacional Autónoma de México*
Lucas dos Reis MARTINS, *University of Hildesheim*
Edward McDOUGALL, *Durham University*
Ramūnas MOTIEKAITIS, *Vilnius University*
Ralf MÜLLER, *University of Hildesheim*
Rossa O. MUIREARTAIGH, *Aichi Prefectural University*

Ono Jun'ichi 小野純一, *Universiteit Gent*
Tony Pacyna, *University of Heidelberg*
Ruben Pfizenmeier, *Freie Universität Berlin*
Niklas Söderman, *Tallinna Ülikool*
Moritz Sommet, *University of Fribourg*
Cody Staton, *Katholieke Universiteit Leuven*
Bernard Stevens, *Université catholique de Louvain*
Jan Gerrit Strala, *Kinjō Gakuen University*
Jacynthe Tremblay, *Nanzan Institute for Religion & Culture*

Printed in Great Britain
by Amazon